PRAXIS
A BRIEF RHETORIC

2nd Edition

Carol Lea Clark
University of Texas | El Paso

PERSPECTIVE

Edited by
Kenneth Gillam

Our green initiatives include:

Electronic Products
We deliver products in non-paper form whenever possible. This includes pdf downloadables, flash drives, & CDs.

Electronic Samples
We use Xample, a new electronic sampling system. Instructor samples are sent via a personalized web page that links to pdf downloads.

FSC Certified Printers
All of our printers are certified by the Forest Service Council which promotes environmentally and socially responsible management of the world's forests. This program allows consumer groups, individual consumers, and businesses to work together hand-in-hand to promote responsible use of the world's forests as a renewable and sustainable resource.

Recycled Paper
Most of our products are printed on a minimum of 30% post-consumer waste recycled paper.

Support of Green Causes
When we do print, we donate a portion of our revenue to green causes. Listed below are a few of the organizations that have received donations from Fountainhead Press. We welcome your feedback and suggestions for contributions, as we are always searching for worthy initiatives.

Rainforest 2 Reef
Environmental Working Group

Carol Lea Clark would like to thank Craig Wynne, her research assistant, for his invaluable help with this second edition of *Praxis*.

Design by Susan Moore

Praxis 2e isbn: 978-1-59871-508-8
Perspective isbn: 978-1-59871-715-0

Books may be purchased for educational purposes.

For information, please call or write:

1-800-586-0330
Fountainhead Press
Southlake, TX 76092

Web site: www.fountainheadpress.com
E-mail: customerservice@fountainheadpress.com

ISBN: 978-1-59871-816-4

Printed in the United States of America

Preface

Praxis is an appropriate name for this composition textbook because the goal of the composition classroom—and this text—is to enable the student to move from thinking about a topic to the action of creating an effective, as well as an ethical, argument for a particular rhetorical situation. This goal echoes the meaning of the Greek word *praxis*, which can be translated as "process," "practice," or "experience." However, the great Greek rhetorician Aristotle used the term in a special way, to specify practical reasoning, for which the goal was action, rather than theorizing. Furthermore, to ancient Greek rhetoricians, *praxis* had the connotation of moral and ethical actions that enhanced the individual's sense of well-being in life.

The content of this expanded and full-color new edition of *Praxis* is a response to the feedback from many composition instructors who made suggestions such as adding stasis theory, more interactive assignments, and additional readings. Moreover, all exercises are labeled with the same icons as the *Fountainhead Press V Series* readers.

Praxis: A Brief Rhetoric 2e takes basic concepts from the rich history of rhetoric—including *kairos, ethos, pathos*, and *logos*—and demonstrates how students can use these concepts together as a critical framework for analyzing the world around them. This framework enables students to become critical consumers of the flood of persuasive media—including books, newspaper articles, television programs, product reviews, social networks, and advertisements—that compete for their attention.

Moreover, *Praxis* encourages students to employ this rhetorical framework of concepts to the creation of their own texts—essays, yes, but also commonplace books, blogs, op-ed arguments, instructions, and a wide variety of other types of writing. Each chapter features readings, activities, and assignments—some serious and thought provoking, and others creativity-inspiring and *fun*.

This textbook is also written for instructors who have essentially the same practical goals as did Aristotle and other rhetors who taught in ancient Greece and Rome. They want to assist their students in developing skills that will enable them to be critical thinkers and critical writers. To achieve these goals, instructors must focus on several distinct but interconnected skills—reading critically; researching subjects formally and informally; understanding audience expectations; utilizing the structure of language to organize and to communicate information for a specific purpose; persuading readers through appropriate use of ethos, pathos, and logos; and revising to improve the effectiveness of a draft. The goal of *Praxis* is to move the student from theory to practical reason to action.

Chapter Highlights

Chapter 1 Practicing Rhetoric

Defines rhetoric and employs classical rhetorical concepts to introduce students to persuasive argument. Introduces visual rhetoric, commonplace books, and blogging.

Chapter 2 Responding Rhetorically

Demonstrates the connection between rhetoric and critical thinking. Introduces the rhetorical triangle, a checklist for rhetorical argument, and techniques for close reading. New assignments include composing a lexicon, considering song lyrics as an argument, and interpreting advertisements.

Chapter 3 Analyzing Rhetorically

Discusses how understanding the *kairos* of an argument enhances critical analysis and provides examples of arguments based on *ethos*, *pathos*, and *logos*. Explains audience analysis, deductive and inductive arguments, and logical fallacies. Assignments include writing a letter to the editor, creating a professional Facebook page, and writing a memo to explain the student's own collage expressing pathos.

Chapter 4 Inventing Rhetorically

Introduces Aristotle's artistic and inartistic proofs and explains how to use the discovery of artistic proofs as an invention strategy. Discusses the similarities and differences between ancient invention techniques and contemporary prewriting. Demonstrates how to use stasis theory to analyze an issue and to construct an effective argument. Includes three related readings that can be used to write a stasis-theory based mini-research paper. Other assignments include analyzing rhetorical techniques in a television courtroom drama, using stasis theory to develop a persuasive argument about a public debate, writing a product review, and composing a rhetorical analysis.

Chapter 5 Writing Rhetorically

Explains how writing allows students to enter the academic conversation. Demonstrates the similarities and differences between ancient and contemporary formats for compositions. Discusses writing basics such as constructing a thesis statement, composing an introduction, weaving in material from sources, and answering opposing arguments. Introduces page design concepts. Assignments include writing an argument-based research paper, a film review, and an op-ed argument.

Chapter 6 Revising Rhetorically

Describes the revision process, which begins with careful rereading, and includes procedures for peer editing. Suggests several ways to consider the qualities of effective writing, such as "William Safire's Rules for Writing" and "Grammar Girl's Top Ten Grammar Myths," as well as more standard criteria. Provides several sample student essays for peer editing.

Chapter 7 Researching Rhetorically

Introduces the research process as developing what Aristotle called inartistic proofs. Describes the difference between primary and secondary research. Assignments include writing a profile of a person, constructing an annotated bibliography, evaluating a website, and avoiding plagiarism.

Appendix

Provides a concise guide to APA and MLA documentation styles.

In summary, the new full-color *Praxis: A Brief Rhetoric 2e*, with its enhanced interactive exercises, celebrates the ancient heritage of the composition classroom and its ability to address the needs of today's students who live in a media-enhanced, technology-complex world.

Praxis Table of Contents

2 RESPONDING RHETORICALLY 33

Perspective Table of Contents

1
PRACTICING RHETORIC

Praxis in Action

Why Rhetoric Is Important in My Writing by Elizabeth Jimenez

Rhetoric is an intangible power that has the ability to motivate and manipulate. If I master rhetoric, I know I possess the ability to move my audience toward my goal.

I communicate effectively when I gain the confidence of the audience. Influencing my class and professor is my number one goal and is done so by my ethos. My use of rhetoric is validated by my credibility in the subject I disseminate. I must possess credibility if I am to be a reputable source of information.

Once I have gained the attention of the audience, I obtain logos when I clearly and logically disseminate my thoughts. I accomplish my purpose when I prove my statements. This is done by substantiating my thoughts with supporting evidence. Many contributing factors that come into play have an influence on my argument, such as bias. If my argument is biased, this can strongly detract from my goal.

Persuasive rhetoric is not necessarily accomplished when I use too much emotion. I find if I overuse pathos, the general idea gets lost. If I want my idea to be well received, it is important for me to communicate with levelheadedness.

These elements help me to establish effective rhetoric, which is crucial as I write for different audiences in college. Rhetoric will open doors throughout my college career as I discover new ways of conveying information and opinions.

Elizabeth Jimenez writes that understanding rhetoric gives her the power to persuade an audience.

Through *Praxis*, Theory Becomes Action

The word **praxis** can be translated as "process" or "practice." Aristotle, the great Greek rhetorician, employed the term in a special way to mean practical reasoning, for which the goal was action. To be practical in the Aristotelian sense is a little different from what being practical means today. It indicates the ability to apply abstract theory to concrete situations and thus, to move from theory to action. Moreover, praxis embodies a creative element that raises it above the mundane or merely pragmatic. Therefore, "practicing rhetoric" is not practice in the sense of rehearsal. Rather, it is performing, or applying, or acting out rhetoric—taking theory and turning it into action.

So, if we understand praxis or the "practicing" part of "practicing rhetoric," what does the "rhetoric" part of the chapter title mean? In common usage, the word *argument* has a narrow definition that emphasizes heated or angry exchanges of clashing and often irreconcilable viewpoints. Moreover, sides in such arguments are limited to black and white opposites and include no shades of gray. If one person is right, then the other must be wrong.

In academia, in contrast, we argue because it causes us to examine critically our own as well as others' ideas. Argument compels us to consider conflicting claims, to evaluate evidence, and to clarify our thoughts. We know that even wise, well-intentioned people don't always agree, so we consider others' ideas respectfully. After one person presents an argument, either orally or in writing, others respond with arguments that support, modify, or contradict the original one. Then, in turn, more individuals counter with their own versions, and thus, the interchange becomes a conversation.

Academic arguments can be divided into several different categories, depending upon the extent of the writer's desire to persuade and the scope of the conversational exchange.

1. **One type of argument simply makes a point about the topic**. For example, later in this chapter you will read an article titled, "San Ysidro Shooting Survivor Lives His Dream of Being a Cop." In the article, the author describes the wounds inflicted on a young man during the McDonald's Massacre in San Ysidro in 1984 and then explains how and why this young man later became a cop. No one is likely to disagree with the writer's line of reasoning, at least not if the author offers sufficient evidence to back up the original statement that, for this man, being a cop is his dream. This article is a profile, a type of argument more often seen in magazines and newspapers than in journals.

one viewpoint

2. **A second type of argument involves a controversial issue, and the writer's aim is to persuade the audience to change its stance on the matter.** The ideal result, for the writer, would be that members of the audience alter their positions to coincide with the writer's viewpoint. In this second type of argument, it is essential that the writer offer the complete structure of thesis, evidence, possible opposition viewpoints which are discussed and countered, and a conclusion. "The Sleepover Question," another reading in this chapter, presents this kind of argument. The author, who has conducted research in both America and Holland, argues the controversial position that if American parents would adopt more liberal attitudes toward their children's sexuality, like the parents in Holland, "the transition into adulthood need not be so painful for parents or children." A reading in Chapter 3, "Why Executions Should Be Televised," offers a more extreme version of this type of argument. Either executions are televised or they aren't, and the writer advocates that they should be.

3. **A third type of argument emphasizes multiple perspectives and viewpoints and tries to find common ground that participants can agree upon.** In Chapter 4, several readings are collected in a casebook called "The $300 House." The *Harvard Business Review* initiated a design competition intended to spark inclusive argument with the aim of gathering ideas about how to build inexpensive but adequate homes for the poor in the world's slums. "Hands Off Our Houses," one response to the competition that appears in the casebook, argues, for example, that bringing $300 houses into the slums of Mumbai is not the answer to the housing problem. In contrast, other responses posted on a website associated with the competition suggest ways the idea of the $300 house might work, while admitting enormous difficulties.

These three types of arguments represent points in a spectrum, and all persuasive texts may not neatly fit into one of the three categories. A crucial thing to remember, though, is that all arguments involve the presentation of a line of reasoning about a topic or an issue—a thesis, hypothesis, or claim—and the support of that reasoning with evidence.

Become Part of the Academic Conversation

As a student, you are expected to join academic conversations that are already in progress. How do you do that? How do you know what kind of response is appropriate? Have you ever entered a party where everyone is talking excitedly? Most likely, you paused near the doorway to get a sense of who was there and what they were discussing before you decided who to talk to and what to say. Or, have you become part of a Facebook group or a listserv discussion group? If so, you know it is a good idea to "lurk" for a while before asking questions or contributing a remark. Writing an academic paper involves a similar process. You read about a subject until you have a good grasp of the points authorities are debating. Then you find a way to integrate your own ideas about that subject with the ideas of others and create an informed contribution to the conversation.

For example, the following students' introductions to movie reviews demonstrate they not only understand the films and have interesting things to say about them; their writing also displays knowledge of what others have written about the films, whether the students agree with those evaluations or not.

- Roger Ebert claims that audience members who haven't seen the first two *Lord of the Rings* films (Peter Jackson, 2001, 2002) will likely "be adrift during the early passages of [the third] film's 200 minutes." But then again, Ebert continues, "to be adrift occasionally during this nine-hour saga comes with the territory" (par. 3). Ebert, though, misses one crucial fact regarding *Lord of the Rings: The Return of the King* (2003). This third installment opens with a flashback intended to familiarize new spectators about what happened in the previous two films. Within these five minutes, the audience discovers how Gollum (Andy Serkis) came to be corrupt through the destructive power of the Ring. The viewer, therefore, will not necessarily be "adrift," as Ebert claims, since the lighting, setting, and sound in the opening of *The Return of the King* show the lighter, more peaceful world before Gollum finds the ring, compared to the darker, more sinister world thereafter.

- "It's hard to resist a satire, even when it wobbles, that insists the most unbelievable parts are the most true" (*Rolling Stone* par. 1). This is Peter Travers's overarching view of Grant Heslov's satire, *The Men Who Stare at Goats* (2009). Travers is correct here; after all, Goats's opening title card, which reads, "More of this is real than you would believe," humorously teases the viewer that some of the film's most "unbelievable parts" will, in fact, offer the most truth. We experience this via Bill Wilson's (Ewan McGregor) interview of an ex "psy-ops" soldier, when Wilson's life spirals out of control, and all the other farfetched actions presenting "reality." But again, it is the film's opening—specifically, its setting, camera

> movements and angles, dialogue, effects, and ambient noise—that sets the foundation for an unbelievably realistic satire.*

In both of these introductions, the students quote reviews by professional film critics and respond to the critics' opinions. Moreover, the students continue their arguments by using the critics' ideas as springboards for their own arguments. These two short examples indicate these students have learned how to counter positions advocated by authorities without losing their own voices. If the rest of their essays continue as they have begun, the students will have written essays to which others can reply, thus continuing the conversation. Later in this textbook, you will have your own chance to enter the conversation of film reviews by reviewing a favorite movie of your own.

Collaborative Groups Help Students Enter the Academic Conversation

Likely, your writing class will include collaborative group work as part of the mix of activities, along with lecture, class discussion, and in-class writing. You may wonder why there is so much talk in a writing class, which is a good question. Use of collaborative groups is based on extensive research, which shows that students who work in small groups as part of their courses tend to learn more and retain the knowledge longer than students who are not asked to work in groups. Also, research shows students who participate in collaborative group work generally are more satisfied with the course. Groups give students a chance to apply knowledge they have learned and provide a change of pace from lectures or other class activities. There are several types of groups, and your class may include one or all of them:

- Informal, one-time pairs or groups. After presenting some material, your instructor may ask you to turn to the person next to you and discuss the topic or answer a question.
- Ongoing small classroom groups. Usually, these groups work together for a significant part of the semester, and your instructor may assign roles to members of the group such as recorder, facilitator, editor, and spokesperson. Often, the roles will rotate, so that everyone has a chance to try out each job. Your instructor may give you a job description for each role or train the class in the tasks for each role.

* Kelli Marshall. "Entering a Conversation, Teaching the Academic Essay," *Unmuzzled Thoughts about Teaching and Pop Culture*, October 23, 2010, http://kellimarshall.net/unmuzzledthoughts/teaching/academic-essay/. Accessed August 30, 2011.

- Task groups. These groups are formed to write a report, complete a project, or do some other task together. These groups meet several times, often outside of class. The products of these groups are usually graded, and your instructor will often require members to rate each other on their performance.

- Peer editing groups. When you have completed a draft of an essay or other text, your instructor may ask you to exchange papers in pairs or within small groups. You will be asked to read your classmate's paper carefully and make comments, either on a peer editing form or on the paper itself. Likewise, your classmate will read and make comments on your paper. Then, when you receive your paper back, you can make revisions based on your classmate's comments.

An added benefit to the use of collaborative groups in writing classes is that students can help each other figure out what the ongoing conversation is for a particular topic or issue before writing about it. Also, groups provide a forum where students can practice making comments that are part of that conversation.

Rhetoric and Argument

The structure of an argument—introduction (including a thesis), supporting evidence, counterarguments, and conclusion—will be familiar to you from previous English classes. What you may not realize is that ancient Greeks developed this argumentative structure out of necessity. Their democratic system of government required that citizens be able to speak persuasively in public, as there were no attorneys or professional politicians. Ancient Greeks called their persuasive strategies rhetoric, and rhetoric became the primary means of education of the elite youth in Athens.

Rhetoric, like argument, is a word that has both a popular meaning and an academic meaning. You have probably heard someone say of a politician's speech, "Oh, that's just rhetoric," meaning the politician's words are empty verbiage or hot air. The politician is attempting to sound impressive while saying nothing that has real meaning. Or perhaps the politician is making promises that listeners believe he or she has no intention of keeping. Politicians who engage in verbal deception often succeed only in acquiring the reputation of dishonesty.

In the field of rhetoric and composition today, rhetoric has a much different meaning. Though definitions vary somewhat from one practitioner to another, rhetoric generally means the study and use of persuasive communication (or argument), a meaning that traces its roots back to the original use of the term by ancient Greeks. Rhetoric, in the form of oratory, was essential to the Greeks, as they used it to resolve disputes in the law courts and to promote political action in the Assembly.

Are We All Greeks?

As Americans, we owe an immense debt to ancient Greek civilization. Our laws, our democratic form of government, our literature, and our art have their roots in ancient Athens. Earlier generations of Americans and Western Europeans, who often studied Latin and Greek, may have had a clearer understanding of the direct connections of our culture to Athens of the 4th and 5th centuries BCE. Indeed, the English poet Percy Bysshe Shelley famously said, "We are all Greeks" because of the essential influence of ancient Greek culture upon Western civilization. However, even translated into 21st century American English, the linkage is still there.

Something quite amazing happened in Athens, around 500 BCE. Instead of being invaded by a foreign country who appointed a puppet ruler or experiencing a coup in which a strong man seized power, the people peaceably chose to put in place a direct democracy. Attica was not the only city-state to have a democracy, but it was the most successful. During the golden age of Greece, from roughly 500 BCE to 300 BCE, art, architecture, and literature thrived.

Direct or radical democracy meant all male citizens of Attica over the age of 20 could vote in the Assembly, the policy-making body of the city-state. They did not elect senators or representatives as we do today. Each of these men *voted directly*. Moreover, they could settle differences with fellow citizens by suing in the law courts. Out of 250,000 to 300,000 residents in Attica, some 30,000 were citizens. Amazingly, it was not unusual for 10,000 of these eligible men to vote in the Assembly. The law courts had juries of 500 or more. Imagine trying to speak to an audience of 10,000 people without modern loudspeakers. Even with the wonderful acoustics in Greek theatres, it would have been a challenge.

Ordinary citizens were required to speak in the Assembly or the courts to promote laws or defend themselves from lawsuits, as there were no attorneys or professional politicians. Certainly, speaking before such large audiences necessitated special skills acquired only through extensive training and practice. Many sought out teachers to help them learn how to speak persuasively, and, indeed, training in rhetoric became the primary method of education for the elite young men of Athens. A few women were also educated in rhetoric, but they were in the minority.

The earliest teachers of verbal persuasive skills we now call rhetoric were Sophists who migrated from Sicily and other Greek states. Some of their viewpoints were curiously modern—for example, that knowledge is relative and that pure truth does not exist. However, they became known for teaching their pupils to persuade an audience to think whatever they wanted them to believe. Sophists such as Gorgias themselves often presented entertainment speeches during which they would argue, on the spur of the moment, on any topic raised by the audience, just to show they were able to construct effective arguments on any subject.

The term rhetoric comes from the Greek word *rhetorike*, which Plato coined as a criticism of the Sophists, claiming the Sophists' rhetoric could be employed to manipulate the masses for good or ill, and that rhetoricians used it irresponsibly. Ironically, Plato demonstrates excellent rhetorical techniques himself when he condemns rhetoric and argues that only the elite who are educated in philosophy are suited to rule, not the rhetoricians. Aristotle, Plato's student, took a more moderate viewpoint toward rhetoric. Indeed, he was the first philosopher to classify rhetoric as a tool for practical debate with general audiences. His book *On Rhetoric* (though it was probably lecture notes possibly combined with student responses, rather than a manuscript intended for publication) is the single most important text that establishes rhetoric as a system of persuasive communication.

Athens, even in its glory days, seethed with controversy and bickering over the many inefficiencies of democracy. Men trained in rhetoric executed two coups, the Tyranny of the Four Hundred in 411 BCE and the Tyranny of the Thirty in 404 BCE, neither of which was an improvement; after each coup, democracy returned. Moreover, Athenians fought wars with Persia (the Battle of Marathon in 490 BCE and the Battle of Thermopylae in 480 BCE) and Sparta (the Peloponnesian War in 431–404 BCE and the Corinthian War of 395–387 BCE). Finally, the armies of Philip II of Macedonia defeated Athens at the Battle of Chaeronea in 338 BCE, ending Athenian independence. Despite coups and wars, democracy remained in place in Athens for nearly 200 years.

If Americans might be called Greeks because our country is based on Greek traditions, this is not to say that rhetoric appears in all cultures. True, one might say that all civilizations have some sort of persuasive negotiation process; but profound differences exist between cultures in terms of what verbal strategies are persuasive. Indeed, disparity in expectations and the actions of individuals and groups from different traditions can be a cause of strife.

Rhetoric and Power

Aristotle defined rhetoric as "the faculty of discovering, in a given instance, the available means of persuasion," which we might paraphrase as the power to see the means of persuasion available in any given situation. Each part of this definition is important. Rhetoric is power; the person who is able to speak eloquently, choosing the most suitable arguments about a topic for a specific audience in a particular situation, is the person most likely to persuade. In both Greece and Rome, the primary use of rhetoric was oratory—persuasion through public speaking. However, the texts of many famous speeches were recorded and studied as models by students, and prominent rhetoricians wrote treatises and handbooks for teaching rhetoric. To Greeks and Romans, a person who could use rhetoric effectively was a person of influence and power because he could persuade his audience to action. The effective orator could win court cases; the effective orator could influence the passage or failure of laws; the effective orator could send a nation to war or negotiate peace.

Skill with rhetoric has conveyed power through the ages, though in our contemporary world, rhetoric is often displayed in written text such as a book, newspaper or magazine article, or scientific report, rather than presented as a speech. Persuasive communication also can be expressed visually, as an illustration that accompanies a text or a cartoon that conveys its own message. Indeed, in our highly visual society, with television, movies, video games, and the Internet, images can often persuade more powerfully than words alone.

Using rhetoric effectively means being able to interpret the rhetoric we are presented with in our everyday lives. Knowledge of persuasive communication or rhetoric empowers us to present our views and persuade others to modify their ideas. Through changes in ideas, rhetoric leads to action. Through changes in actions, rhetoric affects society.

Selected Definitions of Rhetoric

Aristotle, 350 BCE—*Rhetoric is "the faculty of discovering, in a given instance, the available means of persuasion."*

Cicero, 90 BCE—*Rhetoric is "speech designed to persuade" and "eloquence based on the rules of art."*

Quintilian, 95 CE—*Rhetoric is "the science of speaking well."*

Augustine of Hippo, ca. 426 CE—*Rhetoric is "the art of persuading people to accept something, whether it is true or false."*

Anonymous, ca. 1490–1495—*Rhetoric is "the science which refreshes the hungry, renders the mute articulate, makes the blind see, and teaches one to avoid every lingual ineptitude."*

Heinrich Cornelius Agrippa, 1531—*"To confess the truth, it is generally granted that the entire discipline of rhetoric from start to finish is nothing other than an art of flattery, adulation, and, as some say more audaciously, lying, in that, if it cannot persuade others through the truth of the case, it does so by means of deceitful speech."*

Hoyt Hudson, 1923—*"In this sense, plainly, the man who speaks most persuasively uses the most, or certainly the best, rhetoric; and the man whom we censure for inflation of style and strained effects is suffering not from too much rhetoric, but from a lack of it."*

I. A. Richards, 1936—*"Rhetoric, I shall urge, should be a study of misunderstanding and its remedies."*

Sister Miriam Joseph, 1937—*Rhetoric is "the art of communicating thought from one mind to another, the adaptation of language to circumstance."*

Kenneth Burke, 1950—*"[T]he basic function of rhetoric [is] the use of words by human agents to form attitudes or to induce actions in other human agents."*

Gerard A. Hauser, 2002—*"Rhetoric, as an area of study, is concerned with how humans use symbols, especially language, to reach agreement that permits coordinated effort of some sort."*

Activity 1.1 Historical Usage of the Word "Rhetoric"

Read through the list of historical definitions of the word "rhetoric" on the previous page, and choose one that you find interesting. In a discussion, compare your chosen definition with those of your classmates.

Activity 1.2 Contemporary Usage of the Word "Rhetoric"

Find at least two recent but different examples involving use of the word "rhetoric." For example, search your local newspaper for an example of how the word "rhetoric" is being used. A search of the *Dallas Morning News* for the word "rhetoric" led to a story about citizen efforts to clean up a neglected area of town: "He now hopes for help to finally fill the gap between rhetoric and reality." Or ask a friend, fellow employee, or a family member to tell you what the word "rhetoric" means and write down what they say. Discuss your examples in your small group and present the best ones to the class.

Visual Map of Meanings for the Word "Rhetoric"

The word map for the word "rhetoric" shown in figure 1.1 has branches for different meanings of the word, with some branches splitting again to display subtle subsets of connotation. It was created by a website, Visual Thesaurus (www.visualthesaurus.com), which computes visual word maps for any word inputted in its search box. The idea is that words lead to branches that lead to more words, inspiring users to think of language in new ways.

At the Visual Thesaurus site, if you place your cursor over one of the circles connecting the branches, a small box will pop up that defines that connection. One of these connection boxes is visible. Notice it says, "using language effectively to please or persuade." This is the branch of the visual map that is closest to the meaning of "rhetoric" as used in this book. The other branches illustrate other contemporary uses of the word.

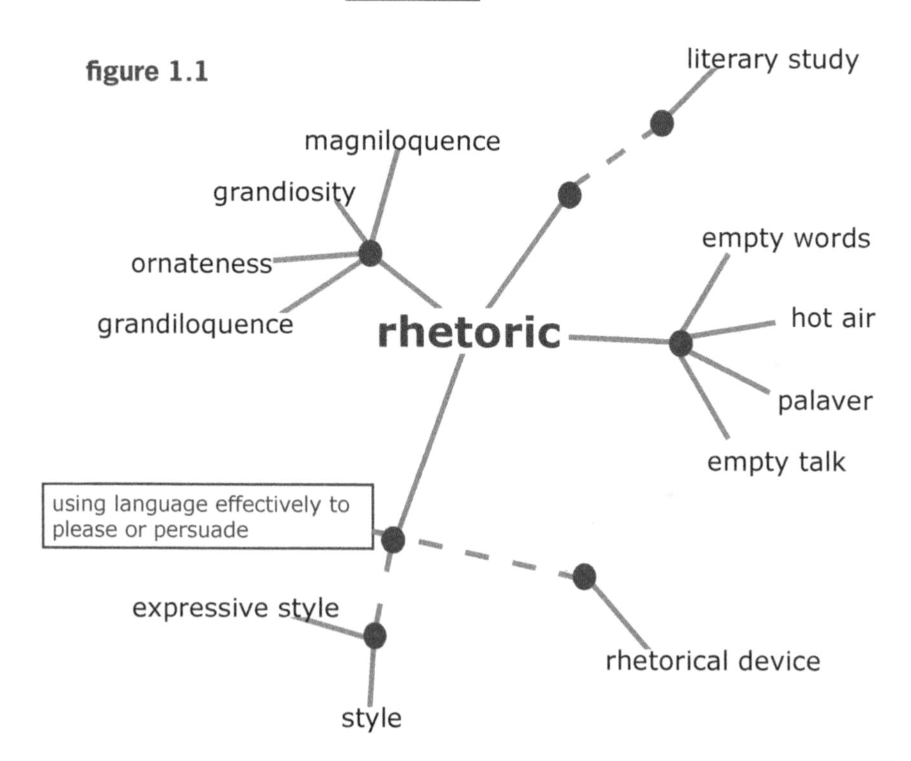

Explore

Activity 1.3 Explore the Visual Map of the Word "Rhetoric"

In your small group, choose one of the five branches of words in the visual map of the word "rhetoric." Go to one or more good dictionaries and explore the meanings of the words in that branch. A good place to start would be the *Oxford English Dictionary*, which your college library may offer online. The *OED* offers intricate analyses of the histories of word meanings. Report to the class what you find out about the words on your particular branch.

Rhetorical Argument

Often, in our culture, the word "argument" is taken to mean a disagreement or even a fight, with raised voices, rash words, and hurt feelings. We have the perception of an argument as something that has victory and defeat, winners and losers. Argument, in the sense of a **rhetorical argument**, however, means the carefully crafted presentation of a viewpoint or position on a topic and the giving of thoughts, ideas, and opinions along with reasons for their support. The persuasive strength of an argument rests upon the rhetorical skills of the rhetor (the speaker or the writer) in utilizing the tools of language to persuade a particular audience.

Aristotle identified three appeals (see figure 1.2) or three ways to persuade an audience, and we are still using these today, though often without using the Greek terms to identify the means of persuasion:

Ethos—The rhetor convinces an audience by means of his character or credibility. In oratory, the speaker projects an air of confidence and authority. In writing, ethos is conveyed by the qualifications of the writer or the authorities that are cited and also by the quality of the writing.

Pathos—The rhetor persuades by playing upon the listener's (or reader's) emotions. He or she may refer to children, death, disaster, injustice, or other topics that arouse pity, fear, or other emotions.

Logos—The rhetor persuades by the use of reasoning and evidence. Arguments based on logos employ deductive or inductive reasoning.

figure 1.2

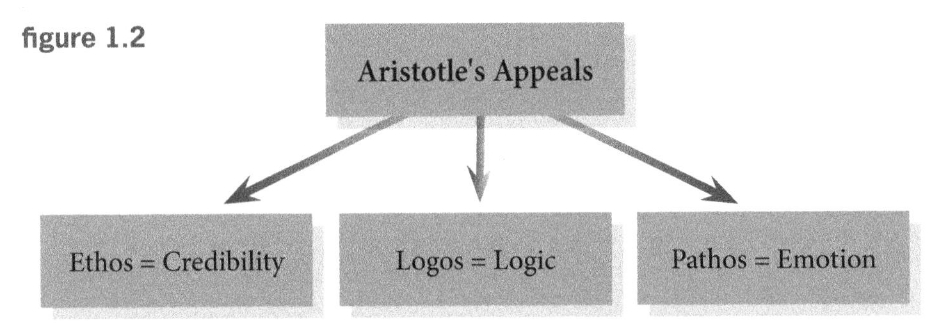

Although a good argument will contain at least traces of all three appeals, skilled rhetors analyze their audiences to determine which of the three would be most persuasive to that particular audience. Then, they construct arguments that emphasize that particular appeal.

In addition, a knowledgeable rhetor considers the time, place, audience, topic, and other aspects of the occasion for writing or speaking to determine the **kairos**, or opportune moment of the composition (see figure 1.3). This factor or critical moment both provides and limits opportunities for appeals suitable to that moment. For example, someone giving a commencement address has certain opportunities and constraints. Likewise, an attorney writing a last-minute appeal for someone on death row has a very different set of options.

figure 1.3

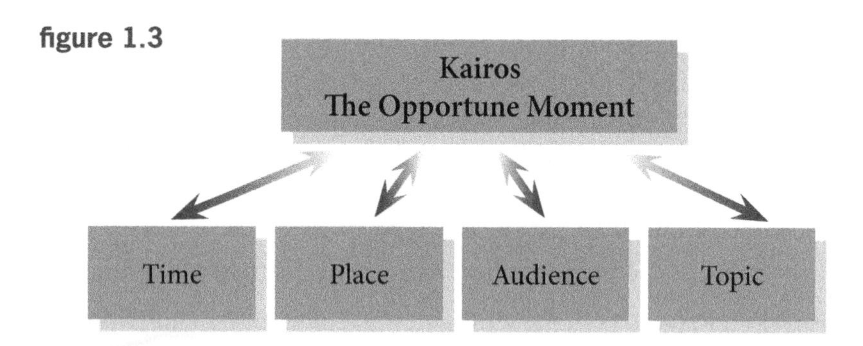

The editorial below addresses the shooting attack on Arizona Congresswoman Gabrielle Giffords that killed six and left Giffords and others seriously wounded. The text, published on *Time* magazine's website shortly after the attack, addresses the kairos of the situation—a United States Congresswoman has been shot, certainly an exceptional moment in many ways. The editorial demonstrates several important things to remember in understanding rhetoric and its use in American society. The author, Nathan Thornburgh, addresses the controversy about whether "overheated rhetoric" (exaggerated pathos) had inspired the shooting, an important question considering the often-inflammatory language of political rhetoric in the United States. However, his text is not filled with rash or harsh words that could further inflame the controversy. Though the text is an opinion piece, taking a position regarding this controversy and offering evidence to support his opinion, it is not itself "overheated rhetoric." As you read the text, think about whether he emphasizes ethos, pathos, or logos. You may or may not agree with his position. Rhetorical language is never neutral; its purpose is to persuade an audience to share the author's opinion. Good arguments, though, do not use "overheated rhetoric," false evidence, or logical fallacies to win over an audience.

Reading 1.1

Violent Rhetoric and Arizona Politics

by Nathan Thornburgh

This editorial by Nathan Thornburgh was originally printed in *Time* shortly after the shooting of Arizona Congresswoman Gabrielle Giffords.

Sometimes, rumors of violence beget actual violence. Saturday's mass shooting at a Safeway on North Oracle Road in Tucson, which killed six and left Democratic Congresswoman Gabrielle Giffords and others gravely wounded, may well be one of those occasions.

It's impossible to know this early what the motivations for the attack were. Was the alleged shooter—who has been identified as 22-year-old Tucsonan

Jared Loughner—angry about immigration? Or perhaps another hot-button issue? YouTube videos ascribed to him bore the mark of mental illness—they were conspiratorial, unintelligible, espousing no particular cause—but no matter his mental state, his crime took place in an overheated political environment. Last March, at the height of the health care reform battle, Giffords's office was vandalized. She mentioned in an MSNBC interview that a Sarah Palin graphic had depicted her district in the crosshairs of a gun sight. "They've got to realize there are consequences to that," she said. "The rhetoric is incredibly heated." The corner next to her office had also become, she said, a popular spot for Tea Party protests.

As Pima County Sheriff Clarence Dupnik put it in an extraordinary and melancholic press conference after the shooting, "we have become the Mecca for prejudice and bigotry." He added that he's "not aware of any public officials who are not receiving threats."

Another shooting victim, a federal judge named John Roll, had been placed under 24-hour security in 2009 after ruling in favor of illegal immigrants in a high-profile case. It's unclear why he was at the supermarket event. But for almost a year now, Arizona's leaders have been grappling with anti-immigration sentiments, inflamed by reports of crossborder violence. National media attention, with its attendant voices of hysteria, only added to the churn. Pundits spoke gravely about a wave of violence, born in Mexico and now flooding Arizona. Arizona's two most famous politicians fueled the fury. Republican Senator John McCain, facing an unexpected reelection challenge from the right, ran a campaign obsessed with crossborder crime. And GOP Governor Jan Brewer, who invited the national spotlight by championing strict anti-illegal immigrant legislation, talked of beheadings in the desert.

The only problem with all this talk about a massive crossborder crime wave is that it wasn't true. Phoenix had not become one of the world's kidnapping capitals. Crime rates in Arizona had been steady or even fallen in some areas. There had been no beheadings in the desert. There were plenty of deaths there, but they were pathetic and meek tragedies: impoverished border-crossers, abandoned by their heartless guides, dying of exposure and dehydration.

But the idea of a state under siege took hold. When I was on the border last year reporting on the murder of rancher Rob Krentz, I talked to many who sincerely believed that they were under attack. Krentz's murder was a terrible event, but it was an isolated event. The relatively small number of home invasions, holdups and other crimes deeply disturbed border communities, but only because they had been living in such calm for so long. Their crime rates still don't match most cities in the states.

The supermarket meet-and-greet where Giffords was shot was actually a testimony to just how safe southern Arizona is. As a press release from her office last week put it, "'Congress on Your Corner' allows residents of Arizona's 8th Congressional District to meet their congresswoman one-on-one and discuss with her any issue, concern or problem involving the federal government." Not exactly the kind of event a politician would hold in a war zone.

It's true that Giffords was not a fan of the state's anti-immigration bill SB1070, but there were higher-profile opponents, such as her fellow Congressional Representative in Tucson, Raul Grijalva. Yet the idea that Arizona is under attack has been pushed hard enough that it's very possible that the coward who shot her (in the head, according to a Tucson paper) believed that the 40-year-old Democrat, who had been tarred by some as soft on immigration because she didn't support SB1070, was contributing to larger-scale violence against Arizonans.

If that is the case, it would only add to the tragedy. The fact is, that among all the overwrought promises and all the panic I heard last summer in Arizona, I found that Giffords was one of the few politicians offering concrete law enforcement steps that would actually work against the drug cartels and other smugglers. It's not just that she fought for more money and police for border protection, although she did that. She co-sponsored legislation last year with a California Republican that aimed to give law enforcement important new tools in cracking down on the cash cards that were a favored method of money-laundering. It was one of the many sensible, pragmatic ideas she had for cracking down on crime.

Whatever dark fantasies drove someone to try to take her life, Giffords is a sensible politician who was likely shot because she dealt with Arizona's reality, not its rumors.

Activity 1.4 Write a Summary of "Violent Rhetoric and Arizona Politics"

Summarizing is an excellent technique to use when preparing for an exam or doing research for an essay. It allows you to discern the main points of a text and how they fit together. With a classmate, review the editorial by Thornburgh. Read the article together carefully, and list the main points individually. After you've listed the main points, put them into paragraph form.

Caution: Beware of the temptation to add your own analysis of what the text is saying. For example, if you are summarizing a scientist's article on global warming, you need to be careful not to reveal your personal opinion about whether or not global warming is occurring or whether or not human actions are to blame. In this assignment, you summarize only. You do not argue or analyze.

When you're finished, compare your summary with that of your partner.

Activity 1.5 Analyzing "Violent Rhetoric and Arizona Politics"

1. What does Nathan Thornburgh mean when he uses the term "overheated rhetoric"?
2. What is the argument that Thornburgh is making about the cause of the attack on Representative Giffords?
3. What evidence does Thornburgh offer to support his argument?
4. Does Thornburgh make his case? Is he convincing? Why or why not?

Reading 1.2

The Sleepover Question

by Amy Schalet

This text by Amy Schalet was first published in *The New York Times*. "The Sleepover Question" hazards an argument that many Americans—or at least American parents—may find controversial. Backed by her credentials as a professor of sociology, she cites research from 130 interviews, both in the United States and the Netherlands, and tackles the issue of whether or not American parents should allow their adolescent children to have sex in the family home. Pay particular attention, for she shows how to argue a subject that is not only controversial but often ignored.

NOT under my roof. That's the attitude most American parents have toward teenagers and their sex lives. Squeamishness and concern describe most parents' approach to their offspring's carnality. We don't want them doing it—whatever "it" is!—in our homes. Not surprisingly, teenage sex is a source of conflict in many American families.

Would Americans increase peace in family life and strengthen family bonds if they adopted more accepting attitudes about sex and what's allowable under the family roof? I've interviewed 130 people, all white, middle class and not particularly religious, as part of a study of teenage sex and family life here and in the Netherlands. My look into cultural differences suggests family life might be much improved, for all, if Americans had more open ideas about teenage sex. The question of who sleeps where when a teenager brings a boyfriend or girlfriend home for the night fits within the larger world of culturally divergent ideas about teenage sex, lust and capacity for love.

Kimberly and Natalie dramatize the cultural differences in the way young women experience their sexuality. (I have changed their names to protect confidentiality.) Kimberly, a 16-year-old American, never received sex education at home. "God, no! No, no! That's not going to happen," she told me. She'd like to tell her parents that she and her boyfriend are having sex, but she believes it is easier for her parents not to know because the truth would "shatter" their image of her as their "little princess."

Natalie, who is also 16 but Dutch, didn't tell her parents immediately when she first had intercourse with her boyfriend of three months. But, soon after, she says, she was so happy, she wanted to share the good news. Initially her father was upset and worried about his daughter and his honor. "Talk to him," his wife advised Natalie; after she did, her father made peace with the change. Essentially Natalie and her family negotiated a life change together and figured out, as a family, how to adjust to changed circumstance.

Respecting what she understood as her family's "don't ask, don't tell" policy, Kimberly only slept with her boyfriend at his house, when no one was home. She enjoyed being close to her boyfriend but did not like having to keep an important part of her life secret from her parents. In contrast, Natalie and her boyfriend enjoyed time and a new closeness with her family; the fact that her parents knew and approved of her boyfriend seemed a source of pleasure.

The difference in their experiences stems from divergent cultural ideas about sex and what responsible parents ought to do about it. Here, we see teenagers as helpless victims beset by raging hormones and believe parents should protect them from urges they cannot control. Matters aren't helped by the stereotype that all boys want the same thing, and all girls want love and cuddling. This compounds the burden on parents to steer teenage children away from relationships that will do more harm than good.

The Dutch parents I interviewed regard teenagers, girls and boys, as capable of falling in love, and of reasonably assessing their own readiness for sex. Dutch parents like Natalie's talk to their children about sex and its unintended consequences and urge them to use contraceptives and practice safe sex.

Cultural differences about teenage sex are more complicated than clichéd images of puritanical Americans and permissive Europeans. Normalizing ideas about teenage sex in fact allows the Dutch to exert *more* control over their children. Most of the parents I interviewed actively discouraged promiscuous behavior. And Dutch teenagers often reinforced what we see as 1950s-style mores: eager to win approval, they bring up their partners in conversation, introduce them to their parents and help them make favorable impressions.

Some Dutch teenagers went so far as to express their ideas about sex and love in self-consciously traditional terms; one Dutch boy said the advantage of spending the night with a partner was that it was "Like Mom and Dad, like when you're married, you also wake up next to the person you love."

Normalizing teenage sex under the family roof opens the way for more responsible sex education. In a national survey, 7 of 10 Dutch girls reported that by the time they were 16, their parents had talked to them about pregnancy and contraception. It seems these conversations helped teenagers prepare, responsibly, for active sex lives: 6 of 10 Dutch girls said they were on the pill when they first had intercourse. Widespread use of oral contraceptives contributes to low teenage pregnancy rates — more than 4 times lower in the Netherlands than in the United States.

Obviously sleepovers aren't a direct route to family happiness. But even the most traditional parents can appreciate the virtue of having their children be comfortable bringing a girlfriend or boyfriend home, rather than have them sneak around.

Unlike the American teenagers I interviewed, who said they felt they had to split their burgeoning sexual selves from their family roles, the Dutch teens had a chance to integrate different parts of themselves into their family life. When children feel safe enough to tell parents what they are doing and feeling, presumably it's that much easier for them to ask for help. This allows parents to have more influence, to control through connection.

Sexual maturation is awkward and difficult. The Dutch experience suggests that it is possible for families to stay connected when teenagers start having sex, and that if they do, the transition into adulthood need not be so painful for parents or children.

Activity 1.6 Analyze "The Sleepover Question"

1. What do you think about the "not under my roof" approach to a parent controlling a teen's sexuality versus the Dutch approach of allowing a teen's partner to sleep over? Discuss in your small group.

2. How do stereotypes play against the argument for a more open approach to teen sex in America? How much of parents' discomfort with their teen potentially having sex is guided by how their parents treated the subject when they were teens?

3. "The Sleepover Question" emphasizes logos. Can you paraphrase the logic of the argument? How does emotion (pathos) play a role in resistance to this argument?

4. In the article, the writer discusses the link between the use of oral contraceptives and lower teen pregnancy rates but does not mention the risk of STDs or condom use. Is it irresponsible of the author not to discuss the risk of STDs and sex, especially when she is willing to discuss teen pregnancy? Does it feel like an incomplete argument without discussing STDs?

5. If you were going to write a letter to the editor about this article, what would you say?

Why Study Rhetoric?

Rhetoric, or persuasive communication, happens all around us every day, in conversation at the grocery store, in blogs, on television, and in the classroom. We Americans constantly air our opinions about almost everything. Sometimes it is to convince others to share our opinions, sometimes the reason is to engage in a dialogue that will help us understand the world around us, and sometimes it is to persuade others to action.

Argument is essential to human interaction and to society, for it is through the interplay of ideas in argument that we discover answers to problems, try out new ideas, shape scientific experiments, communicate with family members, recruit others to join a team, and work out any of the multitude of human interactions essential for society to function. When issues are complex, arguments do not result in immediate persuasion of the audience; rather, argument is part of an ongoing conversation between concerned parties who seek resolution, rather than speedy answers.

Rhetoric provides a useful framework for looking at the world, as well as for evaluating and initiating communications. In the modern world, writing and communicating persuasively is a necessary skill. Those who can present effective arguments in writing are, in the business world, often the ones who are promoted. In addition, those who are able to evaluate the arguments presented to them, whether by politicians, advertisers, or even family members, are less likely to be swayed by logical fallacies or ill-supported research.

Also, writing rhetorically is a tool with sometimes surprising uses. Research shows that, as students, we are more likely to remember material we have written about rather than simply memorized. Also, through the process of writing, writers often find that they initiate ideas and connections between ideas that they might not otherwise have found. Thus, writing may lead to new discoveries.

Rhetoric is a part of our everyday lives. When we're in a conversation with someone, we use rhetoric on a conscious or subconscious level. If you go to class wearing the T-shirt of your favorite musician or band, you're ultimately sending a rhetorical message identifying you as a fan of that artist or group.

If you've ever written a profile on a dating site, you've used rhetorical principles to convince an audience of potential partners to contact you or to write you back if you have chosen to make the first contact. You build ethos by talking about yourself in order to build credibility among potential partners, and you establish pathos when you talk about an interest that is shared by a potential mate.

Being able to use the tools of rhetoric effectively gives you the power to control your communication—both incoming and outgoing—and to affect your environment in a positive way.

Reading 1.3

San Ysidro Shooting Survivor Lives His Dream of Being a Cop

by Janine Zuniga

In this feature story from the *San Diego Union-Tribune*, Janine Zuniga describes vividly how Alberto Leos, then a 17-year-old cook and high school football star, was shot and left for dead during James Oliver Huberty's rampage at a San Ysidro McDonald's in 1984. The 21 dead and 19 wounded made the massacre the worst one-day shooting by a single individual in United States history at the time. But Leos's story did not end there. The young man underwent surgeries and completed rehabilitation, going on to become a policeman. Notice how the author makes use of both ethos and pathos in writing this profile.

The shots fired at point-blank range pierced both arms, his right leg, stomach and chest, and Alberto Leos crumpled to the kitchen floor next to three co-workers at a San Ysidro McDonald's. Even with his injuries, the 17-year-old cook, three weeks into his first job, knew the others were dead. He could tell by the lifeless positions of their bodies.

During a harrowing 77 minutes 20 years ago today, Leos, a high school football star, watched in helpless horror as a heavily armed James Oliver Huberty "executed, killed families, babies, my manager."

In all, 21 people were killed and 19 wounded in what was, up to that time, the worst one-day massacre by a single gunman in U.S. history. "All I remember is saying a prayer," Leos said. "I prayed to see my family one more time . . . before I died."

The McDonald's Massacre, as it came to be called, has faded for many San Diegans during the past two decades, but for those such as Leos who survived, it became the defining moment of their lives.

Leos's recovery included three months in the hospital, where he underwent five surgeries to remove the bullets and repair damage. He spent two years in therapy, for both physical and emotional injuries.

Despite painful rehabilitation, scars and memories, Leos became even more determined to fulfill his childhood dream of becoming a police officer. He has been a cop for 17 years.

After stints with the National City and Chula Vista police departments, Leos is now a San Diego police sergeant working the Southern Division, which includes routine patrols of San Ysidro.

"I was born to do this work," said Leos, who is married and lives in Chula Vista. "I was born to be in this profession. That's how I feel."

Leos said that while growing up in Cudahy, a city southeast of Los Angeles, the only time he saw deputies was when they were taking someone to jail. But that image changed one day when an L.A. County sheriff's deputy visited his third-grade classroom.

"To see him in the school setting, I was in awe—his uniform, his nice, shiny badge," Leos said. "He told us they were there to help people, to help those who can't help themselves. I told myself that when I was older, I wanted to do that."

But Leos's parents quickly and, for a decade, successfully discouraged him from pursuing the dream, saying it was too dangerous a career for their only son. Their opposition vanished on the day he almost lost his life.

Photo by Howard Lipin / Union-Tribune

San Diego police sergeant, Alberto Leos, preparing to go out on patrol recently, overcame five surgeries and two years of painful therapy after the McDonald's Massacre to fulfill his childhood dream of becoming a police officer.

"When I was shot and my friends and co-workers were killed, my parents were very, very supportive of me doing whatever I wanted," Leos said. "I guess they felt I had a second chance."

The short sleeves of Leos's dark-blue uniform can't hide the scars on his arms, but he doesn't often share the details of that day. The 5-foot-8, clean-shaven officer is soft-spoken and somewhat formal.

"Even as a young, young man, I could tell he was a serious kind of person, not in a sober sense, but in that he had a job and wanted to help his folks, that he was a good kid," said Andrea Skorepa, who as an employee of the local social-services agency Casa Familiar helped administer a $1.4 million fund for survivors and those injured in the McDonald's Massacre.

Skorepa, who has remained friends with the officer, said some who lived through it, such as Leos, have accomplished their goals, while others have succumbed to the tragedy.

"For the people who survived, that day was the beginning of a new life for them," Skorepa said. "What they have done with their lives becomes the important story. He doesn't live as a victim. He's not gone that way."

He tries to get assigned to San Ysidro when he can, because he wants to give back to the community and to Casa Familiar. The agency not only helped with the fund but helped get his family through a very tough time.

"That's when I learned about community service and how much it's needed," Leos said.

Said Skorepa, now executive director of Casa Familiar, "I think it gives you a different perspective, if you've come that close to losing your life and are somehow spared, on how to live your life."

In all his years in law enforcement, Leos has never fired his weapon at anyone. He's sure he will if he has to, but his instincts, which he has learned to trust, help guide him more calmly through tense situations.

Now, if a situation doesn't feel right, he will take a few steps back and think it through. Back on that unforgettable day, Leos said something told him not to go to work, but he didn't listen to his gut.

"I woke up with this feeling that I shouldn't go in," said Leos, who will turn 38 next month. "My friends were going to the beach and invited me to go. But it was the first job I ever had, and I talked myself out of it."

Activity 1.7 Consider a Profile

1. In your small group, decide what argument Janine Zuniga is making in this profile of the San Ysidro massacre survivor.

2. Describe what you think are the best specific details the writer includes, either of the shooting or of Leos's subsequent recovery and career as a policeman. How do these details contribute to the story?

3. A profile generally emphasizes the ethos of the subject. In this profile, how does the author do that? How does the author also make use of pathos?

4. As the readers, what conclusion are you left with after you read the article? Is this the impression that the writer wanted you to have, do you think?

Reading 1.4

Memories of McDonald's Rhetorical Actions 20 Years Later

Shortly after the shooting that injured Alberto Leos, wounded 18 others, and killed 21 people (see the reading on page 22), a committee in San Ysidro, California, collected 1,400 signatures asking that the McDonald's be razed and a memorial park built. Although McDonald's was in no way responsible for the attack, it responded to the committee's rhetorical appeal. Bob Kaiser, director of media relations for McDonald's, said, "The concern is for the people, not simply business" and reported that the company's decision whether to reopen the restaurant was being held in abeyance. Later, the company tore down the restaurant and donated the land to the city. After debating what to do with the land, the city used it to build a community college.

In 2004, twenty years after the massacre, a memorial service was held at the site, and the media ran stories about the anniversary. Many people contributed to a blog associated with the anniversary story in the local newspaper:

> Jennifer wrote: "I live in La Jolla, exactly twenty five miles north of the former McDonald's where this tragedy took place some twenty plus years ago. The site is now the home of Southwestern College, but I have seen the memorial and am always filled with sadness when I go there. They have done a wonderful job on the memorial which is just in front of the former McDonald's building which you can tell was once the eatery, but has been painted grey, though the general shape of the building is still there. I am especially touched by the comments in this story and it is great that the memory of what happened not so long ago in our city is kept alive. ALL those that survived or not on that very sad day, were heroes, but their memories will never be in vain and we, as the citizens of this beautiful city will always be proud of their bravery and courage."
>
> Leonor wrote: "I was seven at the time and I lived half a block from McDonald's. I saw bullets flying in the air and I remember police officers not letting us go to our house. They told us to get down in our car and not move. It was scary because we did not know what was going on. We were going to eat at McDonald's but my grandma invited us to her house. I still live in San Ysidro

and I graduated from Southwestern College and I see the area everyday. It's not easy to forget what I do remember."

Armida wrote: "I remember that day. I was there. I had just turned 17. This was my first job. I lost my cousin and two friends because they threw a coffee pot at him to save this guy who became a cop. I saved a co-worker. I never told anybody or wrote about this day till now."

Sergio wrote: "I still remember this event. I'm now 33 years old and I was 9 years old. I still remember the gun shots, many of them. I grew up about 3 blocks away. I remember the countless police officers blocking the streets of Sunset Lane, which was my street. Two of my friends were murdered. I could have been there. My best friend died that day. This has been a funeral I will always remember. I just like to share a tiny bit on that day in the summer of July."

Joe Bloggs wrote: "I remember this happening. I was only about 12 years old at the time and living in Australia, but it is something I never forget about. Why America is so obsessed with guns I will never understand. Nobody except the police and army should have access to firearms. The private ownership of guns should be illegal and there should be gun amnesty days where guns can be handed in to be crushed. This is going to happen time and time again, people, unless you stand up and say no to gun ownership."

The blog entries show the impact of the event, even 20 years later. Notice that there are no negative comments about the McDonald's, nor about what the community decided to do with the land. Nothing McDonald's could have done would have erased the pain of the event, but its rhetorical actions, in both word and deed, did not add to the trauma of the event. McDonald's response to the citizens' request to tear down the building and donate the land to the city continues to be praised 20 years later.

Collaborate Activity 1.8 Blogging and Responding to Blogging

In your group, discuss the blog entries above about the San Ysidro shooting. Which blog entry attracts your attention the most? What do you think was the author's rhetorical purpose?

Write your own blog entry in response to the McDonald's story. What would you say to the citizens who remember the event? What would you say to the people at McDonald's who made the decision to tear down the building and donate the land to the city?

Do you blog? Why? Do you check your blog frequently? How do you feel if there are responses to your comments? How do you feel if there are no responses to your comments? Does it matter if the response is positive or negative?

Compose

Activity 1.9 Write about Everyday Arguments

Read your local newspaper or magazines such as *Time* or *Fortune* or search the Internet and bring to class a copy of a recent text or visual image that makes an argument about an issue. You might find, for example, an editorial in your local newspaper about recycling efforts in your community or a blog entry about parenting practices. Be sure, however, that the text or image takes a position on the issue. Write a paragraph of approximately 100 to 150 words describing the argument to your classmates and your reaction to it.

Encountering Visual Rhetoric

Why is a visual so powerful? Colors, shapes, and symbols impact viewers in ways text alone cannot. Many images present arguments and, because they are visual, they communicate more quickly and, sometimes, more powerfully than words.

The images on the next page are covers from *GQ* magazine. On the left, Sacha Baron Cohen, in the Bruno character, graces the humor edition of the magazine in a pose echoing that of Jennifer Aniston, on the right, which was printed on a cover a few months previously. What do you think when you see a man positioned in a way that is typical for a scantily dressed (or nude) female? Is it funny? Many think so, but not everyone. A posting on a blog called thesocietypages.org says of Cohen, "The contrast between the meaning of the pose (sexy and feminine) with the fact that he's male draws attention to how powerfully gendered the pose is… women look sexy when they pose like this, men look stupid when they do."

A photo's ability to persuade can be significant, whether it is a news photo or an advertisement. However, not everyone interprets images the same way, especially when they evoke stereotypes of gender, race, or religion.

Compare these two cover photos from *GQ* magazine. Though the poses are similar, because the figure on the left is a man and the one on the right is a woman, they evoke very different responses from readers. Some see the photo on the left as paying humorous tribute to the one on the right. Others interpret both images as exploiting feminine gender stereotypes.

Compose

Activity 1.10 Write a Caption for a Photo or a Pair of Photos

Choose a news photo or advertisement from a newspaper, magazine, or the Internet that presents an argument. Alternatively, compare two news photos or advertisements. Copy or paste the photo or photos on a piece of paper and write a caption that expresses the argument(s) you see in the photo.

Rhetorical Arguments Stand the Test of Time

Abraham Lincoln's Gettysburg Address is the short speech that the president delivered at the site of the battle of Gettysburg where, four months previously, the Union Army defeated Confederate forces. His was not the only talk that day at the dedication of the Soldiers' National Cemetery, but it is the only one remembered. In just over two minutes, he was able to reframe the Civil War not just as a victory for the North but as a "new birth of freedom" for all

Americans. Now, during the 150th anniversary of the Civil War, is a good time to remember Lincoln's rhetoric—in terms of both the content and the style of his speech.

Reading 1.5

Text of the Gettysburg Address

Four score and seven years ago our fathers brought forth on this continent, a new nation, conceived in Liberty, and dedicated to the proposition that all men are created equal.

Now we are engaged in a great civil war, testing whether that nation, or any nation so conceived and so dedicated, can long endure. We are met on a great battlefield of that war. We have come to dedicate a portion of that field, as a final resting place for those who here gave their lives that that nation might live. It is altogether fitting and proper that we should do this.

But, in a larger sense, we cannot dedicate—we cannot consecrate—we cannot hallow—this ground. The brave men, living and dead, who struggled here, have consecrated it, far above our poor power to add or detract. The world will little note, nor long remember what we say here, but it can never forget what they did here. It is for us the living, rather, to be dedicated here to the unfinished work which they who fought here have thus far so nobly advanced. It is rather for us to be here dedicated to the great task remaining before us—that from these honored dead we take increased devotion to that cause for which they gave the last full measure of devotion—that we here highly resolve that these dead shall not have died in vain—that this nation, under God, shall have a new birth of freedom—and that government of the people, by the people, for the people, shall not perish from the earth.

Though no actual recording exists of Lincoln giving the speech, you can listen to it if you search on the Internet for "recording of Gettysburg Address." Listen to the speech, noting the phrase "Four score and seven years ago," which is so famous that Americans know instantly, when it is quoted by orators or writers, that it is a reference to Lincoln. Consider what arguments the president makes in his speech. Think about their relevance today.

Activity 1.11 Paraphrase the Gettysburg Address

Rephrase each sentence of the Gettysburg Address, one by one, in your own words, putting it in 21st century wording rather than Lincoln's ceremonial, 19th century phrasing. In a paraphrase, the text does not become shorter; it is recreated in different words. This is a useful technique in helping you understand a text. It is also helpful when you are writing an analysis of a text because you can use your paraphrase rather than long, block quotes. Remember, though, when you are writing an essay, you must cite a paraphrase in the text and also include it in your list of references.

Compose

Activity 1.12 Keep a Commonplace Book

Ancient rhetoricians performed speeches with little warning, often to advertise their services as teachers of rhetoric. Thus, they frequently memorized arguments about specific topics that could be adapted to the audience and situation on a moment's notice. They called these memorized arguments "commonplaces." Commonplace books are an outgrowth of the Greek concept of commonplaces, but they are a little different. They became popular in the Middle Ages as notebooks in which individuals would write down quotes or ideas about a particular topic.

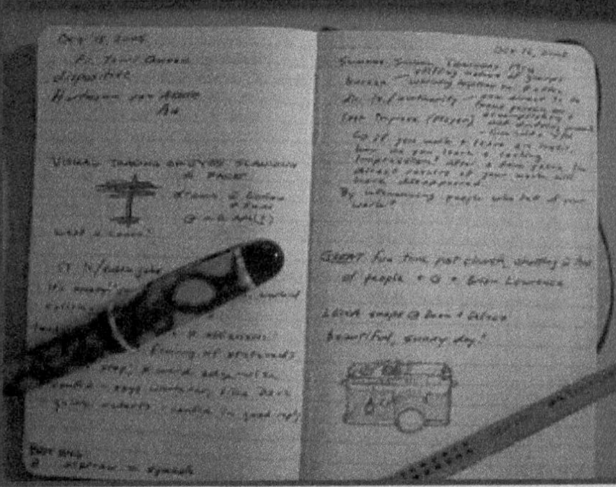

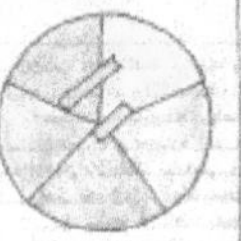

For thousands of years, people have been keeping commonplace books, a kind of journal or diary in which the author includes quotes, drawings, and images.

These notations might later be used to generate an idea for a composition. In more modern times, people have created commonplace books in the form of scrapbooks in which they collect quotes as well as drawings and clippings. Thus, they become a record of a person's intellectual life and can be saved for later reference.

For this class, take a notebook, perhaps one with a colorful or interesting cover, and keep notes, quotes, vocabulary words, and clippings related to the topics discussed in class. As your instructor directs, this commonplace book may be graded as evidence of class participation or it may be a private journal. Take a look at the commonplace books shown here for ideas. Be creative and enjoy adapting this ancient journal form to record ideas that interest you.

Activity 1.13 Create Your Own Blog

Create a home page for a professional blog using a site like Blogger, WordPress, or Live Journal. Blogger is the easiest to use, but the others have more flexible options. Read the help screens for instructions on how to create your blog. Your design choices should reflect your personality. Keep in mind, though, that you are building an "academic self," so all the topics you write about should be of an academic nature and in an academic tone. Some students decide to have two blogs, one for their friends and one for professional networking, so you may want to do this, especially if you already have a blog.

During this class, you'll use the blog to explore different aspects of each chapter in the textbook (and other topics that your instructor directs). You can also blog about other topics related to your writing this semester, and you can link to other blogs that you think your readers would find of interest.

End of the Year... My Favorite Memory

May 15, 2011

Exactly one week ago, I wes at my graduation ceremony receiving my college degree. Normally, graduating would be the last thing a student would do before summer vacation however I am still at CMC working away. You see, me and my RA crew had to stay in the residence halls for a few days after graduation to close down the building. Although they left 2 days ago, I am still here working on a special project. Sitting in an empty 250 bedroom mansion has given me a lot of time to think about my year. With all this reminiscing, I tried to think of my favorite memory of 2nd semester. It was difficult to choose but my 2nd semester Sky Club trip was my favorite memory of all.

For our 2nd semester Sky Club trip, we went to the McDonald Observatory in Fort David Texas. This was the 2nd trip we took and it was my favorite. We embarked out on April Fools Day (no joke) and headed south towards Texas. It was nice because we took two 11 man vans and only had 14 people on the trip so the drive was very comfortable. We stopped in several spots throughout the day and finally 15 hours later we arrived in the famous town of Fort Davis! We were all shocked to actually be in Texas because our amusement for the entire ski season in Steamboat was making fun of Texan tourists. Since we were now tourists in Texas, we began acting like tourists. Immediately we busted out cameras and took pictures of anything and everything we could see.

After you have created the look of your blog, write a first entry that introduces you to your readers. You might include your major, your college, and something interesting that might attract readers to your blog.

2
RESPONDING RHETORICALLY

Praxis in Action

Why I Annotate Readings by Lauren Connolly

Annotating a reading gives me the ability to participate in a conversation with the author of the text in order to develop my ideas for writing and understanding the information presented. My annotation style uses two methods: one is with a pencil and the other is with a highlighter.

As with a conversation, my side comments may be to protest the author's ideas or to make connections with other things in my life, other readings for the class, or my other classes. By making notes, I am actively participating in the conversation, opposed to passively taking in the information presented, and it gives me an opportunity to create something meaningful from the text. Using the highlighter sparingly, I only mark a word or phrase, in order to point out specific ideas or words that I want to reference, understand, or quote in my writing at a later point in time. The meaningful interaction is when, using a pencil, I write comments in the margins in response to these highlights. These comments are frequently a part of my prewriting stage, as I use my marginal comments directly in my early written drafts. Annotating allows me to respond, clarify, and develop my ideas about what I have learned, enabling me to use the ideas later in both my writing and research.

Lauren Connolly likes to annotate readings because it allows her to have a conversation with the writer.

Thinking Critically, Reading Rhetorically

In contemporary times we study texts to encourage students to develop critical thinking, a skill which is essential for understanding the scientific method and for making effective judgments in the workplace and in civil life. This student-centered emphasis would have seemed strange to ancient Greek and Roman rhetoricians and their students. They believed that a rhetor's skill was best developed by honoring the skills of those who excelled in the past. Therefore, a large part of the educational process involved having students study the texts of well-regarded speeches, memorize and recite them, and model new compositions based on their approaches to topics and language style. As Isocrates explained:

> Since language is of such a nature that it is possible to discourse on the same subject matter in many different ways—to represent the great as lowly or invest the little with grandeur, to recount the things of old in a new manner or set forth events of recent date in an old fashion—it follows that one must not shun the subjects upon which others have composed before, but must try to compose better than they . . . (Panegyricus).

Thus, students in ancient Greece or Rome would have been presented with a text, often read aloud by a teacher, and they would be asked to transcribe or copy it down with the idea that they would internalize the skills of the master rhetor who had originally given the speech. Then, they would be asked to write about the same subject in a way that built upon what they had learned from the master text but incorporated their own personal attitudes or perspectives.

Today, rather than being asked to model new compositions based upon the techniques of classic texts, students are asked to read texts carefully and then to engage in critical thinking and discussion about those texts.

Critical thinking involves considering issues thoughtfully and independently. Critical thinkers do not believe facts or opinions just because they are published—whether it is in newspapers, textbooks, on television, or on the Internet. Nor do they focus upon just understanding or memorizing information, as in facts and figures. Critical thinkers examine the reasoning of the information in front of them, looking for premises and considering the inferences drawn from those premises. They are able to think for themselves, making logical connections between ideas, seeing cause and effect relationships, and using information to solve problems.

Reading rhetorically makes use of critical thinking skills, but it also involves looking at texts as arguments and evaluating them for validity, adequacy of evidence, and presence of bias. Moreover, reading rhetorically involves having a knowledge of rhetoric and specialized Greek terms such as logos, pathos, ethos, and kairos—words that were defined briefly in Chapter 1 and will be discussed more extensively in Chapter 3. Practice reading rhetorically as you read the following article on the Strauss-Kahn sexual assault case.

Reading 2.1

In Sex-Crime Cases, Credibility a Thorny Issue

by Paul Duggan

In 2011, Dominique Strauss-Kahn, the head of the International Monetary Fund (IMF), was accused of sexual assault by a housekeeper at the Sofitel New York hotel. He pled not guilty. During the case, the victim's credibility was called into question, as she had reportedly lied to the police in her first statement about the case. The following article, by Paul Duggan, published in *The Washington Post*, talks about the credibility of alleged victims in sex-crime cases, and how, in the Strauss-Kahn case, it could affect the outcome. To begin a critical reading of an article, you want to read the entire piece first for content. Then, reread the introduction. How does the author attempt to capture the audience's attention? How does the author use the Lanigan case as a frame of reference?

A wealthy public figure accused of sexual misconduct in a swanky hotel says that the charge is trumped up, that his alleged victim lacks credibility.

In their eagerness to bag a famous name, the defendant says, investigators have rushed to judgment. He says they have failed to carefully consider whether the woman who reported being accosted had a motive to lie.

That's what Dominque Strauss-Kahn says, through his attorneys.

And that's what lawyer A. Scott Bolden says. He represents Washington Redskins lineman Albert Haynesworth, awaiting trial on a misdemeanor charge that he indecently groped a waitress at the posh W Hotel in Washington.

"Let me tell you something about sex-crimes prosecutors," said Bolden, a former sex-crimes prosecutor. "They tend to be true believers. I mean, they've never met a victim they don't want to save or who they don't believe. . . . And when credibility issues arise, they tend to just want to explain them away."

As authorities Friday acknowledged doubts about the credibility of Strauss-Kahn's accuser in New York, and the rape case against the former head of the International Monetary Fund seemed in jeopardy, Bolden and other lawyers said the news highlights one of the thorniest issues in sex-crimes prosecutions:

Will jurors believe the alleged victim?

Sometimes the believability issue has nothing to do with the allegation itself. The witness may have a troubled past that could cast doubt on her testimony.

Harry O'Reilly, a retired New York City police detective who helped create the department's Special Victims Unit in the early 1970s—the unit that handled the Strauss-Kahn case—said investigators often deal with accusers who have less-than-savory backgrounds and who offer changing accounts of alleged assaults.

"It's quite common for there to be credibility issues," he said. He said detectives initially should focus only on whether the alleged crime occurred, and not be deterred by the woman's personal history, even if it involves dishonesty.

"If someone makes an allegation, we listen," he said. "And then we look for chinks in the story. And if the story begins to dissipate, then we go from there. But at the onset, we're not looking at things in her past that aren't relevant to the allegation."

Attorney Peter Greenspun, who defended Fairfax County teacher Sean Lanigan, acquitted this year of sexually molesting a 12-year-old female student, said authorities have to proceed in such cases with caution.

"These are the kinds of cases where the most care has to be exercised before anyone is charged, because of what allegations like this do to people," Greenspun said.

Jurors in the Fairfax trial later voiced outrage at the dearth of evidence against Lanigan, a married father of three whose life was shattered by the allegations.

"These are devastating charges," Greenspun said. "There's an assumption of guilt by the public, and reputations and life trajectories are destroyed."

In New York, prosecutors acknowledged that the hotel maid who accused Strauss-Kahn of raping her in his luxury suite May 14 later lied to investigators about her personal history and gave them inconsistent accounts of the moments after the alleged assault.

Strauss-Kahn, 62, who was arrested hours after the allegation and resigned from the IMF, was ordered released from home confinement in Manhattan on Friday. But the district attorney's office has not moved to dismiss the rape case.

"She said it happened, and he's sort of a pompous guy with a reputation ... for grabbing women, so they thought, well, of course, it must have happened," Greenspun said. He said police generally spend too little time investigating such cases before making arrests, especially when the suspects are prominent men.

Even if Strauss-Kahn's attorneys have information about his accuser that they could use in court to cast doubt on her veracity, prosecutors have a "moral obligation" to proceed with the case if they believe that the woman is being truthful, said lawyer Mai Fernandez, director of the National Center for Victims of Crime.

"You could have Attila the Hun come to you and say he's a victim, and the truth of the matter is, in this particular case, he may be," Fernandez said.

"You have to look first at the evidence that's directly related to the case at hand," she added. "The victim? Well, everybody has a past. None of us is without sin. There's always something that a defense lawyer can use to tarnish your reputation."

Kristina Korobov, a former prosecutor, agreed with Fernandez, but only to an extent.

"It's true that you can't just say to a victim, 'Well, you have a credibility problem, so too bad,' and then, based on that, you don't proceed with the case," Korobov said. "Because that just rewards offenders who choose victims with credibility problems."

In a case like Strauss-Kahn's, she said, prosecutors are probably weighing whether the woman's credibility is so badly damaged that a conviction would be highly unlikely.

"There were a number of victims in my lifetime who I legitimately believed had been victimized, but I didn't file a charge," said Korobov, now a senior attorney with the National Center for the Prosecution of Violence Against Women. "You've got to be very selective about what cases you bring, based on what you think you can prove."

Activity 2.1 Analyze a Text

In your small group, discuss the following questions and then report your group's opinion(s) to the class.

1. What is the problem that the author is concerned about in regard to prosecuting sex crimes?
2. What court cases does he mention? How was the victim's ethos involved?
3. How does the writer appeal to logos? To pathos?
4. If your group were writing a letter to the editor of the *Washington Post* commenting about this article, what might you say about the controversy the writer presents?

Rhetoric's Visual Heritage and Impact

The first televised presidential debate in September 1960 is a famous example of the power of visual rhetoric and a vivid illustration of the fact that visual elements must be considered when "reading" rhetorical situations. Radio listeners who could hear but not see the debate rated Vice President Richard Nixon as the winner over Senator John F. Kennedy—Nixon's arguments sounded more logical and were more clearly expressed. However, the television audience experienced a new element in the history of presidential debates: They could see the performances of the handsome and tan Senator Kennedy and the pasty-white and ill-looking Vice President Nixon, and they clearly preferred Kennedy. He *looked and acted presidential*, which overcame the drawbacks that had troubled his campaign previously—that he was relatively unknown, young, and Catholic. It overcame any advantage that Nixon may have had in presenting logical arguments and also by being an incumbent vice president. And unfortunately for Nixon, by 1960, 88 percent of Americans had televisions. "It's one of those unusual points on the timeline of history where you can say things changed very dramatically—in this case, in a single night," says Alan Schroeder, a media historian who authored the book, *Presidential Debates: Forty Years of High-Risk TV*.* Indeed, after the unexpected impact of the Kennedy-Nixon debates, presidential candidates were so apprehensive about competing on television that it was 16 years before candidates (President Gerald R. Ford and former Governor Jimmy

* Kayla Webley, "How the Nixon-Kennedy Debate Changed the World" *Breaking News, Analysis, Politics, Blogs, News Photos, Video, Tech Reviews*, September 23, 2010. http://www.time.com/time/nation/article/0,8599,2021078,00.html. Accessed July 30, 2011.

Carter) were again willing to risk presenting themselves side by side on television.

Why did the experience of seeing the two candidates, rather than hearing them or reading their speeches, make such a difference? The ancient Greeks and Romans who developed rhetoric would have understood the reason: It was what they called ethos, which can be translated only imperfectly as credibility. A person's ethos is determined partially by his or her reputation, but as Richard Nixon learned the hard way, it is conveyed even more powerfully by appearance, gestures, tone, and cadence of speech. It is important to remember that the standards and perceptions of Americans are heavily influenced by rhetoric as it was defined and implemented by the Greeks and Romans—first in oral presentations. Many of the attributes of rhetoric translate to written texts, but not all. Thus, when considering a text that was originally presented as a speech, reading rhetorically means thinking about visual rhetoric—the impact the speech would have had on an audience that was *watching and listening to the presentation.*

The first presidential debate between Vice President Richard Nixon and Senator John F. Kennedy illustrated the power of visual rhetoric.

Moreover, the impact of visual rhetoric involves more than speeches: It concerns television shows, films, photographs, paintings, advertisements, and even the typesetting layout of a text that has no illustrations. We will consider these types of visual rhetoric in more detail later in this chapter.

On page 41, we reprint President Barack Obama's speech announcing the death of Osama bin Laden. This speech is available widely on the Internet at such sites as AmericanRhetoric.com, NYTimes.com, and YouTube.com. If possible, watch the speech before you read the text, and as you do so think about the impact of the speech, including the president's verbal presentation and the setting at the White House, as well as the content of the speech. Think about the various audiences President Obama was speaking to—Americans and people around the world who might be watching at that moment, as well as a historic audience of people such as yourself who would be viewing the speech months or years later.

The Rhetorical Triangle

When reading a text or listening to a speech, keep in mind the three parts of the rhetorical triangle—writer, audience, and subject (see figure 2.1). Each of these can be framed as a question:

figure 2.1

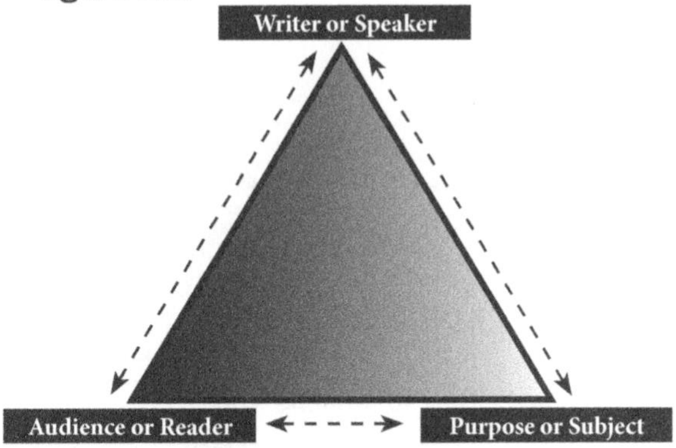

Writer or Speaker

Audience or Reader

Purpose or Subject

- Who is the writer? What is the impression the writer wants to make on the audience? What does the writer do to establish credibility (ethos)? How does the writer create common ground with the audience?

- Who is the intended audience? How would a logical appeal influence the audience? An ethical appeal? An emotional appeal? What does the audience anticipate in terms of organization and format of the presentation or paper? What is the extent of their knowledge about the subject, and do they have prejudices or preferences?

- What is the purpose of the communication? In the case of an argument, the purpose would be to persuade. Is that the case with this reading? Is it clear what the writer wants to persuade the audience to believe or to do? Is the request phrased in a logical manner?

Activity 2.2 Apply the Rhetorical Triangle

For each of the readings presented thus far in the textbook, identify the speaker, the audience, and the purpose. Then analyze how each of those elements affects the content of the reading.

1. "Violent Rhetoric and Arizona Politics" (Chapter 1, p. 14)
2. "The Sleepover Question" (Chapter 1, p. 18)
3. "San Ysidro Shooting Survivor Lives His Dream of Being a Cop" (Chapter 1, p. 22)
4. "In Sex-Crime Cases, Credibility a Thorny Issue" (Chapter 2, p. 35)

Reading 2.2

President Barack Obama on the Death of Osama bin Laden

Good evening. Tonight, I can report to the American people and to the world that the United States has conducted an operation that killed Osama bin Laden, the leader of al Qaeda, and a terrorist who's responsible for the murder of thousands of innocent men, women, and children.

President Barack Obama announced the death of Osama bin Laden.

It was nearly 10 years ago that a bright September day was darkened by the worst attack on the American people in our history. The images of 9/11 are seared into our national memory—hijacked planes cutting through a cloudless September sky; the Twin Towers collapsing to the ground; black smoke billowing up from the Pentagon; the wreckage of Flight 93 in Shanksville, Pennsylvania, where the actions of heroic citizens saved even more heartbreak and destruction.

And yet we know that the worst images are those that were unseen to the world. The empty seat at the dinner table. Children who were forced to grow up without their mother or their father. Parents who would never know the feeling of their child's embrace. Nearly 3,000 citizens taken from us, leaving a gaping hole in our hearts.

On September 11, 2001, in our time of grief, the American people came together. We offered our neighbors a hand, and we offered the wounded our blood. We reaffirmed our ties to each other, and our love of community and country. On that day, no matter where we came from, what God we prayed to, or what race or ethnicity we were, we were united as one American family.

We were also united in our resolve to protect our nation and to bring those who committed this vicious attack to justice. We quickly learned that the 9/11 attacks were carried out by al Qaeda—an organization headed by Osama bin Laden, which had openly declared war on the United States and was committed to killing innocents in our country and around the globe. And so we went to war against al Qaeda to protect our citizens, our friends, and our allies.

Over the last 10 years, thanks to the tireless and heroic work of our military and our counterterrorism professionals, we've made great strides in that effort. We've disrupted terrorist attacks and strengthened our homeland defense. In Afghanistan, we removed the Taliban government, which had given Bin Laden and al Qaeda safe haven and support. And around the globe, we worked with our friends and allies to capture or kill scores of al Qaeda terrorists, including several who were a part of the 9/11 plot.

Yet Osama bin Laden avoided capture and escaped across the Afghan border into Pakistan. Meanwhile, al Qaeda continued to operate from along that border and operate through its affiliates across the world. And so shortly after taking office, I directed Leon Panetta, the director of the CIA, to make the killing or capture of Bin Laden the top priority of our war against al Qaeda, even as we continued our broader efforts to disrupt, dismantle, and defeat his network.

Then, last August, after years of painstaking work by our intelligence community, I was briefed on a possible lead to Bin Laden. It was far from certain, and it took many months to run this thread to ground. I met repeatedly with my national security team as we developed more information about the possibility that we had located Bin Laden hiding within a compound deep inside of Pakistan. And finally, last week, I determined that we had enough intelligence to take action, and authorized an operation to get Osama bin Laden and bring him to justice.

Today, at my direction, the United States launched a targeted operation against that compound in Abbottabad, Pakistan. A small team of Americans carried out the operation with extraordinary courage and capability. No Americans were harmed. They took care to avoid civilian casualties. After a firefight, they killed Osama bin Laden and took custody of his body.

For over two decades, Bin Laden has been al Qaeda's leader and symbol, and has continued to plot attacks against our country and our friends and allies. The death of Bin Laden marks the most significant achievement to date in our nation's effort to defeat al Qaeda.

Yet his death does not mark the end of our effort. There's no doubt that al Qaeda will continue to pursue attacks against us. We must—and we will—remain vigilant at home and abroad.

As we do, we must also reaffirm that the United States is not—and never will be—at war with Islam. I've made clear, just as President Bush did shortly after 9/11, that our war is not against Islam. Bin Laden was not a Muslim leader; he was a mass murderer of Muslims. Indeed, al Qaeda has slaughtered scores of Muslims in many countries, including our own. So his demise should be welcomed by all who believe in peace and human dignity.

Over the years, I've repeatedly made clear that we would take action within Pakistan if we knew where Bin Laden was. That is what we've done. But it's important to note that our counterterrorism cooperation with Pakistan helped lead us to Bin Laden and the compound where he was hiding. Indeed, Bin Laden had declared war against Pakistan as well, and ordered attacks against the Pakistani people.

Tonight, I called President Zardari, and my team has also spoken with their Pakistani counterparts. They agree that this is a good and historic day for both of our nations. And going forward, it is essential that Pakistan continue to join us in the fight against al Qaeda and its affiliates.

The American people did not choose this fight. It came to our shores, and started with the senseless slaughter of our citizens. After nearly 10 years of service, struggle, and sacrifice, we know well the costs of war. These efforts weigh on me every time I, as Commander-in-Chief, have to sign a letter to a family that has lost a loved one, or look into the eyes of a service member who's been gravely wounded.

So Americans understand the costs of war. Yet as a country, we will never tolerate our security being threatened, nor stand idly by when our people have been killed. We will be relentless in defense of our citizens and our friends and allies. We will be true to the values that make us who we are. And on nights like this one, we can say to those families who have lost loved ones to al Qaeda's terror: Justice has been done.

Tonight, we give thanks to the countless intelligence and counterterrorism professionals who've worked tirelessly to achieve this outcome. The American people do not see their work, nor know their names. But tonight, they feel the satisfaction of their work and the result of their pursuit of justice.

We give thanks for the men who carried out this operation, for they exemplify the professionalism, patriotism, and unparalleled courage of those who serve our country. And they are part of a generation that has borne the heaviest share of the burden since that September day.

Finally, let me say to the families who lost loved ones on 9/11 that we have never forgotten your loss, nor wavered in our commitment to see that we do whatever it takes to prevent another attack on our shores.

And tonight, let us think back to the sense of unity that prevailed on 9/11. I know that it has, at times, frayed. Yet today's achievement is a testament to the greatness of our country and the determination of the American people.

The cause of securing our country is not complete. But tonight, we are once again reminded that America can do whatever we set our mind to. That is the story of our history, whether it's the pursuit of prosperity for our people, or the struggle for equality for all our citizens; our commitment to stand up for our values abroad, and our sacrifices to make the world a safer place.

Let us remember that we can do these things not just because of wealth or power, but because of who we are: one nation, under God, indivisible, with liberty and justice for all.

Thank you.

May God bless you.

And may God bless the United States of America.

Activity 2.3 Evaluate the President's Speech

After you have both watched President Obama's speech on the Internet and read the text, discuss these questions in your small group and then present the consensus of your group's answers to the class.

1. Discuss the president's presentation of the speech. Do you think the speech had a different impact on those who watched it on television versus those who heard it on the radio? What about those who neither saw nor heard it but rather read the speech?

2. How would you describe the president's tone, appearance, and mannerisms (all part of his ethos)? What about the location he chose for the speech and the timing just after news agencies had announced Bin Laden's death (the kairos)?

3. Summarize what the president says about the government's reasons for seeking Osama bin Laden and killing him. Does the president make a good argument for the necessity and importance of this act?

4. Notice that the president uses visual imagery in his speech. For example, in paragraph two, immediately after he announces his news, he refers to 9/11—"a bright September day was darkened by the worst attack on the American people in our history." What is the purpose of the visual descriptions in his speech?

5. Do you agree or disagree with what the president has to say? How so?

Activity 2.4 Research Reactions to President Obama's Speech

Using Google or another search engine, research the reactions to the president's speech announcing the death of Bin Laden.

1. In the days after the speech, what did the media report about the attack on Bin Laden's compound?

2. What were some American reactions to the speech and to the killing of Bin Laden?

3. What was the reaction around the world, both in Muslim and non-Muslim countries?

4. Did you learn anything during your research that surprised you? How so?

As your instructor directs, either discuss these questions in class or turn in written answers to the questions.

Reading 2.3

The Lexicon

by Charles McGrath

A *lexicon* is a synonym for dictionary, thesaurus, and wordlist. Charles McGrath, in his *New York Times* essay, "The Lexicon," examines the changes that 9/11 wrought in the English language. The attack on the World Trade Center, unlike other world-changing violent events, hasn't yet created many new words, he decides. Rather, it has brought already-existing words to our everyday vocabulary—such as jihad, T.S.A. shoe bomber, and sleeper cell. These not-so-pretty words are the lexicon of 9/11.

Ground zero, sleeper cells, progressive vertical collapse: The most resonant phrases of 9/11 are imbued with what might be called antipoetry, a resistance to prettification.

Unlike some other momentous events in our history—World War II, say, or the Vietnam War—the attacks that took place on Sept. 11, 2001, have not particularly changed or enriched our vocabulary. Sometimes these things take a while. It wasn't until the 1960s, for example, that the term "holocaust," which used to mean any large-scale massacre, took on the specific connotations it has today. For now, though, you could argue that the events of 9/11 still seem so unfathomable that they have actually impoverished the language a little, leaving us with a vacuous phrase like **war on terror**, which manages to empty both "war" and "terror" of much their meaning, or the creepy, Nazi-sounding **homeland**, which seems a far less pleasant place to live than just plain America.

We do know a lot of words now that we probably should have known before, like **jihad, Taliban, mujahedeen** and **Al Qaeda**. And some that we'd just as soon forget, like **T.S.A., security checkpoint, shoe bomber** and **progressive vertical collapse**. A term like **sleeper cell** probably sticks in our heads because it contains a tiny hint of embedded poetry, and for the same reason it's hard to forget those **72 black-eyed virgins** whom the terrorists believed they were on their way to meet. The "black-eyed" bit is a brilliant touch, even if it's probably a mistranslation.

But the most resonant phrases that have taken residence in our consciousness since that September morning are ones imbued with what might be called antipoetry, a resistance to metaphor or to prettification. **Ground zero**, for example—a term that originated with the Manhattan Project and was originally used in connection with nuclear explosions—seems particularly apt in this new context, with its sense of absolute finality, of a point that is both an end and a beginning and to which everything else refers.

And even **9/11** itself has a kind of rightness. No one says "September 11th" anymore as shorthand for that awful day. (To do so, a friend once joked, would be "so September 10th.") There's a pleasing, no-nonsense simplicity and precision to the expression—the same effect created by "24/7," only starker, and with none of the exaggeration. These four syllables are right at the end of language, where words turn into abstraction. Individually, they're just random, empty numbers, but yoked by that fateful slash they contain volumes. 9/11—everyone knows what that means, and to say any more would be pointless. Sometimes words fail.

Activity 2.5 Develop a Lexicon

Choose one of the following activities and create a lexicon as a group or individually:

1. Reread President Obama's speech about the death of Osama bin Laden. What words have become a more frequent part of the nation's vocabulary as a result of Bin Laden's actions? Al Qaeda and Taliban are two. Can you find others? Do an Internet search for Osama bin Laden, until you have five to seven words. Then write a 250 to 300 word essay, similar to McGrath's, in which you consider how Bin Laden's life and death have affected our country's vocabulary.
2. Do a search on the Internet for "new words." You will find lists of words and phrases that have been added to new editions of dictionaries. Examples may include such words as "aquascape," "soul patch," and "sandwich generation." Choose five to seven new words that are related to each other in some way. Create a lexicon of your own with a paragraph about each word that emphasizes the invention or recent history of the word. Give examples of each word's usage in blogs or other publications.

Ways of Reading Rhetorically

Reading theorist Louise Rosenblatt suggests a technique for analyzing written texts—particularly those with few visual cues other than words on paper or a computer screen. She says that we take the pattern of verbal signs left by the author and use them to recreate the text, not in the exact way the author perceived the text, but guided by it.

So, as we read, there is a constant stream of response to the text. However, Rosenblatt says that even as the reader is recreating the text, he or she is also reacting to it. Thus, there are two interacting streams of response involved as the person moves through the text. The reader, rather than being a passive receptor for the author's text, actually participates in the creative process during reading.

However, we read differently depending on the text and the occasion. For example, if you take a paperback novel on an airplane trip, you probably read simply for entertainment and to pass the time in the air. If you read *King Lear* for a literature class, you read for the plot, characterization, and other elements that you know will be discussed in class. If you read a chapter in your chemistry textbook before an exam, you are focusing on remembering concepts and details that might be on the test. Reading as a writer is another type of reading. You examine the text with an eye for the choices the writer made when crafting the text, such as whether the writer begins with a narrative introduction, a quote from a noted authority, or a startling statement. You notice, for example, what people are mentioned in the text, either as authorities or participants in activities.

Rosenblatt also makes a useful distinction between two main kinds of reading—aesthetic reading and efferent reading. In **aesthetic reading**, the reader is most interested in what happens "during the reading event, as he fixes his attention on the actual experience he is living through," according to Rosenblatt. Readers focus upon the ideas, images, and story of the text that evoke an aesthetic experience in the moment of reading. **Efferent readers**, in contrast, read to learn from the text, and, thus, according to Rosenblatt, "concentrate on the information, the concepts, the guides to action, that will be left with him when the reading is over."

Reading rhetorically is efferent reading, focusing not on the experience of reading but on the information the text conveys and upon the way an argument is established and supported in a text. Some arguments are written in an engaging style that is a pleasure to read, while others are written in a highly emotional tone that arouses a visceral response in the reader. A text that inspires aesthetic reading must sometimes be read several times in order for the reader to focus on the structure of the argument beneath the creative language.

Some theorists say that critical thinking is "thinking about thinking" or "reasoning about reasoning," and that is exactly what reading rhetorically involves—reasoning about whether or not a text presents a reasoned argument. A good way to begin reading rhetorically is to be aware of the essential elements of an argument and identify these elements in the text you are evaluating. See the Checklist of Essential Elements in an Argument presented below.

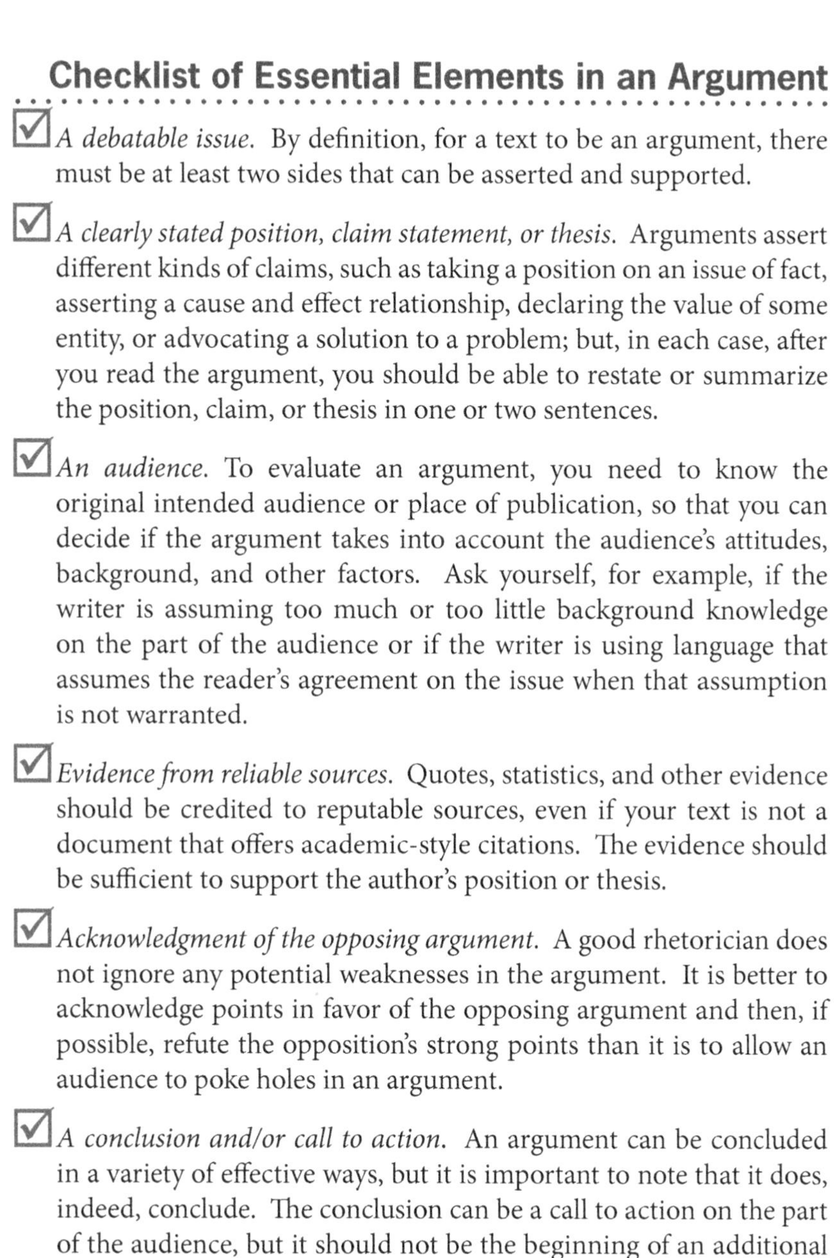

Checklist of Essential Elements in an Argument

- ☑ *A debatable issue.* By definition, for a text to be an argument, there must be at least two sides that can be asserted and supported.
- ☑ *A clearly stated position, claim statement, or thesis.* Arguments assert different kinds of claims, such as taking a position on an issue of fact, asserting a cause and effect relationship, declaring the value of some entity, or advocating a solution to a problem; but, in each case, after you read the argument, you should be able to restate or summarize the position, claim, or thesis in one or two sentences.
- ☑ *An audience.* To evaluate an argument, you need to know the original intended audience or place of publication, so that you can decide if the argument takes into account the audience's attitudes, background, and other factors. Ask yourself, for example, if the writer is assuming too much or too little background knowledge on the part of the audience or if the writer is using language that assumes the reader's agreement on the issue when that assumption is not warranted.
- ☑ *Evidence from reliable sources.* Quotes, statistics, and other evidence should be credited to reputable sources, even if your text is not a document that offers academic-style citations. The evidence should be sufficient to support the author's position or thesis.
- ☑ *Acknowledgment of the opposing argument.* A good rhetorician does not ignore any potential weaknesses in the argument. It is better to acknowledge points in favor of the opposing argument and then, if possible, refute the opposition's strong points than it is to allow an audience to poke holes in an argument.
- ☑ *A conclusion and/or call to action.* An argument can be concluded in a variety of effective ways, but it is important to note that it does, indeed, conclude. The conclusion can be a call to action on the part of the audience, but it should not be the beginning of an additional argument that is not supported by the evidence presented.

Reading 2.4

The Web Means the End of Forgetting

by Jeffrey Rosen

Several years ago, Stacy Snyder was a fairly typical 25-year-old college student training to be a teacher. That all changed forever when she did something that she probably thought was harmless fun—she posted a photo of herself on a social network site. In this article published in *The New York Times*, Jeffrey Rosen uses Snyder's case to illustrate how notions of privacy are changing because of the ever-growing presence and popularity of social networking sites. What is even more alarming, according to Rosen, is that photos and information, once posted on the web, are there forever. The web does not forget, and this lack of forgetting is changing society's ability to forgive and forget.
You may enjoy posting status updates about your life on a MySpace, Facebook, or Twitter account; however, with employers increasingly conducting background checks on such sites, it's very important to be careful about what you choose to post. This includes status updates, photographs, and videos. If you read the following article carefully, you may never look at social networking sites quite the same again.

Four years ago, Stacy Snyder, then a 25-year-old teacher in training at Conestoga Valley High School in Lancaster, Pa., posted a photo on her MySpace page that showed her at a party wearing a pirate hat and drinking from a plastic cup, with the caption "Drunken Pirate." After discovering the page, her supervisor at the high school told her the photo was "unprofessional," and the dean of Millersville University School of Education, where Snyder was enrolled, said she was promoting drinking in virtual view of her underage students. As a result, days before Snyder's scheduled graduation, the university denied her a teaching degree. Snyder sued, arguing that the university had violated her First Amendment rights by penalizing her for her (perfectly legal) after-hours behavior. But in 2008, a federal district judge rejected the claim, saying that because Snyder was a public employee whose photo didn't relate to matters of public concern, her "Drunken Pirate" post was not protected speech.

When historians of the future look back on the perils of the early digital age, Stacy Snyder may well be an icon. The problem she faced is only one example of a challenge that, in big and small ways, is confronting millions of people around the globe: how best to live our lives in a world where the Internet records everything and forgets nothing—where every online photo, status update, Twitter post and blog entry by and about us can be stored forever. With websites like LOL Facebook Moments, which collects and shares embarrassing personal revelations from Facebook users, ill-advised photos and online chatter are coming back to haunt people months or years after the fact.

Examples are proliferating daily: there was the 16-year-old British girl who was fired from her office job for complaining on Facebook, "I'm so totally bored!!"; there was the 66-year-old Canadian psychotherapist who tried to enter the United States but was turned away at the border—and barred permanently from visiting the country—after a border guard's Internet search found that the therapist had written an article in a philosophy journal describing his experiments 30 years ago with LSD. According to a recent survey by Microsoft, 75 percent of U.S. recruiters and human-resource professionals report that their companies require them to do online research about candidates, and many use a range of sites when scrutinizing applicants—including search engines, social networking sites, photo- and video-sharing sites, personal websites and blogs, Twitter and online gaming sites. Seventy percent of U.S. recruiters report that they have rejected candidates because of information found online, like photos and discussion-board conversations and membership in controversial groups.

Technological advances, of course, have often presented new threats to privacy. In 1890, in perhaps the most famous article on privacy ever written, Samuel Warren and Louis Brandeis complained that because of new technology—like the Kodak camera and the tabloid press—"gossip is no longer the resource of the idle and of the vicious but has become a trade." But the mild society gossip of the Gilded Age pales before the volume of revelations contained in the photos, video and chatter on social media sites and elsewhere across the Internet. Facebook, which surpassed MySpace in 2008 as the largest social-networking site, now has nearly 500 million members, or 22 percent of all Internet users, who spend more than 500 billion minutes a month on the site. Facebook users share more than 25 billion pieces of content each month (including news stories, blog posts and photos), and the average user creates 70 pieces of content a month. There are more than 100 million registered Twitter users, and the Library of Congress recently announced that it will be acquiring—and permanently storing—the entire archive of public Twitter posts since 2006.

In Brandeis's day—and until recently, in ours—you had to be a celebrity to be gossiped about in public: today all of us are learning to expect the scrutiny that used to be reserved for the famous and the infamous. A 26-year-old Manhattan woman told *The New York Times* that she was afraid of being tagged in online photos because it might reveal that she wears only two outfits when out on the town—a Lynyrd Skynyrd T-shirt or a basic black dress. "You have movie-star issues," she said, "and you're just a person."

We've known for years that the web allows for unprecedented voyeurism, exhibitionism and inadvertent indiscretion, but we are only beginning to understand the costs of an age in which so much of what we say, and of what others say about us, goes into our permanent—and public—digital files.

The fact that the Internet never seems to forget is threatening, at an almost existential level, our ability to control our identities; to preserve the option of reinventing ourselves and starting anew; to overcome our checkered pasts.

In a recent book, "Delete: The Virtue of Forgetting in the Digital Age," the cyberscholar Viktor Mayer-Schönberger cites Stacy Snyder's case as a reminder of the importance of "societal forgetting." By "erasing external memories," he says in the book, "our society accepts that human beings evolve over time, that we have the capacity to learn from past experiences and adjust our behavior." In traditional societies, where missteps are observed but not necessarily recorded, the limits of human memory ensure that people's sins are eventually forgotten. By contrast, Mayer-Schönberger notes, a society in which everything is recorded "will forever tether us to all our past actions, making it impossible, in practice, to escape them." He concludes that "without some form of forgetting, forgiving becomes a difficult undertaking."

It's often said that we live in a permissive era, one with infinite second chances. But the truth is that for a great many people, the permanent memory bank of the web increasingly means there are no second chances—no opportunities to escape a scarlet letter in your digital past. Now the worst thing you've done is often the first thing everyone knows about you.

THE CRISIS—AND THE SOLUTION?

Concern about these developments has intensified this year, as Facebook took steps to make the digital profiles of its users generally more public than private. Last December, the company announced that parts of user profiles that had previously been private—including every user's friends, relationship status and family relations—would become public and accessible to other users. Then in April, Facebook introduced an interactive system called Open Graph that can share your profile information and friends with the Facebook partner sites you visit.

What followed was an avalanche of criticism from users, privacy regulators and advocates around the world. Four Democratic senators—Charles Schumer of New York, Michael Bennet of Colorado, Mark Begich of Alaska and Al Franken of Minnesota—wrote to the chief executive of Facebook, Mark Zuckerberg, expressing concern about the "instant personalization" feature and the new privacy settings. In May, Facebook responded to all the criticism by introducing a new set of privacy controls that the company said would make it easier for users to understand what kind of information they were sharing in various contexts.

Facebook's partial retreat has not quieted the desire to do something about an urgent problem. All around the world, political leaders, scholars and citizens are searching for responses to the challenge of preserving control of our identities in a digital world that never forgets. Are the most promising solutions going to be technological? Legislative? Judicial? Ethical? A result of shifting social norms and cultural expectations? Or some mix of the above? Alex Türk, the French data protection commissioner, has called for a "constitutional right to oblivion" that would allow citizens to maintain a greater degree of anonymity online and in public places. In Argentina, the writers Alejandro Tortolini and Enrique Quagliano have started a campaign to "reinvent forgetting on the Internet," exploring a range of political and technological ways of making data disappear. In February, the European Union helped finance a campaign called "Think B4 U post!" that urges young people to consider the "potential consequences" of publishing photos of themselves or their friends without "thinking carefully" and asking permission. And in the United States, a group of technologists, legal scholars and cyberthinkers are exploring ways of recreating the possibility of digital forgetting. These approaches share the common goal of reconstructing a form of control over our identities: the ability to reinvent ourselves, to escape our pasts and to improve the selves that we present to the world. [. . .]

[. . .] In the near future, Internet searches for images are likely to be combined with social-network aggregator search engines, like today's Spokeo and Pipl, which combine data from online sources—including political contributions, blog posts, YouTube videos, web comments, real estate listings and photo albums. Increasingly these aggregator sites will rank people's public and private reputations, like the new website Unvarnished, a reputation marketplace where people can write anonymous reviews about anyone. In the Web 3.0 world, Michael Fertik, a Harvard Law School graduate, predicts people will be rated, assessed and scored based not on their creditworthiness but on their trustworthiness as good parents, good dates, good employees, good baby sitters or good insurance risks.

One legal option for responding to online setbacks to your reputation is to sue under current law. There's already a sharp rise in lawsuits known as Twittergation—that is, suits to force websites to remove slanderous or false posts. Last year, Courtney Love was sued for libel by the fashion designer Boudoir Queen for supposedly slanderous comments posted on Twitter, on Love's MySpace page and on the designer's online marketplace-feedback page. But even if you win a U.S. libel lawsuit, the website doesn't have to take the offending material down any more than a newspaper that has lost a libel suit has to remove the offending content from its archive.

Some scholars, therefore, have proposed creating new legal rights to force websites to remove false or slanderous statements. Cass Sunstein, the Obama administration's regulatory czar, suggests in his new book, "On Rumors," that there might be "a general right to demand retraction after a clear demonstration that a statement is both false and damaging." (If a newspaper or blogger refuses to post a retraction, they might be liable for damages.) Sunstein adds that websites might be required to take down false postings after receiving notice that they are false—an approach modeled on the Digital Millennium Copyright Act, which requires websites to remove content that supposedly infringes intellectual property rights after receiving a complaint.

As Stacy Snyder's "Drunken Pirate" photo suggests, however, many people aren't worried about false information posted by others—they're worried about true information they've posted about themselves when it is taken out of context or given undue weight. And defamation law doesn't apply to true information or statements of opinion. Some legal scholars want to expand the ability to sue over true but embarrassing violations of privacy—although it appears to be a quixotic goal.

Daniel Solove, a George Washington University law professor and author of the book, *The Future of Reputation*, says that laws forbidding people to breach confidences could be expanded to allow you to sue your Facebook friends if they share your embarrassing photos or posts in violation of your privacy settings. Expanding legal rights in this way, however, would run up against the First Amendment rights of others. Invoking the right to free speech, the U.S. Supreme Court has already held that the media can't be prohibited from publishing the name of a rape victim that they obtained from public records. Generally, American judges hold that if you disclose something to a few people, you can't stop them from sharing the information with the rest of the world.

That's one reason that the most promising solutions to the problem of embarrassing but true information online may be not legal but technological ones. Instead of suing after the damage is done (or hiring a firm to clean up our messes), we need to explore ways of preemptively making the offending words or pictures disappear.

Zuckerberg said in January to the founder of the publication TechCrunch that Facebook had an obligation to reflect "current social norms" that favored exposure over privacy. "People have really gotten comfortable not only sharing more information and different kinds but more openly and with more people, and that social norm is just something that has evolved over time," he said.

However, norms are already developing to recreate off-the-record spaces in public, with no photos, Twitter posts or blogging allowed. Milk and Honey, an exclusive bar on Manhattan's Lower East Side, requires potential members to sign an agreement promising not to blog about the bar's goings on or to post photos on social-networking sites, and other bars and nightclubs are adopting similar policies. I've been at dinners recently where someone has requested, in all seriousness, "Please don't tweet this"—a custom that is likely to spread.

But what happens when people transgress those norms, using Twitter or tagging photos in ways that cause us serious embarrassment? Can we imagine a world in which new norms develop that make it easier for people to forgive and forget one another's digital sins? [. . .]

[. . .] Perhaps society will become more forgiving of drunken Facebook pictures in the way Samuel Gosling, the University of Texas, Austin, psychology professor says he expects it might. And some may welcome the end of the segmented self, on the grounds that it will discourage bad behavior and hypocrisy: it's harder to have clandestine affairs when you're broadcasting your every move on Facebook, Twitter and Foursquare. But a humane society values privacy, because it allows people to cultivate different aspects of their personalities in different contexts; and at the moment, the enforced merging of identities that used to be separate is leaving many casualties in its wake. Stacy Snyder couldn't reconcile her "aspiring-teacher self" with her "having-a-few-drinks self": even the impression, correct or not, that she had a drink in a pirate hat at an off-campus party was enough to derail her teaching career.

That doesn't mean, however, that it had to derail her life. After taking down her MySpace profile, Snyder is understandably trying to maintain her privacy: her lawyer told me in a recent interview that she is now working in human resources; she did not respond to a request for comment. But her success as a human being who can change and evolve, learning from her mistakes and growing in wisdom, has nothing to do with the digital file she can never entirely escape. Our character, ultimately, can't be judged by strangers on the basis of our Facebook or Google profiles; it can be judged by only those who know us and have time to evaluate our strengths and weaknesses, face to face and in context, with insight and understanding. In the meantime, as all of us stumble over the challenges of living in a world without forgetting, we need to learn new forms of empathy, new ways of defining ourselves without reference to what others say about us and new ways of forgiving one another for the digital trails that will follow us forever.

Activity 2.6 Discuss "The Web Means the End of Forgetting"

1. What is the significance of the title, "The Web Means the End of Forgetting"?
2. What does Jeffrey Rosen mean when he suggests that in the future Stacy Snyder may be an icon?
3. What is the main point in Jeffrey Rosen's main essay? What is he arguing?
4. Does Rosen offer sufficient evidence to make you take his argument seriously? Why or why not?
5. Are you a member of any social networking sites? What can you do in order to protect your reputation?
6. A woman interviewed in the article said, in regard to being tagged in online photos, "you have movie-star issues—and you're just a person." If you are a member of any social networking sites, do you tag friends in photos? Is it important to be careful about this? Why or why not?

Explore

Activity 2.7 What Is the Current State of Identity Protection in Social Networking Sites?

In your group, explore news, watchdog, and government sites to see if any new laws or other protections have been implemented to safeguard individuals posting personal information on the web. Report what you learn to the class.

Close Reading of a Text

Rhetorical reading involves careful and patient attention to the text, even reading the text several times. Following are several strategies for reading critically. You do not need to use all of the reading strategies suggested for each essay you read, but as you begin to read critically, you should try all of the strategies at least once to see which ones supplement your natural reading and learning style.

1. **Learn about the author.** Knowing whether an author is a biologist, a professional writer, or a politician can guide your expectations of the essay. If you are reading in a magazine or journal, you can often discover information in the contributor's notes at the beginning or end of the essay or at the beginning or end of the magazine. Many books have a dust jacket or a page giving a short biography of the author. As you learn about the author, jot down any impressions you may have about the author's purpose in writing the essay. Does the author have an obvious agenda in promoting a certain viewpoint on the topic?

2. **Skim the text.** Once you've gotten to know the author a little, it is helpful to read the essay quickly and superficially by reading the introduction, the first sentence in every paragraph, and the conclusion. Read quickly. When you skim a text, you are not trying to understand it. You are preparing for the more careful read that will follow. If the essay tells a story, skimming will give you a good sense of the chronology of the story. When is the story taking place? How much time seems to pass? If the essay is argumentative, skimming will provide knowledge of the basic structure of the argument and will introduce you to the main points of support. If the essay is primarily informative, you will learn some of the important distinctions and classifications the author uses to organize the information.

   It may be interesting to note whether you can get the gist of the reading by skimming. Has the writer provided topic sentences for paragraphs or sections? If so, the writer is trying to make his or her message easily accessible.

3. **Explore your own knowledge and beliefs on the subject.** Make a list of what you already know about the topic of the text. Then make a list of what you believe about this topic. Finally, make a note beside each entry that marks where that information or belief came from.

4. **Reflect on the topic.** The final step before reading is reflecting on what you expect from the essay before you begin a careful reading. What does the title lead you to expect from the essay? Does your quick glance at the essay seem to support the title? How do you feel about the essay so far? Does it anger you, interest you, bore you? Do you think you have any experience that relates to the essay? Will your experience and the

author's experience lead you to the same conclusions? One effective way to reflect is to freewrite on the topic of the essay. Exploring what you know before you embark on a careful reading of the essay can deepen your responses.

5. **Annotate.** Read the essay slowly, thinking about what meaning the author is trying to convey. It is a good idea to annotate as you read, particularly points that seem important and/or raise questions in your mind. If you don't want to write in your text, try photocopying assigned essays so you can annotate them. You'll probably develop your own system of annotation as you begin to use this technique more often, but here are some basic guidelines to help you begin your annotations:

   - Underline sentences, phrases, and words that seem important to the essay.
   - Circle words you don't know but think you understand from the context. Then you can look them up later to see if the dictionary definition matches the definition you assumed from the context.
   - Write questions in the margins. If the margins aren't large enough to write a complete question, a couple of words to remind you of what you were thinking and a question mark will do. You can also write brief comments in the margins, again just a few words to remind you of your thoughts.
   - Number or put check marks in the margin by major points. Careful annotation of each point in the margin will help you later if you choose to outline.
   - Use arrows, lines, and symbols in the margins to connect ideas in the essay that seem related or depend on each other.
   - Note transitions, sentence structures, examples, topic sentences, and other rhetorical moves that seem particularly effective in the essay by writing a brief comment or an exclamation mark in the margin next to the underlined text.

   See figure 2.2 on page 60 for an example of an annotated article.

6. **Outline.** An excellent way to distill the meaning of a text is to create an informal outline of the argument. If, as part of annotating the essay, you jot down the main subject of each paragraph in the margin, this will allow you to see the organization of the essay and outline it easily. An outline should list the focus of the essay and track how that focus unfolds paragraph by paragraph. If you are outlining a narrative essay,

the outline will probably follow the chronology of the events. Outlining an informative essay, you might find that the outline tracks the steps of a process or reveals divisions and classifications. Outlining an argumentative essay, you'll probably find your outline works to prove a thesis by making statements which support that thesis, raising objections and refuting them, or, perhaps, proposing solutions to solve a problem.

7. **Freewrite about the text.** Another way to distill the meaning of a text after you have read it carefully is to lay the essay aside and freewrite for a few minutes about the content and purpose of the essay. If you have not tried freewriting before, it is easy. You simply put your pen to the paper, focus the topic in your mind, and write whatever comes to mind about the topic for a set period of time, perhaps five minutes. If you cannot think of anything to write, you write, "I can't think of anything to write," and then you continue writing what is in your mind. You may find it helpful to begin your freewriting by writing, "This essay is about . . ." and continue writing, explaining to yourself what you think the essay is about.

8. **Summarize the text.** Write a summary of what you consider to be the primary meaning of the text. Your summary should answer these questions about claims, support, purpose, and audience:

   - What is the author of the essay trying to show or prove (claim)?
   - What does the writer use to convince me that he or she is well informed or right (support)?
   - Why did the writer choose to write this essay (purpose)?
   - Who is the author addressing or writing for (audience)?

   To write a clear summary, you have to understand the essay. You might test your understanding by reading the essay again and deciding whether your summary is accurate. Writing summaries helps you understand your assignments and prepares you for the numerous summaries you will complete.

Responding to Oral and Visual Media

Increasingly, young "politically minded viewers" are plugging into YouTube, Facebook, and comedy shows like "The Daily Show" and other alternative media instead of traditional news outlets. According to a *New York Times*

figure 2.2

Reading 2.2

President Barack Obama on the Death of Osama bin Laden

One man affected so many

Good evening. Tonight, I can report to the American people and to the world that the United States has conducted an operation that killed Osama bin Laden, the leader of al Qaeda, and a terrorist who's responsible for the murder of thousands of innocent men, women, and children.

Where was I when it happened?

It was nearly 10 years ago that a bright September day was darkened by the worst attack on the American people in our history. The images of 9/11 are seared into our national memory—hijacked planes cutting through a cloudless September sky; the Twin Towers collapsing to the ground; black smoke billowing up from the Pentagon; the wreckage of Flight 93 in Shanksville, Pennsylvania, where the actions of heroic citizens saved even more heartbreak and destruction.

visual image—good technique

strong verbs

Presidential seal—ethos

President Barack Obama announced the death of Osama bin Laden.

And yet we know that the worst images are those that were unseen to the world. The empty seat at the dinner table. Children who were forced to grow up without their mother or their father. Parents who would never know the

refers to children—pathos

article, surveys and interviews during the 2008 presidential election indicate that "younger voters tend to be not just consumers of news and current events but conduits as well—sending out e-mailed links and videos to friends and their social networks. And in turn, they rely on friends and online connections for news to come to them." **Word of mouth** (via e-mail) is replacing traditional media as the major news filter, at least for young viewers. In this new process, moreover, "viewers" or "writers of e-mail" move seamlessly back and forth between e-mail, text-messaging, television viewing, and Internet surfing, appreciating and sharing the choicest rhetorical pieces with others. "We're talking about a generation that doesn't just like seeing the video in addition to the story—they expect it," said Danny Shea, 23, the associate media editor for *The Huffington Post* (huffingtonpost.com). "And they'll find it elsewhere if you don't give it to them, and then that's the link that's going to be passed around over e-mail and instant message." This multistream, cross-platform method of communication among younger viewers/readers is a fertile forum for rhetorical analysis.

Actually, the lines between oral, written, and visual "texts" have always been somewhat blurred. Speeches delivered orally in person or on television have a visual component, as the audience sees the speaker present the text. A written text is also, in a sense, visual because the audience's mind must process the little squiggles of ink on paper or on the computer screen into words. A visual text such as an advertisement or cartoon often includes written text, and, even if it does not, the image will inspire thoughts that are often distilled into language for expression. Reasonably, many of the same techniques used to analyze written and oral texts also can be applied to visual media (cartoons, advertisements, television, etc.).

Reading 2.5

Let's Roll

by Neil Young

Music lyrics are performance texts, just as are speeches. They are written to be heard, not written to be read. However, you can analyze the argument in song lyrics, such as "Let's Roll," reprinted here, which was written by Neil Young. The song was inspired by the last words of a passenger named Todd Beamer, who died in the hijacking of Flight 93 on September 11, 2001. To analyze the song's lyrics rhetorically, you can consider whether the lyrics have a debatable issue, a clear thesis or claim, evidence to support that claim, a particular audience, and a conclusion. With a song, moreover, you can also consider the impact of the lyrics as they are presented by a vocalist accompanied by musical instruments. How does the musical presentation of the lyrics affect their impact as an argument?

I know I said I love you,

I know you know it's true,
I've got to put the phone down,
and do what we got to do.

One's standing in the aisleway,
Two more at the door,
We've got to get inside there,
Before they kill some more.

Time is runnin' out,
Let's roll.
Time is runnin' out,
Let's roll.

No time for indecision,
We've got to make a move,
I hope that we're forgiven,
For what we got to do

How this all got started,
I'll never understand,
I hope someone can fly this thing,
And get us back to land.

Time is runnin' out,
Let's roll.
Time is runnin' out,
Let's roll.

No one has the answer,
But one thing is true,
You've got to turn on evil,
When it's coming after you,
You've gotta face it down,
And when it tries to hide,
You've gotta go in after it,
And never be denied,

Time is runnin' out,
Let's roll.

Let's roll for freedom,
Let's roll for love,
We're going after Satan,
On the wings of a dove,
Let's roll for justice,
Let's roll for truth,
Let's not let our children,
Grow up fearful in their youth.

Time is runnin' out,
Let's roll.
Time is runnin' out,
Let's roll.
Time is runnin' out,
Let's roll.

Activity 2.8 Respond to Song Lyrics

1. Reflect on what you know about the September 11 attacks. At the end of the first stanza, Young writes, "I've got to put the phone down, and do what we got to do." What is the call to action he is making here? What rhetorical significance does it have in this historical context?

2. Who is Young referring to when he says, "We're going after Satan"? What action is he advocating?

Activity 2.9 Consider a Song as an Argument

In your small group, explore the Internet for a song that seems to make an argument, and answer the following questions. Share your findings with the class.

1. What message is the artist/group trying to transmit with the song?

2. What are some lyrics that help to support this message?

3. How would you describe the musical style of the song? In what ways does the style of singing and instrumentation help the rhetorical message?

Responding to Visual Rhetoric

Methods of analyzing visual rhetoric draw upon several theoretical traditions. In art criticism, viewers may look for symbolism in an image or consider what meaning the artist was trying to convey. Semiotics views images as having intertextuality, as similar images come to have similar meanings, and those meanings may create similar emotions in the viewer. Rhetoricians, as you might expect, consider the argument that an image may present to a viewer. They think about how the subject of the image is presented in relation to other elements in the visual, how the image is cropped, and what types of lighting and colors are present. Rhetoricians also pay particular attention to the interplay between the visual image and any text that may appear with the image and how the two together construct an argument.

Courtesy BMW premium advertising.

In the BMW advertisement shown above, for example, a beautiful blonde-haired young woman is presented without clothes and lying down with her hair artfully arranged in waves. *Salon* magazine reprinted a copy of the BMW advertisement, pointing out that, "in small print scrawled across her bare shoulder, it reads: 'You know you're not the first.' As your eyes drift to the bottom of the advertisement—and the top of her chest—you learn that it's an advertisement for BMW's premium selection of used cars."

Of course, sexual appeal has been used for decades to sell a whole range of products. However, what do you think is BMW's argument here? *Salon* thinks the ad is implying, "Used cars, used women" and that the ad gives a "whole new meaning" to BMW's slogan, printed in the ad: "Sheer Driving Pleasure."

The image that appears below, surprisingly, isn't advertising a car. No, it is selling a community college, West Hills College, capitalizing on the idea that with all the money you would save by going to a community college, you could buy a nice car.

Courtesy West Hills College

Explore

Activity 2.10 Interpret Advertisements

1. What is the symbolism of the beautiful young woman (presumably naked) posed as she is in the BMW advertisement?

2. What meaning do you think the tag line, "You know you're not the first," adds to the image? Then, when you realize that the image is an ad for BMW used cars, does your interpretation of this tag line's meaning change?

3. What are the creators of the West Hills College advertisement trying to say by showing the image of the student sitting on the car?

4. The use of fonts is another important element in transmitting a message in an advertisement. In the West Hills College ad, why are the words "and save" written in a different font and inserted with the caret?

5. As a college student, would you be convinced by the West Hills advertisement? Why or why not? What elements exist in the ad that would or would not convince you to attend the college mentioned?

6. Do you find the BMW advertisement amusing, objectionable, or appealing? Does it make you want to buy a used BMW?

Activity 2.11 Find Advertisements with Effective Arguments

Bring to class an advertisement that you think makes an effective argument. It can be torn from a magazine or downloaded from the Internet. In your small group, evaluate each advertisement for its effectiveness in selling something, and choose the one with the most effective argument. Present your choice to the class along with an explanation of why you think it is effective.

Interaction between Texts and Images

Many of the texts we encounter in everyday life—in newspapers, magazines, and on the Internet—are not texts in isolation but texts combined with images. Indeed, when readers first glance at one of these media, likely their attention is caught first by photos, then by headlines. Only after being engaged by these attention-getting visual elements (for headlines are visual elements as well as written) are readers likely to focus on the written text. Student writers today, like professionals, have access to the use of visual elements in their compositions, and adding photos can not only catch the reader's attention but also emphasize particular points of an argument or create an overall mood.

All-Star Rockers Salute Buddy Holly

by Andy Greene

R&R

All-Star Rockers Salute Buddy Holly

McCartney, Cee Lo, the Black Keys, Kid Rock and more cut killer covers disc

When Buddy Holly died in a plane crash in 1959, he was just 22 years old and had been writing and recording songs for only about two years. But that music—including immortal hits like "Not Fade Away" and "Peggy Sue"—has had an incalculable impact on rock history. "He was a major influence on the Beatles," Paul McCartney told Rolling Stone recently. "John and I spent hours trying to work out how to play the opening riff to "That'll Be the Day," and we were truly blessed by the heavens the day we figured it out. It was the first song John, George and I ever recorded."

NOT FADE AWAY Holly in 1950. McCartney and Cee Lo recorded new songs commemorating Holly's 75th birthday.

A half-century later, McCartney has returned to Holly's catalog, cutting a smoking rendition of "It's So Easy." It's one of 19 newly recorded Holly covers—by an all-star lineup including the Black Keys, My Morning Jacket, Kid Rock Fiona Apple, Patti Smith, and Lou Reed—for the tribute disc *Rave on Buddy Holly*, spearheaded by Randall Poster, music supervisor of movies such as *The Royal Tenenbaums* and *I'm Not There*. "We wanted to commemorate Buddy's 75th birthday," Poster says. "I've used a lot of his songs in movies, and they're so powerful and so ripe for interpretation."

Florence and the Machine cut a New Orleans-flavored version of "Not Fade Away" while on tour in the Big Easy last year. "My grandmother took me to the musical *Buddy: The Buddy Holly Story* when I was a kid, and it changed my life," says singer Florence Welch. "When we were in New Orleans, we decided it would be good to use the environment around us, so we brought in local Cajun musicians." Cee Lo Green tackled the relatively obscure "You're So Square (Baby, I Don't Care)." "We wanted to keep the rockabilly intact," he says. "But we broadened it and gave it a bit of something unique to me. There's something Americana about it, something country and something African." Smith selected "Words of Love." "During the song she talks in Spanish and is sort of channeling [Holly's widow] Maria Elena Holly," says Poster. "It's so romantic and so novel. More times than not, we were just overwhelmed by the power of the renditions that we received." Despite Holly's extremely brief career, Poster thinks the set could have been even longer: "There's probably a half-dozen more songs we could have done. If I had more time and more of a budget, I would have kept on going."

ANDY GREENE

Activity 2.12 Analyze Interaction between Texts and Images

Read the article, "All-Star Rockers Salute Buddy Holly," by Andy Greene, published in *Rolling Stone* magazine. Look at how the images and layout work together and answer the questions:

1. What rhetorical purpose do the photos of these musicians achieve in relation to the article? Hint: think about the ethos (credibility, reputation, power) of these particular musicians, especially when they appear together on the page.

2. Consider the way the text is wrapped around the pictures. In particular, notice how this layout suggests a close relationship between Buddy Holly, Paul McCartney, and Cee Lo Green. What does this layout signify?

Activity 2.13 Write a Summary

Summarizing is an excellent technique to use when preparing for an exam or researching for an essay. It allows you to discern the main points of a text to see what is beneficial for you to know for the exam or paper. With a classmate, search for an article from a newspaper or magazine that presents a strong argument. Read the article, and list the main points individually. After you've listed the main points, put them into paragraph form. Caution: Beware of the temptation to add your own analysis of what the text is saying. For example, if you are summarizing a scientist's article on global warming, you need to be careful not to reveal your personal opinion about whether or not global warming is occurring or whether or not human actions are to blame. In this assignment, you summarize only. You do not argue or analyze.

When you're finished, compare your summary with that of your partner.

Reading 2.7

How to Make a Kindle Cover from a Hollowed Out Hardback Book

by Justin Meyers

The author of the following article explains why you would want to make a Kindle cover out of an old book instead of buying a new Kindle cover. What does the article say are the drawbacks of the Kindle? Think about it. These instructions are an argument, saying in text and photos that as wonderful as the Kindle is, it does not satisfy the needs of a reader to touch and smell a book. The author attempts to rectify the Kindle's shortcomings through these instructions for making a cover out of a book.

Notice also how the author uses photos to illustrate his text. If you had just the text and no photos, following the instructions would be much more difficult.

Kindle users love reading. But let's face it—a book is in your hands.

Sure, Amazon's Kindle makes it possible to read more books, clears up a lot of shelf space, fits snugly in anyone's baggage and can actually be cheaper in the long run. But each reading feels the same. The only difference is the words you read and your reaction to them. You begin to miss that sometimes rough feel of a hardback book, along with the slick, almost slippery design

of a paperback. Each book seems to have a smell of its own, something unique. And getting your hands dirty with ink from the finely written words was half the journey.

The Kindle erases that part of your reading experience. It feels the same, smells the same and even looks the same. Instead of turning pages, which is different sizes, thicknesses and colors from book to book, you're pressing the same button over and over again. In some ways, reading a classic on your Kindle actually devalues its adventure. But the eBook reader is convenient, practically weightless and serves up immediate literature consumption.

So where's the compromise?

Well, you can have the best of both worlds—sort of . . .

ebonical has crafted the perfect Kindle case—out of a hardcover book. Kindle cases can be expensive, so making a homemade Kindle cover is the perfect weekend project. And chances are you already have the perfect book for your Kindle collecting dust on your bookshelf. If not, you'll need to shop the local bookstores.

"I decided to carve out the pages of a printed book and thus complete the poetic circle of digital book readers destroying the printed word.

"Getting the right book turned out to be harder than I thought as most hardcover books are designed to be a particular size and variance is slight. Too small and the edges would be brittle. Too large and it would just become a hassle and ruin the point of having the small digital reader in the first place. With some time spent scouring thrift shops and second hand book stalls I managed, with some luck, to find what seemed to be the right book."

So, then how do you actually make the Kindle book cover?

STEP 1 **Gather the Materials**

- Your perfectly-sized hardcover book
- Hobby PVA glue (polyvinyl acetate) or Elmer's white glue
- Paintbrush
- Scalpel, box cutter or other sharp utility knife
- Ruler
- Pencil
- More books (for use as weights)

STEP 2 **Crafting Your Kindle Case**

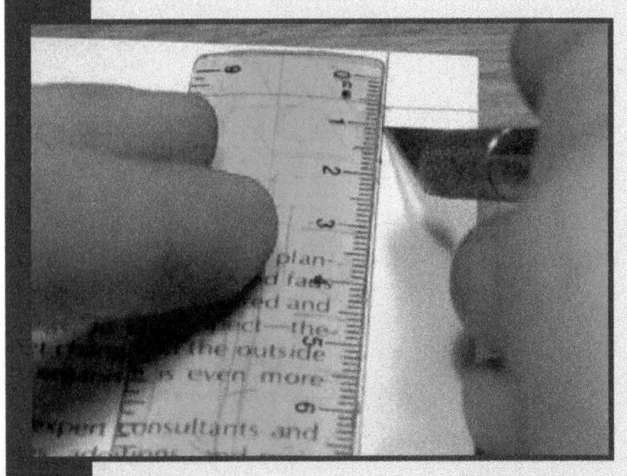

Getting your book ready for your Kindle is an easy process, though a lengthy one.

You begin by choosing where you want your hole to start. Once you have your spot picked, you use the paintbrush to spread the glue onto the edges of the pages where the hole will be cut. Use your extra books to weigh it down during the drying process.

When dry, open the book back up to your chosen starting point. Use the ruler and pencil to mark your hole the size of the Kindle. Once all marked, use your utility knife to start cutting on the outline. It's probably best to use your ruler as a straight edge to help guide the blade along, for a better, straighter cut. This is the longest step, because you have a lot to cut through. The time will vary depending on how deep your book is. I wouldn't recommend *War and Peace.*

Once you've gotten all the way to the back cover, the rest is easy. Just clean up the edges of your cuts as best you can, then use your paintbrush again to spread some glue along the cut edges.

TIP: When choosing your first page to cut, it's good to actually save it for later. Don't cut with the rest of them. When you have your hole fully cut open and have applied the glue, apply another thin line on the top border of your actual first page cut (essentially, the second page). Then close the book and add the weights to the top and let dry. Saving the first page helps reduce the chance of you accidentally gluing unwanted pages to cut ones, causing you to have to cut the pages you didn't want to cut to open the hole back up. Saving your first page makes it premeditated.

After fully dried, open it up and cut the final page (first page) to open the hole up. Then, you'll need to let it dry again, with the book open. After dried, that's it. You're done!

Activity 2.14 Write and Illustrate Instructions

Write and illustrate your own set of instructions for an activity that includes an argument. For example, during a lawn party at the White House, First Lady Michelle Obama served Carrot Lemonade to children who gave the drink rave reviews. Such a recipe could include an introduction explaining that creating healthy adaptations of popular foods and drinks for children only works if they taste good. Or, you might write instructions for how to remove geotags from photos before posting them on Facebook or other social networking sites. In your instructions you could explain that this process prevents people that you don't know from learning where you took the picture—and possibly learning where you live if you took it at home. Your argument would be that it is important to protect your privacy when you post photos on the Internet.

Try out your instructions on a friend, so you are sure you have included all the necessary steps and illustrated them adequately. Don't forget to include a brief statement of your argument, as does the writer of the Kindle cover article.

Activity 2.15 Create Your Own Blog

Read an article on the Internet related to a topic in which you're interested. Make sure the article has a substantial amount of text, as well as related images. In your blog, discuss how the text and the images both contribute to the article's rhetorical message. Include the title of the article, the author, the name of the publication or web page, and a link to the article.

Activity 2.16 Write in Your Commonplace Book

What do you read for fun? Magazines, blogs, books? Do you engage in what Louise Rosenblatt calls "aesthetic reading"? (See the section titled, "Ways of Reading Rhetorically") Write down a quote in your commonplace book from something that you have read for fun. First, reflect about what the quote means to you. Then, comment about why it is important to read things for fun and how that experience is different than reading to learn.

3
ANALYZING RHETORICALLY

Praxis in Action

Analyzing Arguments Improves My Writing by Eurydice Saucedo

Reading enables my creative mind to soar to undreamed-of worlds, to visit the deepest of memories, and to laugh as words describe a child's joy. Yes, reading enables me to be a bigger dreamer, but it also opens my eyes to better understand this world we live in.

Reading essays teaches me definitions and meanings, and, with practice, allows me to discern the validity and reliability of arguments. I can distinguish between fair representation of an issue, embellishment of truth, and bitter sarcasm. Every sentence has more than just simple grammar and punctuation. Every text, just like everything else in life, needs to be taken with a grain of salt, slowly simmered, and thought about before the final evaluation can be made. If I know rhetorical concepts, I can recognize when a text is trying to persuade me of something, and I can decide if the writer presents a good argument and sufficient evidence to merit serious consideration.

Reading and analyzing texts helps me learn how to structure my own argument. I may find a flaw in an argument, for example, a lack of acknowledgement of a counterargument that causes me to distrust a text. This causes me to be more careful to include the counterargument in my own text. And when I read and reread a classic argument such as Martin Luther King's "I Have a Dream" speech, I may make note of a strategy that I can use later. For example, Dr. King's adapting of President Lincoln's memorable language, saying, "five score years ago" instead of Lincoln's "four score and seven years ago" is highly effective. Perhaps I will try adapting a highly memorable quote when it fits in my argument.

One of the best ways to become a better writer is to read good writing.

Eurydice Saucedo writes, "Every text, just like everything else in life, needs to be taken with a grain of salt, slowly simmered, and thought about before the final evaluation can be made."

Discover the Kairos—The Opening for Argument

Kairos is a Greek word often translated as the right or opportune moment to do something, though it has no exact English translation. The first recorded use of the word kairos is in Homer's *Iliad*, where it appears as an adjective referring to an arrow striking the "deadliest spot" on the human body. When the word appears again later in Greek writing as a noun—a kairos—it retains this essential meaning as an opening or aperture. Twelve bronze axes with ring openings for wooden shanks are positioned in a line, so archers can practice by aiming at the kairos or ring opening, with the arrow passing down the line, through each ax. Clearly, launching an arrow through the kairos of twelve axes placed a yard apart required strength, training, practice, and a precise visual and muscle awareness of place. When people today say, "I saw my opening, and I took it, " they are conveying this meaning of kairos as an opening, combined with the idea of kairos as an opportunity.[1]

Ancient Greek archer

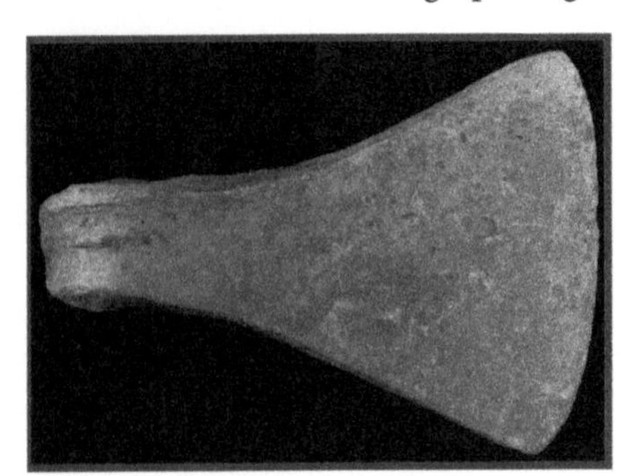

Ancient bronze ax with a ring hole for a wooden shank

Each time a rhetor (a speaker or writer) constructs an argument, he or she is working within a context of a certain moment, a particular time and place, that come together in a unique opportunity or opening for action—a kairos. A kairos both constrains and enables what a rhetor can say or write effectively in a particular situation. So, to compose the most effective text, a rhetor must do more than develop a thesis or statement of the main idea that takes a position about the subject—he or she must discover the kairos of the argument and its ramifications. What opportunities does the kairos present for making a persuasive argument, and what restrictions may be wise in consideration of the audience or occasion?

Use Kairos to Make Your Own Argument

Consider the following suggestions for determining the kairotic moment for your argument—the opening of sensitivity where you can shoot your metaphoric arrow:

- *Consider timeliness.* What is going on right now with the issue and how can you emphasize that in an argument? For example, if you are writing

[1] Thomas Rickert, "Invention in the Wild: On Locating Kairos in Space-Time," in *The Locations of Composition*. eds. Christopher J. Keller and Christian R. Weisser (Albany: SUNY Press, 2007) pp. 72–73.

about the death penalty, choose to write about the current cases on death row or the most recent person to be executed. Or, if your topic is about the unemployed exhausting their government benefits and you have, yourself, recently become unemployed, you can use your own experience as an illustration of the problem.

- *Know your audience.* What are the characteristics of the audience? Do they agree with your position on the issue or not? What is their educational level and the extent of their knowledge about the subject? For example, if you are writing about immigration policy reform, does your audience believe there is a need for reform? Do they have personal experience with illegal or legal immigrants? You can judge the amount of background information you need to provide based upon the characteristics of your audience. Also, the most important members of the audience, so far as an argument is concerned, are not those who already agree with you but those who are neutral or even slightly opposed to your position but willing to listen. Be careful not to phrase your argument in ways that are insulting to people who do not agree with you, for if you do so, they will stop listening to you.
- *Find a place to stand.* In the reading that follows, Martin Luther King, Jr., stood in front of the Lincoln Memorial as he gave his famous speech, "I Have a Dream." This location greatly impacts the speech and increases King's ethos, which we discuss in more detail below. You can make a similar rhetorical move, for example, if you live in a border community because you stand, metaphorically and physically, at an important juncture for issues such as immigration, free trade, and national security.

When Martin Luther King, Jr., gave his "I Have a Dream" speech, his words were carefully crafted to take into consideration the setting in front of the Lincoln Memorial. He said, "Five score years ago, a great American, in whose symbolic shadow we stand today, signed the Emancipation Proclamation." The words "five score" recall the "four score and seven years ago" of Lincoln's words in the Gettysburg Address. And King also pointed out that he and his audience that day stood in the "symbolic shadow" of the president who signed the Emancipation Proclamation. In these ways, he made use of Lincoln's shadow to legitimize what he was saying about civil rights.

In other ways, however, the kairos of the moment limited what he could say. His audience included both the thousands of people in front of him who were dedicated to the cause of racial equality and also the audience of those millions watching on television who may or may not have agreed with his message. Thus, the tone of his message needed to be subtly measured not to antagonize those among his audience, particularly the television audience, who may have opposed aspects of the civil rights movement such as school integration. However, he spoke to let both his supporters and his opponents know, "The whirlwinds of revolt will continue to shake the foundations of our nation until the bright day of justice emerges." Yes, King advocated nonviolent demonstrations, but they were demonstrations nonetheless; he was putting opponents on notice that the disruptions caused by demonstrations would continue "until justice emerges." King consistently took the high road, while maintaining the power of the kairotic moment when he spoke. This is one reason why his words continue to be studied decades after his death.

Reading 3.1

I Have a Dream

by Martin Luther King, Jr.

Martin Luther King, Jr., delivered this speech on August 28, 1963, at the Lincoln Memorial in Washington, D.C., as part of the March on Washington for Jobs and Freedom. A Baptist minister, King received the Nobel Peace Prize in 1964 for his efforts to end racial discrimination through nonviolent means. He was assassinated in 1968.

I am happy to join with you today in what will go down in history as the greatest demonstration for freedom in the history of our nation.

Five score years ago, a great American, in whose symbolic shadow we stand today, signed the Emancipation Proclamation. This momentous decree came as a great beacon light of hope to millions of Negro slaves who had been seared in the flames of withering injustice. It came as a joyous daybreak to end the long night of their captivity.

But one hundred years later, the Negro still is not free. One hundred years later, the life of the Negro is still sadly crippled by the manacles of segregation and the chains of discrimination. One hundred years later, the Negro lives on a lonely island of poverty in the midst of a vast ocean of material prosperity. One hundred years later, the Negro is still languished in the corners of American society and finds himself an exile in his own land. And so we've come here today to dramatize a shameful condition.

In a sense we've come to our nation's capital to cash a check. When the architects of our republic wrote the magnificent words of the Constitution and the Declaration of Independence, they were signing a promissory note to which every American was to fall heir. This note was a promise that all men, yes, black men as well as white men, would be guaranteed the "unalienable Rights" of "Life, Liberty and the pursuit of Happiness." It is obvious today that America has defaulted on this promissory note, insofar as her citizens of color are concerned. Instead of honoring this sacred obligation, America has given the Negro people a bad check, a check which has come back marked "insufficient funds."

But we refuse to believe that the bank of justice is bankrupt. We refuse to believe that there are insufficient funds in the great vaults of opportunity of this nation. And so, we've come to cash this check, a check that will give us upon demand the riches of freedom and the security of justice.

We have also come to this hallowed spot to remind America of the fierce urgency of Now. This is no time to engage in the luxury of cooling off or to take the tranquilizing drug of gradualism. Now is the time to make real the promises of democracy. Now is the time to rise from the dark and desolate valley of segregation to the sunlit path of racial justice. Now is the time to lift our nation from the quicksands of racial injustice to the solid rock of brotherhood. Now is the time to make justice a reality for all of God's children.

It would be fatal for the nation to overlook the urgency of the moment. This sweltering summer of the Negro's legitimate discontent will not pass until there is an invigorating autumn of freedom and equality. Nineteen sixty-three is not an end, but a beginning. And those who hope that the Negro needed to blow off steam and will now be content will have a rude awakening if the nation returns to business as usual. And there will be neither rest nor tranquility in America until the Negro is granted his citizenship rights. The whirlwinds of revolt will continue to shake the foundations of our nation until the bright day of justice emerges.

But there is something that I must say to my people, who stand on the warm threshold which leads into the palace of justice: In the process of gaining our rightful place, we must not be guilty of wrongful deeds. Let us not seek to satisfy our thirst for freedom by drinking from the cup of bitterness and hatred. We must forever conduct our struggle on the high plane of dignity and discipline. We must not allow our creative protest to degenerate into physical violence. Again and again, we must rise to the majestic heights of meeting physical force with soul force.

The marvelous new militancy which has engulfed the Negro community must not lead us to a distrust of all white people, for many of our white brothers, as evidenced by their presence here today, have come to realize that their destiny is tied up with our destiny. And they have come to realize that their freedom is inextricably bound to our freedom.

> We cannot walk alone.
>
> And as we walk, we must make the pledge that we shall always march ahead.
>
> We cannot turn back.

There are those who are asking the devotees of civil rights, "When will you be satisfied?" We can never be satisfied as long as the Negro is the victim of the unspeakable horrors of police brutality. We can never be satisfied as long as our bodies, heavy with the fatigue of travel, cannot gain lodging in the motels of the highways and the hotels of the cities. We cannot be satisfied as long as the negro's basic mobility is from a smaller ghetto to a larger one. We can never be satisfied as long as our children are stripped of their selfhood and robbed of their dignity by a sign stating: "For Whites Only." We cannot be satisfied as long as a Negro in Mississippi cannot vote and a Negro in New York believes he has nothing for which to vote. No, no, we are not satisfied, and we will not be satisfied until "justice rolls down like waters, and righteousness like a mighty stream."[2]

I am not unmindful that some of you have come here out of great trials and tribulations. Some of you have come fresh from narrow jail cells. And some of you have come from areas where your quest—quest for freedom left you battered by the storms of persecution and staggered by the winds of police brutality. You have been the veterans of creative suffering. Continue to work with the faith that unearned suffering is redemptive. Go back to Mississippi, go back to Alabama, go back to South Carolina, go back to Georgia, go back to Louisiana, go back to the slums and ghettos of our northern cities, knowing that somehow this situation can and will be changed.

Let us not wallow in the valley of despair, I say to you today, my friends.

And so even though we face the difficulties of today and tomorrow, I still have a dream. It is a dream deeply rooted in the American dream.

I have a dream that one day this nation will rise up and live out the true meaning of its creed: "We hold these truths to be self-evident, that all men are created equal."

I have a dream that one day on the red hills of Georgia, the sons of former slaves and the sons of former slave owners will be able to sit down together at the table of brotherhood.

I have a dream that one day even the state of Mississippi, a state sweltering with the heat of injustice, sweltering with the heat of oppression, will be transformed into an oasis of freedom and justice.

I have a dream that my four little children will one day live in a nation where they will not be judged by the color of their skin but by the content of their character.

I have a dream today!

I have a dream that one day, down in Alabama, with its vicious racists, with its governor having his lips dripping with the words of "interposition" and "nullification"—one day right there in Alabama little black boys and black girls will be able to join hands with little white boys and white girls as sisters and brothers.

I have a dream today!

I have a dream that one day every valley shall be exalted, and every hill and mountain shall be made low, the rough places will be made plain, and the crooked places will be made straight; "and the glory of the Lord shall be revealed and all flesh shall see it together."[3]

This is our hope, and this is the faith that I go back to the South with.

With this faith, we will be able to hew out of the mountain of despair a stone of hope. With this faith, we will be able to transform the jangling discords of our nation into a beautiful symphony of brotherhood. With this faith, we will be able to work together, to pray together, to struggle together, to go to jail together, to stand up for freedom together, knowing that we will be free one day.

And this will be the day—this will be the day when all of God's children will be able to sing with new meaning:

> My country 'tis of thee, sweet land of liberty, of thee I sing.
> Land where my fathers died, land of the Pilgrim's pride,
> From every mountainside, let freedom ring!
>
> And if America is to be a great nation, this must become true.
>
> And so let freedom ring from the prodigious hilltops of New Hampshire.
> Let freedom ring from the mighty mountains of New York.
> Let freedom ring from the heightening Alleghenies of Pennsylvania.
> Let freedom ring from the snow-capped Rockies of Colorado.
> Let freedom ring from the curvaceous slopes of California.

But not only that:
Let freedom ring from Stone Mountain of Georgia.
Let freedom ring from Lookout Mountain of Tennessee.
Let freedom ring from every hill and molehill of Mississippi.
From every mountainside, let freedom ring.

And when this happens, when we allow freedom to ring, when we let it ring from every village and every hamlet, from every state and every city, we will be able to speed up that day when all of God's children, black men and white men, Jews and Gentiles, Protestants and Catholics, will be able to join hands and sing in the words of the old Negro spiritual:

Free at last! Free at last!

Thank God Almighty, we are free at last![4]

[2] Amos 5:24 (rendered precisely in The American Standard Version of the Holy Bible)

[3] Isaiah 40:4–5 (King James Version of the Holy Bible). Quotation marks are excluded from part of this moment in the text because King's rendering of Isaiah 40:4 does not precisely follow the KJV version from which he quotes (e.g., "hill" and "mountain" are reversed in the KJV). King's rendering of Isaiah 40:5, however, is precisely quoted from the KJV.

[4] "Free at Last" from *American Negro Songs* by J. W. Work.

Activity 3.1 Use Microsoft's Comment Feature to Annotate a Text

Compose

If you download Dr. Martin Luther King's speech from AmericanRhetoric.com, you can make use of Microsoft's Comment feature to annotate the speech with your comments, as is done in the example below. In Microsoft Word, highlight the text you want to annotate, go to the "Insert" pull-down menu, and select "Comment." A box will appear where you can enter your comment.

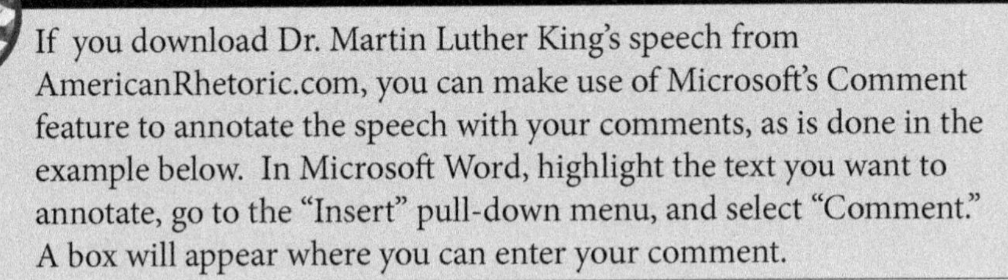

I am happy to join with you today in what will go down in history as the greatest demonstration for freedom in the history of our nation.

Five score years ago, a great American, in whose symbolic shadow we stand today, signed the Emancipation Proclamation. This momentous decree came as a great beacon light of hope to millions of Negro slaves who had been seared in the flames of withering injustice. It came as a joyous daybreak to end the long night of their captivity.

2/7/09 12:38 AM
Comment: Reference to Lincoln's Gettysburg Address

But one hundred years later, the Negro still is not free. One hundred years later, the life of the Negro is still sadly crippled by the manacles of segregation and the chains of discrimination. One hundred years later, the Negro lives on a lonely island of poverty in the midst of a vast ocean of material prosperity. One hundred years later, the Negro is

Activity 3.2 Discuss "I Have a Dream"

Read the "I Have a Dream" speech by Rev. Martin Luther King, Jr., and, if possible, watch the speech. It is archived at http://www.americanrhetoric.com, where it is listed as the most requested speech and #1 in its list of the top 100 American speeches.

1. Discuss the kairos of Dr. King's speech. What was the occasion? Who was his audience, both present and absent? What were the issues he spoke about?
2. How did Dr. King take advantage of the kairos of the situation in the wording of his speech?
3. Why do you think the speech continues to be so popular and influential?

Activity 3.3 Identify the Kairos

Identifying the kairos in Martin Luther King's speech in front of the Lincoln Memorial is easy. In some speeches, however, identifying the kairos is more difficult. Every speech and every text has a kairos, but some rhetors are better at identifying it and utilizing it than others. Identify the kairos in the following readings that have appeared thus far in the text. Then discuss in your group how the writer or speaker does or does not utilize kairos to maximum effect.

1. "Violent Rhetoric and Arizona Politics" (Chapter 1, p. 14)
2. "The Sleepover Question" (Chapter 1, p. 18)
3. "San Ysidro Shooting Survivor Lives His Dream of Being a Cop" (Chapter 1, p. 22)
4. "President Barack Obama on the Death of Osama bin Laden" (Chapter 2, p. 41)
5. "The Web Means the End of Forgetting" (Chapter 2, p. 50)

Activity 3.4 Analyze an Audience

Select a group that you do not belong to and analyze it as a potential audience. As one method, you might locate a blog on the Internet that advocates a point of view different from your own. For example, if you believe in global warming, read a blog frequented by those who do not share that belief. If you are a Democrat, look for a Tea Party or Republican blog. Find a yoga blog if you are a football fan. Read blog entries for a week and write a one-page analysis. Answer these questions:

1. What are the two or three issues of primary interest to the group? What is the general position on each issue?
2. Who are these people? Where do they live? What is their educational level?
3. What is the extent of their knowledge about the issues of primary interest? Are they familiar with the evidence, or do they just repeat opinions?
4. What types of appeals would make a difference to the readers of this blog: ethos, pathos, or logos? How so?

Aristotle's Persuasive Appeals

Some theorists associate the rhetorical triangle directly with Aristotle's **appeals** (or proofs): ethos, pathos, and logos. **Ethos** refers to the writer's (or speaker's) credibility; **pathos** refers to emotion used to sway the audience; and, finally, **logos** refers to the writer's purpose (or subject), for an effective argument will include evidence and other supporting details to back up the author's claims.

Aristotle wrote:

> Of those proofs that are furnished through the speech there are three kinds. Some reside in the character [*ethos*] of the speaker, some in a certain disposition [*pathos*] of the audience and some in the speech itself, through its demonstrating or seeming to demonstrate [*logos*].

Contemporary theorist Wayne C. Booth said something similar:

> The common ingredient that I find in all writing that I admire—excluding for now novels, plays, and poems—is something that I shall reluctantly call the rhetorical stance, a stance which depends upon discovering and maintaining in any writing situation a

> proper balance among the three elements that are at work in any communicative effort: the available arguments about the subject itself [*logos*], the interests and peculiarities of the audience [*pathos*], and the voice, the implied character of the speaker [*ethos*].

Arguments from Logos

Logos or reason was Aristotle's favorite of the three persuasive appeals, and he bemoaned the fact that humans could not be persuaded through reason alone, indeed that they sometimes chose emotion over reason. Aristotle also used the term *logos* to mean rational discourse. To appeal to logos means to organize an argument with a clear claim or thesis, supported by logical reasons that are presented in a well-organized manner that is internally consistent. It can also mean the use of facts and statistics as evidence. However, logos without elements of pathos and ethos can be dry, hard to understand, and boring.

Consider the following logical argument that advocates the televising of executions.

Reading 3.2

Executions Should Be Televised

by Zachary B. Shemtob and David Lat

In this opinion piece published in *The New York Times*, Zachary B. Shemtob and David Lat argue what they know is going to be an unpopular position in the United States—that executions should be televised. Shemtob is an assistant professor of criminal justice at Connecticut State University and Lat is a former federal prosecutor who also founded a legal blog, *Above the Law*. They reason, "democracy demands maximum accountability and transparency." Knowing that their position contradicts present policy, they carefully address possible objections to their position, such as the idea that executions are too gruesome to put on television.

Earlier this month, Georgia conducted its third execution this year. This would have passed relatively unnoticed if not for a controversy surrounding its videotaping. Lawyers for the condemned inmate, Andrew Grant DeYoung, had persuaded a judge to allow the recording of his last moments as part of an effort to obtain evidence on whether lethal injection caused unnecessary suffering.

Though he argued for videotaping, one of Mr. DeYoung's defense lawyers, Brian Kammer, spoke out against releasing the footage to the public. "It's a horrible thing that Andrew DeYoung had to go through," Mr. Kammer said, "and it's not for the public to see that."

We respectfully disagree. Executions in the United States ought to be made public.

Right now, executions are generally open only to the press and a few select witnesses. For the rest of us, the vague contours are provided in the morning paper. Yet a functioning democracy demands maximum accountability and transparency. As long as executions remain behind closed doors, those are impossible. The people should have the right to see what is being done in their name and with their tax dollars.

This is particularly relevant given the current debate on whether specific methods of lethal injection constitute cruel and unusual punishment and therefore violate the Constitution.

There is a dramatic difference between reading or hearing of such an event and observing it through image and sound. (This is obvious to those who saw the footage of Saddam Hussein's hanging in 2006 or the death of Neda Agha-Soltan during the protests in Iran in 2009.) We are not calling for opening executions completely to the public—conducting them before a live crowd—but rather for broadcasting them live or recording them for future release, on the Web or TV.

When another Georgia inmate, Roy Blankenship, was executed in June, the prisoner jerked his head, grimaced, gasped and lurched, according to a medical expert's affidavit. The *Atlanta Journal-Constitution* reported that Mr. DeYoung, executed in the same manner, "showed no violent signs in death." Voters should not have to rely on media accounts to understand what takes place when a man is put to death.

Cameras record legislative sessions and presidential debates, and courtrooms are allowing greater television access. When he was an Illinois state senator, President Obama successfully pressed for the videotaping of homicide interrogations and confessions. The most serious penalty of all surely demands equal if not greater scrutiny.

Opponents of our proposal offer many objections. State lawyers argued that making Mr. DeYoung's execution public raised safety concerns. While rioting and pickpocketing occasionally marred executions in the public square in the 18th and 19th centuries, modern security and technology obviate this concern. Little would change in the death chamber; the faces of witnesses and executioners could be edited out, for privacy reasons, before a video was released.

Of greater concern is the possibility that broadcasting executions could have a numbing effect. Douglas A. Berman, a law professor, fears that people might come to equate human executions with putting pets to sleep. Yet this seems overstated. While public indifference might result over time, the initial broadcasts would undoubtedly get attention and stir debate.

Still others say that broadcasting an execution would offer an unbalanced picture—making the condemned seem helpless and sympathetic, while keeping the victims of the crime out of the picture. But this is beside the point: the defendant is being executed precisely because a jury found that his crimes were so heinous that he deserved to die.

Ultimately the main opposition to our idea seems to flow from an unthinking disgust—a sense that public executions are archaic, noxious, even barbarous. Albert Camus related in his essay "Reflections on the Guillotine" that viewing executions turned him against capital punishment. The legal scholar John D. Bessler suggests that public executions might have the same effect on the public today; Sister Helen Prejean, the death penalty abolitionist, has urged just such a strategy.

That is not our view. We leave open the possibility that making executions public could strengthen support for them; undecided viewers might find them less disturbing than anticipated.

Like many of our fellow citizens, we are deeply conflicted about the death penalty and how it has been administered. Our focus is on accountability and openness. As Justice John Paul Stevens wrote in *Baze v. Rees*, a 2008 case involving a challenge to lethal injection, capital punishment is too often "the product of habit and inattention rather than an acceptable deliberative process that weighs the costs and risks of administering that penalty against its identifiable benefits."

A democracy demands a citizenry as informed as possible about the costs and benefits of society's ultimate punishment.

Collaborate

Activity 3.5 Analyze an Argument from Logos

1. In your small group, go over the Checklist of Essential Elements in an Argument (Chapter 2), and decide if the authors of this article fulfill each one. Be prepared to defend your decisions to the class.

2. Shemtob and Lat present a logical argument about why executions should be televised. Ignoring your own reaction to their editorial, outline the main points.

3. How do the authors handle their audience's possible emotional objections to their argument? Give an example.

4. What is your reaction to the argument that executions should be televised? Did reading and evaluating the article cause you to see the issue differently? If so, in what way?

Deductive Reasoning

Aristotle was the first person in Western culture to write systematically about logic, and he is credited with developing and promoting syllogistic or **deductive reasoning** in which statements are combined to draw a **conclusion**. He wrote that "a statement is persuasive and credible either because it is directly self-evident or because it appears to be proved from other statements that are so." This logical structure is called a **syllogism**, in which premises lead to a conclusion. The following is perhaps the most famous syllogism:

Major premise: All humans are mortal.

Minor premise: Socrates is human.

Conclusion: Socrates is mortal.

The **major premise** is a general statement accepted by everyone that makes an observation about all people. The second statement of the syllogism is the **minor premise**, which makes a statement about a particular case within the class of all people. Comparison of the two premises, the general class of "all humans" and the particular case of "Socrates" within the class of "all humans" leads to the conclusion that Socrates also fits in the class "mortal," and thus his death is unavoidable. Thus, the logic moves from the general to the particular.

Similarly, if you try the pumpkin bread at one Starbucks and like it, you may infer that you will like the pumpkin bread at another Starbucks. The argument would look like this:

Major premise:	Food products at Starbucks are standardized from one Starbucks to another.
Minor premise:	You like the pumpkin bread at one Starbucks.
Conclusion:	You will like the pumpkin bread at another Starbucks.

However, if your major premise is wrong, and the owner of one Starbucks substitutes an inferior stock of pumpkin bread, then your conclusion is wrong. Deductive reasoning is dependent upon the validity of each premise; otherwise the syllogism does not hold true. If the major premise that food products are standardized at all Starbucks franchises does not hold true, then the argument is not valid. A good deductive argument is known as a valid argument and is such that if all its premises are true, then its conclusion must be true. Indeed, for a deductive argument to be valid, it must be absolutely impossible for both its premises to be true and its conclusion to be false.

Inductive Reasoning

Aristotle identified another way to move logically between premises, which he called "the progress from particulars to universals." Later logicians labeled this type of logic as **inductive reasoning**. Inductive arguments are based on probability. Even if an inductive argument's premises are true, that doesn't establish with 100 percent certainty that its conclusions are true. Even the best inductive argument falls short of deductive validity.

Consider the following examples of inductive reasoning:

Particular statement:	Milk does not spoil as quickly if kept cold.
General statement:	All perishable foods do not spoil as quickly if kept cold.
Particular statement:	Microwaves cook popcorn more quickly than conventional heat.
General statement:	All foods cook more quickly in a microwave.

In the first example, inductive reasoning works well because cold tends to prolong the useable life of most perishable foods. The second example is more problematic. While it is true that popcorn cooks more quickly in a microwave oven, the peculiarities of microwave interaction with food molecules does not produce a uniform effect on all food stuffs. Rice, for example, does not cook much, if any, faster in a microwave than it does on a stovetop. Also, whole eggs may explode if cooked in their shells.

A good inductive argument is known as a strong (or "cogent") inductive argument. It is such that if the premises are true, the conclusion is likely to be true.

Collaborate

Activity 3.6 Identify Deductive and Inductive Reasoning

In your small group, identify an example of a deductive argument and list the premises and conclusion. Then identify an inductive argument and identify the particular statement and the general statement. Report to the class.

Logical Fallacies

Generally speaking, a **logical fallacy** is an error in reasoning, as opposed to a factual error, which is simply being wrong about the facts. A **deductive fallacy** (sometimes called a *formal fallacy*) is a deductive argument that has premises that are all true, but they lead to a false conclusion, making it an invalid argument. An **inductive fallacy** (sometimes called an *informal fallacy*) appears to be an inductive argument, but the premises do not provide enough support for the conclusion to be probable. Some logical fallacies are more common than others and, thus, have been labeled and defined. Following are a few of the most well-known types:

Ad hominem (to the man) are arguments that attempt to discredit a point of view through personal attacks upon the person who has that point of view. These arguments are not relevant to the actual issue because the character of the person that holds a view says nothing about the truth of that viewpoint.

> *Example*: Noam Chomsky is a liberal activist who opposes American intervention in other countries. Noam Chomsky's theory of transformational grammar, which suggests that humans have an innate ability to learn language, is ridiculous.

Non sequitur (Latin for "it does not follow") arguments have conclusions that do not follow from the premises. Usually, the author has left out a step in the logic, expecting the reader to make the leap over the gap.

> *Example*: "Well, look at the size of this administration building; it is obvious this university does not need more funding."

Either/or or **false dichotomy** arguments force an either/or choice when, in reality, more options are available. Issues are presented as being either black or white.

> *Example*: With all the budget cuts, "we either raise tuition or massively increase class size."

Red herring arguments avoid the issue and attempt to distract with a side issue.

> *Example*: "Why do you question my private life issues, when we have social problems with which to deal?"

Ad populum (Latin for "appeal to the people") arguments appeal to popularity. If a lot of people believe it, it must be true.

> *Example*: "Why shouldn't I cheat on this exam? Everyone else cheats."

Ad verecundium (Latin for "argument from that which is improper") arguments appeal to an irrelevant authority.

> *Example*: "If the President of Harvard says it is a good idea, then we should follow suit." Or, "That is how we have always done it."

Begging the question arguments simply assume that a point of view is true because the truth of the premise is assumed. Simply assuming a premise is true does not amount to evidence that it *is* true.

> *Example*: A woman's place is in the home; therefore, women should not work.

Confusing cause and effect is a common problem with scientific studies in which the fact that two events are correlated implies that one causes the other.

> *Example*: Obese people drink a lot of diet soda; therefore, diet soda causes obesity.

W

Post hoc (from the Latin phrase "Post hoc, ergo proper hoc," or after this, therefore because of this) is a fallacy that concludes that one event caused another just because one occurred before the other.

Example: The Great Depression caused World War II.

In a **straw man** fallacy, a position of an opponent is exaggerated or weakened, so that it is easier for the opponent to argue against it.

Example: Pro-choice advocates believe in murdering unborn children.

A **slippery slope** argument asserts that one event will inevitably lead to another event.

Example: the Dilbert cartoon below:

DILBERT: © Scott Adams/Dist. by United Feature Syndicate, Inc.

These logical fallacies are summarized in table 3.1.

table 3.1

Chart of Fallacies and Examples		
Fallacy	**The Error in Reasoning**	**Example**
Ad hominem	When speakers attack the person making the argument and not the argument itself.	"We can't believe anything he says; he is a convicted felon."

Fallacy	The Error in Reasoning	Example
Ad populum	When we attempt to persuade people by arguing our position is reasonable because so many other people are doing it or agree with it.	"Why shouldn't I cheat on this exam? Everyone else cheats."
Ad verecundium	An appeal to persuasion based on higher authority or tradition.	"If the president of Harvard says it is a good idea, then we should follow suit." Or, "That is how we have always done it."
Begging the question	When a speaker presumes certain things are facts when they have not yet been proven to be truthful.	"Oh, everyone knows that we are all Christians."
Confusing cause and effect	A common problem with scientific studies in which the fact that two events are correlated implies that one causes the other.	"Obese people drink a lot of diet soda; therefore, diet soda causes obesity."
Either/or	Presents two options and declares that one of them must be correct while the other must be incorrect.	"We either raise tuition or massively increase class size."
Non sequitur	When you make an unwarranted move from one idea to the next.	"Well, look at the size of this administration building; it is obvious this university does not need more funding."
Post hoc	Assumes that because one event happened after another, then the preceding event caused the event that followed.	"Every time Sheila goes to a game with us, our team loses. She is bad luck."
Red herring	When a speaker introduces an irrelevant issue or piece of evidence to divert attention from the subject of the speech.	"Why do you question my private life issues, when we have social problems with which to deal?"
Slippery slope	Assumes that once an action begins it will follow, undeterred, to an eventual and inevitable conclusion.	"If we let the government dictate where we can pray, soon the government will tell us we cannot pray."

Fallacy	The Error in Reasoning	Example
Straw man	When a speaker ignores the actual position of an opponent and substitutes a distorted and exaggerated position.	"Oh, you think we should agree to a cut in our salaries. Why do you want to bleed us dry?"

Activity 3.7 Identify Logical Fallacies

Match the following types of logical fallacies with the examples below:

Types:

Ad hominem
Begging the question
Confusing cause and effect
Post hoc
Straw man
Slippery slope

Examples:

1. Legalization of medical marijuana will lead to increased marijuana use by the general population.
2. Twenty-one is the best age limit for drinking because people do not mature until they are 21.
3. If you teach birth control methods, more teenage girls will get pregnant.
4. The culture wars of the 1960s were a result of parents being unable to control their children after the post–World War II baby boom.
5. Al Gore claims that global warming is a dangerous trend. Al Gore is a liberal. Therefore, there is no global warming.
6. Immigration reform advocates want to separate families and children.

Activity 3.8 Create Examples of Logical Fallacies

In your small group, work through the chart of logical fallacies above and create a new example for each type of fallacy. Then report to the class, one fallacy at a time, with the instructor making a list of each group's examples on the chalk board. Discuss any examples that are not clear cases of a particular fallacy.

Arguments from Pathos

Pathos makes use of emotion to persuade an audience.

Aristotle wrote:

> Proofs from the disposition of the audience are produced whenever they are induced by the speech into an emotional state. We do not give judgment in the same way when aggrieved and when pleased, in sympathy and in revulsion.

Effective rhetors know their audiences, particularly what emotions they hold that are relevant to the issue under consideration. What motivates them? What are their fears, their hopes, their desires, and their doubts? If the audience has the same emotions as you do, fine. However, if they do not already hold those emotions, you need to bring them to share the hurt, the anger, or the joy that will persuade them to share your viewpoint—through the stories you tell, the statistics you cite, and the reasoning you offer.

For example, when Martin Luther King, Jr., in his "I Have a Dream" speech (reprinted earlier in this chapter) referred to the "hallowed spot" of the Lincoln Memorial, he was appealing to his audience's feelings of patriotism and reverence for the accomplishments of President Lincoln. Subtly, he was also garnering this emotion toward Lincoln in contemporary support of civil rights. Lincoln had issued the Emancipation Proclamation that declared all slaves to be free, yet, according to King, America had not lived up to Lincoln's promise.

Reading 3.3

People for Sale
by E. Benjamin Skinner

E. Benjamin Skinner has written on a wide range of topics. His articles have appeared in *Newsweek International, Travel and Leisure*, and other magazines. This essay was adapted from *A Crime So Monstrous: Face-to-Face with Modern-Day Slavery* and appeared in *Foreign Policy*.

Most people imagine that slavery died in the 19th century. Since 1810, more than a dozen international conventions banning the slave trade have been signed. Yet today there are more slaves than at any time in human history.

And if you're going to buy one in five hours, you'd better get a move on. First, hail a taxi to JFK International Airport and hop on a direct flight to Port-au-Prince, Haiti. The flight takes three hours. After landing, take a tap-tap, a flatbed pickup retrofitted with benches and a canopy, three-quarters of the way up Route de Delmas, the capital's main street. There, on a side street, you will find a group of men standing in front of Le Réseau (the Network) barbershop. As you approach, a man steps forward: "Are you looking to get a person?"

Meet Benavil Lebhom. He smiles easily. He has a trim mustache and wears a multicolored striped golf shirt, a gold chain, and Doc Martens knockoffs. Benavil is a courtier, or broker. He holds an official real estate license and calls himself an employment agent. Two-thirds of the employees he places are child slaves. The total number of Haitian children in bondage in their own country stands at 300,000. They are restavèks, the "stay-withs," as they are euphemistically known in Creole. Forced, unpaid, they work in captivity from before dawn until night. Benavil and thousands of other formal and informal traffickers lure these children from desperately impoverished rural parents with promises of free schooling and a better life.

The negotiation to buy a child slave might sound a bit like this:

"How quickly do you think it would be possible to bring a child in? Somebody who could clean and cook?" you ask. "I don't have a very big place; I have a small apartment. But I'm wondering how much that would cost? And how quickly?"

"Three days," Benavil responds.

"And you could bring the child here?" you inquire. "Or are there children here already?"

"I don't have any here in Port-au-Prince right now," says Benavil, his eyes widening at the thought of a foreign client. "I would go out to the countryside."

You ask about additional expenses. "Would I have to pay for transportation?"

"Bon," says Benavil. "A hundred U.S."

Smelling a rip-off, you press him, "And that's just for transportation?"

"Transportation would be about 100 Haitian," says Benavil, "because you'd have to get out there. Plus, [hotel and] food on the trip. Five hundred gourdes"—around $13.

"OK, 500 Haitian," you say.

Now you ask the big question: "And what would your fee be?" Benavil's eyes narrow as he determines how much he can take you for.

"A hundred. American."

"That seems like a lot," you say, with a smile so as not to kill the deal. "Could you bring down your fee to 50 U.S.?"

Benavil pauses. But only for effect. He knows he's still got you for much more than a Haitian would pay. "Oui," he says with a smile.

But the deal isn't done. Benavil leans in close. "This is a rather delicate question. Is this someone you want as just a worker? Or also someone who will be a 'partner'? You understand what I mean?"

You don't blink at being asked if you want the child for sex. "Is it possible to have someone who could be both?"

"Oui!" Benavil responds enthusiastically.

If you're interested in taking your purchase back to the United States, Benavil tells you that he can "arrange" the proper papers to make it look as though you've adopted the child.

He offers you a 13-year-old girl.

"That's a little bit old," you say.

"I know of another girl who's 12. Then ones that are 10, 11," he responds.

The negotiation is finished, and you tell Benavil not to make any moves without further word from you. You have successfully arranged to buy a human being for 50 bucks.

It would be nice if that conversation were fictional. It is not. I recorded it in October 2005 as part of four years of research into slavery on five continents. In the popular consciousness, "slavery" has come to be little more than just a metaphor for undue hardship. Investment bankers routinely refer to themselves as "high-paid wage slaves." Human rights activists may call $1-an-hour sweatshop laborers slaves, regardless of the fact that they are paid and can often walk away from the job.

The reality of slavery is far different. Slavery exists today on an unprecedented scale. In Africa, tens of thousands are chattel slaves, seized in war or tucked away for generations. Across Europe, Asia, and the Americas, traffickers have forced as many as 2 million into prostitution or labor. In South Asia, which has the highest concentration of slaves on the planet, nearly 10 million languish in bondage, unable to leave their captors until they pay off "debts," legal fictions that in many cases are generations old.

Few in the developed world have a grasp of the enormity of modern-day slavery. Fewer still are doing anything to combat it. . . . Between 2000 and 2006, the U.S. Justice Department increased human trafficking prosecutions from 3 to 32, and convictions from 10 to 98. By the end of 2006, 27 states had passed anti-trafficking laws. Yet, during the same period, the United States liberated only about 2 percent of its own modern-day slaves. As many as 17,500 new slaves continue to enter bondage in the United States every year . . . Many feel that sex slavery is particularly revolting—and it is. I saw it firsthand. In a Bucharest brothel, I was offered a mentally handicapped suicidal girl in exchange for a used car. But for every woman or child enslaved in commercial sex, there are some 15 men, women, and children enslaved in other fields, such as domestic work or agricultural labor.

Save for the fact that he is male, Gonoo Lal Kol typifies the average slave of our modern age. (At his request, I have changed his name.) Like a majority of the world's slaves, Gonoo is in debt bondage in South Asia. In his case, in an Indian quarry. Like most slaves, Gonoo is illiterate and unaware of the Indian laws that ban his bondage and provide for sanctions against his master. His story, told to me near his four-foot-high stone and grass hutch, represents the other side of the "Indian Miracle."

Gonoo lives in Lohagara Dhal, a forgotten corner of Uttar Pradesh, a north Indian state that contains 8 percent of the world's poor. I met him one evening in December 2005 as he walked with two dozen other laborers in tattered and filthy clothes. Behind them was the quarry. In that pit, Gonoo, a member of the historically outcast Kol tribe, worked with his family 14 hours a day. His tools were a hammer and a pike. His hands were covered in calluses, his fingertips worn away.

Gonoo's master is a tall, stout, surly contractor named Ramesh Garg. He makes his money by enslaving entire families forced to work for no pay beyond alcohol, grain, and subsistence expenses. Slavery scholar Kevin Bales estimates that a slave in the 19th-century American South had to work 20 years to recoup his or her purchase price. Gonoo and the other slaves earn a profit for Garg in two years.

Every single man, woman, and child in Lohagara Dhal is a slave. But, in theory at least, Garg neither bought nor owns them. The seed of Gonoo's slavery, for instance, was a loan of 62 cents. In 1958 his grandfather borrowed that amount from the owner of a farm where he worked. Three generations and three slave masters later, Gonoo's family remains in bondage.

Recently, many bold, underfunded groups have taken up the challenge of tearing out the roots of slavery. Some gained fame through dramatic slave rescues. Most learned that freeing slaves is impossible unless the slaves themselves choose to be free. Among the Kol of Uttar Pradesh, for instance, an organization called Pragati Gramodyog Sansthan (PGS)—the Progressive Institute for Village Enterprises—has helped hundreds of families break the grip of the quarry contractors.

The psychological, social, and economic bonds of slavery run deep, and for governments to be truly effective in eradicating slavery, they must partner with groups that can offer slaves a way to pull themselves up from bondage. One way to do that is to replicate the work of grassroots organizations such as the India-based MSEMVS (Society for Human Development and Women's Empowerment). In 1996 the group launched free transitional schools where children who had been enslaved learned skills and acquired enough literacy to move on to formal schooling. The group also targeted mothers, providing them with training and start-up materials for microenterprises. . . . In recent years, the United States has shown an increasing willingness to help fund these kinds of organizations, one encouraging sign that the message may be getting through.

For four years, I encountered dozens of enslaved people, several of whom traffickers like Benavil actually offered to sell to me. I did not pay for a human life anywhere. And, with one exception, I always withheld action to save any one person, in the hope that my research would later help to save many more. At times, that still feels like an excuse for cowardice. But the hard work of real emancipation can't be the burden of a select few. For thousands of slaves, grassroots groups like PGS and MSEMVS can help bring freedom. Until governments define slavery in appropriately concise terms, prosecute the crime aggressively in all its forms, and encourage groups that empower slaves to free themselves, however, millions more will remain in bondage. And our collective promise of abolition will continue to mean nothing at all.

Activity 3.9 Analyze an Argument from Pathos

After reading Skinner's essay on slavery, reread the passage in which he negotiated to buy a child slave. Then freewrite for five minutes about how that negotiation made you feel.

Most people feel emotional when they read about a child in distress, and Skinner further highlights that emotional effect by putting this particular episode in dialogue, always a point of emphasis in an essay. Do you think Skinner deliberately appealed to pathos in this part of his essay? Discuss in your group.

List other areas where the essay evokes an emotional response. Consider why, and freewrite on the feelings and beliefs that are brought into play. How did the author know that you would probably react this way?

Although much of Skinner's argument relies on pathos, he also provides statistics and references to authorities to bolster his argument. Identify the paragraphs which provide statistics or other evidence that would qualify as logos.

Arguments from Ethos

No exact translation exists in English for the word *ethos*, but it can be loosely translated as the credibility of the speaker. This credibility generates good will which colors all the arguments, examples, and quotes the rhetor utilizes in his text. Rhetors can enhance their credibility by evidence of intelligence, virtue, and goodwill and diminish it by seeming petty, dishonest, and mean-spirited. In addition, a speaker or writer can enhance his or her own credibility by references to quotes or the actions of authorities or leaders.

Aristotle wrote:

> Proofs from character [ethos] are produced, whenever the speech is given in such a way as to render the speaker worthy of credence—we more readily and sooner believe reasonable men on all matters in general and absolutely on questions where precision is impossible and two views can be maintained.

For example, Martin Luther King, Jr., pointed out in his "I Have a Dream" speech, that, according to the framers of the Constitution and the Declaration of Independence, "unalienable Rights" of "Life, Liberty and the pursuit of Happiness" apply equally to black men and white men. He was, in effect, borrowing the ethos of Thomas Jefferson and the framers of the Constitution in support of the unalienable rights of blacks.

Consider the following article and how the author's credibility or ethos enhances the appeal of his arguments.

Reading 3.4

Alien Life Coming Slowly into View

by Ray Jayawardhana

Ray Jayawardhana, the author of "Alien Life Coming Slowly into View," which was originally published in *The New York Times*, is a professor of astronomy and astrophysics at the University of Toronto. He is also the author of *Strange New Worlds: The Search for Alien Planets and Life Beyond Our Solar System.*

I remember the first time the concept of another world entered my mind. It was during a walk with my father in our garden in Sri Lanka. He pointed to the Moon and told me that people had walked on it. I was astonished: Suddenly that bright light became a place that one could visit.

Schoolchildren may feel a similar sense of wonder when they see pictures of a Martian landscape or Saturn's rings. And soon their views of alien worlds may not be confined to the planets in our own solar system.

After millenniums of musings and a century of failed attempts, astronomers first detected an exoplanet, a planet orbiting a normal star other than the Sun, in 1995. Now they are finding hundreds of such worlds each year. Last month, NASA announced that 1,235 new possible planets had been observed by Kepler, a telescope on a space satellite. Six of the planets that Kepler found circle one star, and the orbits of five of them would fit within that of Mercury, the closest planet to our Sun.

By timing the passages of these five planets across their sun's visage—which provides confirmation of their planetary nature—we can witness their graceful dance with one another, choreographed by gravity. These discoveries remind us that nature is often richer and more wondrous than our imagination. The diversity of alien worlds has surprised us and challenged our preconceptions many times over.

It is quite a change from merely 20 years ago, when we knew for sure of just one planetary system: ours. The pace of discovery, supported by new instruments and missions and innovative strategies by planet seekers, has been astounding.

What's more, from measurements of their masses and sizes, we can infer what some of these worlds are made of: gases, ice or rocks. Astronomers have been able to take the temperature of planets around other stars, first with telescopes in space but more recently with ground-based instruments, as my collaborators and I have done.

Two and a half years ago, we even managed to capture the first direct pictures of alien worlds. There is something about a photo of an alien planet—even if it only appears as a faint dot next to a bright, overexposed star—that makes it "real." Given that stars shine like floodlights next to the planetary embers huddled around them, success required painstaking efforts and clever innovations. One essential tool is adaptive optics technology, which, in effect, takes the twinkle out of the stars, thus providing sharper images from telescopes on the ground than would otherwise be possible.

At the crux of this grand pursuit is one basic question: Is our warm, wet, rocky world, teeming with life, the exception or the norm? It is an important question for every one of us, not just for scientists. It seems absurd, if not arrogant, to think that ours is the only life-bearing world in the galaxy, given hundreds of billions of other suns, the apparent ubiquity of planets, and the cosmic abundance of life's ingredients. It may be that life is fairly common, but that "intelligent" life is rare.

Of course, the vast majority of the extra-solar worlds discovered to date are quite unlike our own: many are gas giants, and some are boiling hot while others endure everlasting chills. Just a handful are close in size to our planet, and only a few of those may be rocky like the Earth, rather than gaseous like Jupiter or icy like Neptune.

But within the next few years, astronomers expect to find dozens of alien earths that are roughly the size of our planet. Some of them will likely be in the so-called habitable zone, where the temperatures are just right for liquid water. The discovery of "Earth twins," with conditions similar to what we find here, will inevitably bring questions about alien life to the forefront.

Detecting signs of life elsewhere will not be easy, but it may well occur in my lifetime, if not during the next decade. Given the daunting distances between the stars, the real-life version will almost certainly be a lot less sensational than the movies depicting alien invasions or crash-landing spaceships.

The evidence may be circumstantial at first—say, spectral bar codes of interesting molecules like oxygen, ozone, methane and water—and leave room for alternative interpretations. It may take years of additional data-gathering, and perhaps the construction of new telescopes, to satisfy our doubts. Besides, we won't know whether such "biosignatures" are an indication of slime or civilization. Most people will likely move on to other, more immediate concerns of life here on Earth while scientists get down to work.

If, on the other hand, an alien radio signal were to be detected, that would constitute a more clear-cut and exciting moment. Even if the contents of the message remained elusive for decades, we would know that there was someone "intelligent" at the other end. The search for extraterrestrial intelligence with radio telescopes has come of age recently, 50 years after the first feeble attempt. The construction of the Allen Telescope Array on an arid plateau in northern California greatly expands the number of star systems from which astronomers could detect signals.

However it arrives, the first definitive evidence of life elsewhere will mark a turning point in our intellectual history, perhaps only rivaled by Copernicus's heliocentric theory or Darwin's theory of evolution. If life can spring up on two planets independently, why not on a thousand or even a billion others? The ramifications of finding out for sure that ours isn't the only inhabited world are likely to be felt, over time, in many areas of human thought and endeavor—from biology and philosophy to religion and art.

Some people worry that discovering life elsewhere, especially if it turns out to be in possession of incredible technology, will make us feel small and insignificant. They seem concerned that it will constitute a horrific blow to our collective ego.

I happen to be an optimist. It may take decades after the initial indications of alien life for scientists to gather enough evidence to be certain or to decipher a signal of artificial origin. The full ramifications of the discovery may not be felt for generations, giving us plenty of time to get used to the presence of our galactic neighbors. Besides, knowing that we are not alone just might be the kick in the pants we need to grow up as a species.

Activity 3.10 Analyzing an Argument from Ethos

1. In the above article, Ray Jayawardhana draws upon the ethos of his position as a professor of astronomy and astrophysics to formulate a convincing argument for the strong possibility of the existence of alien life. In your group, discuss how Jayawardhana's profession increases the credibility of his argument.

2. How do you think this essay would compare to essays by people of more credentials who argue that no alien life exists? What kinds of other evidence could Jayawardhana have offered that would strengthen his argument?
3. Is Jayawardhana appealing to pathos with his opening narrative? What effect does he want to have on his audience by describing this childhood memory?

Combining Ethos, Pathos, and Logos

The ethos, pathos, and logos appeals are equally important and merit equal attention in the writing process. No text is purely based on one of the three appeals, though more of the argument in a particular text may be based on one appeal rather than another. In each writing situation, however, an effective rhetor will think about how each plays into the structure of the argument.

In today's world, for example, a public speaker's effectiveness is affected by the ability to use a teleprompter, or, if one is not available, to memorize a speech well enough so he or she can speak without frequently referring to notes. If a speaker's eyes flit from left to right across the text of a teleprompter, it shows on television. This reduces the credibility, or ethos, of the speaker, no matter how well the other appeals are executed in the speech. The equivalent of presentation for a written text would be to produce a document that is essentially free from grammatical errors, spell-checked, and printed on good paper stock with the correct margins and type size. If the document does not look professional, it will lose credibility or ethos no matter what it says.

To give another example, E. Benjamin Skinner's essay, "People for Sale," relies on the highly emotional image of a child being sold into slavery for its major appeal. However, if you read back through the essay, you will see that it has a clear thesis, which could be stated as the following: Slavery exists in the present time, even in the United States, and it is not even that difficult to buy a slave. The essay is well organized and offers a variety of evidence, including statistics and first-person observation. Logos may not stand out as the primary appeal in Skinner's essay, but it is nevertheless strong in its appeal to logos.

If you want to develop your writing skills, it is essential that you pay attention to each of Aristotle's appeals—ethos, pathos, and logos.

Activity 3.11 Writing about Ethos, Pathos, and Logos

Choose one of the texts in Chapters 1, 2, or 3 and write an essay that identifies the ethos, pathos, and logos of the particular text. Then discuss how the three appeals together are used by the author to produce an effective essay. Alternatively, discuss which of the appeals is weak in the particular essay and how that affects the effectiveness of the essay.

Photos Heighten Ethos or Pathos

When Steve Jobs was in the process of turning over the reins of Apple to Tim Cook, the two appeared in a series of photos in a variety of publications. For example, see the photo below (from wired.com). Notice the "twinning effect," as both Jobs and Cook wear blue jeans and black pullover sweaters. In a not-so-subtle way, Apple was using ethos to visually state that since Jobs and Cook look alike, they must be alike. Thus, Cook would be successful in running Apple.

Photos can be equally effective in presenting pathos, though logos is more problematic.

Meet Tim Cook: The Man in Charge of Apple

For millions of Apple fans, Steve Jobs is irreplaceable. But if there's one man Jobs himself trusts to stand in his shoes it is his second in command Apple Chief Operating Officer Tim Cook.

Activity 3.12 Logos Activity: Write a Letter to the Editor

In the following letter, originally published on the blog, *The Frisky* (www.thefrisky.com), the author uses both humor and logic to argue that *The New Yorker* reviews shouldn't give away the ending of movies.

An Open Letter To The New Yorker

via The Frisky on 4/25/11

Dear *New Yorker*,

Obviously, you are an awesome magazine. However, I have one small, teensy weensy beef. Could you please—possibly—stop ruining the ending of movies for me? Last night, on a 10-hour flight from Buenos Aires to New York, I sat down determined to catch up on your last three issues. In one, I read a review of Jake Gyllenhaal's newish movie, "Source Code." I had been planning to see it. Emphasis on the *had.* While you didn't go into details, you told me how it unfolds in the end. Which sort of takes the wind out of a movie's sail, doesn't it? But even worse, in a fantastic article about Anna Faris and her specific brand of girl humor, you let me know the surprise twist ending of her upcoming click, "What's Your Number?" Which. Doesn't. Even. Come. Out. Until. SEPTEMBER. Reading this reminded me of the collective sigh of 100 students in my Intro to Film Studies class in college when our professor told us the secret to "Chinatown" before we watched.

Choose one of your favorite magazines and write a letter to the editor. You can protest something the magazine has done recently that bothered you, or you can praise something that it has done well. Your letter does not need to be long, but you need to make your argument clear and support it with specific examples. If appropriate for your target publication, use humor as does the author of the letter to the editor of *The New Yorker*.

After you have written your letter to the editor, write a paragraph describing your target publication, what you have written in your letter, and why your letter is an illustration of logos.

Activity 3.13 Pathos Activity: Portray an Emotion in a Collage

Compose

Think of an emotion that you've been feeling lately and that you are willing to explore. Create a collage to express that emotion. Use these criteria.

- You can create your collage with cut and paste paper or you can create it through a computer program.
- Have little white space. Use colors with emotional connotations (blue for calm, for example).
- Have at least three images. You can find these on the Internet or in magazines, or take your own photos.
- Before you begin your collage, write down the emotion you are trying to explore and describe how you plan to represent it. In other words, make a plan, even though you will likely deviate from it.
- When you finish, write a paragraph describing the experience of creating the collage. Turn your paragraph in with your collage.

Activity 3.14 Ethos Activity: Create a Professional Facebook Page

Facebook is not just used to tell your friends about what you did over the weekend. Corporations use it as a networking tool. As you learned in the reading in Chapter 2, "The Web Means the End of Forgetting," it is a good idea to be cautious about what you post about yourself on Facebook because information and photos may be seen by unintended audiences, including future employers. Some individuals choose to have two Facebook pages, one for their personal friends and one for networking.

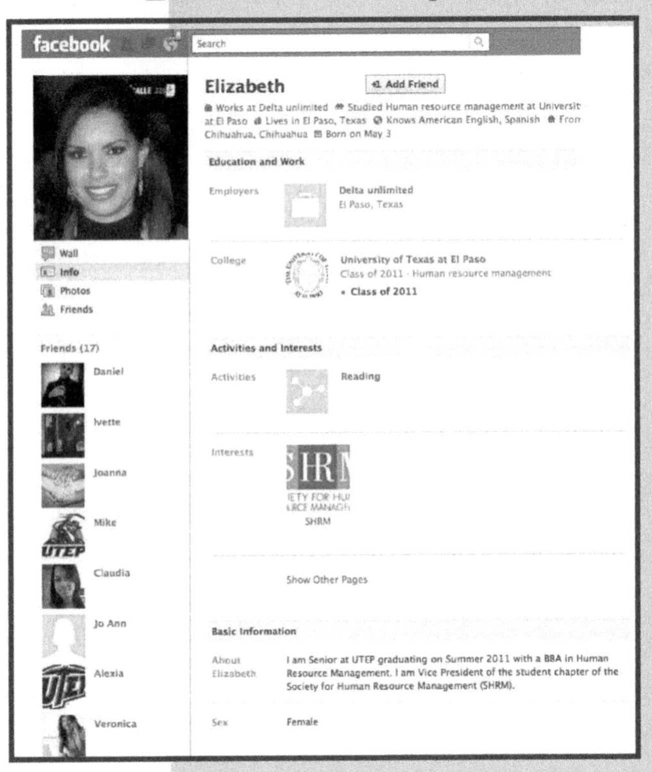

For this assignment, create a professional Facebook page similar to the one shown here. Consider in your small group what information and photos you want to post on a page you will use for networking. In effect, you are creating an ethos for yourself by these choices.

After you have completed your Facebook page, write a paragraph that explains the ethos you wanted to project in your page and how your content choices project that ethos.

Activity 3.15 Write a Rhetorical Analysis

In this essay you will make use of rhetorical vocabulary to analyze a text or combined text and images. The sample student essay in Chapter 7 (see page 190) analyzes a speech archived on the American Rhetoric website (http://www.americanrhetoric.com), which features many presidential and other prominent speeches. Alternatively, you can write a rhetorical analysis of a Facebook page, a newspaper or magazine article, or website.

In your analysis, apply several of the rhetorical concepts you have studied this semester:

- Speaker or writer—Does the speaker's identity affect the text?
- Purpose—What was the speaker or writer trying to achieve?
- Audience—Who was the speech/text directed to? Are there multiple audiences?
- Rhetorical appeals—How does the speaker or writer use ethos, pathos, and logos?
- Kairos—What is special about the rhetorical moment of the text/speech in terms of place and time?

Activity 3.16 Write on Your Blog

In your blog, do a freewrite exercise in which you argue for some type of policy change related to a topic you are interested in writing about. What is the kairos of your topic? Where can you use the three rhetorical appeals (pathos, ethos, and logos)?

Activity 3.17 Write in Your Commonplace Book

Do a search on the Internet for kairos, ethos, pathos, and logos. Print out and paste a short section about each from the Internet. Then comment briefly about each section.

4

INVENTING RHETORICALLY

Praxis in Action

How I Do Invention by Adam Webb

Before I start a research and writing project, I like to explore as many perspectives, arguments, or interpretations of a topic as possible. After I have chosen my topic, I write down everything I know about it. Next, I read broadly about my topic. I call this early stage of the research process "reading around," similar to information gathering.

Then, I usually ask myself a series of questions, such as: (1) Why is this topic important to me? (2) What has been said or written on this topic? (3) Who has already written on this topic? (4) How do these perspectives or arguments relate to my own perspective on this topic? and (5) How has media, such as television or the Internet, portrayed this topic? If I don't know the answers, either from my personal knowledge or my "reading around," I ask individuals who are knowledgeable about my topic. By answering these questions, I usually develop a larger contextual framework in which I can better understand and situate myself within the various perspectives on my topic. This is all before I start to integrate specific material from research sources.

Next, I start locating any recurring terms, themes, symbols, connections, or references as well as listing other ideas, beliefs, or values that might be relevant to my topic. In order to keep track of my ideas and information, I like to use Dragon Dictation, a note-taking and voice recording program application on my smartphone. I sometimes use this application to start writing an outline of my ideas.

By this time, I know what I want to argue and the general framework of my project. Then I can begin adding in specific paraphrases and quotes from my research.

Adam Webb has developed his own process for doing research that he applies to different projects.

Aristotle's Classification of Rhetoric

Aristotle, in *The Art of Rhetoric* (or *On Rhetoric*), laid the groundwork for today's persuasive writing by being the first to write systemically about how to teach rhetoric. His teacher Plato, in contrast, had distrusted rhetoric. Plato deplored the way rhetoricians (or politicians) of his era skillfully manipulated the people of Athens, particularly the masses of up to 10,000 voters in the Assembly or 500 in the juries of the law courts. Aristotle, on the other hand, perceived great potential in rhetoric, when taught properly. Rhetoric, as he envisioned it, could be both persuasive and ethical, and in *The Art of Rhetoric* he laid out an organization and classification of rhetoric as he believed it should be taught.

Aristotle divided the process of writing and delivering a composition into five parts. The first of these was **invention**, during which the writer or speaker expanded a topic into ideas that were later arranged into a text or speech. According to the ancient Greeks, the rhetor *invented* these ideas, though they may have mirrored or adapted thoughts presented by previous rhetors. Today, we call this the **prewriting stage** of the writing process, an adaptation of Aristotle's invention stage.

In the previous chapter, we discussed the three appeals or means that a rhetor can use to persuade an audience: ethos, pathos, and logos. In *The Art of Rhetoric*, Aristotle divides these appeals or means of persuasion into two types of proofs: artistic and inartistic. Today, these proofs are still part of the writing process though we call them by different names.

Artistic Proofs

Artistic proofs are logical arguments constructed by rhetors from ideas plucked from their minds. An individual then develops these thoughts into a line of reasoning and, in the process, explores and narrows the topic, creates a thesis, and determines the ideas that need to be conveyed to the audience. These proofs are the ones that Aristotle and other ancient rhetoricians believed were critically important, for they are the ones developed from the *rhetor's own mind* and, thus, *invented*. These ideas can be shaped into two types of arguments—deductive and inductive—which we will discuss in the next few pages.

Inartistic Proofs

Inartistic proofs are direct evidence that the speaker might use to support the argument, such as testimony, documents, and anything else that rhetors do not invent through their own thinking. Today, we would call these proofs research. They, also, are essential to writing, but they should *support* the writer's ideas, rather than lead them.

For Aristotle's students, the use of artistic and inartistic proofs might not have been a two-step process—first one and then the other, though the proofs are arranged that way in *The Art of Rhetoric*, as they are in this book. Rather, similar to the process used by Adam Webb (see the *Praxis in Action* at the beginning of this chapter), they might have developed both proofs in an alternating or recursive process. After developing basic ideas for a composition through invention, these students would then collect information from authorities (testimony), what Webb refers to as "reading around." Then they would return to inventing artistic proofs about the project, followed by more references to inartistic proofs. Today, we have more resources for research than did the ancient Greeks, but this does not make artistic proofs any less important. The differences between artistic and inartistic proofs are summarized in table 4.1 below.

table 4.1

Aristotle's Artistic and Inartistic Proofs	
Artistic Ideas from the rhetor's own mind, thus *invented*	**Inartistic** Information gained from external sources
Personal knowledge	Authorities
Observation	Testimony
Patterns of reasoning	Documents

The Five Canons of Rhetoric

Greek and Roman teachers of rhetoric divided rhetoric into five parts or canons. These canons corresponded to the order of activities in creating a speech, as they perceived the process: Invention, arrangement, style, memory, and delivery. These five parts are described in many handbooks of rhetorical instruction, including the *Rhetorica ad Herennium*, which was composed by an unknown author between 86 and 82 CE:

> The speaker . . . should possess the faculties of Invention, Arrangement, Style, Memory, and Delivery. Invention is the

> devising of matter, true or plausible, that would make the case convincing. Arrangement is the ordering and distribution of the matter, making clear the place to which each thing is to be assigned. Style is the adaptation of suitable words and sentences to the matter devised. Memory is the firm retention in the mind of the matter, words, and arrangement. Delivery is the graceful regulation of voice, countenance, and gesture.

Today, classes in composition or writing studies still emphasize the necessity of **invention**, now interpreted as prewriting activities that enable writers to develop the logic and words needed for effective arguments. **Arrangement** involves organizing an argument into a logical format that leads the reader easily from the thesis to the conclusion. **Style** has to do with the author's voice and tone and the structure of sentences and paragraphs. **Memory** is used somewhat differently today, as students are no longer required to memorize compositions for oral presentation. Instead, memory is utilized in ways such as remembering how and where to retrieve information from the Internet, books, and other reference materials. Finally, **delivery**, which once involved gestures and tone of voice in an oral presentation, today has to do with document design, so that the final product is presented in a professional manner according to Modern Language Association (MLA) or American Psychological Association (APA) style. Delivery also involves grammatical accuracy because surface errors detract from the effective impact of a document. See table 4.2 below for a summary of the five parts of rhetoric.

table 4.2

The Five Parts (or Canons) of Rhetoric		
English	**Greek**	**Latin**
invention	*heuresis*	*inventio*
arrangement	*taxis*	*dispositio*
style	*lesis*	*elocutio*
memory	*mneme*	*memoria*
delivery	*hypocrisis*	*actin*

The Modern Writing Process Overview

Prewriting (Inventing)

Writing is not only about putting the pen to paper. As did rhetors in ancient Greece and Rome, you have to think deeply and critically about a subject before you begin a composition. The "invention" step of the writer's process is designed to help you find a worthwhile topic and develop your ideas about that topic before you start to write a draft. It includes writing, discussion, and research, as well as informal writing to help you explore your thoughts and feelings about a subject. Whatever method you choose, keep a record of your thoughts and discoveries as you spend this time in close examination of your subject.

Drafting

It may seem odd that writing a draft should come in the middle of the writer's process. However, research has shown that students and professionals alike write more effective essays when they don't reach for the pen too quickly. If you have spent enough time in the invention stage, the actual drafting stage may go more quickly. After writing the first draft, in succeeding drafts you can add details, observations, illustrations, examples, expert testimony, and other support to help your essay entertain, illuminate, or convince your audience.

Revising

Today, we talk more about the revision stage of writing than did ancient rhetoricians. If you are a student who tends to write assigned essays at the last minute, you may have missed this step entirely, yet many writers claim this is the longest and most rewarding step in the writing process. To revise, you must, in a sense, learn to let go of your writing. Some students think their first drafts should stay exactly the way they are written because they are true to their feelings and experience. Many writers find, however, that first drafts assume too much about the reader's knowledge and reactions. Sometimes readers, reading a first draft essay, are left scratching their heads and wondering what it is the writer is trying to convey. Writers who revise try to read their writing as readers would, taking note of gaps in logic, the absence of clear examples, the need for reordering information, and so on. Then they can revise their content with the reader in mind.

Editing and Polishing

Once writers have clarified their messages and the methods by which they will present those messages, one more step must be taken. Particularly because their compositions are written, rather than presented orally, they must go over their work again to check for correct spelling, grammar, and punctuation, as well as the use of Standard Written English. Some students finish with an essay, print it, and turn it in without ever examining the final copy. This is a critical mistake, because misspelled words and typographical and formatting errors can make an otherwise well-written essay lose its credibility. The five canons of rhetoric and the modern writing process are summarized in table 4.3 below.

table 4.3

The Five Canons of Rhetoric and the Modern Writing Process	
Five Canons of Rhetoric	**Modern Writing Process**
Invention—Devising the arguments that will make the case convincing, often basing them on models of famous speeches.	Prewriting—Determining the thesis, points of argument, counterargument, and rebuttal. Researching evidence to support the argument.
Arrangement—Ordering the argument into a logical format. Style—Finding suitable words and figures of speech. [Note: This may have been a recursive process, but the ancients did not consider that aspect important.]	Drafting, revising, and editing—Putting ideas and prewriting into a useable form through a recursive process of drafting, revising, and editing.
Memory—Retaining the argument in the mind, including its content and arrangement.	Remembering how and where to retrieve information from the Internet, books, and other reference materials.
Delivery—Effective use of voice and gestures to present argument.	Publication—Putting text, images, and other elements in a suitable format and releasing the document to an audience.

Collaborate

Activity 4.1 Compare the Five Canons of Rhetoric and the Modern Writing Process

In your group, reread the discussions in this chapter on the five canons of rhetoric and the modern writing process and review the table above. What parts of the five canons correspond to the modern writing process?

What step in the five canons is not included in the contemporary writing process? If the similarities and differences are not clear to you, consult the Internet. If you search for either "Five Canons of Rhetoric" or "Writing Process" you will find resources. What explanations can you offer for the differences? The similarities?

Stasis Theory Identifies Critical Point in Controversy

Stasis theory presents a series of four questions that were developed by Greek and Roman rhetoricians, primarily Aristotle, Quintilian, and Hermagoras. Answering these questions for an issue enabled rhetors to determine the critical (or stasis) point in a disagreement. This was a technique the ancients developed for the law courts to enable advocates to focus their arguments on the crux of the case. Quintilian, the great Roman teacher of rhetoric, explained in regard to a defendant:

> By far the strongest mode of defense is if the charge which is made can be denied; the next, if an act of the kind charged against the accused can be said not to have been done; the third, and most honorable, if what is done is proved to have been justly done. If we cannot command these methods, the last and only mode of defense is that of eluding an accusation, which can neither be denied nor combated, by the aid of some point of law, so as to make it appear that the action has not been brought in due legal form.

Marcus Fabius Quintilianus (Quintilian) was a Roman orator from Spain who taught stasis theory.

In other words, Quintilian is saying that in law cases, advocates have four choices in developing a focus for their arguments. You have probably watched a courtroom drama on television or film and can recall various defenses made on behalf of defendants. The strongest and most obvious defense is that the defendant is not guilty, that is, he or she did not do the deed in question. The same was true in Quintilian's day. However, sometimes an argument of innocence is not possible, perhaps because it seems obvious that the defendant did perform the deed in question. Thus, the advocate must develop a different strategy. For example, in defense of one accused of murder, the attorney may argue self-defense or mitigating circumstances (such as that the killing was an act of war). In rare cases, other defenses are offered; for example, if the supposed victim's body has not been found, the advocate can argue that the victim may still be alive. An attorney can discover these possible defenses by using stasis theory to analyze the situation.

Another great advantage of stasis theory is that, if pursued diligently, it prevents the rhetor from making the mistake of organizing an argument by simply forwarding reasons why he or she is correct and the opposition is wrong. That approach may please people who agree with the rhetor, but it will not likely gain any support from the opposition. Answering the stasis questions carefully forces the writer to consider aspects of the issue that may have been overlooked but are crucial to an effective argument.

The wording of the four questions has varied somewhat over time, but essentially they are questions of fact, definition, quality, and policy. The same questions can be applied to any issue, not only issues of law. The four stasis questions are as follows:

1. What are the facts? (conjecture)
2. What is the meaning or nature of the issue? (definition)
3. What is the seriousness of the issue? (quality)
4. What is the best plan of action or procedure? (policy)

Many writers prefer stasis theory to other prewriting techniques because answering the questions determines whether or not the different sides of an argument are at stasis. Being at **stasis** means that the opponents are in agreement about their disagreement—the stasis point—which can be identified by one of the four stasis questions. If the sides are at stasis, they have common ground to build upon, for they are arguing the same issue. There is, thus, a greater chance the sides can reach a workable consensus or compromise. If opponents are not at stasis, there is much more work to be done to reach consensus.

The point where the opposing sides agree upon their disagreement is the stasis point.

For example, in the argument about the teaching of evolution and/or intelligent design in schools, the two sides are not in agreement about how to discuss the issue. Those in favor of teaching evolution claim intelligent design should not be called science, which is an issue of definition. Those who propose teaching intelligent design along with (or instead of) evolution tend to focus on "proving" evidence, an issue of fact. Until the two sides can agree upon what is the stasis point, or crux of the issue, they cannot debate effectively. They are not presenting arguments about the same question.

The four stasis questions can be broken into the subquestions listed in table 4.4. If you want to find the stasis point, work through the list for your issue, answering all of the subquestions. However, for each question, you must identify not only how *you* would answer the question but also how the opposing side or sides would answer. For example, if you are considering the issue of global warming, people with different positions will not agree on the facts. Thus, you must identify the basic facts of global warming represented by your side, and then identify the facts that might be presented by the opposing side.

table 4.4

Stasis Questions
Fact
• Did something happen? • What are the facts? • Is there a problem/issue? • How did it begin and what are its causes? • What changed to create the problem/issue? • Can it be changed? It also may be useful to ask the following critical questions of your own research and conclusions: • Where did I obtain my data and are these sources reliable? • How do I know they're reliable?
Definition
• What is the nature of the problem/issue? • What exactly is the problem/issue? • What kind of a problem/issue is it? • To what larger class of things or events does it belong? • What are its parts, and how are they related? It also may be useful to ask the following critical questions of your own research and conclusions: • Who/what is influencing my definition of this problem/issue? • How/why are these sources/beliefs influencing my definition of the issue?

Quality
• Is it a good thing or a bad thing? • How serious is the problem/issue? • Who might be affected by this problem/issue (stakeholders)? • What happens if we don't do anything? • What are the costs of solving the problem/issue? It also may be useful to ask the following critical questions of your own research and conclusions: • Who/what is influencing my determination of the seriousness of this problem/issue? • How/why are these sources/beliefs influencing my determination of the issue's seriousness?
Policy
• Should action be taken? • Who should be involved in helping to solve the problem/address the issue? • What should be done about this problem? • What needs to happen to solve this problem/address this issue? It also may be useful to ask the following critical questions of your own research and conclusions: • Who/what is influencing my determination of what to do about this problem/issue? • How/why are these sources/beliefs influencing my determination of what to do about this issue?
Source: Adapted from Purdue Owl Resource on Stasis Theory, http://owl.english.purdue.edu/owl/resource/736/1.

Using Stasis Questions

To illustrate the use of stasis questions, a team of writers working together to compose a report on racism in America might use the stasis questions to talk through information they will later use in their report. In the following sample dialogue, team members disagree about what actions are racist.

> "Flying the Confederate battle flag is racist."
>
> "Flying the Confederate battle flag is *not* racist."
>
> "Yes, it is, because it represents the Confederate states that supported slavery, and it's generally accepted that slavery in America was racist."
>
> "Flying the Confederate battle flag is not racist, because it's a part of American history and Southern heritage."

These two team members disagree about whether or not flying the Confederate battle flag is a racist act. This sort of disagreement might lead to a complete breakdown of group work if common ground cannot be found.

In this example, the team members go on to agree that some people still exhibit the Confederate battle flag (*fact*) on their vehicles and on their clothes, but that the flag is also displayed in museums (*fact*). They go on to agree that the issue is still very important to some people since a number of American states have recently debated the flag in legislatures and assemblies (*quality*). Moreover, group members note that a number of legal suits have been filed for and against the display of the flag in public places, so it's clear the issue still matters to a lot of people (*quality*).

In this sense, the team members have achieved stasis on two of the four stases—*fact* (people still display the flag, though in different places) and *quality* (it's a very important issue). Where the team members disagree, however, is in the stases of *definition* (is the display of the flag "racist"?) and *policy* (what should we do about this?).

Thinking about this disagreement using stasis theory allows people to build common ground so that parties who disagree can move toward resolution and action even if they can't agree on all levels. For example, team members who disagree about whether or not flying the Confederate battle flag is racist might still be able to agree on what to do about it.

> "Ok, we disagree about whether flying the flag is racist, but we can agree that flying the flag is probably protected under the First Amendment to the United States Constitution—that flying the flag is protected by our freedom of speech."
>
> "Yeah."
>
> "So, people are free to display the flag on their vehicles, on their clothes, and on their property, as well as in museums. But,

state legislatures and assemblies will have to debate and vote on whether or not the flag can be displayed on publicly funded property or in public symbols, such as state flags and seals."

"That sounds pretty democratic. Sure."

Not every team situation is going to end this amicably; however, by using the stasis questions to help keep the dialogue going—on a reasonable course—team members can find common ground and work toward action that is acceptable to most, if not all, of the group members.*

Stasis Theory and Kairos

As you will remember from Chapter 3, the *kairos* of an argument is the context, opportune moment, or point in time in which the rhetor, the audience, the issue, and the current situation provide opportunities and constraints for an argument. If you keep kairos in mind as you analyze an issue, you take advantage of timeliness. For example, if you want to write an argument about the death penalty, you might consider that United States courts are increasingly questioning the validity of eyewitness testimony, evidence which has been the deciding factor in many death penalty cases.

As part of your use of stasis theory, consider the four questions in relation to kairos:

1. How do recent developments (new facts) or the local situation affect the issue? Will it change your audience's perception of the facts?
2. Does the current situation affect your audience's definition of the issue? Is it defined differently by an audience in this location than elsewhere?
3. Have recent events made the issue more or less important to your audience? Is it more or less important in your location than elsewhere?
4. Do recent events, locally or widely, affect the need or lack of need for action, in your audience's perception?

As a rhetorician, it is important for you to be aware of the history of a controversy. But it is equally important to have an awareness of the kairos of the argument. Such an awareness enables you to adopt a "ready stance" and adjust your argument, so that it reflects an awareness of your audience's position and interests, as well as contemporary developments in the issue.

* Allen Brizee, "Stasis Theory for Teamwork," *Purdue Owl,* April 17, 2010, http://owl.english.purdue.edu/owl/ (Accessed October 3, 2011).

Such a flexible stance may afford you an opportunity to be persuasive that you might otherwise miss.

Activity 4.2 Identify the Defense in a Television or Film Courtroom Drama

As your instructor directs, watch a courtroom drama on television or film and decide what defense the defendant's attorney is offering. Report your conclusion to your small group or the class. Then, after you have discussed the stasis questions, identify which of the four questions the attorney in the drama is focusing upon as the crux of the defense. Discuss with your group or the class.

Activity 4.3 Use Stasis Theory to Explore Your Topic

Choose an issue that interests you and answer all the stasis questions in the table on pages 117-118, both for your position and for the opposing argument. Elaborate with three or four sentences for each subquestion that is particularly relevant to your topic. Is your issue at stasis for any of the questions? Report to your group or to the class.

Activity 4.4 Evaluate a Public Debate

Locate a public debate that has been reported recently in newspaper editorials, television programs, or other media that can be analyzed by using stasis theory. In a paper of 350 to 500 words, do the following:

- Describe the context (kairos).
- Identify the sides of the argument and their principal points.
- Decide which stasis question each side is primarily addressing.
- Determine whether or not the issue is at stasis and explain your answer.
- Include a citation in MLA or APA format for your source or sources.

Activity 4.5: Use Stasis Theory to Analyze a Case

Professors Vijay Govindarajan and Christian Sarkar launched a competition on the *Harvard Business Network* blog for designs to build $300 houses for the poor. Word of the competition spread quickly, and a wide variety of people began to write about the competition—in editorials in *The New York Times*, the *Economist*, and in a companion blog, http://www.300house.com/blog.

Your Task: Read the four articles written about the $300 house competition that appear on the following pages. Discuss them in class and in small groups. In particular, note that Matias Echanove and Rahul Srivastava write in their *New York Times* op-ed essay, "Hands Off Our Houses," that the idea of a $300 house is impractical and will fail in places such as Mumbai, India. In contrast, "A $300 Idea that Is Priceless," the editorial from the *Economist*, praises the design competition for initiating an "explosion of creativity." Work through the stasis questions, with one side of the controversy being those who support this design initiative. The other side would be those who foresee problems in applying this idealistic initiative in the real world, a viewpoint that is expressed in "Hands Off Our Houses."

Write a paper of approximately 750 words in which you do the following:

- Briefly present the idea of the design competition.
- Summarize the arguments of those in favor of the initiative.
- Explain the reservations expressed in "Hands Off Our Houses."
- Identify a stasis point, if one exists, and explain why you think the sides have common ground on that particular stasis question.
- Discuss whether the discovery of common ground might allow individuals involved in this debate to talk to one another and work toward solutions for the problem of substandard housing in slums worldwide.
- As your instructor directs, cite your sources in APA or MLA style.

Reading 4.1

The $300 House: A Hands-On Lab for Reverse Innovation?

by Vijay Govindarajan

Published in the *HBR Blog Network.*

David A. Smith, the founder of the Affordable Housing Institute (AHI) tells us that "markets alone will never satisfactorily house a nation's poorest citizens . . . whether people buy or rent, housing is typically affordable to only half of the population."

The result? Smith points to a "spontaneous community of self-built or informally built homes—the shanty towns, settlements, and ever-expanding slums that sprout like mushrooms on the outskirts of cities in the developing world."

We started discussing the issue, examining the subject through the lens of reverse innovation.

Here are five questions Christian and I asked ourselves:

1. How can organic, self-built slums be turned into livable housing?
2. What might a house-for-the-poor look like?
3. How can world-class engineering and design capabilities be utilized to solve the problem?
4. What reverse-innovation lessons might be learned by the participants in such a project?
5. How could the poor afford to buy this house?

Livable Housing. Our first thought was that self-built houses are usually built from materials that are available—cardboard, plastic, mud or clay, metal scraps and whatever else is nearby. Built on dirt floors, these structures are prone to collapse and catching fire. Solution: replace these unsafe structures with a mass-produced, standard, affordable, and sustainable solution. We want to create the $300-House-for-the-Poor.

Look and Feel. To designers, our sketch of this house might be a bit of a joke, but it's useful nonetheless to illustrate the concept, to get started. We wanted the house to be an ecosystem of products and solutions designed around the real needs of the inhabitants. Of course it would have to be made out of sustainable, green materials, but more crucially, it would have to be durable enough to withstand torrential rains, earthquakes, and the stress of children playing. The house might be a single room structure with drop-down partitions for privacy. Furniture—sleeping hammocks and fold-down chairs would be built in. The roof would boast an inexpensive solar panel and battery to light the house and charge the mobile phone and tablet computer. An inexpensive water filter would be built in as well.

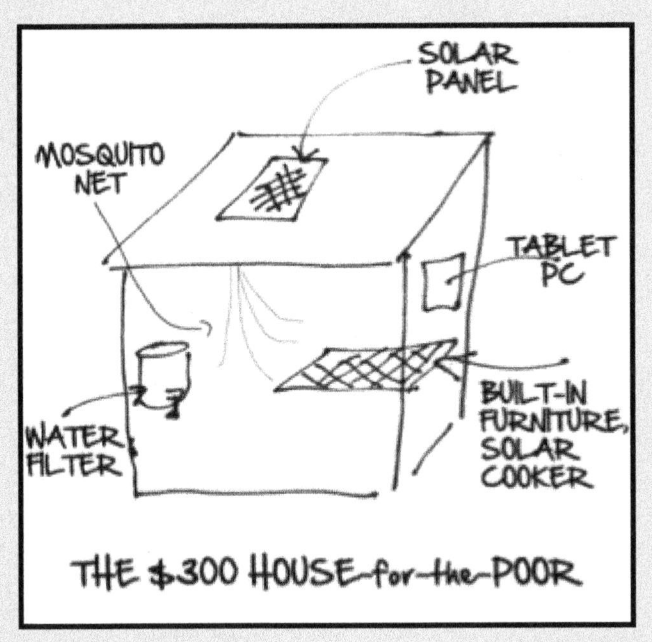

In effect, the house is really a one-room shed designed around the family ecosystem, a lego-like aggregation of useful products that "bring good things to life" for the poor.

World-Class Design. Our next question was: "Who will do this?" We decided that it would have to be a collaboration between global design and engineering companies and non-profits with experience solving problems for the poor. The usual suspects ran through our minds—IDEO, GE, TATA, Siemens, Habitat-for-Humanity, Partners In Health, the Solar Electric Light Fund, the Clinton Global Initiative, the Gates Foundation, Grameen. Governments may play an important part in setting the stage for these types of cross-country innovation projects.

The Reverse Innovation Payoff. Participating companies will reap two rewards. First, they will be able to serve the unserved, the 2.5 billion who make up the bottom of the pyramid. Second, they create new competencies which can help transform lives in rich countries by creating breakthrough innovations to solve several problems (scaled housing for hurricane victims, refugees, and even the armed forces).

A House of One's Own: Affordability. To move beyond charity, the poor must become owners of their homes, responsible for their care and upkeep. The model of social business introduced by Muhammad Yunus resonates strongly with us. Micro-finance must surely play a role in making the $300 House-for-the-Poor a viable and self-sustaining solution.

Of course, the idea we present here is an experiment. Nevertheless, we feel it deserves to be explored. From the one-room shacks in Haiti's Central Plateau to the jhuggi clusters in and around Delhi, to the favelas in São Paulo, the problem of housing-for-the-poor is truly global.

We ask CEOs, governments, NGOs, foundations: Are there any takers?

Reading 4.2

Hands Off Our Houses

by Matias Echanove and Rahul Srivastava

Published in *The New York Times.*

Mumbai, India

Last summer, a business professor and a marketing consultant wrote on The Harvard Business Review's website about their idea for a $300 house. According to the writers, and the many people who have enthusiastically responded since, such a house could improve the lives of millions of urban poor around the world. And with a $424 billion market for cheap homes that is largely untapped, it could also make significant profits.

The writers created a competition, asking students, architects and businesses to compete to design the best prototype for a $300 house (their original sketch was of a one-room prefabricated shed, equipped with solar panels, water filters and a tablet computer). The winner will be announced this month. But one expert has been left out of the competition, even though her input would have saved much time and effort for those involved in conceiving the house: the person who is supposed to live in it.

We work in Dharavi, a neighborhood in Mumbai that has become a one-stop shop for anyone interested in "slums" (that catchall term for areas lived in by the urban poor). We recently showed around a group of Dartmouth students involved in the project who are hoping to get a better grasp of their market. They had imagined a ready-made constituency of slum-dwellers eager to buy a cheap house that would necessarily be better than the shacks they'd built themselves. But the students found that the reality here is far more complex than their business plan suggested.

To start with, space is scarce. There is almost no room for new construction or ready-made houses. Most residents are renters, paying $20 to $100 a month for small apartments.

Those who own houses have far more equity in them than $300—a typical home is worth at least $3,000. Many families have owned their houses for two or three generations, upgrading them as their incomes increase. With additions, these homes become what we call "tool houses," acting as workshops, manufacturing units, warehouses and shops. They facilitate trade and production, and allow homeowners to improve their living standards over time.

None of this would be possible with a $300 house, which would have to be as standardized as possible to keep costs low. No number of add-ons would be able to match the flexibility of need-based construction.

In addition, construction is an important industry in neighborhoods like Dharavi. Much of the economy consists of hardware shops, carpenters, plumbers, concrete makers, masons, even real-estate agents. Importing prefabricated homes would put many people out of business, undercutting the very population the $300 house is intended to help.

Worst of all, companies involved in producing the house may end up supporting the clearance and demolition of well-established neighborhoods to make room for it. The resulting resettlement colonies, which are multiplying at the edges of cities like Delhi and Bangalore, may at first glance look like ideal markets for the new houses, but the dislocation destroys businesses and communities.

The $300 house could potentially be a success story, if it was understood as a straightforward business proposal instead of a social solution. Places like refugee camps, where many people need shelter for short periods, could use such cheap, well-built units. A market for them could perhaps be created in rural-urban fringes that are less built up.

The $300 house responds to our misconceptions more than to real needs. Of course problems do exist in urban India. Many people live without toilets or running water. Hot and unhealthy asbestos-cement sheets cover millions of roofs. Makeshift homes often flood during monsoons. But replacing individual, incrementally built houses with a ready-made solution would do more harm than good.

A better approach would be to help residents build better, safer homes for themselves. The New Delhi–based Micro Homes Solutions, for example, provides architectural and engineering assistance to homeowners in low-income neighborhoods.

The $300 house will fail as a social initiative because the dynamic needs, interests and aspirations of the millions of people who live in places like Dharavi have been overlooked. This kind of mistake is all too common in the trendy field of social entrepreneurship. While businessmen and professors applaud the $300 house, the urban poor are silent, busy building a future for themselves.

Reading 4.3

The $300 House: A Hands-On Approach to a Wicked Problem

by Vijay Govindarajan with Christian Sarkar

Published in the *HBR Blog Network*

When *The New York Times* printed "Hands Off Our Houses," an op-ed about our idea for a $300 House for the poor, we were both delighted and dismayed—delighted because the $300 House was being discussed, and dismayed because authors Matias Echanove and Rahul Srivastava, co-founders of the Institute of Urbanology, didn't seem to have read the series of blog posts about our idea.

Nearly every criticism the authors levy in their op-ed is answered in 12 blog posts, a magazine article from January/February 2011, a video interview, and a slideshow that integrated community and commentary, which were published between last October and this May.

In critiquing our vision, the authors cite Micro Homes Solutions as "a better approach." In fact, the leaders of that venture were invited several months ago to contribute a blog post to our series as a way of joining the discussion and helping us understand what they've seen on the ground there. They declined to be part of the conversation.

The authors also write that students who tried to write a business plan to serve the poor and who visited poor urban areas of India found "the reality here is far more complex than their business plan suggested."

Yet a fundamental tenet of our project and the blog series about it is that slums present complex challenges that can't be fixed with a clever shack alone. Rather than creating an echo chamber of rah-rah rhetoric, we told blog authors to focus on one of the many knotty issues that Echanove and Srivastava cite in their critique. From the start we asked: What are the complexities of financing these homes? How do you get energy and infrastructure into such dwellings? How do you get corporations to invest in a significant way? We acknowledged that we didn't have the answers. "Just because it is going to take longer than it should doesn't mean we should walk away," wrote Seth Godin in one of the posts. "It's going to take some time, but it's worth it."

The op-ed suggests that the $300 House doesn't acknowledge that "space is scarce" in urban poor areas. Yet, Sunil Suri wrote in a post on the urban challenge that "slums by their nature are located where land and space are limited." Suri proposed potential solutions, including innovative materials, new ways of thinking of the construction process, and building up.

The authors also say that "one expert has been left out of the challenge . . . the person who is supposed to live in it." But a post in the series on the co-creation challenge from Gaurav Bhalla addressed this squarely. "It will be unfortunate if the house were to be designed by those who will never live in it," wrote Bhalla. "Investments need to be made understanding the daily habits and practices of people for whom the house is being designed." Bhalla used the case study of the chulha stove, co-created by businesses, NGOs, and slum dwellers, to make his point. We are also bringing students to India and Haiti to do ethnographic research that will inform development of a $300 House, and when prototypes are developed, they will be deployed and tested with those who will live in them.

Echanove and Srivastava also state that a $300 House "would have to be as standardized as possible to keep costs low. No number of add-ons would be able to match the flexibility of need-based construction." While we agree that a one-size-fits-all approach will not work, we disagree that a $300 House would be inflexible. Core tenets from a blog post about the overall design challenge of creating a $300 House by Bill Gross include "give your customers options" and "make it aspirational." And David Smith's entry on the financial challenge shows that flexibility can be born out of financing options as well. A need-based approach alone also ignores the scale of the problem we are facing. "Triple the U.S. population by three. That's how many people around the world live on about a dollar a day," Godin writes. "Triple it again and now you have the number that lives on $2. About 40% of the world lives on $2 or less a day." In any situation where scale is required, so is some level of standardization.

The most puzzling critique in the op-ed was that "construction is an important industry in neighborhoods like Dharavi. Much of the economy consists of hardware shops, carpenters, plumbers, concrete makers, masons, even real-estate agents. Importing prefabricated homes would put many people out of business, undercutting the very population the $300 house is intended to help."

In fact, our contest's design briefing said these dwellings should be "self built and/or self-improvable." It also stated that the design should rely as much as possible on local materials, which of course would be harvested and crafted by local workers. Our goal is to increase demand for local trades, not drive them away. And the idea that jobs would disappear belies the fact that with progress comes new jobs; teachers for the kids who can now go to school; health care professionals for the families that can now afford check-ups; technology professionals who could service solar panels or internet access devices; farmers who could manage shared crop spaces in the neighborhoods. The $300 House project is a housing ecosystem project.

Finally, Echanove and Srivastava state that "The $300 house could potentially be a success story, if it was understood as a straightforward business proposal instead of a social solution."

We disagree completely. We do support other applications for low-cost housing—bringing these dwellings back to the industrialized world for hurricane relief, for example, would be a reverse innovation success story. However, trying to pigeonhole ideas as either "for good" or "for profit" is an outmoded way of thinking.

The authors have an implicit negative view on business. For them, profit seems to be a dirty word. For us, good business and social innovation are one and the same. The rising tide of New Capitalism, what Michael Porter calls "shared value" and what Umair Haque calls "thick value," is perhaps the most important reaction to the corruption and greed that spurred the most recent global economic crisis. The *Economist* was right when it suggested that this is a "can do" moment in history.

Our goal is neither to start yet another charity—one of our advisers, Paul Polak, tells us that "you can't donate your way out of poverty"—nor to start just another business. Rather we must encourage existing businesses to find ways to create new, scalable markets; to get NGOs to share their on-the-ground expertise; and to force governments to make it as simple as possible to work across the hybrid value chain in order to make such a project a reality and begin the process of instilling dignity in and creating options for individuals who now don't have either.

We are happy that Echanove and Srivastava share our passion for the problem of affordable housing, which is a wicked problem. We simply disagree with the idea that if it's a market, it can't also be a socially progressive solution. Trying to categorize the regeneration of slums as either a business problem or social problem is like trying to categorize a flame as either heat or light. It is both, always.

Reading 4.4

A $300 Idea that Is Priceless

from Schumpeter, a column in the *Economist*

Applying the world's business brains to housing the poor.

Friedrich Engels said in "The Condition of the Working Class in England," in 1844, that the onward march of Manchester's slums meant that the city's Angel Meadow district might better be described as "Hell upon Earth." Today, similar earthly infernos can be found all over the emerging world: from Brazil's favelas to Africa's shanties. In 2010 the United Nations calculated that there were about 827m people living in slums—almost as many people as were living on the planet in Engels's time—and predicted that the number might double by 2030.

Last year Vijay Govindarajan, of Dartmouth College's Tuck School of Business, along with Christian Sarkar, a marketing expert, issued a challenge in a *Harvard Business Review* blog: why not apply the world's best business thinking to housing the poor? Why not replace the shacks that blight the lives of so many poor people, thrown together out of cardboard and mud, and prone to collapsing or catching fire, with more durable structures? They laid down a few simple guidelines. The houses should be built of mass-produced materials tough enough to protect their inhabitants from a hostile world. They should be equipped with the basics of civilized life, including water filters and solar panels. They should be "improvable," so that families can adapt them to their needs. And they should cost no more than $300.

Mr. Govindarajan admits that the $300 figure was partly an attention-grabbing device. But he also argues that it has a certain logic. Muhammad Yunus, the founder of Grameen Bank, has calculated that the average value of the houses of people who have just escaped from poverty is $370. Tata Motors has also demonstrated the value of having a fixed figure to aim at: the company would have found it more difficult to produce the Tata Nano if it had simply been trying to produce a "cheap" car rather than a "one lakh" car (about $2,200).

The attention-grabbing certainly worked. The blog was so inundated with positive responses that a dedicated website, 300house.com, was set up, which has attracted more than 900 enthusiasts and advisers from all over the world. On April 20th Mr. Govindarajan launched a competition inviting people to submit designs for a prototype of the house.

Why has a simple blog post led to such an explosion of creativity? The obvious reason is that "frugal innovation"—the art of radically reducing the cost of products while also delivering first-class value—is all the rage at the moment. General Electric has reduced the cost of an electrocardiogram machine from $2,000 to $400. Tata Chemicals has produced a $24 purifier that can provide a family with pure water for a year. Girish Bharadwaj, an engineer, has perfected a technique for producing cheap footbridges that are transforming life in rural India.

Another reason is that houses can be such effective anti-poverty tools. Poorly constructed ones contribute to a nexus of problems: the spread of disease (because they have no proper sanitation or ventilation), the perpetuation of poverty (because children have no proper lights to study by) and the general sense of insecurity (because they are so flimsy and flammable). Mr. Govindarajan's idea is so powerful because he treats houses as ecosystems that provide light, ventilation and sanitation.

Numerous innovators are also worrying away at this nexus of problems. Habitat for Humanity, an NGO, is building durable houses of bamboo in Nepal. Idealab, a consultancy, is on the verge of unveiling a $2,500 house that will be mass-produced in factories, sold in kits and feature breakthroughs in ventilation, lighting and sanitation. Philips has produced a cheap cooking stove, the Chulha, that cuts out the soot that kills 1.6m people a year worldwide. The Solar Electric Light Fund is demonstrating that you can provide poor families with solar power for roughly the same cost as old standbys such as kerosene and candles.

Profits and other problems

These thinkers, like the advocates of the $300 house, must solve three huge problems to succeed. They must persuade big companies that they can make money out of cheap homes, because only they can achieve the economies of scale needed to hit the target price. They need to ensure sufficient access to microloans: $300 is a huge investment for a family of squatters living on a couple of dollars a day. And they need to overcome the obstacle that most slum-dwellers have weak or non-existent property rights. There is no point in offering people the chance to buy a cleverly designed house if they have no title to the land they occupy. Solving these problems will in turn demand a high degree of co-operation between people who do not always get on: companies and NGOs, designers and emerging-world governments.

However, the exciting thing about the emerging world at the moment is a prevailing belief that even the toughest problems can be solved. And a similar can-do moment, in the late 1940s, offers a striking historical precedent for the application of mass-production techniques to housing: as American servicemen flooded home after the second world war to start families, Levitt & Sons built Levittowns at the rate of 30 houses a day by mass-producing the components in factories, delivering them on lorries and using teams of specialists to assemble them.

Some emerging-world governments are beginning to realize that providing security of tenure is the only way to deal with the problem of ever-proliferating slums. And big companies that face stagnant markets in the West are increasingly fascinated by the "fortune at the bottom of the pyramid." Bill Gross of Idealab reckons the market for cheap houses could be worth at least $424 billion. But in reality it is worth far more than that: preventing the Earth from becoming what Mike Davis, a particularly gloomy follower of Marx and Engels, has termed a "planet of slums."

Other Invention Strategies

Great myths have grown up around writers who can supposedly sit down, put pen to paper, and write a masterpiece. If these myths had developed about any other type of artist—a musician or a painter—we would scoff about them and ask about the years of study and practice those artists had spent before they created their masterpieces. Since all of us can write to some degree, perhaps it seems more feasible that great authors simply appear magically amongst us. Alas, it is not so; like all talented artists, good writers must learn their craft through consistent and continuous practice. Similar to how the ancient Greeks used **topoi** (a strategy or heuristic made up of questions about a topic which allows a rhetor to construe an argument) to generate raw material for their compositions, many writers today use the following invention strategies as prewriting activities.

Freewriting

One practice method developed in the 1970s and often attributed to Peter Elbow, author of *Writing without Teachers*, is called freewriting. This method is just what it sounds like—writing that is free of any content restrictions. You simply write what is on your mind. This method is freeform, but there is some structure—you must set a time limit before you begin, and once you begin, you must not stop. The time period is usually 10 to 20 minutes, and you must keep your pen or pencil moving on the page—no hesitations, no corrections, no rereading. Don't worry about spelling, or punctuation, or grammar—just download onto the paper whatever comes to mind. It will seem awkward at best; some have said it is downright painful. But after a few weeks practice, you will realize it is effective and a wonderful individual method of getting at your thoughts on a subject.

Invisible Freewriting

If you just cannot stop paying attention to your spelling and grammar, or if you find yourself always stopping to read what you have written, you can freewrite invisibly. To do this, you will need carbon paper and a pen that is retracted or out of ink. You sandwich the carbon paper, carbon side down, between two sheets of paper and write on the top sheet with your empty pen. You cannot see what you are writing, but it will be recorded on the bottom sheet of paper. If you prefer to work on the computer, you can easily modify this technique by taping a blank sheet of paper over the monitor while you type.

Focused Freewriting

When freewriting, you are writing without sticking to any particular topic. You are exploring many ideas and your sentences may roam from your day at work, the letter you just got from your sister, or a story you read in the paper about a man who tracks the nighttime migrations of songbirds. With focused freewriting, you are trying to concentrate on one particular subject. You can write the name of that subject at the top of the page to remind you of your topic as you write. The rules are the same as the other types of freewriting, but you are focusing on one question or idea and exploring it in depth.

One drawback of focused freewriting is that students sometimes confuse it with a different step in the writing process, drafting. Remember that freewriting is "invention" work, intended only to help you explore ideas on paper. Drafting takes place only after you have explored, analyzed, and organized those ideas. Freewriting helps you think and write critically about a topic while drafting occurs once you have done the critical thinking necessary to come up with a unified, cohesive, and organized plan for an essay.

Listing/Brainstorming

This method of mapping is the least visual and the most straightforward. Unlike freewriting, where you write continuously, with listing you write down words and/or phrases that provide a shorthand for the ideas you might use in your essay, much as you would a grocery or "to-do" list. Brainstorming is a bit looser. Lists usually follow line after line on the page; brainstorming consists of words and phrases placed anywhere you want to write them on the page.

Clustering

When you think of a cluster, you think of several like things grouped together, often with something holding them together. Peanut clusters, a type of candy, are peanuts joined together with milk chocolate. Star clusters are groupings of stars, like the Pleiades or the Big Dipper, connected by their relative positions to each other in space. You can create clusters of like ideas by grouping your ideas around a central topic on a blank sheet of paper.

Organizing or Arranging

The "invention" process is intended to get our ideas out of our heads and onto a piece of paper, but rarely do these ideas arrive in the most logical or effective order. Take some time (an hour or so for a short essay) to analyze your inventions. Place all the ideas in a logical order, and join similar ideas. Next, look for your most significant point, the most important thing you want to say about your subject. This may become your tentative thesis. Then identify which of the other items on your list will help you communicate your point and delete items that are irrelevant to your thesis.

Reading 4.5

Take a Leap into Writing

by Craig Wynne

When I was working at Berkeley's College Academic Support Center, I often tutored second-language learners who struggled with sentences that had awkward constructions. Sometimes, I would say to a student, "What is it you're trying to say here?" The student inevitably could state the point orally with accuracy and clarity. I would then say to the student, "Write down what you just said." The student would write it down with pen and paper. Then I'd say, "Okay, pretend you're the professor. Which do you think is the easier sentence to understand: what you wrote or what you typed?" The student would say, "What I wrote. Whenever I type, I'm always afraid of what the professor will say."

Craig Wynne says, "When jumping out of an airplane, you don't have time to think about consequences. You just have to do it....The same principle applies to writing."

Around that time, I read an article in *Writer* magazine entitled "Forget the Rules and Take a Leap," by an author named Deanna Roy. In this article, Roy had been suffering from writer's block, and she found that skydiving was a way for her to release her thoughts without fear of saying the "wrong thing." So I decided to put this idea into practice myself for the purposes of teaching my students about overcoming their inhibitions when it came to writing.

When jumping out of an airplane, you don't have time to think about consequences. You just have to do it. You can see from the photo, jumping wasn't an easy thing for me to do, but afterwards I was glad I had gone through with taking that leap.

The same principle applies to writing. You need to find a way to write without thinking about whether your words are spelled correctly or whether the professor won't like the idea. Those thoughts get in the way with your writing process. Some students can write with that kind of freedom on a computer, but others find that with the computer comes an uninvited editor who looks over their shoulder and criticizes. Yet, they can escape that editor by talking out their thoughts and then writing with pen and paper. Whatever works. This doesn't mean that writing is ever going to be easy. It's just easier if you can get your thoughts down on a piece of paper before that internal editor starts looking for errors.

A professor named Peter Elbow developed a process called freewriting, which helps writers take that leap from thoughts into words. To freewrite, you put your pen to paper and just write. You don't want to think about whether something is spelled incorrectly or whether the professor will like an idea. Freewriting is the chance for you to get your ideas down on paper (or on the computer). When you freewrite, you don't stop. You just write. Even if you have an idea you think sounds completely stupid or off-the-wall, just write it down. You never know. Sometimes, those "silly" ideas could contain something you might be able to use for your assignment. When I start a project, I begin by letting all my ideas out in words in a row, even if they don't sound quite right. Professor Elbow remarked that freewriting results in a lot of words that are garbage. That's true. However, eventually, I come to words that express an idea I like. In order to get to the point of liking my words, I have to take that leap onto the page. Eventually, I have to worry about grammar, structure, and the end product, but not while I'm freewriting.

Activity 4.6 Consider "Take a Leap into Writing"

1. How do you write most easily? On a computer? With pen and paper? Share your experience getting words onto a page.
2. What do you think of Wynne's comparison of writing to skydiving? What do the two things have in common?
3. Do you have an internal editor that keeps you from writing freely? Can you describe your editor? What does it do?

Activity 4.7 Focused Freewriting

1. Write your topic at the top of a blank sheet of paper.
2. Write a list of at least 10 aspects or characteristics of your topic.
3. Choose two or three items from your list and do a focused freewriting on each item for five to eight minutes.
4. Add more items to your list if you have discovered new ideas during your freewriting.

Activity 4.8 Begin with What You Know

In your small group, make a list of controversial topics that you already have some knowledge about because of personal experience or course work. For example, one of you may be among the millions of Americans without health insurance or you may know someone else in this position. If so, you probably know about some of the failings of the American health care system. Alternatively, you may have lost a job during the 2009 recession or been unable to find a job when you needed one. If so, you probably have some thoughts about the efforts of the federal government to deal with the economic crisis. These personal connections with controversial issues give you a starting point for research on a topic. Share your group's list with the class.

Expand Your Personal Knowledge through Observation

Close observation for descriptive detail can enhance almost any topic. If you are writing a paper on the effectiveness of recycling in your community, you might take a trip to your community's processing area for recycled glass. There you could gather information through observing the glass recycling process. You also might be able to conduct short, informal interviews with the employees about the process.

You may need to call to get permission to visit certain places. You'll need to identify yourself and your topic. Usually you can get permission to visit and observe. However, if you cannot get permission to visit an area, you can ask your contact if there is a similar area nearby. Again, look at your research questions before you visit to decide which questions might be answered by your observations. For example, if you have read about recycling centers in other communities, during your visit to the local center, you could observe the similarities and differences in their procedures. Good writers always gather more detail than they actually use so they have choices about what to include.

The key to successful observation is tuning the senses. Can you remember what your room smelled like when you woke up this morning, the first thing you saw when you opened your eyes, the way your sheets or blanket felt against your skin, the sounds in the room after you turned off your alarm, or the taste of the orange juice or coffee you had with breakfast? Our minds are trained to ignore seemingly unimportant information, so if you can't remember any sensory details from your morning, you're not alone. When conducting an observation, however, those sensory responses are an important part of your research. Sitting in the place you're observing, freewrite for at least five minutes on each of the senses: touch, taste, smell, sight, and sound. You might even freewrite on each of the senses from several different vantage points, depending on the size of the place or the event you're observing. Take notes on the responses given by those you speak with.

Within fifteen minutes of leaving the place you have been observing, take a few minutes to read over your notes and write a few overall impressions or add details you missed in your description. Look again at your research questions and decide which ones have been answered by your visit.

Activity 4.9 Observation Exercise

In this exercise, describe your classroom. Alternatively, go to another setting such as a museum, restaurant, or library and describe that space and the people in it.

- How large is the space, approximately? Describe the shape of the room, and the color and texture of the walls, the ceiling, and the floor.
- How is the space furnished? Describe the color, shape, and style of the furnishings.
- What about representing the other senses? Is the room silent or noisy? Does it have a characteristic smell? Describe.
- How many people are in the room? What are they doing? Describe their ages, general style of dress, and possessions such as computers, backpacks, or purses.
- Pick two or three people that stand out in some way from the other occupants and write a sentence or two about each, describing what it is about each person that caught your attention.

Reading 4.6

BMW 1M: Miniature, Mighty and Miles of Fun

by Dan Neil

Dan Neil, auto columnist for *The Wall Street Journal,* reviewed the new BMW Coupe in his weekly column "Rumble Seat."

As you read the article that follows, pay attention to how the author uses details from both personal knowledge and close observation to enrich his writing.

Typically, car makers will choose a special color for the introduction of a special vehicle, known in the biz as the "launch color." In the case of the 1M Coupe—the Motorsports division variant of BMW's beastly looking 135i—the launch color is a sort of burnt tangerine, a phrase that also describes my own mental citrus after a weekend behind the wheel.

A bratty little barrel-racer of a car, with a spirit that seems to want to bite through the bit, the 1M Coupe is quick, playful, aggressive and laugh-out-loud fun to drive; indeed, it's as much fun as the law will allow. For BMW fanboys, I gather, that's just the problem.

A little history is in order: The M division began in the 1970s building highly tuned versions of the Werks' production cars, with more powerful engines, bigger brakes, more athletic legs and edgier electronics. Some of these cars have been, simply, epic. The M3 that I imprinted on was a '96 Euro-spec yellow coupe. That car is, to this day, the best handling five-seater I've ever driven.

Bratty Little Barrel Racer

(Note to Bavaria: Bring back the narrow-section steering wheel. And stop hogging all the good scenery.)

To describe the pleasures of that M3—known to the geek squad as the E36 model—is to define a kind of atavism that the Bimmerphiles pine for. Those cars were relatively simple (in-line six, manual transmission and spare amenities), with beautifully quick and sensitive steering and an easy progressiveness that meant you could let the rear end slide around without fear of losing it, catching the car with a dab of throttle and counter-steer. It wasn't the fastest car in the world but it was such a sheer limbic pleasure to drive, to wheel, to wield, to control. That's it: a sense of mastery. You got out of that car wearing a cape and a big S on your chest.

Most of all, that car was lightweight. That E36 coupe weighed about 3,200 pounds. By contrast, the current model-year M3 (E92) weighs fully 500 pounds more on a 2.4-inch-longer wheelbase. And while the current M3 has vastly more go-fast hardware—including a 414-horsepower V8, optional dual-clutch gearbox, cybernetic brakes and the M Variable Differential Lock (sounds like an outlawed wrestling hold, doesn't it?)—a certain something, call it a dynamic lucidity, has been lost.

And the fanboys feel betrayed. They whine, they fume, they wear black. You'd think Rudolph Valentino had just died or something. Why does the M3 have to be so heavy? What part of Ultimate Driving Machine does BMW itself not understand?

But everyone's favorite M3 of yore didn't have to have a monster stereo, navi, power seats, umpteen airbags or five-star crash structure. The M3 so fondly remembered has been essentially optioned up and regulated out of existence. Unless BMW discovers the formula for Flubber, that car isn't coming back.

And the bloat isn't confined to the weight scales. The current M3 is also punitively pricey, starting at $61,075 (with gas-guzzler tax) and luxed-out to nearly $70,000. More fanboy despair. Oh, Rudy!

To these disconsolate few, the news last year that the M division was going to hot up the 135i coupe (the E82 platform, in nerd-speak) must have sounded like salvation. The numbers were there. Not quite 3,400 pounds, with a twin-turbo 3.0-liter in-line six delivering 335 hp and 332 pound-feet of torque—with brief computer-summoned overboost of 369 pound-feet—and the sole choice of a six-speed manual transmission, the 1M Coupe sounded like more than just a cool car. It promised a return to form, an end to a kind of despised lavishness, a cure for what ails the BMW brand.

2012 BMW 1M Coupe

Base price: $47,010

Price as tested: $49,000 (est.)

Powertrain: Twin-turbo 3.0-liter in-line six cylinder with variable valve timing; six-speed manual transmission; rear wheel drive with variable differential lock

Horsepower/torque: 335 hp at 5,900 rpm/332 pound-feet at 1,500–4,500 rpm (369 pound-feet at overboost)

Length/weight: 172.4 inches/3,362 pounds

Wheelbase: 104.7 inches

EPA fuel economy: 19/26 mpg, city/highway

Cargo capacity: 8 cubic feet

Now that the car is here, is it? You know, it is, sort of.

To boil it down a bit, the 1M Coupe is the smaller car with the mighty M3's dirty bits, less 400 pounds. The same highly evolved suspension componentry, the same massive brakes behind the same stick-with-a-grip 35-series, 19-inch tires and wheels, the same electronically controlled rear differential, and the same M-tuned dynamics control, which allows drivers to color outside the lines safely at the track. And yes, you can turn the electronic interventions off. But once the nannies are dismissed, be advised, the car has a measure of the old-school, free-gimbaling character of the early M's. In other words, it can get away from you. Me? Oh, please. You'd like that, wouldn't you?

The 1M is certainly track-day ready, with a dry-sump engine-lubrication system with its own heat exchanger as well as a radiator for the heavy-duty six-speed transmission. The car I drove had a brake warning light come on—I think the 14-inch cross-drilled brakes got a little too warm after being lapped at Laguna Seca for a half-hour or so—but they never failed to haul the car down with a precise and determined yank rearward.

Here, at last, is a man's clutch—heavily weighted, with a smooth, precise uptake—and slick-shifting gearshift to go with it. Pedal position is just about perfect for heel-and-toe footwork.

Serene and smooth at low speeds, but with an increasingly impatient growl from the quad exhaust as the revs build, the 1M does several dynamic things particularly well. First, at corner exits, it pulls like hell, like it has deployed some magical torque spinnaker. BMW gives the 0–60 acceleration at 4.7 seconds, but the way this thing gets on the cam in second and third gear will bring a tear to your eye. Like my favorite M3 of olden days, the car is not unnervingly fast but it's hugely willing. This thing hits redline faster than one of the Real Housewives of Atlanta.

Second, it has splendid cornering grip, and the corner-to-corner transitions happen without a lot of heaving, rolling or rebound to unsettle the car or cause you to correct your line. The 1M Coupe has impeccable cornering manners, and the M Sport Seats lock you in driving position.

Third, it trail-brakes like a dream. Turn in to a corner with the brakes on and ease off the binders. The car's rear end slides gracefully to the outside, the world swivels and now you're looking at corner exit. Dig in the spurs, up come the revs. Hi-yo, Silbern, away!

So what could possibly be wrong? Well, for one thing, the 1M Coupe is a total buttaface, one of the ugliest, most disturbingly wrong car designs in modern history. The addition of all the massive wheel arches, lip spoilers, aero mods and the so-called Air Curtain front spoiler helps not at all. This car is the last revenge of former BMW styling head Chris Bangle. Jeez, put a flag over its head and drive for glory.

Second—at least to the fanboys—it's still too heavy, despite the fact it's actually 77 pounds lighter than the standard 135i. But I checked the trunk for lead bars and found none, and I found very little in the way of depleted uranium in the cabin.

I can only conclude that, for some old-schoolers, nothing BMW makes will ever be light enough again. That's too bad. This thing's a tangerine dream.

Activity 4.10 Find Artistic and Inartistic Proofs in a Reading

Much of Dan Neil's column, "BMW 1M: Miniature, Mighty and Miles of Fun," comes from his own personal experience and observation. For example, his description of the car as a, "bratty little barrel-racer of a car, with a spirit that seems to want to bite through the bit," is his own evaluation or thought and, thus, an artistic proof. So is the first sentence, "Typically, car makers will choose a special color for the introduction of a special vehicle, known in the biz as the 'launch color.'" That information comes from his long experience with reviewing cars. Also, his remark that the brake light came on in the car he drove is his observation.

However, the information that the car has "a dry-sump engine-lubrication system with its own heat exchanger as well as a radiator for the heavy-duty six-speed transmission" may have come from the manufacturer's promotional literature.

For this activity, go through the reading and highlight (or underline) the parts that you think come from Dan Neil's own knowledge or observation. These are the artistic proofs. Information he has obtained from other sources (such as the car company) would be inartistic proofs. If you aren't sure whether or not a sentence is his own knowledge or observation, make a note of that in the margin. Discuss this as a class.

Activity 4.11 Write a Product Review

Choose a new product in a category you know well, such as a computer or an MP3 player, and write a review as if you were a columnist for a newspaper, magazine, or blog. Using the techniques explained in this chapter, do prewriting to elicit what you know about the product and the product category. Then, observe the product and try it out, so that you can review its positives and negatives. If you need specific information that you do not know, consult the product advertising, packaging, or instruction manual.

Like Dan Neil's auto product review, you can use vivid language and insider slang in order to provide an enjoyable experience for your reader. Remember, however, that this is an argument. You need to evaluate whether the product is a good or bad selection for its target audience and why.

Activity 4.12 Write on Your Blog

Choose a controversial topic and speculate in your blog whether or not that topic is at a stasis point for any of the stasis questions.

Activity 4.13 Write in Your Commonplace Book

In your commonplace book, freewrite about how you do invention. What methods do you use to extract from your mind what you already know about a subject (what Aristotle would call artistic proofs)?

5
WRITING RHETORICALLY

Praxis in Action

How I Write by Matthew Harding

Writing can seem very daunting at times, especially when you have a major writing assignment that's worth as much as a test. It should be easy since you know about the assignment way ahead of time, but somehow the time ends up getting away from you because it's hard to get started. You end up both stressing about the paper and trying to write it at the last minute. One way that I reduce the pressure of a writing assignment is to start writing long before the paper is due, giving myself enough time to work on it.

If I tell myself that I am only going to write a certain amount at a time, say a page a day, it is less intimidating to write. While this method may seem drawn out, it works. Whenever I come back to the paper the next day, I always review what I have already written, so I can be sure I keep the topic in mind. This way, I avoid burning myself out, getting my ideas confused, or losing track of the topic and, ultimately, rushing to finish by the end. This allows me to come to my paper with a fresh perspective and new ideas with every installment I write. Once I finish that day's work I feel good because I am getting the paper done while also giving it my best effort, which also greatly reduces the stress of having to write it.

Matthew Harding points out that writing can be daunting even for experienced writers.

Through Writing, Enter the Conversation

Cicero's famous work, *On the Ideal Orator*, is not a treatise or handbook about how to be an effective rhetorician. Instead, it is a dialogue, a conversation. The setting is a villa outside Rome belonging to Lucius Licinius Crassus, and the time is 91 CE, an era of dangerous unrest in the Roman Empire. Prominent and respected citizens gather with Crassus to escape, for a while, the political crisis developing in the city. Crassus and his guests settle at leisure under a wide, spreading plane tree, not only to enjoy its shade but also to pay homage to Plato's *Phaedrus*, which similarly took place under a plane tree, though in Greece. They take time this day to dialogue about the attributes of an ideal orator. The purpose of the arguments they present to each other is not to win out over the others but, conversing together, to come to knowledge. It is not a trivial pursuit. Cicero reveals what his characters do not know—soon they will all die horribly as part of the civil unrest in Rome, violence traceable to the failure of leaders to resolve their differences in nonviolent dialogue.

Throughout ancient times, dialogue appears alongside rhetoric. It was through dialogue that rhetoricians such as Aristotle, Isocrates, and Cicero taught their students rhetorical skills. Today, in the writing classroom, group discussion or pairs dialogue is also part of the teaching process. A rhetorical text, too, is a conversation with previous texts, responding to ideas they have presented. In addition, arguments include paraphrases and quotes from others' compositions, making them part of the conversation. Moreover, writers composing texts must anticipate their audiences' reactions—questions they might ask or objections they might raise—so responses to these questions and objects can be included in the argument. This process of responding to audiences in advance continues the conversation.

Organize Your Essay

All texts are conversational, a characteristic reflected in the format or organization. In ancient times, orators began a speech by attracting the audience's attention in what was called the *exordium,* which we would call the opening or introduction. Next, they provided background information in a *narratio* (narration), followed by an *explication* in which they defined terms and enumerated the issues. During the *partition* they would express the thesis or main issue to be discussed, and in the *confirmation* they would provide evidence to support the thesis. Opposition arguments would be addressed in the *refutatio,* and the composition would be wrapped up with a *peroratio* or conclusion. The order of these different elements was not rigid in ancient times, nor is it today. Sometimes one or more sections were eliminated if they were not needed, but then, as now, an effective text included most of these elements. For example, if your audience is very familiar with a particular subject, you may not need to define terms, as you would with an audience who was unfamiliar with the material.

As did the ancient Greeks and Romans, when you write an argument, you begin with an introduction that gains your audience's attention and presents your thesis; likewise, you end with a conclusion that ties together what you have said or presents a call to action. However, you have a choice of several formats for what happens between that introduction and conclusion. Following are three prominent alternatives; your choice of which to use depends on your purpose and the type of evidence you have.

- Created by Stephen Toulmin, the **Toulmin model** for persuasion grew out of the 20th century emphasis upon empirical evidence and is *most effective for arguments that rely on evidence from scientific studies, surveys, or other data.* His model requires six elements. First, rhetors present a claim or statement that they want the audience to accept. Then, they back up the claim with data and facts, what Aristotle would have called inartistic proofs. A warrant links these data to the claim, explaining why the data make the claim valid. Backing provides additional support for the argument, while a counterclaim acknowledges any objections or weaknesses in the argument. And, finally, the rebuttal responds to any counterclaims, removing possible objections to the argument.

- The **Rogerian** (or common ground) **argument** is named for psychologist Carl Rogers. It is *most effective for arguments that attempt to establish common ground between opponents* on an issue. Rogerian argument begins with an introduction that states the problem to be considered. Second, in a much different move than the Toulmin pattern, the rhetor states the opposing argument in neutral language to demonstrate that he or she understands the other side's position, as well as instances when it may be valid. The assumption is that, since the rhetor has been willing to pay attention to the other side's position, they will, in fairness, listen as the rhetor states his or her own position, as well as discusses the instances when it is preferable. The Rogerian argument ends on a positive note, describing how the rhetor's position could, at least in some instances, benefit the opposition.

- The **general modern format** for argument is one that will probably be familiar to you from previous English classes. It is a *format that you can use when your argument does not fit neatly into either the Toulmin or Rogerian patterns.* Moreover, you can adapt it to serve the needs of your argument. It is the standard five-paragraph essay modified for presenting an argument, and, like that pattern, it can be expanded to accommodate longer essays. Similar to the five-paragraph essay, you begin with an introduction that attracts your audience's attention and states your thesis. Then two or three sections each present major points that support your thesis. The next section presents a counterargument, which anticipates audience questions or objections and is followed by a rebuttal of the counterargument. Finally, a conclusion ties the argument together, perhaps by reflecting back to the introduction or issuing a call for action.

Notice that all of these formats include an attempt to dialogue with the audience. In the Toulmin model, the warrant, in particular, is designed to help the audience make the logical link between the claim and the data offered as evidence. In a Rogerian argument, the rhetor carefully and in emotionally-neutral language demonstrates that he or she has been listening to the opposition and can even restate their argument fairly. The arguments produced via these models, even if they do not immediately convince, will not worsen the situation. The aim of well-intentioned rhetors is not to convince at any cost but to continue the conversation until reasonable solutions can be found. For a comparison of the different argument formats, see table 5.1 presented on pages 150–151.

Like the ancient Greeks, you will begin with an opening and end with a conclusion. However, in between the bookends of your essay, you have more flexibility to adapt the basic format than did the Romans.

Write a Thesis Statement

A **thesis** may be a sentence or a series of sentences, or in a few cases it may be implied rather than stated explicitly; but a thesis is at the heart of any piece of writing. If a reader cannot identify your thesis, the meaning of your text is not clear. How do you develop a thesis? First, you determine your occasion for writing—who is your audience, what is your purpose, and what special circumstances are there (if any)? Then you write a working thesis that makes an assertion or claim about your topic, something that will be affected by your audience and purpose. For example, if you are writing a research paper about the advantages and disadvantages of biodiesel fuel, your claim may be stated differently depending on whether your audience is an English class or a chemistry class. In the latter, you might need to use technical language that would be unfamiliar to your English professor.

Working theses are statements that develop and change as essays are written; they are basic frameworks that provide a connection for the ideas you have decided to convey to your reader. Later, after you have completed a draft of your text, examine your working thesis. If needed, rewrite your thesis so that it states the main idea of your essay in a clear and engaging fashion. Consider the following examples of thesis statements.

> The United States should implement a guest worker program as a way of reforming the illegal immigration problem.

> Nuclear power should be considered as part of a program to reduce the United States's dependence on foreign oil.

Compose an Introduction

Experienced writers have different methods of creating a good introduction. One writer who tends to discover his paper as he goes along swears the best way to write an introduction is to write the entire paper and then move the conclusion to the beginning of the essay and rewrite it as the introduction. Another writer lets the paper sit around for a few days before she writes her introduction. A third always writes two or three different introductions and tries them out on friends before deciding which to use. However you choose to write the introduction, make sure it is interesting enough to make your reader want to read on.

The introduction to your essay is an invitation to your reader. If you invite readers to come along with you on a boring journey, they won't want to follow. In magazine and

Essay Starters

If, after you have done extensive invention (prewriting and research), you still find it intimidating to face the blank computer screen, try one of the essay starters below. These are phrases to get the words flowing. Then, later, after you have written a rough draft, go back and revise the beginning. Delete the essay starter and, in its place, write a real introduction. As you probably know, you do not need to say, "In my opinion," because what you write in your essay, unless you attribute it to someone else, is your opinion. See the section in this chapter on writing introductions.

In my opinion . . .

I agree . . .

I disagree . . .

Studies show . . .

Experts say . . .

My paper is about . . .

I am writing this essay because . . .

In the beginning . . .

Argument Formats: A Comparison

Ancient Roman	General Modern Format
Standard pattern the ancients modified to suit the argument.	**Good all-purpose format that can be adapted for the needs of the argument.**
Introduction—Exordium Attracts the interest of the audience and identifies the argument.	**Introduction** Attracts the interest of the audience through its opening strategy and states the thesis.
Background or narration—Narratio Details the history or facts of the issue.	**First main point** Supports the thesis.
Definition—Explication Defines terms and outlines issues.	**Second main point** Supports the thesis.
Thesis—Partition States the particular issue that is to be argued.	**Third main point** Supports the thesis.
Proof—Confirmation Develops the thesis and provides supporting evidence.	**Counterargument** Acknowledges the opposing argument or arguments.
Refutation or opposition—Refutatio Addresses the arguments opposing the thesis.	**Rebuttal of counterargument** Refutes the opposing argument or arguments.
Conclusion—Peroratio Reiterates the thesis and may urge the audience to action.	**Conclusion** Ties together the elements of the composition and gives the reader closure. May summarize the essay and include a call to action.

table 5.1

Toulmin Model	Rogerian Argument
Good for an argument that relies on empirical evidence such as scientific studies or data collection.	**Good when the object is consensus or compromise, so that opponents can work together while retaining their positions.**
Claim Presents the overall thesis the writer will argue.	**Introduction** States the problem to be solved or the question to be answered. Often opponents will also agree there is a problem.
Data Supports the claim with evidence.	**Summary of opposing views** Describes the opposing side's arguments in a neutral and fair manner.
Warrant (also known as a bridge) Explains why or how the data support the claim. Connects the data to the claim.	**Statement of understanding** Concedes occasions when the opposing position might be valid.
Counterclaim Presents a claim that negates or disagrees with the thesis/claim.	**Statement of position** Avoids emotionally charged language, and identifies position.
Rebuttal Presents evidence that negates or disagrees with the counterclaim.	**Statement of contexts** Describes the specific contexts in which the rhetor's position applies/works well.
Conclusion Ties together the elements of the composition (if not included with the rebuttal).	**Statement of benefits** Presents benefits that may appeal to the self-interest of readers who may not yet agree with you; shows how your position benefits them. Ends on a positive note.
	Conclusion Ties together the elements of the composition (if not included in the statement of benefits).

newspaper writing, the introduction is sometimes called a *hook* because it hooks the reader into reading the text. If a magazine writer does not capture the reader's attention right away, the reader is not likely to continue. After all, there are other and possibly more interesting articles in the magazine. Why should readers suffer through a boring introduction? Depending on the topic and pattern of your essay, you might employ one of the following techniques to hook your readers and make them want to keep reading:

- An intriguing or provocative quotation
- A narrative or anecdote
- A question or series of questions
- A vivid sensory description
- A strongly stated opinion

Your introductory paragraph makes a commitment to your readers. This is where you identify the topic, state your thesis (implicitly or explicitly), and give your readers clues about the journey that will follow in the succeeding paragraphs. Be careful not to mislead the reader. Do not ask questions you will not answer in your paper (unless they are rhetorical questions). Do not introduce a topic in your introduction and then switch to another one in your paper.

Although the introduction is the first paragraph or so of the paper, it may not be the first paragraph the writer composes. If you have problems beginning your essay because you cannot immediately think of a good introduction, begin with the first point in your essay and come back to the introduction later.

If you have problems writing anything at all, consider the suggestions offered in the following essay.

Reading 5.1

The Truth about Writer's Block

by Judith Johnson

Judith Johnson suggests in this essay, first published in *Huffington Post Books*, that there is no such thing as writer's block. She suggests what writers experience is the ebb and flow of the writing process.

I don't choose to experience "writer's block" which I see as simply a matter of faulty perception. It is a mislabeling of a very natural part of the ebb and flow of the writing process. To say "I have writer's block" is to judge a temporary or permanent absence of writing momentum and productivity as wrong and therefore to see oneself as a failure in some way. The process of writing is an intricate interplay of conscious and unconscious dynamics and what actually lands on the page is a small part of it all. When we label and judge that process, we interfere with its natural flow and take a position of againstness with ourselves. It's all in how you look at it.

When a writer declares that he or she is experiencing writer's block, it is like grabbing hold of a fear (Fantasy Expectation Appearing Real) and fueling it with emotional distress. A way to reframe this is to simply trust that what appears to be a dry spell is a normal part of the process of being a writer and that either you need time to be away from the writing focus or that the process is largely unconscious at that time. Each writer has to make peace with this by finding their own particular rhythm and honoring that. For example, what works for me is not to have any rigid writing schedule, but rather to let the words come to me—and they always do—sooner or later. When working on a deadline, whether self-imposed or not, I never lose sight of the deadline, it is always there, but I don't beat myself up with it if time keeps passing and nothing is getting on paper. I'll notice that the topic is alive in me—turning this way and that finding its way to the paper. It takes a lot of trust to let this be. So far, it has never failed me.

I have lots of books and articles and projects on the back burner and no fear of running out of things to write about. I know that each piece of writing has a life of its own. For example, I have a poem that I started at the age of 16 that rumbles around in my head from time to time looking for its ending. I know it will end someday, but hasn't so far. That's not a problem to me—just a reality. I also keep what I call a "dump" file for each project and whether I am actively working on it or not, I capture ideas and information there.

In addition to building a strong bond of trust with yourself, here are some other keys to maintaining a good relationship with yourself as a writer:

Just Do It: There is a point at which every writer just has to sit down and write. Whether you write for five minutes or five hours straight doesn't matter, but if you are going to be a writer, you have to sit down and write.

Write with Freedom and Abandon, Then Edit Ruthlessly: It is important to give yourself permission to write whatever comes up without any judgment. Just focus on capturing your thoughts and ideas—forget about grammar, structure and eloquence. Just get a hold of whatever comes up. Then, just as Michelangelo described the sculpting process as discovering a statue inside every block of stone, each writer must ruthlessly revise and refine a piece of work until pleased with it.

Get Out of Your Own Way: If you get into a pattern of negativity and beating up on yourself when writing, find a way to be more loving with yourself and do not feed the negativity.

Patience: Writing takes enormous patience. As with any other art form, you are constantly revising and refining your work. For an artist the equation is never time is money, but rather "do I feel complete with this piece? Is it my best effort given the time I have available?"

Flexibility, Cooperation and Balance: There is always some level of agitation just under the surface that propels a writer forward giving momentum to the working process. But there are always other forces at work and writing is only one of many activities in an individual's life. Finding your own rhythm and being willing to cooperate with the other elements of life that often seem to intrude on the writer's solitary endeavor are like moving between shooting the rapids and gliding along on calm waters, never quite knowing which is going to present itself and when. Experience teaches us all to go with the flow and somehow that seems to yield maximum inner peace and outward productivity.

Keeping a Sense of Humor and Humility: I've learned never to take myself too seriously as a writer. I do my best and need to laugh at myself from time to time when I give too much importance to what I write. If people get value from what I write, that's great and positive feedback is extremely gratifying. However, while writing is ultimately about communication, I find it very funny that I don't write to communicate, but rather because I simply need to write—I am compelled to do so. If the end product of my endeavors is of value to others, that's great, but the solitary process of engaging in the art form itself is entirely for me and I think that is pretty funny.

Letting Go of the Illusion of Control: A really good writer is never in control of the writing process. You may find that having a rigid schedule works well for you or you might be someone who writes when the spirit moves you to do so. Either way, a good writer taps into the wellspring of human consciousness and like love, you can't make that happen on demand.

Is writing challenging? Absolutely! However, it is a great way to learn some profound lessons in life and to be of service to others.

Activity 5.1 **Discuss "The Truth about Writer's Block"**

1. How does Judith Johnson choose to reframe the concept of writer's block?
2. Johnson makes recommendations to deal with the "absence of writing momentum." Which of her suggestions makes the most sense to you? Which makes the least sense to you?
3. What do you think? Is there such a thing as "writer's block"?

Combine Your Ideas with Support from Source Materials

A research paper, by definition, makes use of source materials to make an argument. It is important to remember, however, that it is *your* paper, *not* what some professors may call a "research dump," meaning that it is constructed by stringing together research information with a few transitions. Rather, you, as the author of the paper, carry the argument in your own words and use quotes and paraphrases from source materials to support your argument. How do you do that? Here are some suggestions:

- After you think you have completed enough research to construct a working thesis and begin writing your paper, collect all your materials in front of you (photocopies of articles, printouts of electronic sources, and books) and spend a few hours reading through the materials and making notes. Then, put all the notes and materials to the side and freewrite for a few minutes about what you can remember from your research that is important. Take this freewriting and make a rough outline of the main points you want to cover in your essay. Then you can go back to your notes and source materials to flesh out your outline.
- Use quotes for the following three reasons:
  1. You want to "borrow" the ethos or credibility of the source. For example, if you are writing about stem cell research, you may want to quote from an authority such as Dr. James A. Thomson, whose ground-breaking research led to the first use of stem cells for research. Alternatively, if your source materials include the *New England Journal of Medicine* or another prestigious publication, it may be worth crediting a quote to that source.

2. The material is so beautifully or succinctly written that it would lose its effectiveness if you reworded the material in your own words.
3. You want to create a point of emphasis by quoting rather than paraphrasing. Otherwise, you probably want to paraphrase material from your sources, as quotes should be used sparingly. Often, writers quote source material in a first draft and then rewrite some of the quotes into paraphrases during the revision process.

- Introduce quotes. You should never have a sentence or sentences in quotation marks just sitting in the middle of a paragraph, as it would puzzle a reader. If you quote, you should always introduce the quote by saying something like this: According to Dr. James A. Thomson, "Stem cell research. . . . "
- Avoid plagiarism by clearly indicating material that is quoted or paraphrased. See the appendix (at the end of the book) for more information about citing source material.

Support Your Thesis

After you have attracted the interest of your audience, established your thesis, and given any background information and definitions, you will next begin to give reasons for your position, which further develops your argument. These reasons are, in turn, supported by statistics, analogies, anecdotes, and quotes from authorities which you have discovered in your research or know from personal knowledge. Ideally, arrange your reasons so that the strongest ones come either at the beginning or at the end of this portion of the paper (points of emphasis) and the weaker ones fall in the middle.

Answer Opposing Arguments

If you are aware of a contradicting statistic or other possible objection to your argument, it may be tempting to ignore that complication, hoping your audience will not notice. However, that is exactly the worst thing you can do. It is much better to anticipate your audience's possible questions or objections and address them in your discussion. Doing so prevents you from losing credibility by either appearing to deceive your audience or being unaware of all the facts. Also, acknowledging possible refutations of your position actually strengthens your position by making you seem knowledgeable and fair-minded.

Vary Your Strategies or Patterns of Development

When composing your essay, you have many different strategies or **patterns of development** available to you. You may write entire essays whose sole strategy is argumentation or comparison and contrast, but more often, you will combine many of these different modes while writing a single essay. Consider the following strategies or patterns of development:

- *Analysis* entails a close examination of an issue, book, film, or other object, separating it into elements and examining each of the elements separately through other writing modes such as classification or comparison and contrast.
- *Argumentation* involves taking a strong stand on an issue supported by logical reasons and evidence intended to change a reader's mind on an issue or open a reader's eyes to a problem.
- *Cause and effect* is an explanation of the cause and subsequent effects or consequences of a specific action.
- *Classification* entails dividing and grouping things into logical categories.
- *Comparison and contrast* examines the similarities and differences between two or more things.
- *Definition* employs an explanation of the specific meaning of a word, phrase, or idea.
- *Description* uses vivid sensory details to present a picture or an image to the reader.
- *Exemplification* makes use of specific examples to explain, define, or analyze something.
- *Narration* uses a story or vignette to illustrate a specific point or examine an issue.

Write a Conclusion

After they have read the last paragraph of your essay, your readers should feel satisfied that you have covered everything you needed to and you have shared an insight. You may have heard the basic rules: A conclusion cannot address any new issues, and it should summarize the main points of the essay. Although these are valid and reliable rules, a summary is not always the best way to end an essay. The prohibition against new ideas in the final paragraph also might limit certain effective closures like a call to action or a question for the reader to ponder.

One effective technique for writing a conclusion is to refer back to your introduction. If you began with a narrative anecdote, a sensory description, or a question, you can tie a mention of it to your ending point. Or, if you are composing an argumentative essay, you might choose to summarize by using an expert quote to restate your thesis, giving the reader a final firm sense of ethos or credibility. You might also end with a single-sentence summary followed by a suggestion or a call to action for the reader. Another effective way to end an argument can be a paragraph that suggests further research.

A conclusion doesn't have to be long. As a matter of fact, it does not even need to be a separate paragraph, especially if your essay is short. If your closing comments are related to the final paragraph of the essay, one or two sentences can easily be added to the final body paragraph of the essay.

Consider Elements of Page Design

Professors now take it for granted that you word-process your paper using a professional looking typeface such as Times Roman. However, producing your text on a computer with Internet access gives you the option to do much more—including adding one or more images and other page design elements. Several of the assignments in this chapter offer you the opportunity to be creative with your project presentation. Even if you are required to submit your project in standard MLA or APA essay formats, however, you can still include one or more images, and it is important to consider where you place the images.

Some simple guidelines will help you design effective documents:

- Use space as a design element. Do not overcrowd your pages. Place material so that important parts are emphasized by the space around them.
- Rarely (if ever) use all capital letters. Words in all caps are hard to read, and on the Internet all caps is considered shouting.
- Use headings to group your information and make your pages easy to skim. Readers often like to skim pages before deciding what to read.

Indeed, many people will skim all the headlines, headings, and photo captions first, before reading the body text of any section.

- Put important elements in the top left and lower right parts of the screen. English readers are trained to read from left to right, so our eyes naturally start at the upper left-hand corner of the screen. Our eyes, when skimming, don't flow line by line, but move in a Z pattern, as illustrated in the following diagram (see figure 5.1).

figure 5.1

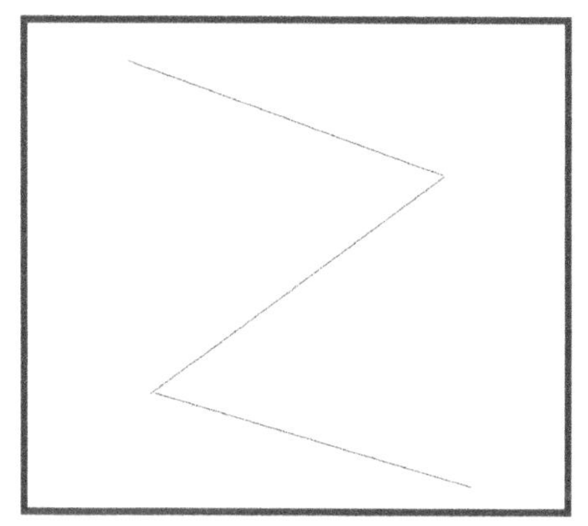

Eye movement when skimming a page

If you want to include a photo in your research paper, for example, you should put it either in the top left or the bottom right corner of the page, points of emphasis in the Z pattern. Today, with a sophisticated word processing program such as Microsoft Word, it is easy to import an image, size it, and move it to the desired place on a page. Once you have imported an image, you can click on it, hold your cursor at a corner, and enlarge or shrink the image by dragging the cursor. Also, by clicking on the image, you can activate the dialogue box that allows you to specify having the text run tightly around the image. Then you can easily move the image around on the page until you have placed it in a pleasing spot. Alternatively, Microsoft Word provides document templates that you can use for newsletters, brochures, and other types of projects.

If you look closely at figure 5.2 on the next page, you may notice that the text surrounding the image does not seem to make any sense (though it is actually Latin). That's because the text is Lorem ipsum text, sometimes called placeholder or dummy text, which designers use to create page layouts before they have the real text from writers. If you want to try using Lorem ipsum yourself, just do a search on the Internet for that name, and you will find sites that provide paragraphs of the nonsense words that you can utilize as placeholder text.

figure 5.2

Ullamcorper Suscipit Lobortis Nisl

Consectetuer Adipiscing Elit

Sed diam nonummy nibh euismod tincidunt ut laoreet dolore magna aliquam erat volutpat. Ut wisi enim ad minim veniam, quis nostrud exerci tation ullamcorper suscipit lobortis nisl ut aliquip ex ea commodo consequat. Duis autem vel eum iriure dolor in hendrerit in vulputate velit esse molestie consequat, vel illum dolore eu feugiat nulla facilisis at vero eros et accumsan et iusto odio dignissim qui blandit praesent luptatum zzril delenit augue duis dolore te feugait nulla facilisi.

Lorem ipsum dolor sit amet, consectetuer adipiscing elit, sed diam nonummy nibh euismod tincidunt ut laoreet dolore magna aliquam erat volutpat. Ut wisi enim ad minim veniam, quis nostrud exerci tation ullamcorper suscipit lobortis nisl ut aliquip ex ea commodo consequat. Duis autem vel eum iriure dolor in hendrerit in vulputate velit esse molestie consequat, vel illum dolore eu feugiat nulla facilisis at vero eros et accumsan et iusto odio dignissim qui blandit praesent luptatum zzril delenit augue duis dolore te feugait nulla facilisi.

Lorem Ipsum Dolor Sit

Amet, consectetuer adipiscing elit, sed diam nonummy nibh euismod tincidunt ut laoreet dolore magna aliquam erat volutpat. Ut wisi enim ad minim veniam, quis nostrud exerci tation ullamcorper suscipit lobortis nisl ut aliquip ex ea commodo consequat. Duis autem vel eum iriure dolor in hendrerit in vulputate velit esse molestie consequat, vel illum dolore eu feugiat nulla facilisis at vero eros et accumsan et iusto odio dignissim qui blandit praesent luptatum zzril delenit augue duis dolore te feugait nulla facilisi. Lorem ipsum dolor sit amet, consectetuer adipiscing

The image in this article has been effectively placed in the lower right corner, which is a point of emphasis.

Including Images in Your Projects: Copyright Implications

United States copyright law includes a provision called "fair use" that allows copyrighted images to be used for educational projects. However, copyright laws are complicated, and the implications of using digital images is still being determined in the courts. Clearly, if you take the photo yourself, you own the copyright. Many photographers post photos on websites such as Flikr.com and give permission for "fair use" of the images on the Internet, so long as their work is credited. Others, however, post their work for viewers to enjoy but do not allow it to be copied. Scanning a photo from a published work and using it once for a class project falls more clearly under the spirit of the "fair use" law than does putting such an image up on the Internet. If you are doing a web page or blog project that includes images, be sure to contact the copyright owner to obtain permission.

Activity 5.2 Write a Research-Based Argument Paper

The Purpose of the Assignment

Writing a research paper gives you the opportunity to practice key academic writing skills, including locating and utilizing research materials, prewriting, drafting, and revision. It also requires you to take a position on a topic, create an argument, and support it with quotes and paraphrases from authoritative sources.

Purpose as a Writer

Your purpose as a writer is to convince readers to consider your argument carefully, and, if possible, to persuade them to agree with your point of view. To do this, include appropriate background material and definitions, as well as a consideration of opposing arguments.

Topic

Your topic should address a current issue about which you can take and support a position in the paper length your instructor specifies. Choose your topic carefully, as it should be one that engages your interest and enthusiasm.

Audience

Unless your instructor specifies otherwise, you can assume that your audience has general awareness of your issue but is unfamiliar with scholarly sources on the topic.

Sources

To do your research, you will need to utilize recent and credible sources that include a mix of recent books, scholarly articles, public speeches, and news articles. You may also use interviews, observation, and personal experience, if they are relevant to your topic. Sources will need to be cited in the text and in a works cited page or references page, according to MLA or APA style.

Information that you gather from your sources should support the argument you have created. A research paper is not an assignment in which you take information from sources and simply reorganize it into a paper. The expectation for this course is that you will use your sources to create an argument that is distinctly your own.

Thesis

Your essay should have a clear thesis that takes a position on an issue that can be supported within the word limitations of the assignment.

Rough Draft

As directed by your instructor, bring two copies of your rough draft essay to class for peer editing. The draft should have your sources credited in the text and should have a works cited page or references page.

Final Draft

Submit your final draft in MLA or APA format in a folder with your rough draft and copies of all of your source materials with the location of quotes or paraphrased material highlighted. If you are using material from a book or books, copy enough of the text before and after your quotes or paraphrases so that your instructor can determine the context of the material being quoted.

Reading 5.2

Film Review: *The Hangover* (2009)

by Owen Gleiberman

This film review by Owen Gleiberman appeared in EW.com. As you read the review, decide what you think is the author's position. How does he support his argument?

Going to Las Vegas for a "wild" bachelor party is now the ultimate middle-class hedonist cliché. It's not just that the jaunt has been done so often, in the movies as well as in life. It's that there's a contradiction embedded in the lure of the Vegas bacchanal. Men—and women too, of course—go there to be as reckless as humanly possible. But the naughtiness is so *organized* that there's not much recklessness left in it. Sure, you can craps-table your way to financial ruin, but the lap dances, the glorified college drinking binges, the ritualized ordering of hookers: It's all about as spontaneous as a shuffleboard tournament on a cruise ship.

The fun of *The Hangover*—what makes it more than just one what-happens-in-Vegas romp too many—is that the film completely understands all this. The four comrades who drive from Los Angeles to the Nevada desert to prepare for the wedding of Doug (Justin Bartha) aren't daring or cool; they aren't born swingers. They're an unglamorous Everyguy quartet, doing what they all think they're supposed to do. They're probably imitating Vegas movies as much as those films imitated reality.

Phil (Bradley Cooper), the one who's good-looking enough to strut into a casino like he owns it, is a junior-high teacher devoted to his wife and kid; Stu (Ed Helms), the group dweeb, is an anxious-eyed dentist who's like the 21st-century version of *American Graffiti*'s Terry the Toad, with a fascist girlfriend (Rachael Harris) who treats him like a slave; and Alan (Zach Galifianakis), so brick-stupid he qualifies as more nutzoid than dorkish, is a pudgy, bearded runt who stands up in the group's cruising convertible and shouts "Road trip!" That's an inside nod to the fact that Todd Phillips, the movie's director, made *Road Trip* as well, though it also indicates that these four think they're living inside a stupid teen comedy.

They arrive at their hotel, and the film then cuts to the next day, when they wake up in their trashed villa. There's a tiger in the bathroom, and a baby in the cabinet. Stu is missing his top right incisor; the groom is nowhere to be seen. And the thing is, none of them remembers . . . anything. *The Hangover* is structured, basically, as one long morning-after *OMG what have I done?*, and the kick of the film is that the discovery of what the characters have, in fact, done becomes the perfect comeuppance to their tidy fantasy of Vegas bliss. A light-buttered comic nightmare, like Martin Scorsese's *After Hours* (or Peter Berg's scandalous, overlooked *Very Bad Things* with things not nearly so bad), *The Hangover* is a riff on what the stuff you do when you're *really* out of control says about you.

The surprises in this movie are everything, so without giving much away, I'll just say that a Vegas chapel figures into the mix. So does a crowbar-wielding Asian gangster (Ken Jeong) who might be the epicene brother of Long Duk Dong in *Sixteen Candles*. There's also a juicy run-in with Mike Tyson. *The Hangover* has scattered laughs (many in the cathartically funny end-credit montage), but overall it's more amusing than hilarious. The most deftly acted character is Stu, played by Helms with a realistic alternating current of horror and liberation. As Alan, Zach Galifianakis makes blinkered idiocy a cartoon rush, though a little of him goes a long way. I wish Phillips, working from a script by the knockabout team of Jon Lucas and Scott Moore (*Ghosts of Girlfriends Past*), had nudged the characters closer to being a true shaggy-dog Apatow-style ensemble. You're always a little too aware that they're types. But it's fun seeing each of them have the "fun" they deserve.

Activity 5.3 Discuss Review of *The Hangover*

1. Owen Gleiberman says that the "wild" bachelor party in Las Vegas has become a cliché. Is this true? What other films portray bachelor parties in Las Vegas?

2. What is different about the Vegas bachelor party in *The Hangover*, according to the review?

3. What is Gleiberman's thesis? What evidence does he offer to support his thesis?

4. Does the review make you want to see the movie, if you haven't? How so?

Activity 5.4 Write a Film Review

In this assignment, you are a film critic. Write a review that could appear in a newspaper, magazine, or blog. Your style and tone will be dictated by your audience, so identify the publication just under the title of your review by saying something like this: "Written for Undergroundfilms .com." Be sure to read several reviews published in your chosen media outlet.

1. Select a film you would like to review. Films that are social commentaries are particularly good for reviewing. It does not have to be a serious movie, but it should be one that makes you think about some social trend or historical event.

2. After you decide on a film, learn about its context. Who are the director, producer, and primary actors? What films have these individuals worked on before? Have they won awards? Are they known for a certain style? Read and annotate other reviews of the film, marking sections that you might paraphrase or quote to support your opinions.

3. What about the historical event or social context? Can you learn more about it to see if the film presents a reasonably accurate picture of that time and place (a kairos)? Is it based on a book? If so, what kind of a job does it do creating the world of the book?

4. Is the film persuasive? Does the film appeal to ethos, pathos, or logos? In what way?

5. Create a working thesis that makes an argument about the film. You can modify this thesis later, but it helps to identify early on what you want to argue.
6. Use some of the invention strategies in Chapter 4 to help you articulate what proofs you can use to support your argument.
7. Near the beginning of your draft, briefly summarize enough of the film that your review will be interesting to those who have not seen it. However, don't be a "spoiler." Don't ruin the film for potential viewers by giving away the ending.
8. Organize your essay into three main points that support your thesis and at least one counterargument that complicates or disagrees with your argument.
9. Write a compelling introduction that uses one of the approaches discussed in this chapter. You want your reader to be interested in what you have to say. For example, you might begin with a startling quote from the film or a vivid description of a pivotal scene.
10. Be sure to include specific examples and colorful details. These are essential to make your review interesting to the reader.

Compose

Activity 5.5: Write an Op-Ed Argument

The Op-Ed Project (www.theop-edproject.org) is an online initiative to "expand the range of voices" submitting op-ed essays to media outlets. According to its statistics, 80 to 90 percent of op-ed pieces are currently written by men, which is something it endeavors to change by helping women and members of other underrepresented groups develop the skills to get published in top media markets. Whether you are male or female, you may belong to an underrepresented group that is not having its voice heard as part of the national conversation about issues.

An op-ed is an opinion piece printed in a newspaper, magazine, blog, or other media outlet. The name derives from earlier times in print journalism when these opinion pieces would be printed on a page opposite the editorial page. Op-eds are written by individuals not affiliated with the publication, as opposed to editorials that are written by the publication's staff.

Tips for Op-Ed Writing from the Op-Ed Project

1. **Own your expertise**
Know what you are an expert in and why—but don't limit yourself. Consider the metaphors that your experience and knowledge suggest.

2. **Stay current**
Follow the news—both general and specific to your areas of specialty. If you write about Haiti, read the Haitian press. If you write about pop culture, read the media that cover it.

3. **The perfect is the enemy of the good**
In other words: write fast. You may have only a few hours to get your piece in before the moment is gone. But also . . .

4. **Cultivate a flexible mind**
Remember that a good idea may have more than one news hook; indeed, if the idea is important enough it can have many. So keep an eye out for surprising connections and new news hooks—the opportunity may come around again.

5. **Use plain language**
Jargon serves a purpose, but it is rarely useful in public debate, and can obfuscate–sorry, I mean cloud–your argument. Speak to your reader in straight talk.

6. **Respect your reader**
Never underestimate your reader's intelligence or overestimate her level of information. Recognize that your average reader is not an expert in your topic and that the onus is on you to capture her attention–and make the argument compel.

This assignment asks you to write an op-ed piece suitable for submission to a major newspaper or other media outlet. It does not require you to submit your text. That is up to you.

For this assignment, you need to do the following:

1. Read op-eds that appear in the major regional newspaper or other media outlet for your city, such as the *Chicago Tribune*, the *Washington Post*, or the *Arizona Republic*. The Op-Ed Project provides a list of the top 100 U.S. media outlets on its website. Read several op-eds to get a sense of the topics and style of the articles that the newspaper or other media outlet prints.

2. Notice that op-eds are not academic writing. They must be well-researched, but they also generally are written in a more casual and engaging style than traditional academic writing. You must first attract your audience's attention in order to present your case. Analyze how each op-ed you read captures the reader's interest.

3. Choose a topic that is timely and of interest to the readers of the publication that you choose. Research that topic using some of the tools in the research chapter of this textbook.

4. The length and structure of your op-ed should follow the pattern of pieces recently published in your publication.

5. Keep your audience in mind—the readers of the publication.

6. Follow the basic op-ed structure recommended by the Op-Ed Project, reprinted below.

7. Read the "Tips for Op-Ed Writing from the Op-Ed Project," in the sidebar.

(*Note*: A *lede* (or lead) is a journalism term that means the beginning of your article that catches your reader's attention and establishes your topic.)

Basic Op-Ed Structure from the Op-Ed Project

(*Note*: This is not a rule—just one way of approaching it.)

Lede (around a news hook)

Thesis (statement of argument—either explicit or implied)

Argument (based on evidence, such as stats, news, reports from credible organizations, expert quotes, scholarship, history, and first-hand experience)

- 1st Point
    - Evidence
    - Evidence
    - Conclusion
- 2nd Point
    - Evidence
    - Evidence
    - Conclusion
- 3rd Point
    - Evidence
    - Evidence
    - Conclusion

Note: In a simple, declarative op-ed ("policy X is bad; here's why"), this may be straightforward. In a more complex commentary, the 3rd point may expand on the bigger picture (historical context, global/geographic picture, mythological underpinnings, etc.) or may offer an explanation for a mystery that underpins the argument (e.g., why a bad policy continues, in spite of its failures).

"To Be Sure" paragraph (in which you preempt your potential critics by acknowledging any flaws in your argument and address any obvious counterarguments)

Conclusion (often circling back to your lede)

Activity 5.6 Write on Your Blog

Write an informal review of a film you have seen recently. What did you like and what did you dislike? Would you recommend the film to a friend?

Activity 5.7 Write in Your Commonplace Book

Find a piece from the Opinion/Editorial section of your local newspaper that interests you. If you were going to write a letter to the editor in response, what might you say?

The Casebook: In 2011, two professors launched a competition on the *Harvard Business Network* blog for designs to build $300 houses for the poor. Word of the competition spread quickly, and a wide variety of people began to write about the competition—in editorials in *The New York Times* and the *Economist* and in a companion blog, http://www.300house.com/blog.

Your Task: In Chapter 4 you read four articles about the $300 house competition. Read and discuss them in class and in small groups. Make a list of the different positions being argued in these texts and what evidence the writers offer to support their opinions. Then construct your own short research-based argument about the design competition or an op-ed essay (as your instructor specifies) agreeing with one of the positions or developing your own.

6 REVISING RHETORICALLY

Praxis in Action

How I Revise by Amber Lea Clark

Revising is an essential part of the writing process. One of the first things I do when I revise a paper is read with organization in mind. How is my introduction? Does my argument make sense? Did I transition well between points? Next, I look for words and phrases I have repeated too many times and look for other ways to say what I'm trying to say.

For me, a very necessary part of the revision process is reading the paper out loud to see how it flows. I look for any awkwardly worded sentences. It also helps me find typos and misused words. If I'm in a lab setting, I read very quietly, just mouthing the words. I might get a couple of funny looks but I don't care, it is a must when it comes to the revising process for me.

One of the best things to do in the revising process is set your paper aside and come back to it several hours or a day later. This requires some planning and an attempt not to procrastinate too much. Doing this allows me to look at my paper again with fresh eyes and see what I might have left out or want to say differently.

My mother always told me to have someone else give me feedback on my papers before I turn them in. This is valuable advice. I always have someone look over my papers and try to help others when they need someone to look at their papers. I ask the person who is proofing my paper to look for typos but also any sentences that do not make sense as they are worded. Is my argument coming through clearly?

Also, I always run my paper through the computer's spell check and grammar check. The computer will flag things as grammatically wrong that aren't, so I don't follow everything it says; but the computer also finds errors I haven't. Oh, be sure to spell the proper names right!

Amber Lea Clark says that one important part of her revision is setting her paper aside for a few hours or overnight and then looking at it with fresh eyes.

Revision Is Part of the Writing Process

In ancient times, the focus of the rhetor was upon the presentation of oral arguments in the form of speeches and students trained to perform in pressured situations before a law court or assembly. Though a speaker might spend time in preparation, most speeches were one-time opportunities. If the words were not well-chosen and well-spoken the first time, there was no second chance to influence an audience.

With modern written documents, a composition does not have to be perfect when the words first appear on the page. A document is not truly finished until it is transmitted to an audience, and, even then, important documents are often circulated in draft stages to colleagues for comments before they are presented to an audience.

Many writers claim that revising is the most rewarding step in writing, the time when they have words on a page to work with and can manipulate them to create a composition that communicates effectively. Yet, many students feel that their first drafts should stay exactly the way they've written them because these writings are truest to their feelings and experience. They are sure they have made their point clearly. In reality, a first draft often leaves the reader scratching his or her head and wondering what it was the writer meant to say. To communicate effectively, a writer must learn to interact with his reader to ensure he has communicated his message clearly.

Begin Revision by Rereading

The first step of revising is rereading. This step can be simple, if you are reading something written by someone else. When it is your own writing, it becomes infinitely more difficult. After all, you know what you meant to say—you know the research behind the writing and why you chose certain words or phrases. You even know how every sentence is supposed to read—even though you may have left out a word or two or three—and your mind can trick you into seeing the missing words right where they belong. Unfortunately, the reader does not have your understanding, and communication can break down. You need to learn to read your own work critically, as if it were written by a stranger. One of the first aids in this process is to read your work aloud. You can often hear stumbling blocks quicker than you can see them.

You can also learn to read your own work more objectively by reading and commenting on other writers' work. Look at the structure of essays, at the way the writers use transitions and topic sentences, and at the sentence structure and choice of words. As you learn to see how good writers put ideas and words together, you will begin to think about the readings in a more thorough manner—thinking of alternative, perhaps even better, ways to express the message of each essay. You will also learn to read your own work with a more critical eye.

Qualities of Effective Writing

Reading the work of some professional writers, you may have developed the idea that the best writing is writing that is difficult to understand, writing that sends the reader to the dictionary with every sentence, or writing that uses many technical or specialized terms. Often, we think something difficult to read must be well written. Although it is sometimes difficult to read about topics that are new to us because we're learning new vocabulary and struggling with complex ideas, it simply is not true that the best writing is hard to read. Indeed, the most effective writing, the kind of writing you want to produce in your classes, is simple, concise, and direct.

Keep It Simple

Simple means "unadorned" or "not ornate." *Writing simply* means saying something in common, concrete

William Safire's Rules for Writing

William Safire, long-time language enthusiast, political columnist, and contributor to "On Language" in the *New York Times Magazine*, has a little fun with grammar rules and myths.

- Remember to never split an infinitive.
- The passive voice should never be used.
- Do not put statements in the negative form.
- Verbs has to agree with their subjects.
- Proofread carefully to see if you words out.
- If you reread your work, you will find on rereading a great deal of repetition can be avoided by rereading and editing.
- A writer must not shift your point of view.
- And don't start a sentence with a conjunction. (Remember, too, a preposition is a terrible word to end a sentence with.)
- Don't overuse exclamation marks!!
- Place pronouns as close as possible, especially in long sentences, as of 10 or more words, to their antecedents.
- Writing carefully, dangling participles must be avoided.
- If any word is improper at the end of a sentence, a linking verb is.
- Take the bull by the hand and avoid mixing metaphors.
- Avoid trendy locutions that sound flaky.
- Everyone should be careful to use a singular pronoun with singular nouns in their writing.
- Always pick on the correct idiom.
- The adverb always follows the verb.
- Last but not least, avoid clichés like the plague; seek viable alternatives.

language without too much complication in the sentence structure. Writing simply doesn't mean you have to use only short or easy words. It doesn't mean that all your sentences will be simple sentences. It doesn't mean that you can't use figures of speech or intricate details. Simple writing means that you try to get your point across in a direct and interesting way. You aren't trying to hide your ideas. Instead, you are trying to amplify those ideas and begin an intelligible conversation with your reader.

Rely on Everyday Words

When writing about computers or other technical subjects, it's tempting to use **jargon** or specialized words you might use when talking to others with the same knowledge, interest, and background. When writing for a limited audience whose members are familiar with technical terms, a bit of jargon might be acceptable. However, most of the writing you will do in college and later in the workplace will address a larger audience. You will want to avoid the use of highly technical terms, acronyms, and abbreviations.

If it seems that the writers in this text use many big words or technical terms, stop for a minute to consider the original audience for each of the essays. Consider how your vocabulary grows each year as you read, discuss, and consider new ideas. The everyday words of a tenth grade student will probably be fewer in number than the everyday words of a junior in college. Similarly, the everyday words of a college freshman will be different from the everyday words of a computer professional with three years of work experience. Use words that are comfortable and familiar to you and your readers when you write, and you will write clear, effective essays.

Use Precise Words

We sometimes assume that the reader will know what we mean when we use adjectives like "beautiful," "quiet," or "slow." However, the reader has only his or her own ideas of those adjectives. You can make your writing more interesting and effective by adding concrete details to give the reader an image that uses at least two of the five senses.

You can use details from all of the senses to make your writing even more concrete and precise. What are some of the sensual qualities of the experience or thing? Can you compare it to another thing that your readers may be familiar with to help them understand it better? Can you compare it to something totally unlike it? Can you compare it to a different sense to surprise readers and help them understand the image you are trying to create?

A good way to practice your ability to write original concrete images is to expand on a cliché. A **cliché** is an overused saying or expression. Often, clichés begin as similes that help make images more concrete. They become clichéd or overused because they lose their originality or they don't contain enough detail to give us the entire picture. Choose a cliché and write a sentence that expands the cliché and uses the senses to create a clear picture of the thing described. You might try some of the following clichés:

She is as pretty as a picture.

It smelled heavenly.

It was as soft as a baby's bottom.

His heart is as hard as stone.

It tastes as sour as a pickle.

We stared at the roaring campfire.

We listened to the babbling brook.

Precise details allow us to experience the world of the writer. We leave our own views and perceptions and learn how someone else sees the world. We learn what "quiet" is like for one writer and what "beautiful" means to another. Fill in the gaps between your words and ideas with vivid images and your writing will become more interesting and more effective.

Be Concise

Rid your writing of excess words and leave only that which makes your meaning clear and concrete. Becoming aware of several common problems can help you make your writing more concise. When you begin a sentence with either "it is" or "there is," you transfer all the meaning of the sentence to the end of the sentence. This is known as a **delayed construction**. You have delayed the meaning. The reader must read on to find out what "it" or "there" refer to. They don't get anything important from the beginning of the sentence.

Examine the following sentences:

It is important to change the oil in older gasoline engines.

There is an apple on the table.

There isn't anything we need to fear except our own fear.

We can rewrite these sentences, making them more concise, by deleting the "there is" or the "it is" and restructuring the sentence.

> Changing the oil in older gasoline engines is important.
>
> An apple is on the table.
>
> We have nothing to fear but fear itself.

Notice that the second group of sentences is shorter and the important information is no longer buried in the middle. Revising this type of sentence can make your writing more concise and get information to the reader more effectively.

If you think you may be guilty of using "it is" and "there is" (or "it's" and "there's") too often, you can use most word processing programs to seek these constructions out. Use the "search" or "find and replace" tool that's found in the Edit portion of your pull-down menu. Type "it is" and ask your computer to find every place you use this construction in your document. When you find a sentence that begins with "it is," revise the sentence to make it more concise. Do the same with "there is," "it's," and "there's." After you become more aware of these errors by correcting them, you'll find that you notice the errors before or as you make them. You will begin to write more concisely, and you'll have fewer delayed constructions to revise.

You can also make your writing more concise by avoiding common wordy expressions. Sometimes when we're nervous about writing or insecure about our knowledge of a topic, we try to hide that insecurity behind a wall of meaningless words, such as in the following sentence:

> At this point in time, you may not have the ability to create a web page due to the fact that you've avoided using computers for anything other than playing Solitaire.

This sentence is full of deadwood phrases that add no meaning to the sentence. If we take out the unneeded words, we have this sentence:

> You may not be able to create a web page because you've only used your computer to play Solitaire.

Your computer may have a grammar checker that will identify some commonly used wordy expressions. If your computer doesn't have a grammar checker, or if your instructor has asked you not to use the grammar checker in your computer, you can still learn to revise the wordiness out of your paragraphs. Use the computer to separate a paragraph of your writing into sentences. As you scroll through the paragraph, hit the hard return or "Enter" key on your keyboard twice every time you find a period. Once you have separated the sentences, look at each sentence. What is the important idea in the sentence? What words are used to convey that idea? What words don't add any meaning to the sentence? Delete words that don't convey meaning, and revise the sentence to make it more concise.

Use Action Verbs

Action verbs are words that convey the action of a sentence. They carry much of our language's nuance and meaning. Many inexperienced writers use only "to be" verbs: *am, is, are, was, were, be, been,* and *being.* If you use too many of these verbs, you risk losing much of the power of language. If I say someone is coming through the door, I've created a picture of a body and a doorway. If I say someone marches or slinks through the door, I've added information not only about movement but also about the quality of that movement. I've given my subject the attitude of a soldier or a cat. For example, consider this sentence written by Howard Rheingold:

> Thirty thousand years ago, outside a deceptively small hole in a limestone formation in the area now known as southern France, several adolescents shivered in the dark, awaiting initiation into the cult of toolmakers.

By using the verb "shivered," especially when accompanied by the words "in the dark," Rheingold paints a word picture much more vivid than he would have conveyed with the use of a "to be" verb. Using interesting verbs can enliven your writing.

If you want to focus upon using more action verbs, skim through your essay and circle all the "to be" verbs. Read the sentences with circled "to be" verbs more closely, and choose several to rewrite using active verbs in place of the "to be" verbs. You won't be able to do this for every sentence, but replace them where you can and your writing will become more lively, more concise, and more effective.

Fill in the Gaps

When we write, we sometimes forget that we are writing to an audience other than ourselves. We expect that our readers are people just like us, with our experiences, memories, and tastes. Because we have assumed they're so much like us, we expect our readers to be able to read more than what we've written on the page. We expect them to read our minds. We may leave large gaps in our essays, hoping the reader will fill in exactly the information we would have included.

If I'm writing an essay about my childhood in the South and I say it was always so hot in the summer that I hated to go outside, I might think my reader knows what I mean by hot. However, there are many different ways to be "hot." In east Texas where I grew up, the hot was a sticky hot. Eighty degrees made me long for a big glass of sweetened iced tea with lots of ice. The heat made my clothes cling. Sweating didn't help because the sweat didn't dry. I spent the day feeling as if I'd never dried off after my morning shower. In New Mexico, I never really felt hot unless the temperature got above 110 degrees. At that point, the heat would rush at me, making it difficult to breathe. I would open the door to leave the house, and it felt as if I had opened the oven door to check on a cake. If I say I was hot in the summer without describing how heat felt to me, my reader may not get the message I'm trying to convey. Don't expect your reader to know what you mean by "hot" or by any other general description. Instead, take a minute to add details that will fill in the gaps for the reader.

Speak Directly

To *speak directly* is to say, up front, who is doing what. Sometimes we don't tell the reader who is completing the action or we tell them too late. Let's look at the following sentences:

> The steak was stolen from the grill.
>
> The decisive battle was fought between the Confederate and the Union armies in Vicksburg, Mississippi.
>
> The red truck has been driven into the side of the green car.

Although we might be able to guess who the actors are in each of the sentences, the first and last sentences don't tell us directly. Even if the reader can guess that it was a dog who stole the steak from the grill or my neighbor who drove the red truck into the side of the green car, the reader has to stop and figure out who is doing what before he or she can read on. This slows the reader down and diminishes the effectiveness of your writing.

Language professionals call this **passive voice**. The action comes before the actor. Note that sometimes, as in the first and last sentences above, the writer doesn't mention the actor at all. To identify passive verbs in your writing, look for verbs coupled with another action word that ends in "-ed" or "-en" such as "was stolen" or "was forgotten."

Find the action and the actor in the sentence to make sure that they are in the most effective order. The most effective sentence order is actor first, then action. If the sentence does not specify the actor but leaves it implied, chances are that it is a passive sentence. For example, read this sentence: "The red truck was driven into the green car." It does not say who the driver was, and thus it is a passive sentence.

Rewriting some of your sentences to eliminate use of the passive voice will make your writing stronger and more interesting.

President Barack Obama has won high marks for his verbal eloquence, as illustrated by this cartoon published in the *International Herald Tribune*. His 2004 Keynote Speech at the Democratic National Convention and his best-selling book, *The Audacity of Hope*, helped propel him to national prominence.

Activity 6.1 When You Reeeaaallly Want to Describe Something

This activity requires a thesaurus or access to the Visual Thesaurus website (http://www.visualthesaurus.com).

1. Strunk and White's *The Elements of Style,* in an entry on "Misused Words and Expressions," says,

   "*Very*. Use this word sparingly. Where emphasis is necessary, use words strong in themselves."

   With a partner, paraphrase and discuss this Strunk and White writing tip.

2. To demonstrate Strunk and White's advice in (1) above, revise the following sentence, getting rid of the adverb "very."

   Julie is very pretty.

   No, don't say, "Julie is beautiful." Make a list of more precise and vivid words that could be used instead. Refer to a thesaurus (or the Visual Thesaurus website) to find words such as "stunning" and so on.

3. As a class, brainstorm other intensifying adverbs such as "awfully" or "extremely" that you tend to use as words of emphasis (in writing or in everyday speech) and list those words on the board.

4. In pairs again, compose a short paragraph of two or three sentences about a subject or event (e.g., a tornado, a celebrity sighting, a sports event, a news event, a concert, etc.) and intentionally use as many common or trite intensifying words as possible.

5. Exchange the short paragraph you composed in (4) above with another pair of classmates. Revise the other partnership's dialogue with the use of a thesaurus. The revised dialogue should not contain any "intensifiers" or trite words of emphasis. Replace such words and phrases with more powerful and concise language. For example, "I was really happy to see the Hornets win. They totally beat the Giants," could be revised to read (with the help of more concise and powerful words): "I was euphoric to see the Hornets thrash the Giants."

6. Read your "before" and "after" dialogues to the class. Afterward, discuss which words were eliminated and how the words that replaced those intensifiers changed the tone and/or meaning of the dialogue.

Source: Adapted from a lesson plan, "When You Reeeaaallly Want to Say Something," from the Visual Thesaurus website, http://www.visualthesaurus.com/cm/lessons/1450.

Remember to Proofread

It is understandably difficult to find the errors in an essay you have been working on for days. A few tricks used by professional writers might help you see errors in your essay more clearly.

1. With pencil in hand, read the essay aloud, slowly—and preferably to an audience. When you are reading aloud, it is more difficult to add or change words, so you tend to catch errors you would not see reading silently to yourself. Plus the reactions of your audience may point out areas where future readers may become confused or lose interest.

2. Another trick is to read the essay backwards, sentence by sentence. This forces you to look at sentence structure and not at the overall content of the essay. If you are working on a computer, another way to accomplish this is to create a final edit file in which you hit the hard return twice at the end of every question or statement. You might even go so far as to number the sentences so they look more like grammar exercises. Then look at each sentence individually.

Reading 6.1

Grammar Girl's Top Ten Grammar Myths

by Mignon Fogarty, quickanddirtytips.com

In this blog entry by Mignon Fogarty, she offers her top-ten list of grammar mistakes and misunderstandings.

10. **A run-on sentence is a really long sentence.** Wrong! They can actually be quite short. In a run-on sentence, independent clauses are squished together without the help of punctuation or a conjunction. If you write "I am short he is tall," as one sentence without a semicolon, colon, or dash between the two independent clauses, it's a run-on sentence even though it only has six words.

9. **You shouldn't start a sentence with the word "however."** Wrong! It's fine to start a sentence with "however" so long as you use a comma after it when it means "nevertheless."

8. **"Irregardless" is not a word. Wrong!** "Irregardless" is a bad word and a word you shouldn't use, but it is a word. "Floogetyflop" isn't a word—I just made it up and you have no idea what it means. "Irregardless," on the other hand, is in almost every dictionary labeled as nonstandard. You shouldn't use it if you want to be taken seriously, but it has gained wide enough use to qualify as a word.

7. **There is only one way to write the possessive form of a word that ends in "s." Wrong!** It's a style choice. For example, in the phrase "Kansas's statute," you can put just an apostrophe at the end of "Kansas" or you can put an apostrophe "s" at the end of "Kansas." Both ways are acceptable.

6. **Passive voice is always wrong. Wrong!** Passive voice is when you don't name the person who's responsible for the action. An example is the sentence "Mistakes were made," because it doesn't say who made the mistakes. If you don't know who is responsible for an action, passive voice can be the best choice.

5. **"i.e." and "e.g." mean the same thing. Wrong!** "e.g." means "for example," and "i.e." means roughly "in other words." You use "e.g." to provide a list of incomplete examples, and you use "i.e." to provide a complete clarifying list or statement.

4. **You use "a" before words that start with consonants and "an" before words that start with vowels. Wrong!** You use "a" before words that start with consonant sounds and "an" before words that start with vowel sounds. So, you'd write that someone has an MBA instead of a MBA, because even though "MBA" starts with "m," which is a consonant, it starts with the sound of the vowel "e"—MBA.

3. **It's incorrect to answer the question "How are you?" with the statement "I'm good." Wrong!** "Am" is a linking verb and linking verbs should be modified by adjectives such as "good." Because "well" can also act as an adjective, it's also fine to answer "I'm well," but some grammarians believe "I'm well" should be used to talk about your health and not your general disposition.

2. **You shouldn't split infinitives. Wrong!** Nearly all grammarians want to boldly tell you it's OK to split infinitives. An infinitive is a two-word form of a verb. An example is "to tell." In a split infinitive, another word separates the two parts of the verb. "To boldly tell" is a split infinitive because "boldly" separates "to" from "tell."

1. **You shouldn't end a sentence with a preposition. Wrong!** You shouldn't end a sentence with a preposition when the sentence would mean the same thing if you left off the preposition. That means "Where are you at?" is wrong because "Where are you?" means the same thing. But there are many sentences where the final preposition is part of a phrasal verb or is necessary to keep from making stuffy, stilted sentences: "I'm going to throw up," "Let's kiss and make up," and "What are you waiting for" are just a few examples.

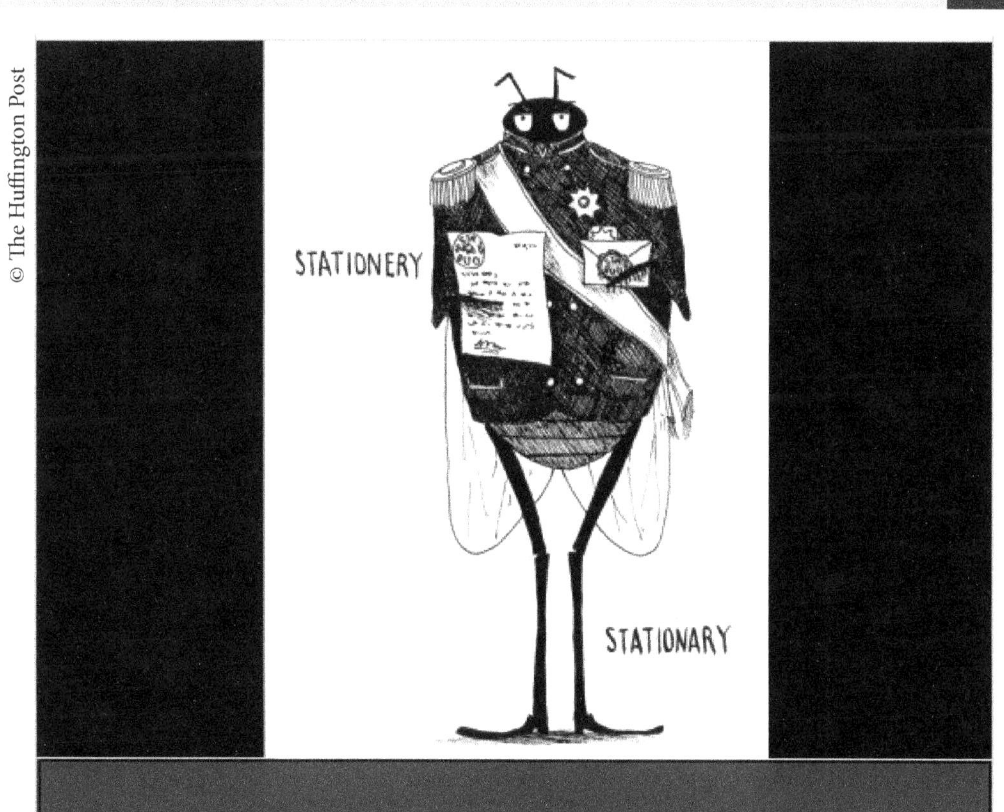

Stationary means "fixed in place, unable to move;" ***stationery*** is letterhead or other special writing paper. (Hint: ***Stationery*** with an **e** comes with an envelope.) Examples: Evan worked out on his ***stationary*** bike. The duke's initials and crest appeared atop his personal ***stationery***.

Eminent means "distinguished or superior"; ***imminent*** means "impending, sure to happen." Also, ***eminent*** domain is the right of a government to take over private property for public use. Examples: The rain was ***imminent***; it would arrive soon, soaking the ***eminent*** dignitaries on the stage. (Think of ***imminent*** and ***impending***, which both begin with the same letters.)

Reading 6.2

Top Ten Distractions for Writers, or Any Job Really

by Sam Scham

The following list, "Top Ten Distractions for Writers, or Any Job Really," by Sam Scham, was published in the Yahoo Contributor Network.

When you have a set goal in mind, whether it is for personal or work reasons, so many other things can become easy distractions. For writers in particular, life seems to get in the way. There are other pressing matters that we have to worry about.

1. The Internet

The Internet is a very huge distraction these days. For writers who do research online for their great idea, it is easy to stumble upon different links and steer away from the main point in focus. If you find yourself doing this, try to limit the time you do research therefore getting off the Internet earlier and allow more time for writing.

2. The Radio

Music can help a writer generate ideas and feelings. Listening to the radio can be a distraction if you leave it on for too long. If you are like me, you are able to write the best in silence. You need to be able to hear yourself think. If you are listening to the radio and it is hard to turn away from it, listen to it in segments. Listen to some music and when a commercial comes on, mute the radio and start writing. Maybe, before you know it, you will forget that you were ever listening to the radio.

3. The Television

The television and the radio are similar in many ways. For one, it is hard to turn off, especially if you are in the middle of a show that you want to finish. But then, you see a commercial for what is coming up next and you are intrigued to watch it. At the end of the current show, turn off the TV and get writing. Soon, you will not notice the absence of the picture box.

4. Own Procrastination

You want to sit down and write, but at the same time you don't, you have no motivation. The solution is to take a day off, do not think of it at all. Work on any other pressing matters like home chores or calling up an old friend that you've been meaning to catch up with. On the next day, wake up and get writing. Just jump right into it and it will be like you never took a break.

5. Other People

Especially if you live with family or friends other people always being around can be a huge distraction. In order to solve this, find out when everyone will be out and fit in time to write while they are gone. If that just doesn't work with your everyday schedule, find a nice place outside or at the local library where you can work in peace without other people bugging you.

6. Other Responsibilities

Work, chores, walking the dog; these everyday responsibilities are tiring and at the end of the day you just cannot get the energy to write. Try writing in the morning, even if it is just for a few minutes. Get the best out of what you got and do not get discouraged.

7. Telephones

With cell phones these days, you can be getting texts at every minute either from friends or social networks. When you are writing, the best way to refrain from your cell phone is by turning it completely off and leaving it somewhere out of sight so that you are not tempted to check it.

8. Outdoor Activities

Especially on a really nice day, you may want to forget the writing and spend some time outdoors. That is completely fine. Enjoy life to the fullest. If you end up not writing for the day, remember that there is always tomorrow. But be careful not to put it off for too long and too often. If you really want to spend time outside, take the writing with you and kill two birds with one stone.

9. Everyday Needs

You need to eat sometime and when you work and do everything else, cooking can really tire you out and make you not want to write. On those days, try to make simple meals if you absolutely do not want to order out. There is nothing wrong with having a bowl of cereal for dinner.

10. Being Bored

We all get bored sometimes, even of our own writing. Take a break. Do not work on writing your big project, but work on something else. A day or two later go back to that big project and start working on writing it again and if you are still bored, put it to the side again. At least you cannot say that you did not try.

Compose

Activity 6.2 Write a List of Your Writing Habits

As you write an essay assigned by your instructor, keep notes about your writing process. What distracts or keeps you from writing? What works well when you write? What kind of prewriting do you do? What are the best (or worst) conditions for you when you write?

Organize your notes about your writing process into a theme such as "Best Places to Write" or "Ways to Avoid Procrastinating." As Sam Scham does, write two or three sentences about each of your writing habits.

Gain Feedback by Peer Editing

Your instructor may schedule class periods for peer workshops. These workshops are opportunities for you to get responses from your readers. Often, you will be divided into groups of three or four students and you will be given a list of questions to answer about your peers' essays. Your peers will get copies of your essay, and they will give you comments as well. The first peer workshop can be a difficult experience. It is never easy to take criticism, constructive or not. Taking criticism in a small group is even more difficult. There are several things you can do to make your peer groups more productive.

When Your Essay Is Being Reviewed

1. Write down everything the reviewers say. You think you will remember it later, but often you will forget just that piece of advice you need. More importantly, writing while the reviewers speak is an effective way to keep the channels of communication open. It is hard to come up with a defense for your paper if you are busy writing.

2. Save your comments until all the reviewers are done. If you have specific questions, write them in the margins of your notes. If they ask you questions, make a note to answer them when everyone is done. If you allow yourself to speak, you will be tempted to start defending your essay. Once you start defending your essay, two things happen. First, you stop listening to the comments. Second, you offend your reviewers, making it less likely that they will give you honest criticism in the future.

3. The first comment you should make to your reviewers is "Thank you." The second comment can be anything but a defense. Your readers are only telling you how they have interpreted your essay. They are giving you their opinions; you do not have to make the changes they suggest.

4. Save all the comments you get on your essay. Set them aside for a day or so. Then make the changes that you think will make your essay better.

When You Are the Reviewer

1. Read an essay through, at least one time, just to browse the content of the essay. Appreciate the essay for what it does well. Try to ignore any problems for now. You will get back to them the second time you read

and begin your comments in the margins. Every essay will have at least one thing about it that is good.

2. Always begin your comments with a sincere discussion of what you like about the essay.

3. Be specific in your comments. Your peers will probably understand you better if you say, "The topic sentence in paragraph four really sets the reader up for what the essay accomplishes in paragraph four. But I can't really find a topic sentence for paragraph six, and the topic sentences in paragraphs two and three could be improved." Note how this statement gives a positive response and then identifies specific places where the author can improve the essay. This works much better than a generalized statement like, "Topic sentences need work."

4. Be descriptive in your comments. It is often helpful for students to hear how you are reading their essays. "Paragraph five seems to be telling me . . . " or "I got the feeling the essay's overall message is . . . " are good ways to start descriptive sentences.

5. Realize that you are analyzing a paper and not a person. Directing your comments toward the essay, "Paragraph nine doesn't really have anything new to add, does the paper need it?" sounds better to the listener than "You repeat yourself in paragraph nine. Do you really need it?"

Independent Reviewing

If your instructor does not require peer editing, you can ask someone to review your essay. Choose someone you trust to give you an honest opinion. It might not be effective to ask a parent, spouse, or girlfriend/boyfriend to give you a critique if you know they are going to like anything you write, just because you wrote it. It might be better to ask another student who has recently had an English class or one of your current classmates. In exchange, you might offer to look over their work. Remember, you learn to read your own essays better by reading other peoples' essays more critically.

Sample Questions for Peer Review

When you have revised your paper several times, have someone answer these questions regarding its overall content, paragraph development, and word choice and sentence structure.

Overall Content

1. What is the thesis or main point of the essay? Where does the writer state this main point? If the main point is implied rather than stated, express it in a sentence. Does the main point give a subject and an opinion about the subject? How might the writer improve his/her thesis?

2. What is the purpose of this essay? What are the characteristics of the audience the writer seems to be addressing (formal, fun-loving, serious, cynical, laid-back, etc.)?

Paragraph Development

1. Do each of the paragraphs in the essay work to support the main point of the essay? Which paragraphs seem to wander from that main point? What other information needs to be added to develop the main point?

2. List two places in the essay where the writer uses vivid sensory details. How effective are those details? Are they used to support the thesis of the essay? Identify two places in the essay where the writer needs more effective details. What kind of details might he or she include?

3. What grade would you give the introduction? How does it draw the reader into the essay? What specific things can the writer do to make the introduction more inviting?

4. Which paragraph do you like the best? Why? Which paragraph in the essay do you like the least? Why? What can the writer do to improve his/her paragraphs?

5. What grade would you give the conclusion? How does it provide closure for the essay? What specific things can the writer do to make the conclusion more effective?

Word Choice and Sentence Structure

1. Are adequate transitions used between the paragraphs? Find an effective paragraph transition and identify it. Why does it work? Find two places between paragraphs that need more or better transitions. What can the writer do to improve these transitions?

2. Are a variety of sentences used? Where might the writer vary the sentence structure for better effect? What two sentences in the essay did you find most effective? Why?

3. Are there any words that seem misused or out of place? What positive or negative trigger words are used? Do they enhance the message of the essay or detract from it?

Activity 6.3 Peer Editing of Sample Student Essay

As your instructor directs, either individually or in groups, peer edit one of the following sample student papers and then answer the questions regarding overall content, paragraph development, and word choice and sentence structure listed in the above section, Sample Questions for Peer Review. Then discuss your peer editing in your small groups, comparing your answers to those of others in your group.

Sample Student Essay for Peer Editing, Profile Assignment

Longing for Better Days

As she sits in her cramped room in Amman, Jordan, watching the recent news, Aysha Mustafa, 92, is saddened by the world she lives in today. As she places her wrinkled hands on her lap and begins to recall a time when things were pleasant, tears begin to flow down her cheeks. Those times are long gone she says. Aysha moved from Palestine to Jordan after the sudden death of her husband in 1995. Moving here was tough she says, "It was hard to leave my country." Aysha's story goes back 60 years ago, where she lived in her homeland Palestine. She recalls her childhood as being peaceful and joyous. She smiles as she describes memories of her and her brother riding in the back of her father's wagon. "Life was good," she says. Although her family had very little to live on, she was still happy.

Like many Palestinians, Aysha still dreams to one day return back and live in her homeland Palestine, where she longs to rekindle sweet memories there. "Jordan is fine she says but I rather live on the land that is mine." As we sit in the living room watching the crisis in Gaza in January 2009, Aysha begins to wipe the tears from her sad yet hopeful eyes, and reiterates with a sigh in her voice, "May God be with them." The appalling images of young children being killed by Israeli rockets leave 92 year old Aysha in distress. How many more men, women and children will die before both sides reach an agreement she questions? As her grandson flips through the channels, he crosses upon the Al-Jazeera news that announces that the number killed in Gaza has reached the disturbing number of 781. She suddenly lowers her head and gazes into space. . "It kills me to see my people getting killed like this," she stutters trying to hold back tears. The Israeli and Palestinian conflict has been going on for more than 60 years now. Many innocent civilians of both sides have been killed due to this grotesque war.

Despite all of this, it is people like Aysha that still carry hope that one day they will return back to their homeland and live in peace and harmony. Aysha's wish like many others is for all Palestinians to live a life of security and freedom, freedom to make their own choices and decisions on their own land. Aysha struggles to explain how as a child she used to run around in the fields freely, fearing no one or anything. "The feeling of freedom is indescribable," she says. "I was free to walk and go as I pleased, with no blockades to hold me back."

Today however, boys and girls in Palestine do not share the same luxury that Aysha experienced before the occupation. It is heart breaking watching this old yet strong willed woman recalling her childhood memories. Suddenly, Aysha begins to hold her chest and breathe heavily; her grandson approaches her and gives her her heart medicine. He explains that talking about such a personal and stressful topic leaves his grandmother feeling tired and overwhelmed. She has a weak heart, "My days are getting shorter," she says. Aysha is an inspiration, throughout this interview she kept calm and never wavered or seemed weak. One would think she would be vulnerable to everything surrounding her, but on the contrary she was full of wisdom. When asked what she hoped for, she said with a confident tone, "My people will see better days than this; I know this for a fact. They will be happy again; mothers will no longer be forced to bury their children. The day of justice and freedom is near, I can feel it." As she said this, Aysha seemed certain that this war will not last very long. Many Palestinians have the same hopes as Aysha, they too are confident that the day will come when their people will believe in security again.

Aysha is one of many Palestinians who shares the same dream as millions, which is a liberated and a prosperous Palestine. As she stands up and leans on her cane she says, "We want our rights, we want justice, we want freedom on our land, and we want Palestine."

Aysha's final words were that she prays that once her soul rests, she hopes to be buried next to her husband's grave on the holy land of Palestine.

Sample Student Essay for Peer Editing, Rhetorical Analysis Assignment

Rhetorical Analysis of President Reagan's "Challenger Speech"

FIVE, FOUR, THREE, TWO, ONE, WE HAVE LIFT OFF! THE SPACE SHUTTLE CHALLENGER HAS CLEARED THE LAUNCH PAD. This was supposed to be a glorious day in American history, a mile stone in the United States Space Program. Instead this day quickly turned into one of the most horrific scenes witnessed live by the American public, which included thousands of school children, who watched from the comfort and safety of their classrooms.

On January 28, 1986, the space shuttle Challenger was scheduled for launch in Florida. It would mark the second flight by the United States Space program and it was the first educational launch program. On this particular flight there was to be a teacher on board, she was the first teacher on a space shuttle as a result of a special program from NASA. Although there were some clear concerns regarding whether the shuttle should launch, NASA officials gave the green light and the mission moved forward. Within seconds of lift off, the space shuttle Challenger burst into flames and disintegrated in mid flight, instantly killing all seven passengers aboard. The nation was shocked, especially thousands of young children who eagerly watched the live coverage on television. Within hours of the explosion President Ronald Reagan went on live television and addressed the nation from the White House. President Reagan was scheduled to address the nation on that particular day to report on the state of the Union, instead he went on television and paid tribute to the Challenger Seven. President Reagan delivered one of the most inspirational, and motivational speeches of his tenure as the President of the United States. It is a speech, like all great speeches, that would out live his presidency, and be regarded as one of the great speeches of our time.

The nation stood still, not knowing what to make of the days events. In such times of sorrow people tend to need support, guidance, and reassurance. The American people needed someone to follow, a shoulder to lean on, a vision of the future, a leader. President Reagan went on live television and paid tribute to the "Challenger Seven" in a speech from the White House. President Reagan sat alone behind a large desk surrounded in the background by family pictures. President Reagan used his ethos as a credible individual; he was the leader of the free Nation. He gave the speech from the White House, which is clearly recognized by the American public as a symbol of power and security. The image of him sitting behind a great desk flanked by pictures of family and loved ones borrowing once again from their ethos. This was a not only the President of the United States delivering this speech, this was a husband, a father, and a son too.

The occasion for the speech was obvious: The Nation had just witnessed seven brave individuals perish before their very eyes. These brave souls were, husbands, sons, daughters, fathers, and they had paid the ultimate sacrifice for mankind. President Reagan portrayed all of these different roles played by each of the "Challenger Seven" from behind that desk. As the speech proceeded, President Reagan was careful to not down play the Challenger incident, but he appealed to logos, or logic, by saying "But we have never lost an astronaut in flight. We've never had a tragedy like this one." Here he used pathos to emphasize the severity of the incident while at the same time letting the nation know that there have been other brave astronauts who have also paid the ultimate price for the visions and progress of mankind. President Reagan throughout his speech used his words very carefully and with great insight. His words and the double meaning or relation to the events of the day made a huge impact on the delivery and acceptance of his speech by the American public. As he stated "Your loved ones were daring and brave, and they had that special grace, that spirit that says, Give me a challenge, and I'll meet it with joy." As one can see, President Reagan is using the word challenge here, this is a direct reference to the space shuttle Challenger.

President Reagan goes on to address the thousands of children who also witnessed the event, addressing the emotion or pathos of the occasion. He states, "And I want to say something to the schoolchildren of America who were watching the live coverage of the shuttle's take-off. I know it's hard to understand, but sometimes painful things like this happen. It's all part of the process of exploration and discovery. It is all part of taking a chance and expanding man's horizons. The future doesn't belong to the fainthearted; it belongs to the brave. The Challenger crew was pulling us into the future, and we'll continue to follow them." Here President Reagan's audience is the children, who in turn are the future of the nation. By saying that the Challenger was taking them towards the future, he is saying what everybody already knows. The children are the future of the nation and he is telling them that they must continue to move forward, for one day they will be the leaders of the country.

President Reagan's message is very clear: This was a tragedy, yet we as a nation must continue to move forward in order to honor the memory of the "Challenger Seven." President Reagan, utilizing logos, then mentions the

NASA employees in his speech. Here he does not blame or degrade the space program or its employees. Instead he praises there hard work and dedication to the American people and the space program. He does not speculate on the cause of the explosion nor does he address any issues related to who is to blame. He completely omits any negative or accusatory comments in his speech. This was a very tactful and extremely intelligent move by Reagan. He knew the American public had many questions regarding the explosion. He also knew that those questions needed to be answered and that it was his responsibility to provide those answers to the nation. Yet on this day, and in this speech, it was not the right time to do so.

President Reagan in closing his speech borrows from the ethos of the past when he stated "There's a coincidence today. On this day three hundred and ninety years ago, the great explorer Sir Francis Drake died aboard ship off the coast of Panama... a historian later said, He lived by the sea, died on it, and was buried in it. Well, today, we can say of the Challenger crew: their dedication was, like Drake's complete."

President Reagan's speech on the space shuttle Challenger served several purposes. First, it paid tribute to the seven astronauts who lost their lives in the explosion. Second, it provided the nation with a much needed reassurance that everything was going to be all right. And although this was terrible accident and set back for our country, he also left no doubt that the Nations commitment to NASA and the space program would not only survive, but continue to advance forward into the future.

Sample Student Essay for Peer Editing, Short Op-Ed Argument

Women in Combat

It is without a doubt that most of us have seen, read, or even heard about women in foreign countries, specifically the Middle East, being victims of sexual discrimination in male dominated work. But, would anyone possibly imagine, that even at a smaller scale, it occurs right here right now. This op-ed piece focuses on women in combat. While some countries do allow women to fight in combat, it seems archaic that the leader of the free world and by many referred as the #1 nation in the world, that we still bar women from certain roles in the military.

The most common fallacies believed by many include, women's enervated strength. Or, there psychological structure is so that they are considered nurturers not murderers. The most archaic mentality yet is that women are a distraction to men. The list can go on, but the above seems to be the most common misconceptions.

The case against the strength of a woman seems irrefutable. No one can argue that in general men are stronger than women. But there are many factors to be considered in arguing the rebuttal. For instance, the double standards set by our military. The annual Physical fitness test clearly subordinates the female's potential physical ability. A study conducted in Great Britain by the Ministry of Defense concluded that "women can be built to the same levels of physical fitness as men of the same size and build" (Shepard, 2007). How can we expect a woman to perform closer to a man's standards when we delude her understanding of what it really takes to achieve physical fitness? Would it be any different if we took a male chef and only taught him how to cook appetizers, then graded him for the entire meal including entre and desert?

Psychological structure is also a hot topic. Women are nurturers, not murderers. Kingsley Browne, author of Co-Ed Combat, The New Evidence Why Women shouldn't Fight the Nation's Wars, made a diluted attempt to answer this question by stating "There are large differences in men and women and willingness to take Physical risks. For example something like 93% of work place deaths are men" (Traders Nation, 2007). While men seem quite capable to murdering, Browne failed to cite that women are also capable of committing heinous crimes, as evidenced by the 2.1 million women serving sentences in American Prisons for violent crimes (Shepard, 2007).

Psychological Structure is an important factor in wars, as Browne reiterates. "Women's greater fear of death and injury and greater aversion to physical risks are likely to affect their combat performance negatively" (Arron, 2007). Clearly not all women are cut out for combat. But if we use this formula, it is also evidenced that not all men are cut out for combat. It is said that over 100,000 men panicked at the thought of going to the Vietnam War and fled the country to avoid the draft (Shepard, 2007). Surely any veteran of any War would consider this a perfect paradigm of a coward?

Another myth is that, women are a distraction to men. While the idea may rain ring true one could also conclude that any soldier, male or female, that is so easily distracted may be a danger not only to themselves but also to the unit they serve. While this conclusion does not rectify that argument, it does show the weak rationales that women face. Furthermore this mentality sends society the message that it's acceptable to punish/exclude women from full participation due to men's personal failings. Since World War One female nurses have served on the front line, and it has never been documented that women distract men (Jericho, 2008, p. 8).

This topic clearly incites emotions from opponents and proponents of women in combat. Women deserve attention to the matter starting with the Pentagon ensuring our women are properly trained and given the tools to succeed. But the story doesn't begin there, it begins at home. If we cannot treat a boy and a girl the same when growing up, why should we expect anyone to treat them any different as adults. How many times do we see a girl with a dole while the father teaches the son to hunt? Or watch a father rough house with his son, while the mother teaches her daughter how to apply makeup? Give your sister the tools and she will build you a bridge.

References

Arron. (2007) The Clock Stopped. Retrieved from: http://thestoppedclock.blogspot.com/2007/12/cowardly-untrustworthy-women.html

Jericho, J. (2008) Effectiveness of the Sex Discrimination Act. Retrieved from: http://www.aph.gov.au/Senate/committee/legcon_ctte/sex_discrim/submissions/sub02.pdf

Sheppard, c. (2007) Women in Combat. Strategy Research Project. Retreived from: http://www.carlisle.army.mil/usawc/Registar/policies.cfm

Traders Nation. (2007) Retrieved from: http://www.youtube.com/watch?v=1VgAd3WdaD0

Activity 6.4 Write on Your Blog

Choose one of your previous blog postings, and revise it using the suggestions provided in this chapter.

Activity 6.5 Write in Your Commonplace Book

Choose one of the readings in this chapter that you think could be improved, and write in your commonplace book about how it could be changed. Give specific examples.

7
RESEARCHING RHETORICALLY

Praxis in Action

How I Do Research by Jane Concha

You have your topic and you're ready to go. But now you think, "Where do I go from here?" I have definitely been there. Sometimes, I am so nervous that I don't even research until the last minute, thinking that the Internet would grant me some great sources. Unfortunately, that *never* works.

What I have now realized is that research takes time; with patience and a clear path, I have always managed to find sources that are geared to my topic and add depth to my paper.

To start, I brainstorm ideas of where I want to go with my research. Sometimes, a quick search on Google can help give me some hints on where to start. For example, if I choose to write on the desert in El Paso, a quick search can help me find the name of the desert, the type of climate, and the habitat. From there, I could easily go on the library database and search the keywords I have based on my online search.

I like to use online databases from my library website like Jstor and Academic Search Complete (EBSCO) because I can access print articles from my computer, and that satisfies professors who require that you have a certain number of print sources.

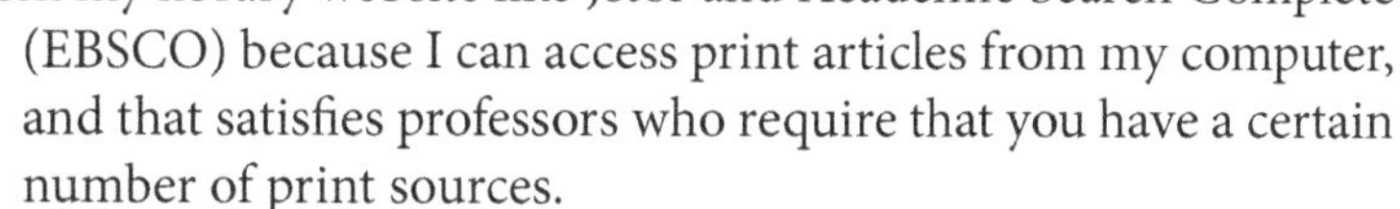

However, I'd recommend to fellow students that it's a good idea to get over their fear of actually going to the library in person except to use the computers or have study dates. Yes, you may be able to access articles and even books (Google Books, etc.) from your computer, but the library does have one great advantage—the research ninjas called librarians. These are people to cultivate, not once but throughout your academic career. They can help you find sources you wouldn't have thought of and can be invaluable when you can't find that essential bit of information.

Jane Concha uses the Internet, online databases, and librarians when conducting research for a paper.

Even when websites look useful, I'm careful with a *.com* website because those sites usually get their information from research that is easily accessible on a database or information that is slanted toward a certain point of view. However, I do like *.gov* websites because they usually have great statistics I can add to my paper.

Once I find my sources, I pick out the ones that I don't want and discard them. I usually don't look at anything over five years old. I also reject information that pertains to my topic, but is too boring to be interesting to my reader.

Once I'm done finding great sources, it is a lot easier to write my paper.

Research Provides Inartistic Proofs

As discussed in Chapter 4, ancient Greeks began the writing process with invention, a stage in which they searched their memories for data related to the topic at hand. This information constituted artistic proofs, knowledge that rhetors invented from their own minds, emotions, and observation. However, rhetors also supplemented their invented proofs with information that was gleaned from other sources such as the testimony of witnesses, evidence given under torture, and written contracts. Yes, evidence given under torture was considered a legitimate proof. None of these inartistic proofs were generated from the rhetor's mind or "invented." As such, the Greeks considered these sources of information to be inartistic proofs.

Today, the range of inartistic proofs available to writers and speakers is vastly expanded—scientific studies, opinions from authorities, videotapes of events, government documents, and so on. You can locate these in the traditional way—library books and print periodicals—but more likely you will begin your search with the Internet, a resource the ancients could not have imagined. However, as in ancient times, it is still the task of today's rhetor to locate available resources, sift through them to locate those that are relevant, evaluate their reliability and validity, and incorporate them into a text to support an argument.

Researching rhetorically, the title of this chapter, refers to making use of your ethos or credibility as a writer by incorporating your expert knowledge because of everyday experiences and the subjects you have studied. It also involves maximizing as well as"borrowing" the credibility of source materials you quote or paraphrase in your text. When you quote or paraphrase an expert, your paper gains authority that it would not otherwise have. For example, if you are the parent of a child with attention deficit hyperactivity disorder (ADHD), your experiences caring for that child and interacting with the health care and educational systems, as well as the reading you have done to seek out effective treatment, qualifies you to speak with authority about what it is like to raise such as child. If you are writing a paper about educational options for children with ADHD, you can cite some of your own experiences, but you will also want to quote or paraphrase opinions of authorities about the best ways to provide a quality educational environment for these children. These opinions of experts can be found in books, periodicals, and possibly government documents, and including them will increase your power to convince an audience.

You Do Research Every Day

Although the words "research paper" sound imposing to many students, research is really a natural part of your experience. You do research every day, often without being aware of the process, whether it is determining the calorie count of a serving of sugar-free ice cream or calculating the dollar amount you will spend on gasoline for a weekend trip. The information-gathering you do for a research paper builds on the informal research skills you already have by adding additional places to look for information and additional tools to use in that search.

How do you go about finding the best reference sources to support your general knowledge? A key factor to keep in mind is the credibility of each of the sources you choose. Citing information from a source written in the last three years is generally more credible than a source published ten years ago because the information is obviously more current. Peer-reviewed journals and books published by reputable publishers are probably the most credible sources. Information from a news magazine such as *Time* has more credence than material found in popular magazines such as *Glamour* or *People*, which are designed for entertainment rather than covering the news. Indeed, many instructors will forbid the use of Wikipedia as a source, not because all the information is inaccurate (because it is not) but because the reader has no way of evaluating whether information is correct or not since the entries were written by volunteers and the content has not been vetted by a reputable publisher or other authoritative organization.

Don't be reluctant to ask for help. Your instructor may be willing to suggest resources on your topic, as will librarians. Instructors may refer you to specific books or authors. Others may demonstrate a journal search for you, in the process finding you valuable sources. As noted by Concha in the chapter opener, librarians can be valuable allies in your search, as their job is to serve your needs as a library patron. If you ask for help, a librarian will often run a search for you in the online catalog or may even walk with you into the stacks to find appropriate source materials.

Primary and Secondary Research

If you've ever purchased a major consumer product, say a computer, chances are you already knew quite a bit about what was available before you took out your charge card. For example, many of your friends probably have computers as well as definite opinions about what brands and models are preferable. Perhaps you already own a computer and like it so much that you want to upgrade to the next model or maybe you have complaints about its performance. Still, before you made your purchase, you probably did some research on the Internet, reading product specifications and reviews. Maybe you tried out a computer or two at the local Apple Store or another retailer. If you went through this sort of process before buying a computer or another consumer product, you already know the basics about primary and secondary research.

Primary research involves personal interaction with your subject. Interviews with people on the scene of an event and questionnaires are all primary sources. Novels, poems, diaries, and fictional films are also primary sources because they stand alone and are not interpreting anything else. To return to the computer purchase analogy, when you visited the Apple Store or other retailers to examine computers, you were doing primary research. When you looked at product reviews in magazines, you were doing secondary research. Similarly, when you read a *Time* magazine article that analyzes climate change and quotes prominent experts in the field, you are conducting secondary research.

A little later in this chapter, Activity 7.1 asks you to interview someone who has had an unusual life experience and write a profile of that person. You may be able to gather all the information you need for this assignment by doing an interview, though it might be a good idea to revisit the observation exercise (Activity 4.10) in Chapter 4. If you know the person personally, you can also utilize that prior knowledge.

Other writing assignments ask you to combine your own experience or primary research with information gained from secondary research in books or periodicals. For example, you might be asked to write an essay about recycling. You can include your own experience with recycling or visit a recycling center in your community and report what you see. You can also support this primary research with secondary research in books or periodicals in which authorities offer facts and opinions about the effectiveness of recycling. In addition, you can interview an authority on recycling, perhaps a professor or chairperson of a community committee, as an additional secondary source.

You may notice that many magazine articles or books refer to other books, statistical studies, or additional evidence but do not document sources in the text or give a bibliography. In this course, however, your instructor will probably ask you to document outside references following the Modern Language Association (MLA) or American Psychological Association (APA) format. The purpose is to train you in academic writing, which differs from journalism or popular writing in that all sources are credited both in the text and in a works cited page. Documentation also benefits those who read your essays and might want to use the same sources for additional research of their own. It is, therefore, not a check against plagiarism but an important tool for other researchers.

Reading 7.1

Bringing History to Life with Primary Sources

by Alexander A. Aimes

In this article, Alexander A. Aimes argues that primary sources add depth and help bring a research topic to life.

History sometimes bores because of the way it is taught. Often, educators merely present students with information they are supposed to remember, rather than encourage students to explore historic documents and draw conclusions. As a Museum Studies intern at Mystic Seaport, a maritime history museum in Mystic, Connecticut, I worked with other interns to create history education programs targeted at high school audiences. We presented students with primary sources and asked them to think critically about the documents, to develop their own ideas about history.

My favorite program we developed related to the Temperance Movement, a mid-nineteenth century social reform movement that aimed to put an end to alcohol consumption. Members of the Greenman family, prominent shipbuilders and storeowners who lived in Mystic, became involved in Temperance as the movement gained national momentum. We traced the development of their beliefs through historic documents relating to their business and civic activities. For example, we showed students pages from the 1840s account books of the family-owned Greenman General Store that had frequent references to the sale of alcohol. By the 1850s, those references had vanished. Also, we gave students newspaper articles from the 1870s in which the Greenmans publicly stated their support of Temperance, indicating the passion with which the Greenmans advocated against alcohol. The text of the education program encouraged students to discover the Greenmans apparently stopped selling alcohol, a decision that affected the company's profits, *before* their public announcement of their change in attitude toward alcohol.

Students going through the educational program realized they would not know this fascinating detail, which hints the Greenmans were willing to lose company revenue in support of their beliefs, if they had not scrutinized account books from the 19th century. Moreover, we asked students to think about whether they could cite negative evidence—that is, the *absence* of liquor sales in the 1850s account books—as sufficient grounds for assuming the Greenmans changed their business practices by that decade? What other evidence would help support this conclusion—an open ended question students can answer in a variety of ways.

Focusing on historical evidence allows us to ask deeper questions about our conclusions. The questions we encouraged the students at Mystic Seaport to think about show the debatable nature of historical conclusions based on primary sources. While applied here to a museum activity, this strategy of poring over primary sources can be used in almost any research context. Original documents get us as close as possible to whatever subject we are studying. They also add depth to our interpretations by encouraging critical analysis of sources.

Interviews

Depending on your topic, your community probably has some excellent sources sitting behind desks at the nearest college, city hall, or federal office building. If you are looking into the environment, you could contact the Environmental Protection Agency, an attorney who specializes in environmental law, a professional employee of the park system or the Bureau of Land Management, a college professor who works in the natural sciences, or a group in your area dedicated to beautification and restoration efforts.

If you don't know anyone connected with these organizations, a look in the yellow pages or blue government pages of the phone book should give you the information you need.

When you contact the person you'd like to interview, identify yourself and your reason for wanting to speak with him or her. Most people are happy to assist college students in their research, and almost everyone is flattered by the attention. If your first choice refuses, ask him or her if they know anyone who might be knowledgeable about your topic and available for an interview. When you get a positive response, arrange an hour and a location convenient for both of you. If the interview is scheduled more than a week from the initial contact, you can write a letter confirming your appointment, or you can call the day before the scheduled interview to confirm the time and location.

Once you've scheduled the interview, make a list of questions you will ask your interview subject. There are two types of questions you can ask your subject: open and closed. **Open questions** such as the following leave room for extended discussion because they don't have a yes, no, or specific answer:

> Could you tell me about the most positive experience you've had with [topic]?
>
> When did you decide to study [topic]?
>
> What's the most negative experience you've had with [topic]?

Questions like these allow for extended discussions. Even if it seems your subject has finished his or her response to the question, let a few moments of silence pass before you ask another question. Silence can be uncomfortable for some people, and he or she might feel compelled to expand on the response to your question in interesting ways.

Closed questions are useful for gathering specific information. Questions such as "When did you graduate?" and "How long have you been involved in [topic]?" are closed questions. Although closed questions are important to an interview, be sure they're balanced by questions that allow your subject room to talk and expand on his or her ideas.

Before the interview, confirm the exact location of your appointment. If you are unfamiliar with the planned meeting place, go by the day before to make sure you can find it. Take several pens or pencils with you to the interview in addition to a writing tablet with a stiff back. If possible, use a recorder to record the interview, but be sure to ask your subject if it is okay. Most people will allow recording, if you assure them that the recording is only for your use in collecting information for your research paper. If you are using a recorder, test its operation before you get to the interview location so you won't have any surprises when you're with your subject or discover later that the machine was not working.

Although you've prepared a list of questions to follow, don't be afraid to ask a question that isn't on your list. If your subject mentions briefly an experience that seems relevant to your topic, you might want to ask him or her more about that experience, even though it isn't on your list of questions. Indeed, the best way to interview may be to read over your questions just before you meet your subject, then not refer to them during the interview. Before you leave, however, look over your list to see if you have missed any questions of importance.

Remember to let lulls in the conversation work for you by drawing your interview subject into further explanations or illustrations of previous comments. If you interview a talkative person who strays from the topic, try to steer him or her back to the questions you've prepared, but if you can't, don't worry. You'll probably get useful information anyway. Be courteous and attentive. Even if you're recording the interview, take notes. It makes both the subject and the interviewer feel more comfortable and serves as a backup, should your recording not work.

Within 15 minutes after leaving the interview, jot down some notes about your subject's appearance; the sights, sounds, and smells of the place where you conducted the interview; and any overall impressions of the meeting. Make sure you have the date and location of the interview in your notes because you will need it for documentation on your works cited page.

Compose

Activity 7.1 Write a Profile of a Person

Write a profile of a person that is unusual in some way. Your profile should include description, quotes, and whatever background explanations are needed to provide a context, so that the story flows logically from one element to another. The length should be approximately 750 to 1,000 words. Answering the following questions will help you elicit information you need to write your profile.

1. **History**—What is the history of the person? Does the history affect the present?
2. **Qualities**—What qualities make this person worth writing about? Can you give examples that *show* the qualities?
3. **Values and standards**—What does the subject believe in most strongly? How does this shape his/her actions? Can you give specific examples?
4. **Impact**—How does the subject affect those around him or her? This may include both positives and negatives. Give examples.
5. **Description**—Write a physical description of the person, including any unusual aspects that make the person stand out in a crowd. Describe the setting where you interviewed the person or where the person works or lives.

Secondary Research Sources Expected by Professors

You have been assigned a research paper or project. What does your professor expect? First of all, you need to understand the assignment: What specifically does your professor want you to research? Do you have instructions about what kinds of sources your professor wants? Are restrictions put on what Internet or database sources you can use? Possibly, your instructor has specified that you need to use books, journals, major magazines and newspapers, and certain web-based information. This means that you are to use reputable sources to obtain a balanced, impartial viewpoint about your topic. So, how do you find these sources?

Neither you nor your professor should be surprised that you can find enough material for your research paper through the Internet, even if your professor says you can use only print sources. Your library has full-text databases such as Jstor and Academic Search Complete (EBSCO) that will provide you with PDF images of actual journal pages, not web pages. Moreover, Google and other online libraries have the full-text versions of many book chapters or entire books.

However, in many cases the latest books in a field are not online, so you need to venture into the actual library building to find some of the best sources for your research. This is also true of primary sources such as letters and maps. Moreover, librarians can aid you in finding the research materials you need.

Consider the following secondary research sources:

Books: In these days of easy-to-find resources on the Internet, students may wonder why they should bother with books at all. However, scholarly books treat academic topics with in-depth discussion and careful documentation of evidence. College libraries collect scholarly books that are carefully researched and reviewed by authorities in the book's field. Look for recently published books rather than older books, even if they are on your topic. Academic books or well-researched popular books often have bibliographies or lists of additional references at the end of the book. These lists are useful for two reasons: First, if such lists of books are present, it is a good clue this is a well-researched book, and, second, it gives you a ready list of other possible resources you can consult for your research project.

Scholarly journals: Just having the word "journal" in the title does not mean it is a journal. *Ladies Home Journal,* or *The Wall Street Journal,* for example, are not journals. Your instructor means peer-reviewed journals in which the authors have documented their sources. Peer-reviewed means that articles have been reviewed by experts in the field for reliability and relevance before being published. Your library should have print indexes to journals in which you can look up your topic. You may also be able to find journal articles—sometimes in full text—through the online databases offered by your college library.

Major magazines and newspapers: These publications report the news based on the actual observation of events and interviews with experts and also present informed editorial opinions. Examples are magazines such as *Time* and *Fortune* and newspapers such as *The New York Times,* the *Boston Globe, The Wall Street Journal,* and the *Washington Post.* You can locate full-text articles directly from the online versions of major print magazines and newspapers. Often, these publications charge a fee for articles not published recently. However, you can often find the same articles free through one of your library databases.

Special interest publications: These are periodicals that focus on a specific topic but are written for a wider audience than scholarly journals. Authors of articles base their articles on interviews with experts, recent scholarly books and journals, and other reputable sources. Examples include *Psychology Today* and *Scientific American*.

Government documents: Government documents present a wealth of information for many contemporary events and issues. Your library may be a federal depository, which means that users can locate many federal documents onsite. If so, you can look up government sources in the online library catalog. Government documents are also available through online databases.

Encyclopedias: Encyclopedias can be useful to browse when you are looking for topics. They are also helpful for providing background information such as dates when events occurred. However, most instructors prefer that you do not use encyclopedias as sources in your paper. This is particularly true for Wikipedia, the online encyclopedia that is assembled by volunteers who have specialized knowledge on topics and, thus, has no systematic vetting of the contents. However, Wikipedia entries often include bibliographies which can be useful in pointing you to books, articles, or other websites that can be used as references.

Web pages: The problem with web-based information is that anyone with some knowledge of computers can put up a website on the Internet. Thus, information from websites must be carefully evaluated as to author, publishing organization, etc. One way to deal with this problem is to find web information through librarian-generated indexes and search engines that are designed to screen websites for credibility (see the section titled "Find Internet Information," which appears later in this chapter).

As you use the categories above to find secondary sources for your paper or project, realize that your topic influences your choice of reference materials. If you are writing about a literary topic such as Shakespeare's *Othello*, you will find a number of relevant books and journal articles. If your topic is more contemporary, such as the current status of the country's housing market, you may be able to find some books or journal articles for background information, but you will need to use recent magazine and newspaper articles to find the latest information.

As you examine your sources, remember that gathering the information should help you discover what you think about your topic, not just what others think. This will enable you to create a paper based on *your* ideas and opinions, with source materials supporting your position.

Employ Computerized Library Catalogs

Public Access Catalogs (PACs) or computerized catalogs, accessed through the Internet, have replaced card catalogs. A library computerized catalog provides bibliographical information about the library's collection, including thousands of books, photos, videos, journals, and other items. Generally, catalogs can be accessed by any of the following methods: keyword, subject, author, title, or call number. You may also find books that are available in digital form through the catalog. In addition, on the library home page, you will find links to other information and services such as database searches, interlibrary loans, and course reserves.

Types of Computerized Searches

Conducting a computerized search involves accessing the library's catalog using one of the following search methods:

- ***Keyword***—Unless you know the author or title of a book, keyword is the best type of search because it finds the search word or words anywhere in the bibliographical citation.

    Example: water quality

- ***Title***—Type the exact order of words in the title.

    Example: History of the United Kingdom

- ***Author***—Type the author's name, putting the last name first. You don't need to include a comma.

    Example: Miller Henry J.

- ***Subject***—Type the exact Library of Congress subject heading.

    Example: Spanish language—Grammar, Historical

- ***Call Number***—Type the exact call number.

    Example: B851.P49 2004

If you have a general topic, you probably want to use the keyword search, for subject search actually refers to the exact Library of Congress subject-search designations, and, unless you use the precise search terms specified by that classification system, you may not get the results you want. The use of keywords, however, will lead you to hits on your topic. Then, once you have found one book that is in your topic area, you can examine the screen for Library of Congress subject headings and click on those to browse for more books.

An invaluable resource of any library is the Interlibrary Loan department. Here you can request books your library does not own, as well as journal articles from periodicals not in the library's collection or obtainable through the library's databases. Books and articles are obtained for you by the staff on a minimal or no-fee basis. This is extremely helpful because you can request books you find in bibliographies. However, it generally takes seven to ten days to obtain books through an interlibrary loan, so you need to plan well in advance. To request an item, you simply go to the Interlibrary Loan department in your library or fill out a form on the library's website.

Activity 7.2 **Locate Books on Your Topic**

Using the online card catalog at the library, locate three books about your topic. Write down the titles, authors, publishers, dates of publication, and catalog numbers. Now, go to the stacks and find the books. While you are there, find two other books nearby on the same topic. Check the table of contents and index to see if they contain information you can use.

Utilize Electronic Library Resources

College and university libraries increasingly rely on databases to provide digital versions of articles published in journals, magazines, newspapers, and government documents, as well as other publications and materials. Generally, the databases are available to students and faculty through the Internet via the library home page, though a library card and a password may be required for off-campus access.

Library databases make use of online forms similar to those of a library computerized catalog. Searches are by subject, title, author, and name of publication. Advanced search features are available. Some databases provide the full-text versions of articles published in newspapers, journals, and magazines. Others give publication information only, such as title, author, publication, date of publication, and an abstract of the article. Popular databases include Lexis-Nexis, Academic Search Complete (see figure 7.1), Periodical Archive Online (ProQuest), Project Muse, and JSTOR.

figure 7.1

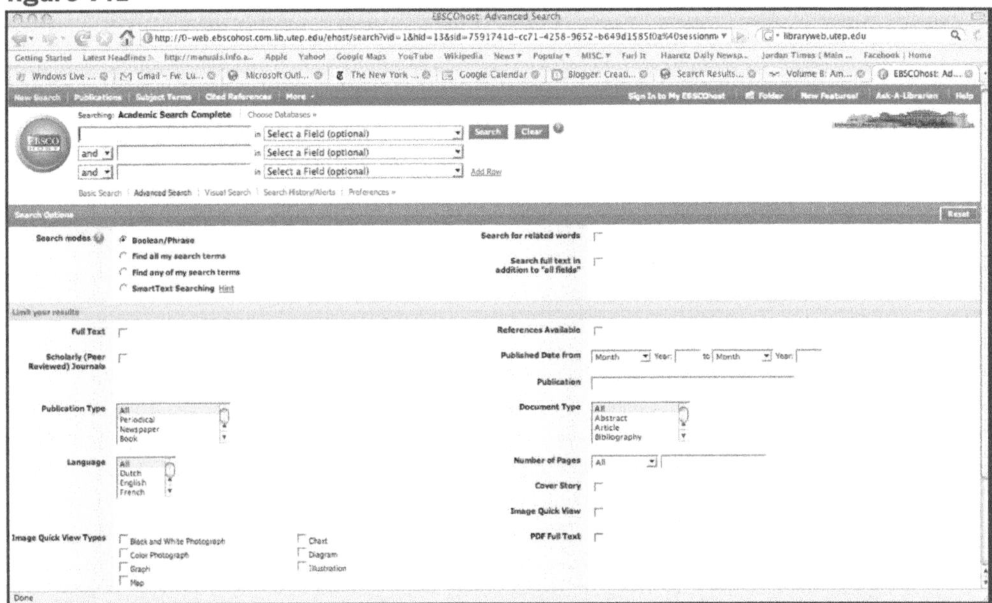

Academic Search Complete is one of EBSCO's popular online databases that can be accessed by students through their library's website. The database indexes full-text articles on a wide variety of topics.

Activity 7.3 Locate Newspaper and Magazine Articles

Go to your library's online databases and choose one that relates to your topic. Then access it and type in your topic. Try using various key words. Jot down titles, authors, and publication information concerning any articles that look interesting. If full-text versions are available, save them to your computer or disk drive or e-mail them to yourself. If not, find out if your library has a hard copy version or microfilm of the articles.

Find Internet Information

The World Wide Web is an incredible resource for research. Through it, you can find full texts of pending legislation, searchable online editions of Shakespeare's plays, environmental impact statements, stock quotes, and much, much more. Finding credible research sources is not always easy. Anyone with an Internet connection and a little knowledge can put up a web page and claim to be an expert on a chosen topic. Therefore, information from the Internet must be scrutinized with even more diligence than print sources. For example, if you enter the word "environment" in one of the keyword search engines, you may receive thousands of "hits," or sites that relate to that topic from all over the world. How do you sift through all of that feedback in order to find information relevant to your topic? It is a problem that has not been completely solved on the Internet.

However, the search engine Google now provides Google Books, http://books.google.com, which offers the full-text versions of millions of books, though usually not the full text of the entire book unless the book is no longer copyrighted. Also, Google Scholar, http://scholar.google.com, provides access to scholarly papers, though if your library has computerized databases (see figure 7.2), it will likely have a more extensive collection available to you. Also, the Directory of Online Open Access Journals, http://www.doaj.org, enables you to search online journals that offer free access.

figure 7.2

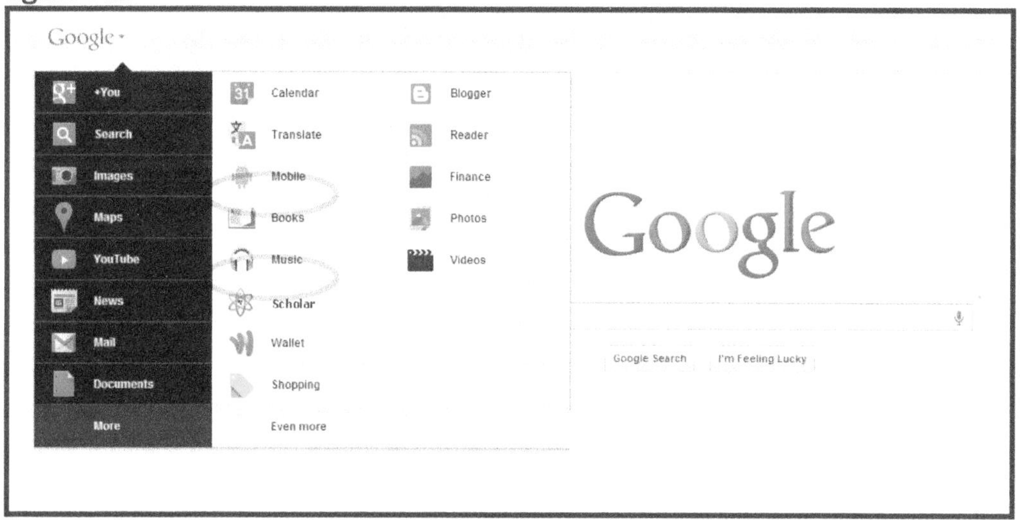

Click on the menu bar on the left side of the Google.com search page to find links to Google Books and Google Scholar. Google Books offers the full-text versions of millions of books, though usually not the full text of the entire book unless the book is no longer copyrighted. Also, Google Scholar, at http://scholar.google.com, provides access to scholarly papers, though not always full text.

One of the best ways for students to find Internet resources is through indexing projects sponsored by major libraries. In the case of each directory/search tool, librarians have personally reviewed and selected websites that are of value to academic researchers, including both students and faculty. These indexing websites may be organized by subject area, in addition to having keyword search engines. Thus, you might quickly locate the most authoritative websites without having to wade through masses of sites looking for the reliable ones. The following websites offer links to a variety of reputable sources:

IPL2: Information You Can Trust, http://www.ipl.org (see figure 7.3)

Infomine, http://infomine.ucr.edu

figure 7.3

IPL2: Information You Can Trust is a public library on the Internet. It offers links to resources by subject, newspapers and magazines, and special collections created by the Internet Public Library.

Government documents also can be found easily through the Internet and are indexed at a variety of sites, including these:

FirstGov, http://www.firstgov.gov

Thomas Legislative Information, http://thomas.loc.gov

Federal Citizen Information Center, http://www.pueblo.gsa.gov/

FedWorld.Gov, http://www.fedworld.gov/

Explore Activity 7.4 Find a Journal Article in Google Scholar

Go to Google Scholar either through Google.com or directly at http://scholar.google.com and search for a journal article on your chosen topic. If the Google link does not offer you full text, then go to the index of electronic journals on your college library website and search for the journal. Likely, your library will offer a database that provides full text for the article. Note: The advantage of this method of finding journal articles is that Google Scholar indexes articles from journals available in many different databases.

Evaluate Sources

Many people tend to believe what they see in print. They may think that if information is in a book or a news magazine, it must be true. If you read critically, however, you know that all sources must be evaluated. With the Internet, perhaps even more than with print texts, it is important to evaluate your sources. Here are some guidelines to consider when evaluating sources.

- **Who is the author?** This question is equally important, whether the source in question is a book, a magazine, or a website. If you have the dust jacket of the book, the back flap will quickly provide you with essential information to screen the author. In the short biographical sketch, usually included along with a photo, you can learn the author's academic credentials and university affiliation, what previous books the author has published, and other qualifications that the publisher thinks qualifies the author to write this particular book. If there is no dust jacket (as is often true with library books), you can try to find information about the author through an Internet search engine or a reference text such as *Contemporary Authors*. A magazine or journal will often provide brief biographical information at the end of the article or on a separate authors' page. If the text is on a website, determining the authorship is more complex, as authors often are not named. In that case, you are forced to rely on the credibility of the entity publishing the website. Many websites have a link called something like "About Us" or "Mission Statement," and that page will give you some idea about the motivations of the entity sponsoring the site. Is it selling something? Is it part of an organization that has a political agenda? These are things to keep in mind when considering the bias of the site's content.

- **For what audience is the text written?** Determining this may require some detective work. In the case of a book, the preface or introduction may give you some clues. With magazines and journals, consider the demographics of the readership. With a website, a little clicking around in the site and a look at the kind of texts, graphics, and advertising used (if any) should tell you what readers the site is designed for.

- **What sources does the author rely upon?** If you are working with an academic text, the sources should be clearly cited in the text by author and page number, footnotes, or endnotes. If it is a more popular book or article, sources are acknowledged less formally; however, a credible author will still make an effort to credit sources. For example, an article might say, "According to the March issue of the *New England Journal of Medicine*. . . . "

- **Does the text have an obvious bias?** Ask yourself if the argument is logical and if sources are mentioned for any statistics or other evidence. Are any opposing viewpoints discussed fairly? Does the author engage in name calling (a clear sign of bias)? Are there obvious holes or contradictions in the argument? For most purposes, you are looking for texts which do not appear to have been written with a biased agenda. However, in some cases, the opposite is true. If you are looking for a political candidate's position on a certain issue, then reading the candidate's book or going to the candidate's website will provide you with a biased viewpoint but one which you can analyze for the purposes of your paper. When dealing with information from sources with an obvious agenda, though, you must be careful not to represent the material as unbiased in your text.

- **What do others think of the text?** For a book, you can look for a review in *Book Review Digest* or *Book Review Index*, two publications you can find in the reference section of the library. Also, *The New York Times* and other newspapers review prominent popular books. Most magazines and newspapers print letters to the editor, which may offer comments on controversial articles. The Scout Report, which can be found at the *Scout Project*, http://scout.wisc.edu, reviews selected websites. If you locate a review of your text, you can cite the review in your research paper to provide additional evidence of the text's credibility.

Activity 7.5 Locate and Evaluate a Source

Locate one source (book, magazine or newspaper article, or website page) which you think would be a credible source for a research paper. For that source, answer the questions in the Evaluate Sources section above.

Activity 7.6 Evaluate a Website

Go to the Internet and look up a website related to a topic you are researching. Answer these questions as fully as you can.

1. Who is the author of this source? Is the author credible on this topic? Why or why not?
2. What does the text focus on? Is it thoughtful and balanced, or does it seem one-sided? What gives you that impression?
3. When was the website last updated?

4. What is the purpose of this site? Is it to provide information? Or is it trying to persuade readers to accept a particular point of view?
5. How professional is the tone, and how well-designed is the site? How carefully has it been edited and proofread? Are there any grammatical and spelling errors that compromise its credibility?
6. What kinds of links does the site provide? Do they add to the website's credibility or detract from it?

Avoid Plagiarism

Plagiarism is defined as follows by the Writing Program Administrators (WPA), a group of English professors who direct college composition programs: "In an instructional setting, plagiarism occurs when a writer deliberately uses someone else's language, ideas, or other original (not common-knowledge) material without acknowledging its source." A keyword here is "deliberately." Instructors, however, may have difficulty distinguishing between accidental and deliberate plagiarism. The burden is upon you as the writer to give credit where credit is due. These are some examples of plagiarism:

- Turning in a paper that was written by someone else as your own. This includes obtaining a paper from an Internet term paper mill.
- Copying a paper or any part of a paper from a source without acknowledging the source in the proper format.
- Paraphrasing materials from a source without documentation.
- Copying materials from a text but treating it as your own, leaving out quotation marks and acknowledgement.

The guidelines provided in table 7.1 can help you identify when it is appropriate to give credit to others in your writing.

table 7.1

Choosing When to Give Credit	
Need to Document	**No Need to Document**
• When you are using or referring to somebody else's words or ideas from a magazine, book, newpaper, song, TV program, movie, web page, computer program, letter, advertisement, or any other medium. • When you use information gained through interviewing another person. • When you copy the exact words or a "unique phrase" from somewhere. • When you reprint any diagrams, illustrations, charts, and pictures. • When you use ideas given to you by others, whether in conversation or through e-mail.	• When you are writing your own experiences, your own observations, your own insights, your own thoughts, or your own conclusions about a subject. • When you are using "common knowledge"—folklore, common-sense observations, or shared information within your field of study or cultural group. • When you are compiling generally accepted facts. • When you are writing up your own experimental results.

The Online Writing Lab (OWL) at Purdue University provides an excellent handout on avoiding plagiarism, including the information about when to give credit to sources in the table above.
See http://owl.english.purdue.edu.

Activity 7.7 Plagiarism Exercise

In this exercise you will intentionally plagiarize a text. Then you will collaborate with a partner to produce a text that paraphrases and cites sources.

1. With a partner, choose a public figure currently in the news. On your own, write a brief bio of the individual you have both chosen, intentionally quoting extensively from one source without using quotation marks or citing the source.
2. Exchange your text with your partner by e-mail. Now, paste into Google or another search engine a sentence or long phrase copied in your partner's text, putting the copied text in quotation marks. Search. Repeat until you are able to identify the source of the text that your partner has intentionally plagiarized. Your partner should follow the same exercise using your text.
3. Finally, back in class, work with your partner to compose a brief bio of the individual that paraphrases these texts (and others, if needed).

4. Turn in the final version, along with the plagiarized versions. Describe your experience in trying to locate the source of your partner's plagiarized text.

Reading 7.2

Anatomy of a Fake Quotation

by Megan McArdle

In this article, originally published in *The Atlantic,* Megan McArdle tells the story of how a fake Martin Luther King, Jr. quote was created and posted on the Internet.

Yesterday, I saw a quote from Martin Luther King Jr. fly across my Twitter feed: "I mourn the loss of thousands of precious lives, but I will not rejoice in the death of one, not even an enemy."—Martin Luther King, Jr. I was about to retweet it, but I hesitated. It didn't sound right. After some Googling, I determined that it was probably fake, which I blogged about last night.

Here's the story of how that quote was created.

It turns out I was far too uncharitable in my search for a motive behind the fake quote. I assumed that someone had made it up on purpose. I was wrong.

Had I seen the quote on Facebook, rather than Twitter, I might have guessed at the truth. On the other hand, had I seen it on Facebook, I might not have realized it was fake, because it was appended to a long string of genuine speech from MLK Jr. Here's the quote as most people on Facebook saw it:

> I will mourn the loss of thousands of precious lives, but I will not rejoice in the death of one, not even an enemy. Returning hate for hate multiplies hate, adding deeper darkness to a night already devoid of stars. Darkness cannot drive out darkness; only light can do that. Hate cannot drive out hate, only love can do that.

Everything except the first sentence is found in King's book, *Strength to Love*, and seems to have been said originally in a 1957 sermon he gave on loving your enemies. Unlike the first quotation, it does sound like King, and it was easy to assume that the whole thing came from him.

So how did they get mixed together?

Thanks to Jessica Dovey, a Facebook user, that's how. And contrary to my initial assumption, it wasn't malicious. Ms. Dovey, a 24-year-old Penn State graduate who now teaches English to middle schoolers in Kobe, Japan, posted a very timely and moving thought on her Facebook status, and then followed it up with the Martin Luther King, Jr., quote.

> I will mourn the loss of thousands of precious lives, but I will not rejoice in the death of one, not even an enemy. "Returning hate for hate multiplies hate, adding deeper darkness to a night already devoid of stars. Darkness cannot drive out darkness; only light can do that. Hate cannot drive out hate, only love can do that." MLK Jr.

At some point, someone cut and pasted the quote, and—for reasons that I, appropriately chastened, will not speculate on—stripped out the quotation marks. Eventually, the mangled quotation somehow came to the attention of Penn Jillette, of Penn and Teller fame. He tweeted it to his 1.6 million Facebook followers, and the rest was Internet history. Twenty-four hours later, the quote brought back over 9,000 hits on Google.

The quote also went viral on Twitter, and since the 140-character limit precluded quoting the whole thing, people stripped it down to the most timely and appropriate part: the fake quote. That's where I saw it.

The speed of dissemination is breathtaking: mangled to meme in less than two days. Also remarkable is how defensive people got about the quote—though admirably, not Penn Jillette, who posted an update as soon as it was called to his attention. The thread for my post now has over 600 comments, and by my rough estimate, at least a third of them are people posting that I need to print a retraction, because of the nonfake part of the quotation. But I didn't quote that part; I was only interested in the too-timely bit I'd seen twittered.

Even more bizarrely, several of these readers, who clearly hadn't read too closely, started claiming that I had retroactively edited the post to make them look like idiots, even going so far as to scrub all the versions in RSS readers so that they, too, showed that I was talking about the truncated version. Even if you think I am the sort of low scoundrel who would do such a thing, this seems like a lot of work for not much reward. I'm not sure whether it's even possible to completely scrub an RSS feed, but even if it were, I'd have had to notify my bosses, who tend to frown on retroactive editing.

Meanwhile, several other people began confabulating a provenance for it. *Obviously*, he was talking about Vietnam, and what sort of moral midget couldn't understand that? This even though the latest citation for the true part of the quote was a book published in 1967, which would have been written earlier than that, when U.S. casualties in Vietnam were still relatively low. Moreover, the ambiguity with which the antiwar movement viewed the North Vietnamese makes "enemy" a hard fit.

It is, of course, not strange that people might look for possible confirming facts. What's strange is that they were sure enough of themselves to make fun of anyone who disagreed. Yet several other people on the comment thread had linked to a version of the quotation from 1957. I am second to no one in my admiration for Dr. King. But I do not think that he prefigured Vietnam by seven years.

Which only illustrates why fake quotes are so widely dispersed. Though one commenter accused me of trying to make people feel stupid for having propagated the quote, that was hardly my intention—we've all probably repeated more fake quotations than real ones. Fake quotations are pithier, more dramatic, more on point, than the things people usually say in real life. It's not surprising that they are often the survivors of the evolutionary battle for mindshare. One person actually posted a passage which integrated the fake quotation into the larger section of the book from which the original MLK words were drawn.

We become invested in these quotes because they say something important about us—and they let us feel that those emotions were shared by great figures in history. We naturally search for reasons that they could have said it—that they could have felt like us—rather than looking for reasons to disbelieve. If we'd put the same moving words in Hitler's mouth, everyone would have been a lot more skeptical. But while this might be a lesson about the need to be skeptical, I don't think there's anything stupid about wanting to be more like Dr. King.

Ms. Dovey's status now reads: "has apparently gone back in time and put her words into one of MLK's sermons. I'm somewhere between nervous and embarrassed and honored . . . I really hope I haven't said anything he wouldn't agree with . . . Only what I feel in my heart."

A lot of us were feeling the same thing—and I think it's clear from his writings that MLK would have too. There's no reason to be embarrassed about that.

Activity 7.8 Discuss "Anatomy of a Fake Quotation"

1. How was the fake quotation created? How did it spread on the Internet?
2. Note the speed and the reach of the fake quote. What does Megan McArdle suggest the story of this fake quote says about why fake quotes can become so widely disbursed?
3. What is your reaction to this story of the fake quotation?

Activity 7.9 Prepare an Annotated Bibliography

An annotated bibliography is a list of bibliographical citations with a few sentences or a paragraph for each entry that offers explanatory information or critical commentary about the source. Many instructors request an annotated bibliography as a step in writing a research paper because it is an indication of the scope and direction of your research.

1. Select 10 quality sources about your topic. These should be, as your instructor directs, a mix of books, scholarly journal and magazine articles, government documents, and selected texts from websites.
2. Skim the text of each source and read portions more closely that seem relevant to your topic.
3. Write a bibliographical citation for each source in MLA style. (See the appendix that follows this chapter for MLA style samples.)
4. Write a few sentences for each source in which you do the following:
   (a) Summarize the content and purpose of the source.
   (b) Explain how you might use the source in your research paper.

Sample Annotated Bibliography on the Federal Aviation Administration User Fees

Horne, T. A. (2007, February). User Fee Debate. *AOPA Pilot Magazine*, *50*, 27.

The author of this article is an experienced, commercial rated pilot that has flown for over 30 years. He also sits on the Aircraft Owners and Pilots Association (AOPA) board. This article explains what the Federal Aviation

Administration (FAA) has proposed and what it means to pilots. Congress is cutting the budget for the FAA and in turn wants to impose fees for anyone who flies into a controlled airspace. This would have a very tragic effect on general aviation. This is huge because if anyone is flying anywhere around a decent-sized city, they are going to fly through these airspaces. Also, the FAA wants to charge for approaches into airports and landing on airport runways. This is bad because all of these charges would add up to more than $200. This would discourage people from flying, making them sell their aircraft. This would slowly dissolve the general aviation industry. I can use this article to explain what is going on and why the government wants to charge these fees.

Boyer, P. (Director) (2007, October 6). AOPA's Reasonable Analysis of User Fee Issues at AOPA Expo. *AOPA Expo 2007*. Lecture conducted from AOPA, Hartford, CT.

This lecture was given by the president of AOPA, Phil Boyer. He spoke of the fees that the FAA is trying to impose and what they would mean for general aviation pilots. He explains that the fees that the FAA wants are directed toward general aviation and not toward the airlines. He also gave some examples of what would be better for everyone, if the FAA really is in a crisis. This source is important because it provides an explanation and breakdown of these user fees and gives some examples of what could be put in place of these proposed fees.

Fact Sheet—Impact of Administration's Financing Proposal on General Aviation. (2007, April 23). *FAA: Home*. Retrieved March 2, 2011, from http://www.faa.gov/news/fact_sheets/news_story.cfm?newsid=8747.

This website is the official FAA website that has all of its information. This one fact sheet lists all the facts and myths related to this issue. It goes over what the FAA wants to put into place and where and when it will happen. It brings up all of the more important issues regarding the topic, but leaves some out as well. For example, nowhere in the sheet does it say anything about controlled airspace fees, which is one of the biggest fees it would implement. It does mention another, which is the fuel tax hike. This would weaken general aviation because a lot of pilots cannot afford higher fuel prices. This will be important to have a government agency's point of view on the topic.

AOPA Online: What's the FAA's user fee proposal? (2006, November 30). *AOPA Online: Aircraft Owners and Pilots Association.* Retrieved March 2, 2011, from http://www.aopa.org/whatsnew/newsitems/2006/061130userfees.html.

This website is the official website for AOPA, which is a foundation that protects flying and everything related to aviation. This article goes over what the user fees would be, but it goes into greater detail about what the fuel prices would be after the legislation is put into place. Fuel is needed for all flights and is already expensive. What the government wants to do in addition to implementing user fees is to put more tax on fuel. This would make it much harder for the average pilot to afford flying his/her aircraft. This is beneficial to the argument because it focuses on one of the major fees that the FAA would implement: the fuel hikes.

User Fees—NBAA Calls Proposed FAA Budget a 'Sweetheart Deal' For the Airlines. (2006, November 30). *California Pilots Association.* Retrieved March 2, 2011, from http://www.calpilots.org/index.php?option=com_content&view=article&id=1141&catid=45:pre-2008-archived-articles&Itemid=81.

Cal Pilots is an organization similar to the AOPA, but it has a defined area. It is also very concerned with this issue. The article is from the NBAA which is the National Business Aviation Association. The article explains that the airline industry is getting it easy with this proposal. It says that the government is trying to move fees from the airlines to general aviation. The problem with this is that the airline industry can handle it, general aviation cannot. General aviation includes every aspect of aviation excluding the airlines and the military. The majority of general aviation pilots are your everyday, fly-for-fun kinds of people. These people cannot afford all the fees that would be put into place. This would destroy the industry. This is important because it ties the airline industry into the argument.

Network, A. (2009, October 12). Aero-TV: AirVenture Meet the Boss—Randy Babbitt Tackles User Fees. Retrieved from http://www.youtube.com/watch?v=J14ut3O_j3M.

This video is from AirVenture, which is a fly-in expo. Randy Babbitt is one of the head officials for the FAA and he explains that the FAA needs money to meet the needs of the industry. He says that the planes now are more efficient, making them use less fuel which means that the fuel tax in effect now is less effective. He goes on to explain that the FAA needs to make up this deficit, but it does not know exactly where it is going to come from.

This is important because it is a government official who is explaining the situation the FAA is in and what he thinks will happen.

Wald, M. L. (2006, March 7). F.A.A. Seeks New Source of Revenue in User Fees. *The New York Times*. Retrieved March 2, 2011, from http://query.nytimes.com/gst/fullpage.html?res=9507E0D91531F93 4A35750.

Matthew L. Wald is a journalist for *The New York Times*. In the article, he interviews some very influential people in the aviation industry. Another important fact about him is that he is also a general aviation pilot. This article explains that because of the drop of airline tickets that the FAA needs to find new ways to make money because the tax implemented on tickets is not getting the job done. It says that the FAA is going to tax the users of the air traffic control system. This article is important because it gives specific numbers on how much the FAA is in debt and what the budget proposal is.

Activity 7.10 Compare and Contrast Media

Your instructor will select an article on a topic or event that is currently in the news. Find another article on the same subject either from the same news outlet or another major news source (*The New York Times, The Wall Street Journal, CNN, Time*, etc.). Compare and contrast how the reporting of the event is similar or different in the two texts. Note: You are not to write a report on the content of the articles themselves; instead, identify the author's perspective in each text and how it influences how the news is portrayed to readers.

Look for opinions, adjectives with positive or negative connotations, facts or evidence presented, the tone of the headline, and the text itself. Also consider the target audience.

Organize your observations in a one- to two-page report with a clear thesis that presents your evaluation of the two texts.

Activity 7.11 Write on Your Blog

In your blog, write a summary and a response to a source you might use to research your topic. Is it useful for your research? Why or why not?

Activity 7.12 Write in Your Commonplace Book

Copy a quote from a source that you think makes a critical point about the argument paper you are writing. Then comment about the quote—what does it mean and why is it important?

A
APPENDIX
CITING SOURCES

Praxis in Action

How I Cite by Craig Wynne

Make no mistake about it: Doing the citations can be an annoying part of the writing process. I don't know of anyone who enjoys doing citations because it is not easy to get the information in the right order, as well as put periods and commas where they are required; but citations are necessary, so your instructor knows from where you obtained your sources. If your instructor doesn't specify a format, ask if you should use MLA or APA. Also, if you are lucky enough to have an instructor who will take a look at a rough draft of your Works Cited page or bibliography, be sure to take advantage of that opportunity!

I find it can be stressful trying to put together citations at the end of a paper, as it can take a few hours trying to remember where you got your sources. I prefer to do them as I write, as it actually saves time to do that. Whenever I insert a quote or a paraphrase, I cite it immediately after I've written it. I do the internal citation, and I add the reference to my Works Cited page. I find it helps me to complete this part of the process, and it saves me time at the end having to go back through sources.

I'm also careful about using citation generators such as EasyBib and RefWorks. Many students find they can be effective time-savers, but I don't recommend relying on them entirely. Generators do a good job in setting up the order of a citation, but citations have to look a certain way, and the generators don't always get the periods and the capitals in the right places. They also won't cite inside the text. Personally, I find it easier and faster just to do the citations myself without using a citation generator. If you decide to try out EasyBib, RefWorks, or another citation generator, remember to allow yourself enough time to double-check all your citations against a handbook or handout that gives you the correct formats.

To save time and avoid undue stress, Craig Wynne prepares citations as he writes.

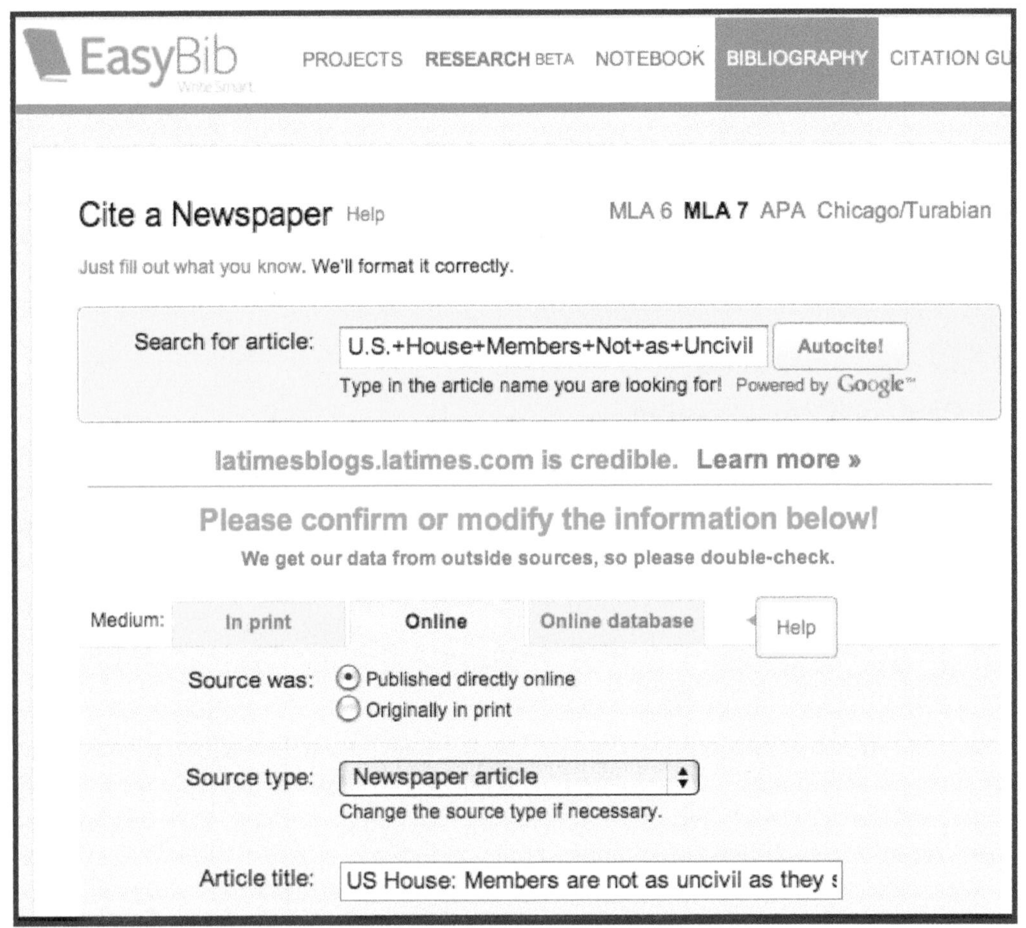

EasyBib is one of the citation generators available on the Internet through a keyword search. Most offer a free version, with upgraded features for a subscription fee. Note that EasyBib encourages users to double-check their entries both for content and form. Citation generators assist with documentation format, but they cannot eliminate errors.

Evolving Formats of Document Citation

The widespread use of the Internet for research is changing the way sources are cited in documents. This is certainly true of electronic sources because of the ephemeral nature of web pages. Although documents may look like print sources (often with title, author, and publication information), they also share a characteristic of live performances in that you can access them after they have occurred only if you can find a recorded version. Once web pages are removed from a website, you cannot view them unless they have been archived. Also, web pages can be updated or changed, while retaining the same appearance, which makes systematic documentation difficult.

In the past, Modern Language Association (MLA) style recommended including the URL (web address) of web page documents in the Works Cited list. However, more recently MLA has taken the position that including that information has limited value because URLs are prone to change and are cumbersome in any case. The current recommendation is that students include URLs only when the material would otherwise be difficult to locate or if the instructor requires it. If you do include a URL, enclose it with an angle bracket and follow with a period. For example, the web page for *The New York Times* would be <http://nytimes.com>.

APA style suggests including the elements of a citation in the same order as you would for a print source, adding information about electronic retrieval after the standard information. However, APA also recognizes that information such as author, publication date, publisher, or even title may be missing in an electronic source. APA suggests giving the DOI (Digital Object Identifier) a unique alphanumeric string that is a persistent link, whenever possible. If it is not available, APA recommends giving the URL of the item being cited.

Interestingly, the prevalence of Internet sources is changing the way print sources are cited. MLA style recommends adding the word "print" after printed source citation information, as you would add "web" after a source accessed on the Internet.

When You Have a Choice of Electronic Source Format, Choose a PDF

When searching for articles in online databases or web pages, you may be offered a choice of formats: HTML or PDF. If you have that choice, select the PDF because it will have page numbers. Essentially, a PDF document reproduces print documents exactly, so that reading one is just like reading the original article except that it is not surrounded by the other content of the original publication.

If you are utilizing electronic documents as sources and they are not PDFs, you may be missing several of the usual elements of document citation, such as author name, publisher or sponsoring organization, page numbers, and even a title. In this case, give as much information about these traditional elements of citation as you can, and review the examples that follow for help with format. As an easy rule of thumb, though, keep this in mind: The more of the traditional elements used to classify and place a document within the scholarly world that are missing, the less likely the text is to be credible and reliable. If readers cannot tell where the information originated, how are they to trust it?

Note that MLA and APA both specify that documents should be double-spaced. The following examples are single-spaced to save space.

MLA Style

For MLA style, you may refer to the *MLA Handbook for Writers of Research Papers* and the MLA website, http://www.mla.org. The Purdue Owl, http://owl.purdue.english.edu, is also an excellent reference.

A paper written in MLA style should be double-spaced, with margins set at one inch on all sides. Choose a standard typeface such as Times Roman in 12 pt. type.

Beginning on the first page, generate a heading on the upper right-hand side of the page that gives the page number.

Do not create a cover page unless your instructor specifies one. Instead, on the upper left-hand side of the first page, give your name, your instructor's name, the course, and the date. These items should all be flush left, double-spaced, and set on separate lines.

Double-space again and center the title. Follow the title with another double-space and indent the first line of text. Indent each paragraph.

Bibliographical Documentation

In MLA style, this is called either the Works Cited page or an Annotated Bibliography. The title, either Works Cited or Annotated Bibliography, should appear centered on the top margin of the last page of a researched essay. The Works Cited page should be double-spaced with no extra line spacing between entries. The first line of each entry begins at the margin, and all subsequent lines of a particular entry are indented 5 spaces on the left margin. All entries should be in alphabetical order. The Annotated Bibliography is formatted like the Works Cited page with the addition of an annotation or description of the source in a paragraph following the citation. The following entries are typical citations prepared according to MLA style.

Examples are offered for both print, online, and database versions, when applicable.

Book

Egan, Jennifer. *A Visit from the Goon Squad.* New York: Alfred A. Knopf, 2010. Print.

Book with Two Authors

Friedman, Thomas L. and Michael Mandelbaum. *That Used to Be Us: How America Fell behind in the World It Invented and How We Can Come Back.* New York: Farrar, Straus and Giroux, 2011. Print.

Two or More Selections from the Same Print Collection or Anthology

Note: To avoid repetition on the list of works cited, cite an anthology or reader as a separate entry. Then cross-reference entries to the anthology as in the example below.

Burns, Gary. "Marilyn Manson and the Apt Pupils of Littleton." Petracca and Sorapure 284–90. Print.

Fox, Roy. "Salespeak." Petracca and Sorapure 56–72. Print.

Petracca, Michael and Madeleine Sorapure, eds. *Common Culture: Reading and Writing About American Popular Culture.* 5th ed. Upper Saddle River: Pearson, 2007. Print.

Note: Alphabetize each entry among other entries on the Works Cited page. Do not group the entries from the anthology together unless they fall next to one another alphabetically. Also, remember that you will have no parenthetical citation referencing the editors Petracca and Sorapure. You should cite Burns and Fox in the parenthetical citations in your paper.

Book with Multiple Editors

Mennuti, Rosemary B., Arthur Freeman, and Ray W. Christner, eds. *Cognitive-Behavioral Interventions: A Handbook for Practice.* New York: Routledge, 2006. Print.

Online Edition of Book or Novel

James, Henry. *The American.* 1877. Fiction: *The Eserver Collection.* Web. 15 June 2008.

(This book was published before 1900, so the name and city of the publisher are not needed. For more recent books, give the print information first, then the information about web publication.)

Macfie, A. L. *Orientalism: a Reader.* New York: New York UP, 2000. *Google Books.* Web. 26 Sept. 2011.

Scholarly Article in Print Journal

Thompson, Jason. "Magic for a People Trained in Pragmatism: Kenneth Burke, and the Early 9/11 Oratory of George W. Bush." *Rhetoric Review* 30.4 (2011): 350–71. Print.

Scholarly Article Found in Online Database

Angel, R. J. "Immigrants and Welfare: The Impact of Welfare Reform on America's Newcomers." *Contemporary Sociology: A Journal of Reviews* 39.5 (2010): 568–69. Academic Search Complete. Web. 10 September 2011.

Scholarly Article from Journal Published Online

Gustafsson, Amanda. "Beware the Invisible." *Papers from the Institute of Archeology* 20 (2010): n. pag. Web. 29 Sept. 2011.

Note: MLA specifies including page numbers for scholarly publications, so if the online journal does not provide page numbers, include n. pag. (no page).

Book Review

Schneider, Robert J. Rev. of *Modern Physics and Ancient Faith*, by Stephen M. Barr. *Anglican Theological Review* 86 (2004): 506–07. Print.

Book Review Published Online

Garner, Dwight. "An Unearthed Treasure That Changed Things." Rev. of *The Swerve: How the World Became Modern. The New York Times*, 27 Sept. 2011. Web. 28 Sept. 2011.

An Editorial

Wolfe, Gregory. "The Operation of Grace." Editorial. *Image: A Journal of the Arts and Religion* 70 (Summer 2011): 3–4 Print.

An Editorial Published Online

"U.S. House: Members Are Not as Uncivil as They Seem." Editorial. *Nation Now. Los Angeles Times*, 28 Sept. 2011. Web. 29 Sept. 2011.

Note: This editorial was published in a blog called *Nation Now* that is published by the *Los Angeles Times.*

Magazine Article

Perry, Alex. "Epidemic on the Run." *Time* 26 Sept. 2011: 46–49. Print.

Magazine Article from Online Database

Neuwirth, Robert. "Global Bazaar: Shantytowns, Favelas and Jhopadpattis Turn Out to Be Places of Surprising Innovation." *Scientific American* Sept. 2011: 56–63. *Academic Search Complete.* Web. 29 Sept. 2011.

Online Magazine Article

Leonard, Andrew. "Inside the Shadow Economy: The Growing Underwater Bazaar." *Salon.* Salon Media Group, 29 September 2011. Web. 29 September 2011.

Note: The title of the magazine is followed by the publisher or sponsor of the site, a comma, and the date of publication. MLA uses this format because it does not consider online-only magazines to be periodicals. If no publisher is given, add n.p., and if no date is given, add n.d.

Interview

"Samantha Stosur, U.S. Open Champion." Interview by Cassandra Murnieks. *Time.* Time Inc., 23 Sept. 2011. Web. 29 Sept. 2011.

Online Speech

King, Jr., Martin Luther. "I Have a Dream." Speech. March on Washington for Jobs and Freedom. Lincoln Memorial, Washington, D.C. 28 Aug. 1963. *Americanrhetoric.com*. Michael E. Eidenmuller. n.d. Web. 29 Sept. 2011.

Note: The citation includes n.d. (no date) because the date when the speech was posted on the site is not given.

Page on a Website

Coe, Jennifer. "How to Refinish a Dresser." *How To*. SheKnows LLC, 3 Aug. 2011. Web. 29 Sept. 2011.

Note: The blog *How To* lists its publisher as SheKnows LLC. If the publisher were not given, then you would use n.p. (no publisher).

Image from a Website

Gogh, Vincent Van. *Cypresses*. 1889. Oil on canvas. *The Metropolitan Museum of Art*, New York. The Metropolitan Museum of Art. Web. 29 Sept. 2011.

Blog Posting

"Respect Your Audience." Web log post. *Writer's Block*. NIVA Inc., 2009. Web. 15 Sept. 2011.

Note: The blog does not list an author for the posting, so the citation begins with the title.

Government Document

"El Chamizal Dispute: Compliance with Convention of the Chamizal." 1964. *U.S. Senate Hearing*. Cleofas Calleros Papers. University of Texas at El Paso Library Special Collections. 33–9. Print.

Government Document Online

Travis, William Barret. "Letter from the Alamo, 1836." Texas State Library & Archives Commission. Web. 15 Apr. 2011.

Government Document from Online Database

"United Nations Resolutions on Operation Desert Storm." Aug–Nov 1990. Essential Documents in American History: 1492–Present. 1–17 Academic Search Premier. Web. 8 May 2011.

A Film on DVD

The Lord of the Rings: The Return of the King. Dir. Peter Jackson. New Line, 2003. DVD-ROM.

Television Program

Martin, David. "The Pentagon's Ray Gun." *60 Minutes.* CBS. New York, New York, 2 Mar. 2008. Television.

MLA Parenthetical or (In-Text) Documentation

Parenthetical documentation refers to the process of citing sources within the text. Citing sources within the text is necessary for students to indicate when they are using the words, thoughts, or ideas that are not their own and borrowed from an outside source. Whether students use a direct quote, a paraphrase, or a summary of the information, they must properly provide credit to the original author(s) of that source. Using appropriate sources for support and documenting these sources accurately adds to the credibility and value of a student's essay. The following examples provide a guideline to proper parenthetical documentation.

Direct Quote (three lines or less)

"Scientists estimate that the rangewide population of the San Joaquin kit fox prior to 1930 was 8,000 . . . " (Conover 44).

Direct Quote (more than three lines)

Conover's 2001 study of the San Joaquin kit fox found the following:

> For the most part, in the "real" world, kit foxes escape their predators and the high temperatures of their desert environment by spending the day underground in a den. In Bakersfield, they follow suit. Kit foxes move every couple of weeks to a new den.

> Moving to different dens may be one reason why they have persisted; the constantly changing abodes provided new places to hide. (199)
>
> **Note**: For a direct quote that is more than three lines, the passage should be indented 10 spaces and set as a block, as shown here.

Direct Quote When the Author Is Named in the Text

Hildebrand states that "generals of Alexander the Great brought news to Europe of vegetable wool which grew in tufts of trees in India" (144).

Information from Printed Source (but not a direct quote)

It is common to see an Osprey make its nest on an electric power pole (Askew 34).

Electronic Sources

Many electronic sources are not numbered with pages unless they are presented in a PDF file. If paragraphs are numbered, use numbers following the abbreviation, par. Most often the source will not have page, paragraph, section, or screen numbers. In this case, include no numbers in the parentheses. Instead, include the words that come first in the bibliographic citation.

(Coe, Jennifer. "How To")

APA Style

For APA style, you will want to refer to the *Publication Manual of the American Psychological Association* and the website provided by the American Psychological Association, http://www.apastyle.org, which offers free tutorials for APA style. The Purdue Owl also offers excellent information at http://owl.english.purdue.edu.

APA specifies that your essay should be typed in 12 pt. Times Roman type and double-spaced, with one-inch margins. In addition, APA style specifies the following general rules for formatting a paper or essay:

- Running heads—Create running heads for your page numbers, flush left, beginning on the title page. Also, on the title page, you should have a running head that reads like this:

  Running head: Title of Your Paper

  with the title actually being your paper title. On succeeding pages, the flush left header should include only the title of your paper, not the words "Running Head."

- Title page—In addition to the running heads, your title page will contain the title of the paper (one- or two-line title), followed by your name on the second line, and then the name of your college on the third line, all centered.

- Unless your instructor specifies otherwise, the second page of your paper is a 150- to 200-word abstract that summarizes the major aspects of your paper.

- Begin your essay on the third page, after the running head, which is the title of your paper and the centered title. Indent each paragraph and double-space.

- At the end of your paper, include your References, which lists your sources according to APA citation style.

Bibliographical Documentation

In APA style, this is called either the References or the Annotated Bibliography. The title, either References or Annotated Bibliography, should appear centered on the top margin of the last page of a researched essay. The References or Annotated Bibliography page should be double-spaced with no extra line spacing between entries. The first line of each entry begins at the margin, and all subsequent lines of a particular entry are indented on the left margin 5 spaces for a References Page. All entries should be in alphabetical order. The Annotated Bibliography is formatted like the References page with the addition of an annotation or description of the source in a paragraph following each citation.

> **Note**: APA suggests that when you are citing a source from the web or an online database you should give the DOI (Digital Object Identifier) of the source in the References List. If the DOI is not available, you can give the URL (web address) for the

text. APA does not require that you give the date you access a source on the Internet unless you have reason to believe that the text may change or disappear from the Internet. Also note that if you cite an entire website, simply include the website address in parentheses in the text with no entry in the References page. The following entries are typical citations for APA style. Examples are offered for both print, online, and database versions, when applicable.

Book

Egan, J. (2010). *A visit from the Goon Squad.* New York: Alfred A. Knopf.

Book with Two Authors

Friedman, T. L., & Mandelbaum, M. (2011). *That used to be us: how America fell behind in the world it invented and how we can come back.* New York: Farrar, Straus & Giroux.

Book with Multiple Editors

Mennuti, R.B., Freeman, A., & Christner, R.W. (Eds.). (2006). *Cognitive-behavioral interventions in educational settings: A handbook for practice.* New York: Routledge.

Book Online Edition

James, H. (1960). The American. Retrieved from http://eserver.org/fiction /novel.html

(If the book has a DOI, then give that instead of the URL).

Online Edition of Book

Macfie, A. L. (2000). *Orientalism: a reader.* New York: New York University Press. Retrieved September 26, 2011, from Google Books.

Scholarly Article in Print Journal

Thompson, J. (2011). Magic for a people trained in pragmatism: Kenneth Burke, and the early 9/11 Oratory of George W. Bush. *Rhetoric Review, 30* (4), 350–371.

Scholarly Article Found in Online Database

Angel, R. J. (2010). Immigrants and welfare: the impact of welfare reform on America's newcomers. *Contemporary Sociology: A Journal of Reviews*, 39(5), 568–569.

> **Note:** APA does not require that you list the database where you obtained an article unless the article would be difficult to locate. Instead, use the citation format you would if it were a print source.

Scholarly Article from Journal Published Online

Gustafsson, A. (2010). Beware the invisible. *Papers from the Institute of Archeology*, 20. Retrieved September 29, 2011, doi:10.5334/pia.343.

> **Note**: This citation includes a doi (digital object identifier), which provides a permanent way to locate an article, even if databases or websites change.

Book Review

Schneider, R. J. (2004). [Review of the book *Modern physics and ancient faith]. Anglican Theological Review, 86*, 506–07.

Book Review Published Online

Garner, D. (2011, September 27). An unearthed treasure that changed things [Review of *The Swerve: How the world became modern*]. *The New York Times.*

An Editorial

Wolfe, G. (2011). The operation of grace [Editorial]. *Image: A Journal of the Arts and Religion*, 70, 3–4.

An Editorial Published Online

U.S. House: Members are not as uncivil as they seem [Editorial]. (2011, September 28). *Nation Now*. Retrieved September 29, 2011, from http://latimesblogs.latimes.com/nationnow/2011/09/us-house-more-civil-than-the-mid-90s-but-trouble-could-lay-ahead-.html.

Note: This editorial was published in a blog called *Nation Now* that is published by the *Los Angeles Times.*

Magazine Article

Perry, A. (2011, September 26). Epidemic on the run. *Time*, 46–49.

Magazine Article from Online Database

Neuwirth, R. (2011, September). Global bazaar: Shantytowns, favelas and jhopadpattis turn out to be places of surprising innovation. *Scientific American*, 56–63.

Note: APA does not require you to cite the database where you obtained the article unless you think the article would be difficult to find.

Online Magazine Article

Leonard, A. (2011, September 29). A growing underworld bazaar. *Salon.* Retrieved September 29, 2011, from http://www.salon.com/news/inside_the_shadow_economy/?story=/politics/feature/2011/09/29/shadowintro.

Interview

Samantha Stosur, U.S. Open Champion [Interview by C. Murnieks]. (2011, September 23). In *Time.* Retrieved September 29, 2011, from http://www.time.com/time/arts/article/0,8599,2094349,00.html.

Online Speech

King, Jr., M. L. (1963, August 28). *I have a dream.* Speech presented at March on Washington for Jobs and Freedom at the Lincoln Memorial, Washington, D.C. Retrieved September 29, 2011.

Page on a Website

Coe, J. (2011, August 3). How to refinish a dresser. *How To.* Retrieved September 29, 2011.

Image from a Website

Van Gogh, V. (1889). *Cypresses* [Painting found in The Metropolitan Museum of Art, New York]. Retrieved September 29, 2011.

Blog Posting

Respect your audience [Web log post]. (2009). Retrieved September 15, 2011, from http://www.writersblock.ca/tips/monthtip/tipjan98.htm.

Government Document

El Chamizal dispute: Compliance with convention of the Chamizal. (1964). *U.S. Senate Hearing.* Cleofas Calleros Papers. University of Texas at El Paso Library Special Collections (#33–9).

Government Document Online

Travis, W. B. (2005). Letter from the Alamo, 1836. Retrieved from Texas State Library & Archives Commission, http//www.tslstate.tx.us/treasures/republic/Alamo/travis01.gov.

A Film or DVD

Coen, E. & Coen, J. (Producers and directors). (2007). *No country for old men* [Motion picture]. United States: Paramount Vantage.

Television Program

Martin, D. (Reporter). (2008, March 2). The Pentagon's ray gun [Television series episode]. In M. Walsh (Producer) *60 Minutes*. New York, New York: CBS.

APA Parenthetical or (In-Text) Documentation

Direct Quote (three lines or less)

"Scientists estimate that the rangewide population of the San Joaquin kit fox prior to 1930 was 8,000 . . . " (Conover, 2001, p. 44).

Direct Quote (more than three lines)

Conover's 2001 study of the San Joaquin kit fox found the following:

> For the most part, in the "real" world kit foxes escape their predators and the high temperatures of their desert environment by spending the day underground in a den. In Bakersfield, they follow suit. Kit foxes move every couple of weeks to a new den. Moving to different dens may be one reason why they have persisted; the constantly changing abodes provided new places to hide. (p. 199)
>
> **Note**: For a direct quote that exceeds three lines, indent the passage 5 spaces and set as a block, as shown here.

Direct Quote When the Author Is Named in the Text

Hildebrand (2004) stated that "generals of Alexander the Great brought news to Europe of vegetable wool which grew in tufts of trees in India" (p. 144).

Information from Printed Source (but not a direct quote)

It is common to see an Osprey make its nest on an electric power pole (Askew, year, p. 34).

Naming the Author of a Reference in Your Text, but Not Using a Direct Quote

Thompson (2002) maintained that . . .

In 2002, Thompson discovered . . .

Electronic or Other Sources Missing Author, Date, or Page Numbers

If your source provides section notations or paragraph numbers, indicate those. Use the paragraph ¶ symbol or the abbreviation para. and number.

(Bussell, 2000, ¶ 9)

If you include a quote from a text that has neither page numbers nor paragraph or section numbers, then simply give the author and the date:

(Bussell, 2000).

If there is no author, as in an editorial, then give part of the name of the text and the date:

("Respect your audience," 2009).

If there is no date, then use n.d. If you have no date, no page number, and no author, your in-text citation will look as follows:

("The future of space," n.d.)

Works Cited

"20 Years Later, San Ysidro McDonald's Massacre Remembered." Web log post. *North County Times*. Lee Enterprises Inc., 2004. Web. 17 July 2004.

"A $300 Idea that Is Priceless." *The Economist* 28 Apr. 2011. Print.

Adams, Scott. "Dilbert." Comic Strip. *United Feature Syndicate*. Print.

Aimes, Alexander. "Bringing History to Life with Primary Sources." Student essay. Used by permission.

"Choosing When to Give Credit." *The Purdue Online Writing Lab*. Purdue University. 9 June 2009. Web. 12 Nov. 2011.

Davey, Monica M. "Meet Tim Cook." 12 August 2007. Photograph. European Pressphoto Agency, Frankfurt.

Duggan, Paul. "In Sex-Crime Cases, Credibility a Thorny Issue." *The Washington Post* 1 July 2011. Print.

Echanove, Matias, and Rahul Srivastava. "Hands Off Our Houses." *The New York Times* 1 June 2011: A27. Print.

Fogarty, Mignon. *Grammar Girl: Quick and Dirty Tips for Better Writing*. New York: St. Martin's Press, 2008. Print.

Gleiberman, Owen. "Film Review: The Hangover." Rev. of *The Hangover*, by Dir. Todd Phillips. *EW.com* 2 June 2009. Web. 15 Nov. 2010.

Govindarajan, Vijay. "The $300 House: A Hands-On Lab for Reverse Innovation?" Web log post. *HBR Blog Network*, Harvard Business School Publishing, 26 Aug. 2010. Web. 22 Oct. 2011.

Govindarajan, Vijay. "The $300 House: A Hands-On Approach to a Wicked Problem." Web log post. *HBR Blog* Network, Harvard Business School Publishing, 7 June 2011. Web. 22 Oct. 2011.

Greene, Andy. "All Star Rockers Salute Buddy Holly." *Rolling Stone.* Straight Arrow Publishers, 7 July 2011. Print.

Jayawardhana, Ray. "Alien Life, Coming Slowly into View." *The New York Times.* 27 March 2011: WK10. Print.

Johnson, Judith. "The Truth about Writer's Block." *The Huffington Post*. HuffPost News, 25 July 2011. Web. 11 Nov. 2011.

King, Jr., Martin Luther. "I Have a Dream." Speech. March on Washington for Jobs and Freedom. Lincoln Memorial, Washington, D.C. 28 Aug. 1963. *Americanrhetoric.com*. Michael E. Eidenmuller. n.d. Web. 12 Nov. 2011.

Lincoln, Abraham. "Gettysburg Address." Speech. Dedication of the Soldiers' National Cemetary. Gettysburg, Pennsylvania 19 Nov. 1863. *Ourdocuments.gov*. n.d. Web. 15 Nov. 2011.

McArdle, Megan. "Anatomy of a Fake Quotation." *The Atlantic* 2 May 2011. Print.

McGrath, Charles. "The Lexicon." *NYTimes.com* 8 Sept. 2011. Web. 9 Sept. 2011.

Meyers, Justin. "How to Make a Kindle Cover from a Hollowed Out Hardback Book." *Wonder How To*. n.p., March 2011. Web. 12 Nov. 2011.

Neil, Dan. "BMW 1M: Miniature, Mighty and Miles of Fun." *The Wall Street Journal* 3 Sept. 2011. Print.

Obama, Barack. "Remarks by the President on Osama bin Laden." Speech. Address to the Nation that Osama bin Laden is dead. The White House, Washington, D.C. 1 May 2011. *The White House Blog.* Macon Phillips. 2 May 2011. Web. 29 Sept. 2011.

Rosen, Jeffrey. "The Web Means the End of Forgetting." *The New York Times* 25 July 2010: MM30. Print.

Schalet, Amy. "The Sleepover Question." *The New York Times* 23 July 2011: SR9. Print.

Scham, Sam. "Top Ten Distractions for Writers, or Any Job Really." *Yahoo*.com 12 Aug. 2008. Web. 12 Nov. 2011.

Shemtob, Zachary, and David Lat. "Executions Should Be Televised." *The New York Times* 31 July 2011: SR4. Print.

Skinner, E. Benjamin. "People for Sale." *Foreign Policy.* March–April 2008. Print.

Thornburgh, Nathan. "Violent Rhetoric and Arizona Politics." Editorial. *Time* 9 Jan. 2011. Print.

Wright, Don. "Obama Grammarian Cartoon." *International Herald Tribune* 20 January 2009. Print.

Wynn, Craig. "Take a Leap Into Writing." Student essay. Used by permission.

Young, Neil. "Let's Roll." *Are You Passionate?* Reprise Records, 2002. CD.

Zuniga, Janine. "San Ysidro Shooting Survivor Lives His Dream of Being a Cop." *San Diego Union-Tribune* 18 July 2004. Print.

PERSPECTIVE

Edited by
Kenneth Gillam

Associate Editors

Kathryn Bennett
Megan Hoelting
Tristin Hooker
Cynthia Johnson
Aubrey Larimore
Kandice McKee
Heather Messick
Natalie Monzyk
Andrew Myers
Eden Olena
Shiloh Peters
Erik Renth
Linda Tinson
Wendy Wallace
Satarah Wheeler
Bambi Whitaker

INTRODUCTION

By Erik Renth

"...I started the class by picking up a chair and placing it in front of me. What do you see? I asked the class. A chair. Then I placed the chair upside down. Not what do you see? Still a chair. Then I straightened the chair and asked a few students to stand in different places around the room, and asked both those standing and those sitting to describe the same chair. You see this is a chair, but when you come to describe it, you do so from where you are positioned, and from your own perspective, and so you cannot say there is only one way of seeing a chair, can you? No, obviously not. If you cannot say this about so simple an object as a chair, how can you possibly pass absolute judgment on any given individual?"

Reading Lolita *in Tehran: A Memoir in Stories*
–Azar Nafisi

You have your own perspective. Your experiences, your religion, your thoughts, your political affiliations, and so many other facets of you—they all make up a unique perspective that cannot be replicated, at least not in whole. No one else can see the chair from the exact point that you are sitting; no one else can experience that vision in quite the same way. Your perspective is unique, but it isn't the only perspective that exists—it isn't the only valid perspective. There will always be others sitting at a different point in the room, seeing from a different place. Such is the nature of life, though. There will always be others seeing life unfold from a different locale, a different angle, a different perspective.

As every individual approaches the same issue, he or she brings all of those experiences and thoughts as well. Those things that we bring to our perspective are our understanding and make up our culture. We find commonality through our cultural identities; we are able to identify with similar viewpoints, and those bind us to other people who share our cultural identities. We have the propensity to share many things and many views through our culture, and that helps to shape a collective viewpoint.

Think of the chair at the front of the classroom once more. You're the only person who can see the chair from that very angle, but think of the commonality you all see in the chair. It is made of wood. It has a red seat, a crooked leg. You all see this, and this is your common experience. It binds you all, in a way. That isn't to say that culture is universal, though. Wonder what it would be like to experience it from another perspective. Would it be different? You could go stand in the same spot as one of your peers and try to see what they see. But could you experience that viewpoint in the exact same way? It would be difficult to notice the sloped back, the red seat, or the type of wood in quite the same way. What you call a maroon, another might call crimson. But more than that; how your culture uses chairs, if it has chairs at all, will inform your experiences and memories, which go on to shade all meanings. Though you're standing in the same place, the experiences vary.

In the same way, personal cultures vary. All of the cultures and experiences that make up each individual in the room means that each will experience it in in a novel way. It is by embracing and empathizing with those differences that we can learn to reach a level of understanding with others. No one person is more right about how the chair looks, though. It's all about where each person in the room is coming from. And, just as important as the way see the chair is that we think of how everyone else in the room can see the chair—those perspectives are all integral to the collective experience. In much the same way, it is important to be sensitive to the cultures we encounter in an increasingly global society. In *Education for the Intercultural Experience,* Milton J. Benett presents a model of intercultural sensitivity, which is defined as seeing one's own culture as central to reality. As an individual moves from Ethnocentric to Ethnorelative stages, he or she becomes more able to relate within diverse cultural spheres and usurps the tendency to view his or her own cultural identity as a paragon. The stages are shown below.

ETHNOCENTRIC STAGES

Denial: This is the first of the stages, and people in this stage are the most ethnocentric. People in in the denial stage often fail to see differences between cultures, ignore those differences, or intentionally isolate themselves from such differences to protect their own worldview. Those in denial are genuinely disinterested in understanding other cultures.

Defense: The stage of defense is the first stage in which cultural differences are recognized. However, a person in the defense stage is denigrating to other cultures and openly vocal about the superiority of his or her own culture. While this may not seem like a less ethnocentric viewpoint, the willingness of those people in the defense stage to recognize cultural differences is an important, albeit small, step forward.

Minimalization: In this last stage of ethnocentrism, there is a shift toward understanding the global population as a whole. While the denigration of other cultures has weaned in a person in the minimalization stage, differences between the cultures are, in this stage, minimalized or romanticized. Thus, a person in this stage is susceptible to stereotyping.

ETHNORELATIVE STAGES

Acceptance: Acceptance is the first stage in which a person not only recognizes that there are multiple, complex worldviews but also accepts those as valid. While a person in this stage may still think his or her culture is the most valid, he or she has the ability to recognize that his or her thoughts are born out of a particular cultural experience.

Adaptation: In the adaptation stage, people become more empathetic to the cultures of others, and they have developed the interpersonal communication skills to effectively communicate crossculturally. This is the first stage in which a person may see the world through several integrated worldviews and has the insight to behave appropriately across a broad range of cultural situations.

Integration: The final stage of the continuum, integration, sees the breakdown of traditional cultural roles. A person in this stage of the continuum may be able to see past traditional cultural barriers to evaluate a situation. The "I" becomes more than merely a viewpoint from any particular culture; rather, it is a constantly changing and evolving perspective.

No two people will ever see the world in exactly the same way. However, it is our duty to continue in the pursuit of understanding the vision of others in an attempt to find a more global perspective. This book was assembled with that end in mind. The editors chose the specific articles in the book to illustrate the various aspects of culture. From the pageantry of Bollywood to the advancement of robotics for use by the aging population and Walt Whitman and the Civil War, these articles help *Perspective* to illuminate the diversity of global culture, to move the reader toward ethnorelativity and the integration of cultures into his or her own viewpoints. It is our hope that these articles will help you to think of other perspectives—ones you may not have been able to experience before—as you move through your everyday life and to see the world as something that is more than just what you can see from where you stand.

Max Fisher is a current blogger for the Washington Post, *focusing on foreign affairs and international policies. He is is a former author and editor at* The Atlantic.

WELCOME TO AMERICA, PLEASE BE ON TIME

By Max Fisher

WHAT GUIDE BOOKS TELL FOREIGN VISITORS TO THE U.S.

Such tips as "don't hand out cash to dinner guests" reveal what foreign tourists find surprising about coming to America.

The United States is the second greatest tourist draw in the world, with 60-million-plus visitors in 2010 alone (France, number one, attracted almost 80 million). Flipping through a few of the many English-language tourist guides provides a fascinating, if non-scientific and narrow, window into how people from the outside world perceive America, Americans, and the surprises and pitfalls of spending time here.

Of the many pieces of advice proffered, four of the most common are eat with your fingers (sometimes), arrive on time (always), don't drink and drive (they take it seriously here!), and be careful about talking politics (unless you've got some time to spare). But they say more than that.

One of the first things you notice in picking up *Lonely Planet USA* or *Rough Guides: The USA* or reading WikiTravel's United States of America page, as I did (traditional guides such as *Fodor's* or *Frommer's* are more circumspect and not nearly as interesting), is the surprising frankness in discussing the warts of American history and society. The destruction of native communities and slavery both get long sections, the latter usually including some comments on still-present racial sensitivities.

"Gifts of cash, prepared ready-to-serve foods, or very personal items (e.g. toiletries) are not appropriate."

Politics get heavy treatment in the books, as do the subtleties of discussing them, maybe more so than in any other guidebook I've read (what can I say, it's an addiction). *Lonely Planet* urges caution when discussing immigration. "This is the issue that makes Americans edgy, especially when it gets politicized," they write, subtly suggesting that some Americans might approach the issue differently than others. "Age has a lot to do with Americans' multicultural tolerance."

Rough Guide doesn't shy away from the fact that many non-Americans are less-than-crazy about U.S. politics and foreign policy and encouragingly notes that many Americans are just as "infuriated" about it as visitors might be. Still, it warns that the political culture saturates everything, and that "The combination of shoot-from-the-hip mentality with laissez-faire capitalism and religious fervor can make the U.S. maddening at times, even to its own residents." They go on:

> Vigour and passion are animating forces in politics and culture here. While this tendency has deep roots in the country's religious heritage (modern evangelism was perfected here), it affects everything from the firm opinions people hold over even trivial matters, to the public stand they make over God, government, guns, and other incendiary topics.

Lonely Planet even offers a helpful tip for navigating the polarized politics, in which political truth can be hard to come by, particularly "during election cycles." They recommend fact.check.org: "It's a great resource for parsing truth from political bombast." Sometimes, the books seem to assume that foreign visitors might have a tough time navigating the redder parts of America. "Texas is the country's capital for oil-drilling, BBQ-eating and right-wing politicking, with huge expanses of land and equally domineering attitudes," says *Rough*

Guide. Lonely Planet says that solo women travelers in "rural" areas can sometimes attract raised eyebrows.

But maybe the topic that gets the most attention in these books is food, which they praise for its quality and variety (and portion size) in a tone of near-disbelief. As in any culture, the niceties of dining—especially at someone's home—can get complicated. Here, from Wikitravel, is some sage advice on a ritual that even I did not realize was so complicated until I read this passage:

> When invited to a meal in a private home, it is considered polite for a guest to ask if they can bring anything for the meal, such as a dessert, a side dish, or for an outdoor barbecue, something useful like ice or plastic cups, plates. The host will usually refuse except among very close friends, but it is nonetheless considered good manners to bring along a small gift for the host. A bottle of wine, box of candies or fresh cut flowers are most common. Gifts of cash, prepared ready-to-serve foods, or very personal items (e.g. toiletries) are not appropriate.

Wikitravel has you covered for going out to restaurants: don't plop down at a stranger's table, don't slurp, and don't pick up your cell phone. There is one piece of good news: it is not considered rude to leave some food on your plate. If you've ever made the mistake of over-ordering in a culture where eating less than everything can be a profound insult, you know how much of a relief this American standard can be:

> It is usually inappropriate to join a table already occupied by other diners, even if it has unused seats; Americans prefer this degree of privacy when they eat. Exceptions are cafeteria-style eateries with long tables, and at crowded informal eateries and cafes you may have success asking a stranger if you can share the table they're sitting at. Striking up a conversation in this situation may or may not be welcome, however.
>
> Table manners, while varying greatly, are typically European influenced. Slurping or making other noises while

> eating are considered rude, as is loud conversation (including phone calls). [...] Offense isn't taken if you don't finish your meal, and most restaurants will package the remainder to take with you, or provide a box for you to do this yourself (sometimes euphemistically called a "doggy bag," implying that the leftovers are for your pet). If you want to do this, ask the server to get the remainder "to go"; this term will be almost universally understood and will not cause any embarrassment. Some restaurants offer an "all-you-can-eat" buffet or other service; taking home portions from such a meal is either not allowed or carries an additional fee.

You might say that global food cultures tend to fall into one of two categories: utensil cultures and finger cultures. The U.S., somewhat unusually, has both: the appropriate delivery method can vary between cuisines, and even between dishes, and it's far from obvious which is which. Baked chicken is a fork food, but fried chicken a finger food, depending on how it's fried. If you get fried pieces of potato, it's a finger food, unless the potato retains some circular shape, in which case use your fork. And so on. Confused yet?

The books emphasize that the U.S. is safe, with one big exception they all note: "inner cities," which are described with a terror that can feel a little outdated. "When driving, under no circumstances should you stop in any unlit or seemingly deserted urban area," *Rough Guide* warns, going on to describe dangerous scams - a strange man waving you down for "auto trouble," another car hitting yours out of nowhere so that you'll get out - in a way that makes them sound commonplace.

Gay and lesbian travelers are urged to stick to the big cities. "In the rural heartland, however, life can look more like the Fifties - homosexuals are still oppressed and commonly reviled. Gay travelers need to watch their step to avoid hassles and possible aggression," according to *Lonely Planet*.

Despite the divides, there is one thing that Americans agree on, according to the guides: punctuality is a big deal. *Lonely Planet*, in the same paragraph, notes that "Americans are notoriously informal in their dining manners" but that "it's polite to be prompt . . . arrive within 15 minutes of the designated time." They repeat, later, "Do be on time. Many folks in the U.S. consider it rude to be kept waiting." *Rough Guide* hammers home, in asides in many sections, that things happen on time here, and lateness doesn't get forgiven easily.

Another common tip has to do with personal space: Americans like it *a lot*. "Don't be overly physical if you meet someone," says *Lonely Planet*. *Rough Guide* suggests keeping arms-length distance except in the most crowded urban circumstances. Books gently deter cheek-kissing - especially outside of coastal cities - and, when it comes to the intricacies of when to hug or not hug, suggest simply following the Americans' lead.

For travel, there are long sections on visas and how to navigate airport security, along with warnings that Amtrak service can be, as the *Rough Guide* puts it, "skeletal." WikiTravel features a yellow-highlighted section warning against overstaying your visa - the country takes it quite seriously. There are three paragraphs reiterating the importance of carrying travel documents on your person when near the border.

In many ways, the tour books say as much about the world as they do about the U.S., by highlighting the ways in which American practices and standards deviate. Anyone who's traveled widely, particularly in the developing world, will understand why these books are so emphatic about, for example, punctuality, personal space, and the unreliability of our trains.

Still, these are guides for people who want to spend their time and money seeing America, and this excitement shines through even the sourest sections.

"Many of the stereotypes do hold true - this is a place where you'll find real life cowboys, gangsters, and other Hollywood standbys," *Rough Guide* says. "The palpable sense of newness here creates an odd sort of **optimism**, where anything seems possible and fortune can strike at any moment."

Update, June 3: A number of commenters ask about tipping. As I note in the comments, the books tend to include long sections on the nuances of American tipping. They also strongly encourage visitors to adhere to the unusually high tipping rates, explaining both that service jobs tend to pay very poorly and that the tipping system is partially responsible for the exceptional quality and consistency of service here. A commenter on Reddit posts this excerpt, from a guide book for the U.S. that the commenter says was translated from Japanese, explaining tipping in unusually blunt terms.

> Americans have a social institution called a "gratuity." Basically, the price on the menu at any place which serves food is not the real price. The real price is 20% higher. You have to calculate 20%, write it under the subtotal, and sum to arrive at the real price. Taxis work the same way. It is considered very rude not to pay the "gratuity."

Does Fisher's viewpoint give you a new perspective on how foreign visitors view the United States? Do you think Fisher makes any unfair observations about the United States?

Fisher discusses several issues—like physical space, tipping, and punctuality—as very important, which might imply that these are less important in other cultures. What might this article say about how people of different cultures and perspectives see similar situations?

A well known anthropologist, Dr. Horace Mitchell Miner, earned his doctorate from the University of Chicago in 1937. He served in the U.S. Army as a counterintelligence agent during World War II and became an assistant professor of sociology at the University of Michigan upon completing his service. He received many scholarly awards, including a Fulbright Research Grant, and had several publications. "Body Rituals among the Nacirema," published in American Anthropologist *in June of 1956, is his most famous work. Dr. Miner died as a result of Alzheimer's disease in 1993.*

BODY RITUALS AMONG THE NACIREMA

By Horace Mitchell Miner

The anthropologist has become so familiar with the diversity of ways in which different peoples behave in similar situations that he is not apt to be surprised by even the most exotic customs. In fact, if all of the logically possible combination of behavior have not been found somewhere in the world, he is apt to suspect that they must be present in some yet undescribed tribe. This point has, in fact, been expressed with respect to clan organization by Murdock (1949:71). In this light, the magical beliefs and practices of the Nacirema present such unusual aspects that it seems desirable to describe them as an example of the extremes to which human behavior can go.

Professor Linton first brought the ritual of the Nacirema to the attention of anthropologists twenty years ago (1936: 326), but the culture of this people is still very poorly understood. They are a North American group living in the territory between the Canadian Cree, the Yaqui and Tarahumare of Mexico, and the Carib and Arawak of the Antilles. Little is known of their origin, although tradition states that they came from the east. According to Nacirema mythology, their nation was originated by a culture hero, Notgnihsaw, who is otherwise known for two great feats of strength—the throwing of a piece of wampum across the river Pa-To-Mac and the chopping down of a cherry tree in which the Spirit of Truth resided.

Nacirema culture is characterized by a highly developed market economy which has evolved in a rich natural habitat. While much of the people's time is devoted to economic pursuits, a large part of the fruits of these labors and a considerable portion of the day are spent in ritual activity. The focus of this activity is the human body, the appearance and health of which loom as a dominant concern in the ethos of the people. While such a concern is certainly not unusual, its ceremonial aspects and associated philosophy are unique.

The fundamental belief underlying the whole system appears to be that the human body is ugly and that its natural tendency is to debility and disease. Incarcerated in such a body, man's only hope is to avert these characteristics through the use of the powerful influences of ritual and ceremony. Every household has one or more shrines devoted to this purpose. The more powerful individuals in the society have several shrines in their houses and, in fact, the opulence of a house is often referred to in terms of the number of such ritual centers it possesses. Most houses are of wattle and daub construction, but the shrine rooms of the more wealthy are walled with stone. Poorer families imitate the rich by applying pottery plaques to their shrine walls.

While each family has at least one such shrine, the rituals associated with it are not family ceremonies but are private and secret. The rites are normally only discussed with children, and then only during the period when they are being initiated into these mysteries. I was able, however, to establish sufficient rapport with the natives to examine these shrines and to have the rituals described to me.

The focal point of the shrine is a box or chest which is built into the wall. In this chest are kept the many charms and magical potions without which no native believes he could live. These preparations are secured from a variety of specialized practitioners. The most powerful of these are the medicine men, whose assistance must be rewarded with substantial gifts. However, the medicine men do not provide the curative potions for their clients, but decide what the ingredients should be and then write them down in an ancient and secret language. This writing is understood only by the medicine men and by the herbalists who, for another gift, provide the required charm.

The charm is not disposed of after it has served its purpose, but is placed in the charm-box of the household shrine. As these magical materials are specific for certain ills, and the real or imagined maladies of the people are many, the charm-box is usually full to overflowing. The magical packets are so numerous that people forget what their purposes were and fear to use them again. While the natives are very vague on this point, we can only assume that the idea in retaining all the old magical materials is that their presence in the charm-box, before which the body rituals are conducted, will in some way protect the worshipper.

Beneath the charm-box is a small font. Each day every member of the family, in succession, enters the shrine room, bows his head before the charm-box, mingles different sorts of holy water in the font, and proceeds with a brief rite of ablution. The holy waters are secured from the Water Temple of the community, where the priests conduct elaborate ceremonies to make the liquid ritually pure.

In the hierarchy of magical practitioners, and below the medicine men in prestige, are specialists whose designation is best translated "holy-mouth-men." The Nacirema have an almost pathological horror of and fascination with the mouth, the condition of which is believed to have a supernatural influence on all social relationships. Were it not for the rituals of the mouth, they believe that their teeth would fall out, their gums bleed, their jaws shrink, their friends desert them, and their lovers reject them. They also believe that a strong relationship exists between oral and moral characteristics. For example, there is a ritual ablution of the mouth for children, which is supposed to improve their moral fiber.

The daily body ritual performed by everyone includes a mouth-rite. Despite the fact that these people are so punctilious about care of the mouth, this rite involves a practice which strikes the uninitiated stranger as revolting. It was reported to me that the ritual consists of inserting a small bundle of hog hairs into the mouth, along with certain magical powders, and then moving the bundle in a highly formalized series of gestures.

In addition to the private mouth-rite, the people seek out a holy-mouth-man once or twice a year. These practitioners have an impressive set of paraphernalia, consisting of a variety of augers, awls, probes, and prods. The use of these objects in the exorcism of the evils of the mouth involves almost unbelievable ritual torture of the client. The holy-mouth-man opens the client's mouth and, using the above mentioned tools, enlarges any holes which decay may have created in the teeth. Magical materials are put into these holes. If there are no naturally occurring holes in the teeth, large sections of one or more teeth are gouged out so that the supernatural substance can be applied. In the client's view, the purpose of these ministrations is to arrest decay and to draw friends. The extremely sacred and traditional character of the rite is evident in the fact that the natives return to the holy-mouth-men year after year, despite the fact that their teeth continue to decay.

It is hoped that, when a thorough study of the Nacirema is made, there will be careful inquiry into the personality structure of these people. One has but to watch the gleam in the eye of a holy-mouth-man, as he jabs an awl into an exposed nerve, to suspect that a certain amount of sadism is involved. If this can be established, a very interesting pattern emerges, for most of the population shows definite masochistic tendencies. It was to these that Professor Linton referred in discussing a distinctive part of the daily body rituals which is performed only by men. This part of the rite involves scraping and lacerating the surface of the face with a sharp instrument. Special women's rites are performed only four times during each lunar month, but what they lack in frequency is made up in barbarity. As part of this ceremony, women bake their heads in small ovens for about an hour. The theoretically interesting point is that what seems to be a preponderantly masochistic people have developed sadistic specialists.

The medicine men have an imposing temple, or *lati pso*, in every community of any size. The more elaborate ceremonies required to treat very sick patients can only be performed at this temple. These ceremonies involve not only the thaumaturge, but a permanent group of vestal maidens who move sedately about the temple chambers in distinctive costume and headdress.

The *lati pso* ceremonies are so harsh that it is phenomenal that a fair proportion of the really sick natives who enter the temple ever recover. Small children whose indoctrination is still incomplete have been known to resist attempts to take them to the temple because "that is where you go to die." Despite this fact, sick adults are not only willing but eager to undergo the protracted ritual purification, if they can afford to do so. No matter how ill the supplicant or how grave the emergency, the guardians of many temples will not admit a client if he cannot give a rich gift to the custodian. Even after one has gained admission and survived the ceremonies, the guardians will not permit the neophyte to leave until he makes still another gift.

The supplicant entering the temple is first stripped of all his or her clothes. In every-day life the Nacirema avoids exposure of his body and its natural functions. Bathing and excretory acts are performed only in the secrecy of the household shrine, where they are ritualized as part of the body-rites. Psychological shock results from the fact that body secrecy is suddenly lost upon entry into the *lati pso*. A man, whose own wife has never seen him in an excretory act, suddenly finds himself naked and assisted by a vestal maiden while he performs his natural functions into a sacred vessel. This sort of ceremonial treatment is necessitated by the fact that the excreta are used by a diviner to ascertain the course and nature of the client's sickness. Female clients, on the other hand, find their naked bodies are subjected to the scrutiny, manipulation and prodding of the medicine men.

There remains one other kind of practitioner, known as the "listener." This witch-doctor has the power to exorcise the devils that lodge in the heads of people who have been bewitched. The Nacirema believe that parents bewitch their own children. Mothers are particularly suspected of putting a curse on children while teaching them the sacred body rituals. The patient simply tells the "listener" all his troubles and fears, beginning with the earliest difficulties he can remember. The memory displayed by the Nacirema in these exorcism sessions is truly remarkable. It is not uncommon for the patient to bemoan the rejection he felt upon being weaned as a babe, and a few individuals even see their troubles going back to the traumatic effects of their own birth.

In conclusion, mention must be made of certain practices which have their base in native esthetics but which depend upon the pervasive aversion to the natural body and its functions. There are ritual fasts to make fat people thin and ceremonial feast to make thin people fat. Still other rites are used to make women's breasts larger if they are small and smaller if they are large. General dissatisfaction with breast shape is symbolized in the fact that the ideal form is virtually outside the range of human variation. A few women afflicted with almost inhuman hyper-mammary development are so idolized that they make a handsome living by simply going from village to village and permitting the natives to stare at them for a fee.

Reference has already been made to the fact that excretory functions are ritualized, routinized, and relegated to secrecy. Natural reproductive functions are similarly distorted. Intercourse is taboo as a topic and scheduled as an act. Efforts are made to avoid pregnancy by the use of magical materials or by limiting intercourse to certain phases of the moon. Conception is actually very infrequent. When pregnant, women dress so as to hide their condition. Parturition takes place in secret, without friends or relatives to assist, and the majority of women do not nurse their infants.

Our review of the ritual life of the Nacirema has certainly shown them to be a magic-ridden people. It is hard to understand how they have managed to exist so long under the burdens which they have imposed upon themselves. But even such exotic customs as these take on real meaning when they are viewed with the insight provided by Malinowski when he wrote (1948:70):

> Looking from far and above, from our high places of safety in the developed civilization, it is easy to see all the crudity and irrelevance of magic. But without its power and guidance early man could not have mastered his practical difficulties as he has done, nor could man have advanced to the higher stages of civilization.

References Cited

Lenton, Ralph; 1936, *The Study of Man.* New York, D. Appleton-Century Co.

Malinowski, Bronislaw; 1948, *Magic, Science, and Religion.* Glencoe, The Free Press.

Murdock, George P.; 1949, *Social Structure.* New York, The Macmillan Co.

1. What is your opinion of the importance of body ritual? If you lived among the Nacirema, would you tell them of your opinion? To what extent can you identify with the article?

2. Compare and contrast the rituals of the Nacirema with some of your own body rituals.

3. Write "Nacirema" backwards. In small groups, discuss your reactions to this article and its implications.

Journalist Jane Flanagan writes for the South African bureau of the British news source The Telegraph. *Her articles and reports often appear on the news source's online version at www.telegraph.co.uk.*

DRUNK BABOONS PLAGUE CAPE TOWN'S EXCLUSIVE SUBURBS

By Jane Flanagan

Groot Constantia, in the heart of Cape Town's wine country, can deal with inebriated holidaymakers—but it is invading baboons which have developed a taste for its grapes that the wine makers are struggling with.

Each day, dozens of Cape Baboons gather to strip the ancient vines—the sauvignon blanc grapes are a particular favourite—before heading into the mountains to sleep. A few, who sample fallen fruit that has fermented in the sun, pass out and don't make it home.

"They are not just eating our grapes, they are raiding our kitchens and ripping the thatch off the roofs. They are becoming increasingly bold and destructive," said Jean Naude, general manager at the vineyard, which is celebrating its 325th birthday this year. Guards banging sticks and waving plastic snakes have been deployed with only limited success, and not even a blast of a vuvuzela, the plastic horn made famous at the World Cup, seems to frighten them.

It is not just the vineyards in South Africa which are under siege, however, but also the exclusive neighbouring suburb of Constantia, home to famous residents including Earl Spencer, Wilbur Smith, and Nelson Mandela.

Crisis meetings between animal welfare groups and traumatised locals are struggling to find a workable solution.

"Where there's a mountain, there's a baboon," said Justin O'Riain of the Baboon Research Unit at the University of Cape Town. "As we take up more and more of their land, the conflict increases."

The baboons lived in the mountains of Cape Town long before humans took up residence, but development has forced the unlikely neighbours into increasingly closer contact.

Before laws afforded baboons a protected status a decade ago, troublesome animals were regularly killed or maimed by home owners and farmers. Now around 20 full-time "baboon monitors" are employed to protect them and guide them away from residential areas. It has proved mission impossible. Last week, a 12-year-old boy was left traumatised after confronting a troop who had broken into his family home.

Hearing noises from the kitchen, he went to investigate and found the beasts ransacking cupboards. When the child fled upstairs to find his babysitter, three males gave chase and surrounded him as he made a tearful phone call to his mother, while the animals pelted him with fruit.

"When he called me he was terrified. They had him surrounded," said the Constantia housewife, who did not wish to be identified.

Chickens, geese, peacocks and even a Great Dane dog have been killed in recent weeks by the marauding baboons—the males have huge and terrifying canine teeth. Roof tiles, electric fences, orchards and vegetables gardens have been trashed.

"Lunch parties in the garden are now just impossible," a homeowner complained. "It is so unrelaxing. Rather than chatting over our meal, we are looking over our shoulders and bolting the food as quickly as we can before it is stolen. We can't even leave a window open in summer. We are under siege."

In a concession to despairing residents, wildlife authorities have begun collaring baboons identified as "troublesome" and imposed a strict "three strikes" policy whereby animals which repeatedly break into homes are humanely destroyed.

Fourteen year-old William, a large male known officially as GOB03, who had terrorised the coastal suburb of Scarborough for as long as anyone can remember, was the first to fall foul of this controversial rule.

His death last month was greeted with outrage and jubilation in equal measure and dominated the letters pages of the local newspapers for weeks.

Meanwhile, For Sale signs are sprouting up in suburbs with baboon populations. Families which have lived in the same house for generations are giving up, moving away to get away from their animal tormentors.

Initially the title of this article may sound amusing, but in reality it is a serious issue. Whose rights should take precedence, "Families (human property rights) which have lived in the same house for generations" or Baboons (Animal rights) who lived in the mountains "long before humans took up residence"?

The article mentions that "the exclusive neighbouring suburb of Constantia, home to famous residents including...Nelson Mandela" is under attack. Why is this information important? How might this impact the local and/or global economics?

How do you, an American, connect with this story from across the world? Think about all of the elements in this story that may be similar and those that are different. What inferences can you make from this that may impact your life? Your future world?

Think about how the rhetoric of the article contributes to your reaction after your first reading. Now, read it again. How does the rhetoric affect you? Is there a difference? Are some voices more emotionally effective? Are some more logically effective?

This article was originally published on August 30, 2010 in the weekly satirical newspaper The Onion. The Onion *parodies current political events and social issues in the United States.*

MAN ALREADY KNOWS EVERYTHING HE NEEDS TO KNOW ABOUT MUSLIMS

By The Onion

MAN ALREADY KNOWS EVERYTHING HE NEEDS TO KNOW ABOUT MUSLIMS

SALINA, KS—Local man Scott Gentries told reporters Wednesday that his deliberately limited grasp of Islamic history and culture was still more than sufficient to shape his views of the entire Muslim world.

Gentries, 48, said he had absolutely no interest in exposing himself to further knowledge of Islamic civilization or putting his sweeping opinions into a broader context of any kind, and confirmed he was "perfectly happy" to make a handful of emotionally charged words the basis of his mistrust toward all members of the world's second-largest religion.

"I learned all that really matters about the Muslim faith on 9/11," Gentries said in reference to the terrorist attacks on the United States undertaken by 19 of Islam's approximately 1.6 billion practitioners. "What more do I need to know to stigmatize Muslims everywhere as inherently violent radicals?"

"And now they want to build a mosque at Ground Zero," continued Gentries, eliminating any distinction between the 9/11 hijackers and Muslims in general. "No, I won't examine the accuracy of that statement, but yes, I will allow myself to be outraged by it and use it as evidence of these people's universal callousness toward Americans who lost loved ones when the Twin Towers fell."

"Even though I am not one of those people," he added.

When told that the proposed "Ground Zero mosque" is actually a community center two blocks north of the site that would include, in addition to a public prayer space, a 500-seat auditorium, a restaurant, and athletic facilities, Gentries shook his head and said, "I know all I'm going to let myself know."

Gentries explained that it "didn't take long" to find out as much about the tenets of Islam as he needed to. He said he knew Muslims stoned their women for committing adultery, trained for terrorist attacks at fundamentalist madrassas, and believed in jihad, which Gentries described as the thing they used to justify killing infidels.

"All Muslims are at war with America, and I will resist any attempt to challenge that assertion with potentially illuminating facts," said Gentries, who threatened to leave the room if presented with the number of Muslims who live peacefully in the United States, serve in the country's armed forces, or were victims themselves of the 9/11 attacks. "Period."

"If you don't believe me, wait until they put your wife in a burka," Gentries continued in reference to the face-and-body-covering worn by a small minority of Muslim women and banned in the universities of Turkey, Tunisia, and Syria. "Or worse, a rape camp. That's right: For reasons I am content being totally unable to articulate, I am choosing to associate Muslims with rape camps."

Over the past decade, Gentries said he has taken pains to avoid personal interactions or media that might have the potential to compromise his point of view. He told reporters that the closest he had come to confronting a contrary standpoint was tuning in to the first few seconds of an interview with a moderate Muslim cleric before hastily turning off the television.

"I almost gave in and listened to that guy defend Islam with words I didn't want to hear," Gentries said. "But then I remembered how much easier it is to live in a world of black-and-white in which I can assign the label of 'other' to someone and use him as a vessel for all my fears and insecurities."

Added Gentries, "That really put things back into perspective."

1. According to Gentries, all Muslims believe in jihad, which he describes as "the thing [Muslims] use to justify killing infidels." The authors of *The Onion* are aware that this is one potential perspective that people may have, but does that mean that this version of jihad is true? Research the concept of jihad. What is it? According to whom?

2. "For reasons I am content being totally unable to articulate, I am choosing to associate Muslims with rape camps." –Gentries

   Do you think it is necessary for a person's credibility as a speaker or writer to be able to provide evidence to support his or her beliefs? Why? What kinds of evidence are needed?

3. In what ways does this article resemble an actual newspaper article? In what ways does it differ? Why do you think the authors would try to recreate the tone of a newspaper article for this spoof?

Azar Nafisi, born in 1955, is a scholarly writer and former professor. After receiving her Ph.D. in Literature from the University of Oklahoma, Nafisi returned to her native Iran and taught at multiple universities. In 1997, she and her family emigrated to the United States, and she began writing her memoir of times teaching and leading a book club of women. Reading Lolita in Tehran, *published in 2003, was on the* New York Times *bestsellers list for over two years and received both praise and criticism for Nafisi's portrayal of life in Iran.*

READING *LOLITA* IN TEHRAN

By Azar Nafisi

In the fall of 1995, after resigning from my last academic post, I decided to indulge myself and fulfill a dream. I chose seven of my best and most committed students and invited them to come to my home every Thursday morning to discuss literature. They were all women—to teach a mixed class in the privacy of my home was too risky, even if we were discussing harmless works of fiction. One persistent male student, although barred from our class, insisted on his rights. So he, Nima, read the assigned material, and on special days he would come to my house to talk about the books we were reading.

I often teasingly reminded my students of Muriel Spark's *The Prime of Miss Jean Brodie* and asked, Which one of you will finally betray me? For I am a pessimist by nature, and I was sure at least one would turn against me. Nassrin once responded mischievously, "You yourself told us that in the final analysis we are our own betrayers, playing Judas to our own Christ." Manna pointed out that I was no Miss Brodie, and they, well, they were what they were. She reminded me of a warning I was fond of repeating: *do not*, under *any* circumstances, belittle a work of fiction by trying to turn it into a carbon copy of real life; what we search for in fiction is not so much reality but the epiphany of truth. Yet I suppose that if I were to go against my own recommendation and choose a work of fiction that would most resonate with our lives in the Islamic Republic of Iran, it would not be *The Prime of Miss Jean Brodie* or even *1984* but perhaps Nabokov's *Invitation to a Beheading* or better yet, *Lolita.*

A couple of years after we had begun our Thursday morning seminars, on the last night I was in Tehran, a few friends and students came to say good-bye and to help me pack. When we had deprived the house of all its items, when the objects had vanished and the colors had faded into eight gray suitcases, like errant genies evaporating into their bottles, my students and I stood against the bare white wall of the dining room and took two photographs.

I have the two photographs in front of me now. In the first there are seven women, standing against a white wall. They are, according to the law of the land, dressed in black robes and head scarves, covered except for the oval of their faces and their hands. In the second photograph the same group, in the same position, stands against the same wall. Only they have taken off their coverings. Splashes of color separate one from the next. Each has become distinct through the color and style of her clothes, the color and the length of her hair; not even the two who are still wearing their head scarves look the same.

The one to the far right in the second photograph is our poet, Manna, in a white T-shirt and jeans. She made poetry out of things most people cast aside. The photograph does not reflect the peculiar opacity of Manna's dark eyes, a testament to her withdrawn and private nature.

Next to Manna is Mahshid, whose long black scarf clashes with her delicate features and retreating smile. Mahshid was good at many things, but she had a certain daintiness about her and we took to calling her "my lady." Nassrin used to say that more than defining Mahshid, we had managed to add another dimension to the word *lady*. Mahshid is very sensitive. She's like porcelain, Yassi once told me, easy to crack. That's why she appears fragile to those who don't know her too well; but woe to whoever offends her. As for me, Yassi continued good-naturedly, I'm like good old plastic; I won't crack no matter what you do with me.

Yassi was the youngest in our group. She is the one in yellow, bending forward and bursting with laughter. We used to teasingly call her our comedian. Yassi was shy by nature, but certain things excited her and made her lose her inhibitions. She had a tone of voice that gently mocked and questioned not just others but herself as well.

I am the one in brown, standing next to Yassi, with one arm around her shoulders. Directly behind me stands Azin, my tallest student, with her long blond hair and a pink T-shirt. She is laughing like the rest of us. Azin's smiles never looked like smiles; they appeared more like preludes to an irrepressible and nervous hilarity. She beamed in that peculiar fashion even when she was describing her latest trouble with her husband. Always outrageous and outspoken, Azin relished the shock value of her actions and comments and often clashed with Mahshid and Manna. We nicknamed her the wild one.

On my other side is Mitra, who was perhaps the calmest among us. Like the pastel colors of her paintings, she seemed to recede and fade into a paler register. Her beauty was saved from predictability by a pair of miraculous dimples, which she could and did use to manipulate any an unsuspecting victim into bending to her will.

Sanaz, who, pressured by family and society, vacillated between her desire for independence and her need for approval, is holding on to Mitra's arm. We are all laughing. And Nima, Manna's husband and my one true literary critic—if only he had had the perseverance to finish the brilliant essays he started to write—is our invisible partner, the photographer.

There was one more: Nassrin. She is not in the photographs—she didn't make it to the end. Yet my tale would be incomplete without those who could not or did not remain with us. Their absences persist, like an acute pain that seems to have no physical source. This is Tehran for me: its absences were more real than its presences.

When I see Nassrin in my mind's eye, she's slightly out of focus, blurred, somehow distant. I've combed through the photographs my students took with me over the years, and Nassrin is in many of them but always hidden behind something—a person, a tree. In one,

I am standing with eight of my students in the small garden facing our faculty building, the scene of so many farewell photographs over the years. In the background stands a sheltering willow tree. We are laughing, and in one corner, from behind the tallest student, Nassrin peers out, like an imp intruding roguishly on a scene it was not invited to. In another I can barely make out her face in the small V space behind two other girls' shoulders. In this one she looks absentminded; she is frowning, as if unaware that she is being photographed.

How can I describe Nassrin? I once called her the Cheshire cat, appearing and disappearing at unexpected turns in my academic life. The truth is I can't describe her: she was her own definition. One can only say that Nassrin was Nassrin.

For nearly two years, almost every Thursday morning, rain or shine, they came to my house, and almost every time, I could not get over the shock of seeing them shed their mandatory veils and robes and burst into color. When my students came into that room, they took off more than their scarves and robes. Gradually, each one gained an outline and a shape, becoming her own inimitable self. Our world in that living room with its window framing my beloved Elburz Mountains became our sanctuary, our self-contained universe, mocking the reality of black-scarved, timid faces in the city that sprawled below.

The theme of the class was the relation between fiction and reality. We read Persian classical literature, such as the tales of our own lady of fiction, Scheherazade, from *A Thousand and One Nights*, along with Western classics—*Pride and Prejudice, Madame Bovary, Daisy Miller, The Dean's December* and, yes, *Lolita*. As I write the title of each book, memories whirl in with the wind to disturb the quiet of this fall day in another room in another country.

Here and now in that other world that cropped up so many times in our discussions, I sit and reimagine myself and my students, my girls as I came to call them, reading *Lolita* in a deceptively sunny room in Tehran. But to steal the words from Humbert, the poet/criminal of *Lolita*, I need you, the reader, to imagine us, for we won't really exist if you don't. Against the tyranny of time and politics, imagine us the way we sometimes didn't dare to imagine ourselves: in our most private and secret moments, in the most extraordinarily ordinary instances of life, listening to music, falling in love, walking down the shady streets or reading *Lolita* in Tehran. And then imagine us again with all this confiscated, driven underground, taken away from us.

If I write about Nabokov today, it is to celebrate our reading of Nabokov in Tehran, against all odds. Of all his novels I choose the one I taught last, and the one that is connected to so many memories. It is of Lolita that I want to write, but right now there is no way I can write about that novel without also writing about Tehran. This, then, is the story of *Lolita* in Tehran, how *Lolita* gave a different color to Tehran and how Tehran helped redefine Nabokov's novel, turning it into this *Lolita*, our *Lolita*.

1. In the first chapter of the book, Nafisi writes about a conversation that questions the differences between fiction and reality. How is this discussion similar to the one about actual versus perceived culture?

2. If you were under a regime such as the one in the book that restricted learning, would your education have continued to flourish? Is such a desire for knowledge irrepressible?

3. How powerful is clothing in a culture?

Heather Carreiro, English Department Head at the International School of Ho Chi Minh City's American Academy, while teaching English, works as a freelance writer. She has contributed to Matador Network, BootsnAll, GoNOMAD, *and* Journey Beyond Travel. *In addition to teaching in Vietnam, she spent three years teaching and developing English language courses in Pakistan.*

DEFINITIONS OF MODESTY: BIKINIS IN THE SUPERMARKET, BURKINIS AT THE POOL

By Heather Carreiro

Does any culture have the right to define modesty, nudity or "freedom" for everyone else?

In the wake of Facebook's decision to remove photos of women breastfeeding, a lively debate sparked on *Matador Life* about cultural perceptions of breastfeeding, misogynistic attitudes toward women's bodies and the definition of pornography.

This led to the questioning of our definitions of concepts like "modesty" and "nudity." Is there a universal standard of what should be considered modest or lewd? If one culture considers showing certain body parts as public nudity while another does not, does the second culture have the right to see the first as backward, oppressive or uneducated because of its differing views of modesty?

There are organizations, such as the Topfree Equal Rights Society (TERA), that promote the legal right for women be topless in public places. The TERA website states, "We do believe that since men may choose to do so [go topless] in many situations, women must also be able to at least in the same situations. Without penalty of any kind."

TERA questions the premise of what is defined legally as nudity and why women who go topless are often considered to be in violation of public decency laws while men who go topless are not. While TERA focuses only on the United States and Canada, the existence of organizations like TERA, along with the following examples, make me wonder what the limitations are when it comes to determining what is a 'right'; what is a violation of other people's rights, and if it is even possible to agree to national or universal standards when it comes to issues like modesty and public nudity.

BIKINIS IN THE SUPERMARKET, BURKINIS AT THE POOL

In the U.S. it is common to see cleavage in public and skimpy bathing suits on the beach, but why is it that if a woman showed up in a bikini in the supermarket she would elicit stares? What if a man went to his office wearing only boxer shorts?

In American culture it is generally not acceptable to expose that amount of skin in public. A woman in a matching g-string and a bra could not go to the neighborhood ATM without being noticed, yet if she happened to be standing on sand or near a body of water nobody would blink an eye. Well, unless of course they were checking her out.

Even in current-day Western culture, we can see that there are no clear lines. What is modest at the beach is immodest at the workplace. We have different standards of what is appropriate and inappropriate based on different contexts.

In some cases it can even be taboo to wear too much clothing. Just this month a French Muslim woman was banned from a public swimming pool in Paris. Her crime: having too much skin covered. She showed up wearing a burkini, a wetsuit-like garment that also covers the hair. Not only was she prevented from swimming with her children, but a local government official deemed her decision to wear the suit as "obviously a provocation by a militant."

In France right now, there is significant debate over whether the burka should be banned. French President Sarkozy has made it clear that "the burka is not welcome in France" and has called it "a sign of subservience…a sign of lowering."

The question here is: Is it naïve to assume that all women who wear a burka or burkini are oppressed? Should we completely discount the idea that some of these women choose to wear such garments from their own personal conviction or preference, whether or not similar garments serve as a sign of oppression for other women?

Just as most of us in the West would feel embarrassed if we were stripped to our underwear in public, could it not be that some of these women simply feel uncomfortable and shamed at the thought of showing their legs, knees, or even their faces?

NAKED BRITNEY SPEARS

In Japan, posters of a pregnant, naked Britney Spears were temporarily banned from subway stations. The poster portrayed the cover of *Harper's Bazaar* August 2006 magazine issue, and at the time many Western bloggers criticized Japanese officials for being prude and not promoting the beauty of a pregnant female body.

Eventually the subway company caved and ran the ad, but if other nude ads similar to the Spears photo had been rejected in the past, why should the fact that the singer was pregnant force the company to treat the Spears ad differently? A spokesman for Toyko Metro explained that, "Our earlier request to cover the photo from the waist down was because of nudity, not because we had anything against pregnant women."

This is an example of how one culture, represented by the editorial team at *Harper's Bazaar,* did not take into account the norms of another culture regarding what constitutes public nudity. Just because we may not be phased seeing a naked singer on billboards or magazine covers, does that mean other cultures should be forced to get used to it too?

MINI-SKIRTS, CAR ACCIDENTS AND GUERILLA WARFARE

In response to a 1970 mini-skirt ban in Malawi, one European expat wrote about how the country's "paradise was shattered" due to the ban, and it was now "a question of guerilla warfare. Chins up, hems up is the order of the day." The article relates stories of expat women ignoring the ban, getting deported for breaking the mini-skirt rule and conspiring ways to get around it.

Throughout southern Africa, the waist, hips and butt are often seen as the most sexual part of a woman's body. Countrywide mini-skirts bans have also been enacted in Swaziland and Uganda after an increase in traffic accidents allegedly caused by immodestly dressed woman. Mini-skirt wearers, both locals and foreigners, have been accused of indecency and public nudity.

Something makes me question the ethnocentrism of the European expat's attitude toward the Malawi mini-skirt ban. It is really our place to engage in "guerilla warfare" against another culture's concept of modesty? Glimpse contributor Saman Maydani wrestled with a similar issue when it came to wearing pants in Zambia. After a local man shared with her that wearing pants was considered to be "morally degenerative," she chose a different course of action than the expat women in Malawi. She started wearing skirts.

In the West, we sometimes hold to this ideas that less clothing inherently equals more freedom, and that any culture that promotes differing views of modesty is either behind the times, fundamentalist or oppressive. I see the situation as much more complicated than that, and to assume to that our view of what modesty is defines freedom or lack of it just serves as another face of cultural imperialism.

1. How do you define modesty? What cultural ideals, such as religion or nationality, affect your definition? Could your definition be considered wrong by a different culture? Why?

2. Many countries, France especially, are accusing women of being too modest and promoting an oppressive culture. Do you agree that one can be "too modest?" Can modesty be oppressive?

Arlie Russell Hochschild is a Professor Emerita of Sociology at The University of California at Berkeley. She has received the Lifetime Achievement Award from the American Sociological Association for her pioneering work in the Sociology of Emotions. Her most recent book, The Outsourced Self: Intimate Life in Market Time, *was chosen as one of* Publisher's Weekly's *Best Books of 2012.*

THE NANNY CHAIN

By Arlie Russell Hochschild

Vicky Diaz, a 34-year-old mother of five, was a college-educated schoolteacher and travel agent in the Philippines before migrating to the United States to work as a housekeeper for a wealthy Beverly Hills family and as a nanny for their two-year-old son. Her children, Vicky explained to Rhacel Parrenas,

> were saddened by my departure. Even until now my children are trying to convince me to go home. The children were not angry when I left because they were still very young when I left them. My husband could not get angry either because he knew that was the only way I could seriously help him raise our children, so that our children could be sent to school. I send them money every month.

In her forthcoming book *Servants of Globalization*, Parrenas, an affiliate of the Center for Working Families at the University of California, Berkeley, tells an important and disquieting story of what she calls the "globalization of mothering." The Beverly Hills family pays "Vicky" (which is the pseudonym Parrenas gave her) $400 a week, and Vicky, in turn, pays her own family's live-in domestic worker back in the Philippines $40 a week. Living like this is not easy on Vicky and her family. "Even though it's paid well, you are sinking in the amount of your work. Even while you are ironing the clothes, they can still call you to the kitchen to wash the plates. It ... [is] also very depressing. The only thing you can do is give all your love to [the two-year-old American child]. In my absence from my children, the most I could do with my situation is give all my love to that child."

Vicky is part of what we could call a *global care chain*: a series of personal links between people across the globe based on the paid or unpaid work of caring. A typical global care chain might work something like this: An older daughter from a poor family in a third world country cares for her siblings (the first link in the chain) while her mother works as a nanny caring for the children of a nanny migrating to a first world country (the second link) who, in turn, cares for the child of a family in a rich country (the final link). Each kind of chain expresses an invisible human *ecology of care*, one care worker depending on another and so on. A global care chain might start in a poor country and end in a rich one, or it might link rural and urban areas within the same poor country. More complex versions start in one poor country and extend to another slightly less poor country and then link to a rich country.

Global care chains may be proliferating. According to 1994 estimates by the International Organization for Migration, 120 million people migrated legally or illegally from one country to another. That's two percent of the world's population. How many migrants leave loved ones behind to care for other peoples' children or elderly parents, we don't know. But we do know that more than half of legal migrants to the United States are women, mostly between ages 25 and 34. And migration experts tell us that the proportion of women among migrants is likely to rise. All of this suggests that the trend toward global care chains will continue.

How are we to understand the impact of globalization on care? If, as globalization continues, more global care chains form, will they be "good" care chains or "bad" ones? Given the entrenched problem of third world poverty, which is one of the starting points for care chains, this is by no means a simple question. But we have yet to fully address it, I believe, because the world is globalizing faster than our minds or hearts are. We live global but still think and feel local.

FREUD IN A GLOBAL ECONOMY

Most writing on globalization focuses on money, markets, and labor flows, while giving scant attention to women, children, and the care of one for the other. Most research on women and development, meanwhile, draws a connection between, say, World Bank loan conditions and the scarcity of food for women and children in the third world, without saying much about resources expended on caregiving. Much of the research on women in the United States and Europe focuses on a chainless, two-person picture of "work-family balance" without considering the child care worker and the emotional ecology of which he or she is a part. Fortunately, in recent years, scholars such as Ernestine Avila, Evelyn Nakano Glenn, Pierette Hondagneu-Sotelo, Mary Romero, and Rhacel Parrenas have produced some fascinating research on domestic workers. Building on this work, we can begin to focus on the first world end of the care chain and begin spelling out some of the implications of the globalization of love.

One difficulty in understanding these implications is that the language of economics does not translate easily into the language of psychology. How are we to understand a "transfer" of feeling from one link in a chain to another? Feeling is not a "resource" that can be crassly taken from one person and given to another. And surely one person can love quite a few people; love is not a resource limited the same way oil or currency supply is. Or is it?

Consider Sigmund Freud's theory of displacement, the idea that emotion can be redirected from one person or object to another. Freud believed that if, for example, Jane loves Dick but Dick is emotionally or literally unavailable, Jane will find a new object (say, John, Dick and Jane's son) onto which to project her original feeling for Dick. While Freud applied the idea of displacement mainly to relations within the nuclear family, the concept can also be applied to relations extending far outside it. For example, immigrant nannies and au pairs often divert feelings originally directed toward their own children toward their young charges in this country. As Sauling C. Wong, a researcher at the University of California, Berkeley, has put it, "Time and energy available for mothers are diverted from those who, by kinship or communal ties, are their more rightful recipients."

If it is true that attention, solicitude, and love itself can be "displaced" from one child (let's say Vicky Diaz's son Alfredo, back in the Philippines) onto another child (let's say Tommy, the son of her employers in Beverly Hills), then the important observation to make here is that this displacement is often upward in wealth and power. This, in turn, raises the question of the equitable distribution of care. It makes us wonder, is there in the realm of love an analogue to what Marx calls "surplus value," something skimmed off from the poor for the benefit of the rich?

Seen as a thing in itself, Vicky's love for the Beverly Hills toddler is unique, individual, private. But might there not be elements in this love that are borrowed, so to speak, from somewhere and someone else? Is time spent with the first world child in some sense "taken" from a child further down the care chain? Is the Beverly Hills child getting "surplus" love, the way immigrant farm workers give us surplus labor? Are first world countries such as the United States importing maternal love as they have imported copper, zinc, gold, and other ores from third world countries in the past?

This is a startling idea and an unwelcome one, both for Vicky Diaz, who needs the money from a first world job, and for her well-meaning employers, who want someone to give loving care to their child. Each link in the chain feels she is doing the right thing for good reasons, and who is to say she is not?

But there are clearly hidden costs here, costs that tend to get passed down along the chain. One nanny reported such a cost when she described (to Rhacel Parrenas) a return visit to the Philippines: "When I saw my children, I thought, 'Oh children do grow up even without their mother.' I left my youngest when she was only five years old. She was already nine when I saw her again but she still wanted for me to carry her [weeps]. That hurt me because it showed me that my children missed out on a lot."

Sometimes the toll it takes on the domestic worker is overwhelming and suggests that the nanny has not displaced her love onto an employer's child but rather has continued to long intensely for her own child. As one woman told Parrenas, "The first two years I felt like I was going crazy. . . . I would catch myself gazing at nothing, thinking about my child. Every moment, every second of the day, I felt like I was thinking about my baby. My youngest, you have to understand, I left when he was only two months old. . . . You know, whenever I receive a letter from my children, I cannot sleep. I cry. It's good that my job is more demanding at night."

Despite the anguish these separations clearly cause, Filipina women continue to leave for jobs abroad. Since the early 1990s, 55 percent of migrants out of the Philippines have been women; next to electronic manufacturing, their remittances make up the major source of foreign currency in the Philippines. The rate of female emigration has continued to increase and includes college-educated teachers, businesswomen, and secretaries. In Parrenas's study, more than half of the nannies she interviewed had college degrees and most were married mothers in their 30s.

Here are men in this picture? For the most part, men especially men at the top of the class ladder leave child-rearing to women. Many of the husbands and fathers of Parrenas's domestic workers had migrated to the Arabian peninsula and other places in search of better wages, relieving other men of "male work" as construction workers and tradesmen, while being replaced themselves at home. Others remained at home, responsible fathers caring or helping to care for their children. But some of the men tyrannized their wives. Indeed, many of the women migrants Parrenas interviewed didn't just leave; they fled. As one migrant maid explained:

> You have to understand that my problems were very heavy before I left the Philippines. My husband was abusive. I couldn't even think about my children, the only thing I could think about was the opportunity to escape my situation. If my husband was not going to kill me, I was probably going to kill him... . He always beat me up and my parents wanted me to leave him for a long time. I left my children with my sister... . In the plane ... I felt like a bird whose cage had been locked for many years... . I felt free... . Deep inside, I felt homesick for my children but I also felt free for being able to escape the most dire problem that was slowly killing me.

Other men abandoned their wives. A former public school teacher back in the Philippines confided to Parrenas: "After three years of marriage, my husband left me for another woman. My husband supported us for just a little over a year. Then the support was stopped. . . . The letters stopped. I have not seen him since." In the absence of government aid, then, migration becomes a way of coping with abandonment.

Sometimes the husband of a female migrant worker is himself a migrant worker who takes turns with his wife migrating. One Filipino man worked in Saudi Arabia for 10 years, coming home for a month each year. When he finally returned home for good, his wife set off to work as a maid in America while he took care of the children. As she explained to Parrenas, "My children were very sad when I left them. My husband told me that when they came back home from the airport, my children could not touch their food and they wanted to cry. My son, whenever he writes me, always draws the head of Fido the dog with tears on the eyes. Whenever he goes to Mass on Sundays, he tells me that he misses me more because he sees his friends with their mothers. Then he comes home and cries."

THE END OF THE CHAIN

Just as global capitalism helps create a third world supply of mothering, it creates a first world demand for it. The past half-century has witnessed a huge rise in the number of women in paid work from 15 percent of mothers of children aged 6 and under in 1950 to 65 percent today. Indeed, American women now make up 45 percent of the American labor force. Three-quarters of mothers of children 18 and under now work, as do 65 percent of mothers of children 6 and under. In addition, a recent report by the International Labor Organization reveals that the average number of hours of work per week has been rising in this country.

Earlier generations of American working women would rely on grandmothers and other female kin to help look after their children; now the grandmothers and aunts are themselves busy doing paid work outside the home. Statistics show that over the past 30 years a decreasing number of families have relied on relatives to care for their children and hence are compelled to look for nonfamily care. At the first world end of care chains, working parents are grateful to find a good nanny or child care provider, and they are generally able to pay far more than the nanny could earn in her native country. This is not just a child care problem. Many American families are now relying on immigrant or out-of-home care for their *elderly* relatives. As a Los Angeles elder-care worker, an immigrant, told Parrenas, "Domestics here are able to make a living from the elderly that families abandon." But this often means that nannies cannot take care of their own ailing parents and therefore produce an elder-care version of a child care chain caring for first world elderly persons while a paid worker cares for their aged mother back in the Philippines.

My own research for two books, *The Second Shift* and *The Time Bind*, sheds some light on the first world end of the chain. Many women have joined the law, academia, medicine, business but such professions are still organized for men who are free of family responsibilities. The successful career, at least for those who are broadly middle class or above, is still largely built on some key traditional components: doing professional work, competing with fellow professionals, getting credit for work, building a reputation while you're young, hoarding scarce time, and minimizing family obligations by finding someone else to deal with domestic chores. In the past, the professional was a man and the "someone else to deal with [chores]" was a wife. The wife oversaw the family, which in pre-industrial times, anyway, was supposed to absorb the human vicissitudes of birth, sickness, and death that the workplace discarded. Today, men take on much more of the child care and housework at home, but they still base their identity on demanding careers in the context of which children are beloved impediments; hence, men resist sharing care equally at home. So when parents don't have enough "caring time" between them, they feel forced to look for that care further down the global chain.

The ultimate beneficiaries of these various care changes might actually be large multinational companies, usually based in the United States. In my research on a Fortune 500 manufacturing company I call Amerco, I discovered a disproportionate number of women employed in the human side of the company: public relations, marketing, human resources. In all sectors of the company, women often helped others sort out problems both personal and professional at work. It was often the welcoming voice and "soft touch" of women workers that made Amerco seem like a family to other workers. In other words, it appears that these working mothers displace some of their emotional labor from their children to their employer, which holds itself out to the worker as a "family." So, the care in the chain may begin with that which a rural third world mother gives (as a nanny) the urban child she cares for, and it may end with the care a working mother gives her employees as the vice president of publicity at your company.

HOW MUCH IS CARE WORTH?

How are we to respond to the growing number of global care chains? Through what perspective should we view them?

I can think of three vantage points from which to see care chains: that of the primordialist, the sunshine modernist, and (my own) the critical modernist. The primordialist believes that our primary responsibility is to our own family, our own community, our own country. According to this view, if we all tend our own primordial plots, everybody will be fine. There is some logic to this point of view. After all, Freud's concept of displacement rests on the premise that some original first object of love has a primary "right" to that love, and second and third comers don't fully share that right. (For the primordialist as for most all of us those first objects are members of one's most immediate family.) But the primordialist is an isolationist, an antiglobalist. To such a person, care chains seem wrong not because they're unfair to the least-cared-for children at the bottom of the chain, but because they are global. Also, because family care has historically been provided by women, primordialists often believe that women should stay home to provide this care.

The sunshine modernist, on the other hand, believes care chains are just fine, an inevitable part of globalization, which is itself uncritically accepted as good. The idea of displacement is hard for the sunshine modernists to grasp because in their equation seen mainly in economic terms the global market will sort out who has proper claims on a nanny's love. As long as the global supply of labor meets the global demand for it, the sunshine modernist believes, everything will be okay.

If the primordialist thinks care chains are bad because they're global, the sunshine modernist thinks they're good for the very same reason. In either case, the issue of inequality of access to care disappears.

The critical modernist embraces modernity but with a global sense of ethics. When the critical modernist goes out to buy a pair of Nike shoes, she is concerned to learn how low the wage was and how long the hours were for the third world factory worker making the shoes. The critical modernist applies the same moral concern to care chains: The welfare of the Filipino child back home must be seen as some part, however small, of the total picture. The critical modernist sees globalization as a very mixed blessing, bringing with it new opportunities such as the nanny's access to good wages but also new problems, including emotional and psychological costs we have hardly begun to understand.

From the critical modernist perspective, globalization may be increasing inequities not simply in access to money and those inequities are important enough but in access to care. The poor maid's child may be getting less motherly care than the first world child. (And for that matter, because of longer hours of work, the first world child may not be getting the ideal quantity of parenting attention for healthy development because too much of it is now displaced onto the employees of Fortune 500 companies.) We needn't lapse into primordialism to sense that something may be amiss in this.

I see no easy solutions to the human costs of global care chains. But here are some initial thoughts. We might, for example, reduce the incentive to migrate by addressing the causes of the migrant's economic desperation and fostering economic growth in the third world. Thus one obvious goal would be to develop the Filipino economy.

But it's not so simple. Immigration scholars have demonstrated that development itself can *encourage* migration because development gives rise to new economic uncertainties that families try to mitigate by seeking employment in the first world. If members of a family are laid off at home, a migrant's monthly remittance can see them through, often by making a capital outlay in a small business or paying for a child's education.

Other solutions might focus on individual links in the care chain. Because some women migrate to flee abusive husbands, a partial solution would be to create local refuges from such husbands. Another would be to alter immigration policy so as to encourage nannies to bring their children with them. Alternatively, employers or even government subsidies could help nannies make regular visits home.

The most fundamental approach to the problem is to raise the value of caring work and to ensure that whoever does it gets more credit and money for it. Otherwise, caring work will be what's left over, the work that's continually passed on down the chain. Sadly, the value ascribed to the labor of raising a child has always been low relative to the value of other kinds of labor, and under the impact of globalization, it has sunk lower still. The low value placed on caring work is due neither to an absence of demand for it (which is always high) nor to the simplicity of the work (successful caregiving is not easy) but rather to the cultural politics underlying this global exchange.

The declining value of child care anywhere in the world can be compared to the declining value of basic food crops relative to manufactured goods on the international market. Though clearly more essential to life, crops such as wheat, rice, or cocoa fetch low and declining prices while the prices of manufactured goods (relative to primary goods) continue to soar in the world market. And just as the low market price of primary produce keeps the third world low in the community of nations, the low market value of care keeps low the status of the women who do it.

One way to solve this problem is to get fathers to contribute more child care. If fathers worldwide shared child care labor more equitably, care would spread laterally instead of being passed down a social-class ladder, diminishing in value along the way. Culturally, Americans have begun to embrace this idea, but they've yet to put it into practice on a truly large scale [see Richard Weissbourd, "Redefining Dad," *TAP*, December 6, 1999]. This is where norms and policies established in the first world can have perhaps the greatest influence on reducing costs along global care chains.

According to the International Labor Organization, half of the world's women between ages 15 and 64 are working in paid jobs. Between 1960 and 1980, 69 out of 88 countries for which data are available showed a growing proportion of women in paid work (and the rate of increase has skyrocketed since the 1950s in the United States, Scandinavia, and the United Kingdom). If we want developed societies with women doctors, political leaders, teachers, bus drivers, and computer programmers, we will need qualified people to help care for children. And there is no reason why every society cannot enjoy such loving paid child care. It may even remain the case that Vicky Diaz is the best person to provide it. But we would be wise to adopt the perspective of the critical modernist and extend our concern to the potential hidden losers in the care chain. These days, the personal is global.

1. Diagram a global care chain as described by Hochschild. Describe the costs and benefits of people at each link in the chain. What things could be described as a deficit or surplus at each link? How do you think the perception of what is lost and gained change based on the perspective of people who represent different links in the chain?

2. Hochschild ends the essay by saying "the personal is global." What else does this apply to in your life? Think about anything from your clothes to your phone, or even your education.

3. Hochschild describes three perspectives of global care chains: the primordialist, the sunshine modernist, and the critical modernist. Which of these perspectives is closest to your own? How do you justify your position? What has led you to adopt this perspective?

Hungry Planet: What the World Eats *is the result of the collaborative efforts of husband-and-wife team Peter Menzel, photojournalist, and Faith D'Aluisio, writer. Previously a television news producer, D'Aluisio has co-authored a number of other works with Menzel, including* Women in the Material World *(1996),* Man Eating Bugs: the Art and Science of Eating Insects *(1998),* Robo Sapiens: Evolution of a New Species *(2000), and* What I Eat: Around the World in 80 Diets *(2010). Menzel's photography has appeared in* National Geographic *and* Smithsonian.

HUNGRY PLANET: WHAT THE WORLD EATS

By Faith D'Aluisio and Peter Menzel

Peter Menzel and I invited ourselves to dinner with 30 families in 24 countries to explore humankind's oldest social activity, eating. Anyone who remembers grocery shopping 20 years ago knows that the U.S. diet has changed rapidly, but fewer people realize that this transformation is worldwide. Some dietary changes are due to globalization, as largescale capitalism reaches new places. Others are due to rising affluence, as people in formerly impoverished places gain the means to vary their diet—first eating more meat and fish, then pizza and burgers. And some changes are due to the tides of migration, as travelers, immigrants, and refugees bring thier own foods to new lands and acquire new tastes in return. To learn more, we watched typical families the world over as they farmed, shopped, cooked, and ate. At the end of each visit, we created a protrait of the family surrounded by a week's worth of their groceries. The sum, we hope, is a culinary atlas of the planet at a time of extraordinary change.

This book began with a single mouthful of noodles. In the mid-1990's, Peter and I found ourselves in a small covered motorboat off the southeastern coast of the island of New Guinea speeding through the Arafura Sea. It was early spring—typhoon season was approaching. At this time of year, storms can come up so quickly that the local charter planes suspend operations at the slightest hint of bad weather, and even the illegal fishing trawlers plundering the tropical seas around the island are extra careful. Because our assignment schedule was tight, we couldn't wait for a less stormy day. Instead, we hunted for an experienced boat captain willing to make the seven-hour journey to the Asmat— heavily forested section of the Indonesian province of Papua—one of the most remote places on earth.

Peter is a photojournalist and I am a writer, and we have worked together in almost 50 countries over the last 12 years. We generally focus on international stories, and that day eight years ago we were headed to the Asmat to document the lives of its hunting and gathering inhabitants.

From the Asmat's ramshackle capital, Agars, we took a 40-foot longboat three hours up the Pomats River to the village of Sitwa. It was a small, poor place deep in the rain forest, a collection of wooden huts without running water, electricity, telephones, or roads of any kind. Its people live hand to mouth, felling towering sago palm trees and mashing the pulp to make their staple food, a kind of bread. When they can get them, they eat sago grubs. Occasionally, they get fish from the river. It was the steamiest, swampiest place I'd ever been. And it was there, an hour or two after our arrival, that this book began.

Peter and I were (respectively) photographing and talking with a tall skinny man and his two sons, all three of whom showed the marks of hard living. Like many in the village, the man was blind in one eye from vitamin deficiencies: the children had skin diseases and looked seriously undernourished. As we were talking, the older boy pulled a dry brick of instant ramen noodles out of its wrapper and munched it down. His naked, pot-bellied little brother tipped the ramen's flavoring packet into his own mouth and worked the powder around with his tongue until it dissolved. I was mesmerized. I saw this scene play out again and again during our time in Sawa, a place with next to no connection to the rest of the world—children eating an uncooked convenience food intended to simplify the busy lives of people very far away.

I asked a Catholic priest, a longtime resident missionary, about the noodles. He said that logging money had begun to trickle into the villages of these hunters and gatherers. Accompanying the cash came the first merchant to Sawa, a Sulawesian who sold dried food and snacks. Now there's nothing intrinsically wrong with the occasional quick snack of ramen noodles in processed broth, but your don't have to be a food activist to wonder if it is a good idea for the Asmatian, already struggling to find basic nourishment, to dose themselves with jolts of sugar, salt, and artificial flavors.

Since that visit to the Asmat we've seen similar scenes worldwide and have noticed that something odd—even revolutionary—is going on in the world of food. Producing and consuming food is one of humankind's oldest and most basic activities, but the signs of change are everywhere. Riding in taxis through Beijing, we'd see scads of Kentucky Fried Chicken outlets springing up. A grandfather in rural China who remembers the pain of hunger railed against the young Chinese he sees now, wasting food. Here at home, on assignment in the Midwest, we saw endless rows of corn and soy and learned that much of it is now genetically modified. (For better or worse, we Americans don't know when we are eating GM foods—and when we aren't.) In the suburbs of Paris, we met French teenagers whose favorite meals were Pad Thai and sushi. A young mother living in Mexico told me that she had no idea what were the ingredients of soft drinks. Her sedentary family of five was drinking six gallons of Coca-Cola a week, to the exclusion of most other beverages, even as she worried about the family's growing weight and dental problems.

The global marketplace has changed the way people are eating. Societies that are becoming less physically active are also increasing their consumption of energy-dense foods. Even without the academic studies, it's easy to spot—just look around. Many affluent countries are overfed. And unfortunately, it seems that in the developing world, even before people attain a level of influence that helps ensure their adequate nutrition, they are eating in ways almost guaranteed to make them less healthy. As charitable organizations continue their desperately important campaigns against world hunger, others begin equally important campaigns against world obesity. Meanwhile, activists left, right, and center denounce food corporations, food scientists, food conservationists, and food regulators.

To try to make sense of this fascinating, baffling, important muddle, we worked our way around the world and looked at the everyday food of everyday people everywhere—the heaping plates at middle-class mealtimes, the meager communal bowls shared by families crushed by poverty, the sacks of grain served up by overworked aid organizations, the clamorous aisles in hypermarkets, the jam-packed shelves in mom-and-pops, the foods prescribed by religious doctrine, the foods of celebration, subsidized foods. We met people along the way who helped us illustrate the bewildering diversity of what humankind eats in the 21st century: global food, snack food, fast food, junk food, health food, functional food, complimentary food, fortified food, organic food, processed food.

The result—the book in your hands—is not a diet book. Nor is it a jeremiad about supposedly evil corporations, or the supposed enemies of progress, or any of the other sides in the debate about the politics of food. Rather, it is an attempt at a global portrait at a time of momentous change—a freeze-frame snapshot of a fast-moving target.

PROCESS

Gathering information for any project that spans multiple countries is dauntingly difficult, but this one was particularly hard, not least because I often had to introduce concepts that are taken for granted in the developed world. Take, for instance, the idea of a recipe. At Breidjing Refugee Camp in eastern Chad, I asked our translator, Hassane, about the recipe for *aiysh*, the thick porridge that is the staple food of the Sudanese families in the camp. Hassane asked, "There is no such plan for cooking. She learned it from her mother." "I realize that," I replied, "but I must write down how *aiysh* is made, so that the people who read this book can make sense of the food and the process that D'jimia uses to make it." "They only make it, they don't talk about it," he argued. "I realize that, Hassane," I tried again, "but D'jimia will talk about it if we ask her. Please tell her that I have watched many women make *aiysh*, and now I want to ask about the method she uses, so I can write it down for the book."

Peter had exited this conversation, understandably enough, and was photographing at the next tent block, where a group of men were slaughtering a goat for the celebration of the end of Ramadan. D'jimia and the chief of her tent block—who was translating Hassane's Arabic into D'jimia's native Massalit—watched our exchange with interest.

"This is much too difficult," Hassane repeated, shaking his head, as we began anew—from English to Arabic, Arabic to Massalit, and back again. Within a short time, D'jimia had outlined the instructions for making *aiysh*, and we had moved on to talking about the life she and her five children used to lead and the plentiful food they'd had in Sudan, before being forced into Chad by the Janjawiid.

But the flow of information was not just one-way. Sometimes the project taught our subjects as much as it taught us. After our visit to the British village of Collingbourne Ducis in Wiltshire and the subsequent family food portrait, Deb Baintone e-mailed: "I can't believe that I was honest enough to let you photograph the amount of Mars bars I ate in a week—the average British family will be pleased to see that! I eat hardly any these days, so I suppose I've moved on to something equally unhealthy—scary thought, if I've started to get remotely healthy!"

In Shingkhey, a remote hillside village of a dozen homes, Nalim and Namgay's family assembles in the prayer room of their three-story rammed-earth house with one week's worth of food for their extended family of thirteen. Family members: Sangay Kandu, 39, Sangay, 35, holding Tandin Wangchuk (7 months), Sangay Zam (12, daughter of Sangay Kandu and Sangay), Chato Namgay (14, monk, son of Sangay Kandu and Sangay), Chato Geltshin (12, son of Sangay Kandu and Sangay).

The Mustapha family in their courtyard in Dar es Salaam village, Chad, with a week's worth of food. Gathered around Mustapha Abdallah Ishakh, 46 (turban), and Khadidja Baradine, 42 (orange scarf), are Abdel Kerim, 14, Amna, 12 (standing), Nafissa, 6, and Halima, 18 months. Lying on a rug are (left to right) Fatna, 3, granddaughter Amna Ishakh (standing in for Abdallah, 9, who is herding), and Rawda, 5. Cooking method: wood fire. Food preservation: natural drying.

The Madsen family in their living room in Cap Hope village, Greenland, with a week's worth of food. Standing by the TV are Emil Madsen, 40, and Erika Madsen, 26, with their children (left to right) Martin, 9, Belissa, 6, and Abraham, 12. Cooking method: gas stove. Food preservation: refrigerator-freezer. Favorite foods? Emil: polar bear. Erika: narwhal skin. Abraham and Belissa: Greenlandic food. Martin: Danish food.

The Ayme family in their kitchen house in Tingo, Ecuador, a village in the central Andes, with one week's worth of food. Ermelinda Ayme Sichigalo, 37, and Orlando Ayme, 35, sit flanked by their children (left to right): Livia, 15, Natalie, 8, Moises, 11, Alvarito, 4, Jessica, 10, Orlando hijo (Junior, held by Ermelinda), 9 months, and Mauricio, 30 months. Not in photograph: Lucia, 5, who lives with her grandparents to help them out. Cooking method: wood fire.

1. What kind of factors determine the quality and quantities within a family's diet?

2. Think about previous attempts to feed the hungry in other countries. Why do you think that hunger is a persistent problem in the world?

Patrick Symmes is a writer and freelance journalist for magazines including Harper's, Outside, *and* Conde Nast Traveler. *Symmes specializes in issues such as insurgencies, global environmental problems, and the geopolitics involved with each.*

THIRTY DAYS AS A CUBAN

By Patrick Symmes

Pinching pesos and dropping pounds in Havana

In the first two decades of my life I don't believe I ever went more than nine hours without eating. Later on I was subjected to longer bouts—in China in the 1980s, traveling with insurgents in remote areas of Colombia and Nepal, crossing South America by motorcycle, deeply broke—but I always returned home, feasted, ate whatever, whenever, and put back on what weight I'd lost—and more. I'd undergone the usual trajectory of American life, gaining a pound a year, decade after decade. By the time I resolved to go to Cuba, and live for a month on what a Cuban must live on, I was 219 pounds, the most I'd ever weighed in my life.

In Cuba the average salary is $20 a month. Doctors might make $30; many people make only $10. I decided to award myself the salary of a Cuban journalist: $15 a month, the wages of an official intellectual. I'd always wanted to be an intellectual, and $15 was a substantial kick above the proles building brick walls or cutting cane for $12, and almost twice the $8 paid to many retirees. With this money I would have to buy my basic ration of rice, beans, potatoes, cooking oil, eggs, sugar, coffee, and anything else I needed.

I knew it would be hard to give up food, and so I began my Cuban diet while still in New York City, shaking off nine pounds in the two months before my departure. Time and again, as I prepared for this trip, horrified friends speculated on what food I was gorging on, what special items I was rushing to consume. Their operating assumption was that being deprived of some cherished item for thirty days was an unbearable test. They were worried about ice cream. In my experience, no one who is hungry craves ice cream.

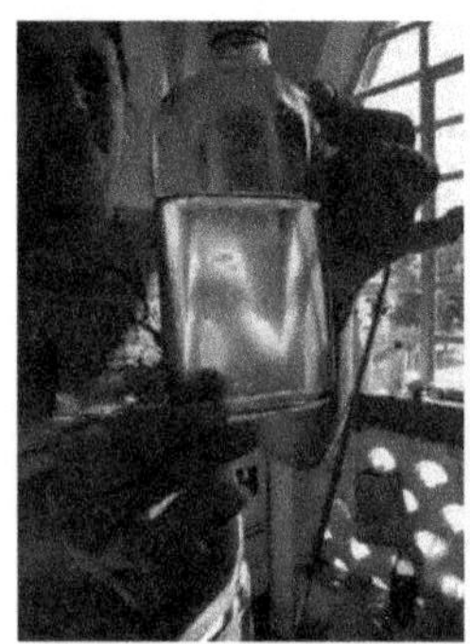

A monthly oil ration, photograph by Patrick Symmes; A shop on Calle Industria, photograph © Lorenzo Castore/Agence VU/Aurora Photos; A standard ration board, photograph by Patrick Symmes

My first half hour inside Cuba was spent at the metal detectors. Then, as part of a new regimen, unknown in my previous fifteen years coming here, I was given an intense but amateurish interrogation. This had nothing to do with me: all foreigners on the small turboprop from the Bahamas were separated out and questioned at length. The Cuban government was nervous about solitary foreign travelers because Human Rights Watch had recently been through, on tourist visas, and a State Department contractor, also traveling on a tourist visa, had been caught distributing USB drives and satphones to opposition figures. Tourists were dangerous.

As in Israel, an agent in plain clothes asked me detail-oriented questions of no importance ("What town are you going to? Where is that?"), designed to provoke me, reveal some inconsistency, or show nervousness. He didn't look in my wallet and ask why, if I was staying in Cuba for a month, I had less than twenty dollars. The supervisor's gaze settled on the other passengers. Passed. "Thirty days," I told the lady who stamped my tourist visa. The maximum.

There was a sign hanging from the airport ceiling with a drawing of a bus on it. But there was no bus. Not now, a woman at the information desk explained. There would be a bus—one—tonight, around 8 p.m., to take the airport workers home.

That was six hours from now. Central Havana was ten miles away. Since taxis cost about $25—more than my total budget for the next month—I was going to have to walk.

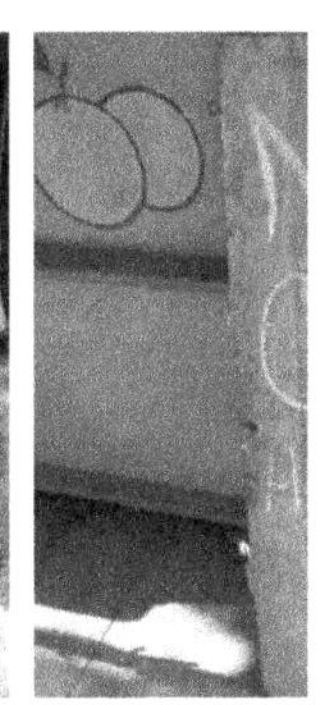

A daily bread ration, photograph © Alfredo Falvo/Contrasto/Redux; An agro, photograph by Patrick Symmes; The meat annex of an agro, photograph by Patrick Symmes

The same woman pulled from her uniform pocket a couple of aluminum coins, which she gave to me: 40 centavos, or about 2 U.S. cents. Out on the highway, a few miles from here, I might find a city bus. And in Havana I might find, must find, a way to survive for a month. I had to shoulder my knapsack and start walking, the aluminum coins clicking in my pocket. I strolled out of the terminal, across the parking lot, out the driveway, and turned down the only road, putting the outside world behind me with a steady slog. Every few minutes a taxi would pull up, beeping, or a private car would stop, offering to take me for half the official price. I walked on, slowly, past the old terminals, along scrubby fields. Billboards trumpeted old messages: *Bush Terrorist.* After forty minutes I passed over a railroad crossing, came out to the highway, and got lucky. The bus for Havana was right there. An hour later I was in central Havana and on foot, searching for an old friend.

The first people I spoke to in the city—total strangers who lived near my friend[1]—brought up the ration system. With no prompting from me, they pulled out their ration book and bitched.

The book—called the *libreta*—is the foundational document of Cuban life. Nothing important about the ration system has changed: although it is now printed in a vertical format, the book looks identical to the one issued annually for decades.

What has changed is the ink: there is less written in the book. There are fewer entries, for smaller amounts, than even in 1995, during the starving time of the "Special Period." In the intervening years, the Cuban economy has recovered; the Cuban ration system has not. In 1999, a Cuban development minister told me that the monthly ration supplied enough food to last just nineteen days, but predicted that the amount would soon climb. It has declined. Although the total amount of food available in Cuba is greater, and caloric consumption is up, that is no thanks to the ration system. The growth has occurred in privatized markets and cooperative gardens and through massive imports, while state food production fell 13 percent last year and the ration shrank with it. It is commonly agreed that a monthly food ration now contains just twelve days of food. I was here to make my own calculation: how could anyone survive the month on twelve days of food?

There is one ration book per family. Goods are distributed at a series of neighborhood bodegas (one for dairy and eggs; another for "protein"; another for bread; the largest for dry goods and everything from coffee to cooking oil to cigarettes). Each store has a clerk who writes in the amount issued to the family. My friend's neighbors—husband, wife, and grandson—had received a standard ration of staples, which was, per person:

4 pounds refined sugar

1 pound crude sugar

1 pound grain

1 piece fish

3 rolls

They laughed when I asked if there was beef.

"Chicken," the wife said, but this produced howls of protest. "When was there chicken?" her husband asked. "Well, that's true," she said. "It has been a few months." The "protein" ration was delivered every fifteen days and was ground mystery meat, mixed with a large amount of soy paste (if the meat was pork, this was falsely called *picadillo*;

if it was chicken, it was called *pollo con suerte,* or chicken and luck). Usually there was enough for about four hamburgers a month, but so far in January they had received only one fish each—usually a dried, oily mackerel.

And there were eggs. The most reliable of all protein sources, these were called *salvavidas,* or lifesavers. There used to be an egg a day; then it became an egg every other day; now it was an egg every third day. I would have ten for the next month.

The husband spent a full quarter of his tiny salary on the electric bill. The family survived only because, in his job as a state chauffeur, he could steal about five liters of gasoline every week.

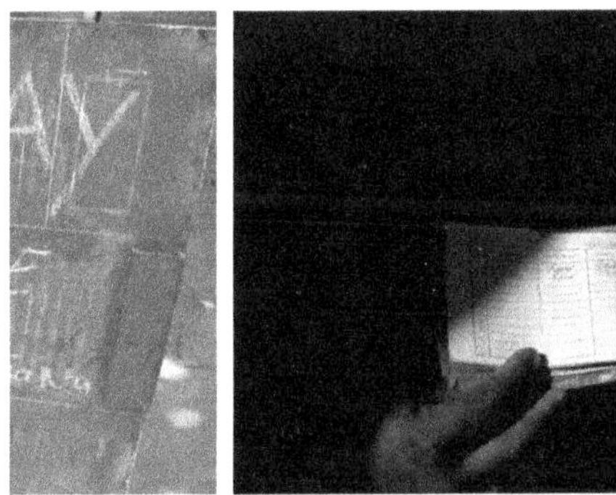

A daily bread ration, photograph © Alfredo Falvo/Contrasto/Redux; An agro, photograph by Patrick Symmes; The meat annex of an agro, photograph by Patrick Symmes

Eventually my friend appeared and squired me off to a private home in the Plaza neighborhood, where I had arranged to rent an apartment for the month—the one expense left out of my accounting here. It was spartan, in the Cuban style: two rooms, cushionless chairs, a double burner on a countertop, and a half-size refrigerator. I unloaded my pockets, stashing away the food I had bought in the Bahamian airport: some bagels, a can of fruit punch, sandwiches, and—my emergency stash—a packet of sesame sticks from the airplane. With a fourteen-hour trip from New York behind me, I ate one of the sandwiches and went to sleep.

On my second day, I gnawed on a sesame bagel, absentmindedly consuming the whole thing, as if there would always be another. According to a calorie-counting application on my cell phone, the bagel had 440 calories. Everything I ate for the next month would be entered on that little keypad, recorded, summed up by day and week, divided into protein, carbohydrates, and fat, graphed in scrolling bars. An active man of my size (six foot two, 210 pounds) needs about 2,800 calories a day to maintain his weight. I had no other food supplies yet, and I finished breakfast when the housekeeper working for my landlord gave me two thimbles of coffee, larded with sugar (75 calories).

Just as Cubans exploit loopholes to survive, I worked my obvious foreignness to my benefit, wandering that day in and out of fancy hotels few Cubans could enter. This gave me access to air-conditioning, toilet paper, and music. I blew past security at the Habana Libre, the old Hilton, and rode the elevator to the top floor, which offered commanding views of Havana at dusk. The nightclub wasn't open yet, but I barged in anyway, discovering a rehearsal in progress. A Russian rocker, backed by more than thirty musicians, was working through his set in preparation for some later gig. They had been issued bottled water and tea, which I consumed in large amounts. Tea's astringent taste—mediated by lots of sugar—finally made sense to me. This was the drink of the novice monk, the cold and hungry. It was an appetite killer.

There had been catering. Only one and a half cheese sandwiches remained, abandoned on a napkin near the string section; during a crescendo I stuffed them into my pockets. I walked the hour back across Havana to my room, passing dozens of new stores, butcher shops, bars, cafeterias and cafés, pizza joints, and other prolific suppliers of hard-currency food. I lingered, looking at the immense frozen turkey breasts for sale in a shop window.

By the time I got to my room, the sandwiches had disintegrated in my pockets, a mass of crumbs, butter, and cheese product, but I ate them, slowly, dragging the experience out. I'd always scorned the Cubans who cheered the regime for a sandwich, but by day two I was ready to denounce Obama for a cookie.

On the morning of the third day I walked for more than two hours through Havana in search of food, burning 600 calories, the equivalent of those cheese sandwiches. I had wrongly assumed that I could simply buy the food I needed for the month. But as an American I was ineligible for the ration, through which rice costs a penny a pound. As a "Cuban" living on $15 a month I could not afford to buy food outside the system, in the expensive dollar stores. Cubans called these small stores, which sold everything from batteries and beef to cooking oil and diapers, *el shopping.* After hours of frustration, unable to buy any food at all, I rode the bus back to my apartment.

I had no lunch. I tried reading, but I had brought only books about hardship and suffering, like *Les Misérables.* I started with an easier, more comic take on loneliness and deprivation, *Sailing Alone Around the World* by Joshua Slocum, and consumed 146 pages on my first day. Slocum got across the Atlantic on little more than biscuits, coffee, and flying fish, and I took particular satisfaction when, mid-Pacific, he discovered that his potatoes were ridden with moths and was forced to chuck the valuable rations overboard. But then he would do something unconscionable, like cook an Irish stew or call on some reserve of smoked venison from Tierra del Fuego. A passing boat even tossed him a bottle of Spanish wine once, the bastard. Reading at this rate, books were another thing I would run out of.

Finally, unable to lie still any longer, I raced out of the house and, following a tip, found a house a few blocks away with a cardboard sign on the gate reading cafe. Behind the house there was a barred window, and I put the equivalent of 40 cents through the bars. A woman passed out a roll filled with processed lunch meat. For another 12 cents I got a small glass of papaya juice. Although I tried to eat slowly, lunch vanished within moments. At this rate—half a dollar a meal—my entire cash supply would be eaten up, and I left her back yard vowing to eat almost nothing for dinner.

Worse news awaited me in the morning when, upon dressing, I discovered that the zipper on my pants was broken. In another effort to look and feel Cuban, I had brought only two pairs of pants. Pants are one of the many non-food items distributed by ration, and that meant, typically, one pair a year. Most Cubans got along with just a couple of items of clothing of each type. So the broken zipper would have to be repaired—there were no pants in January. A few feeble attempts to repair it myself failed. I was going to have to spend some money, or trade something, for a tailor's work. Breakfast: coffee, two cups, with sugar. 75 calories total.

I went food shopping on day four, a ludicrous experience. By chance I had ended up taking an apartment near the largest and best market in Havana, which was neither large nor good. The market was an *agro,* meaning a place for farm produce. These are sometimes referred to as farmers' markets, but there was no farmer meets-consumer bonhomie, only a roaring, crowded, sweaty pen of stalls selling the same narrow band of goods at prices set by the state: pineapples, eggplants, carrots, green peppers, tomatoes, onions, yucca, garlic, plantains, and not much else. There was a separate room specializing in pork, with quivering heaps of dull pink meat turned over by bare-handed men and measured out by dull knives. Meat was beyond my reach, though "fat" was listed at only 13 pesos (or 49 cents) a pound.

I waited in line to change my entire stock of money—eighteen hard currency *pesos convertibles*—into the regular Cuban pesos.[2] The resulting pile of worn, dirty bills added up to 400 pesos, worth about $16 at the Havana street rate. Then I fought through the crowds to buy one eggplant (10 pesos), four tomatoes (15), garlic (2), and a small bunch of carrots (13). At a bakery counter a woman selling bread rolls affirmed they were only for people with ration books—but then threw me five rolls and greedily snatched 5 pesos out of my hand. The only love came from the tomato vendor, who threw in an extra nightshade.

I bought three pounds of rice for a little more than a dime, and some red beans, spending a catastrophic $2 for what would, in the end, produce only a handful of meals.

Young hustlers followed me to the exit muttering, "Shrimp, Shrimp, Shrimp." Outside, a man saw me coming and climbed into a tree, descending again with five limes, which he offered me (it was not a lime tree but a drop zone for his black-market produce). I staggered home under the weight of the rice and vegetables, looking, as my landlady later observed, like a divorced man starting his new life.

The accumulated calories inevitably led me to speculate on the other side of things: money. How would I survive a couple of weeks from now, if I was spending the equivalent of $2 at a pop? I continued to hoof it everywhere, taking the hour-long walk just to wander through the tourist hotels of Vedado (without ever spotting another stray sandwich), or stand with my face pressed to the iron grille of some restaurant, watching, with four or five Cubans, the band play a mambo for foreigners.

Every day I was approached by Cubans who said, in one phrase or another, *Give me money.* My own options would be grim in the weeks ahead. Should I stand on the street corner, demanding dollars from strangers? How hungry did you have to get before you became like the teenage girl I overtook on a Vedado sidewalk that afternoon, who, holding a baby on her hip, turned to me and said, *Deseas una chica sucky sucky?*

If I was going to suck something, I knew what it would be. I found myself watching the Ladas as they rolled past, trying to see how many had locking gas caps. With some tubing and a jug, I could get five liters of gasoline and sell it through a friend in Chinatown. But all the cars in Cuba had locking gas caps or were themselves locked behind gates at night. Too many men, harder than I, were already working that line. This was no island for amateur thieves.

I needed coffee, but all stores were barren of this staple. Even the hard-currency shopping in the neighborhood carried no coffee, and repeated tours of the dollar supermarkets in Vedado and at various hotels had revealed no coffee all month. I had once seen a pound of Cubacafe, the dark, export-grade stuff, for sale at a movie theater in Old Havana. But it was 64 pesos, and even while jonesing I could not pay that much or walk that far. From the window of my bathroom I could see that the ration store was open, and so I wandered over.

There were five satchels of coffee on the shelf. It was the light-brown domestic brand, Hola, which sells for a little more than a peso for the first four-ounce bag, and 5 pesos a sack after that. A dozen people were jostling for bread and rice, so I had time to study the two chalkboards listing which goods were available. The larger board listed basic ration goods. Your first four pounds of rice cost 25 centavos; the next pound was 90 centavos. No more than six pounds of rice were allowed in a month, to prevent overselling for profit. The smaller chalkboard listed "liberated products," a briefer list of cigarettes and other items that could be bought without limit.

I called out *El último*, and was now holding a place in line behind the previous last customer. Pretty soon a woman with a plastic bag arrived, cried *El último*, and I lifted a finger. Now she was last. I was served by a smiling but agitated man. He was tall, black, with a scruffy partial beard. He waved his hand when I asked for coffee. No words were necessary: a foreigner cannot buy on the ration, and there was no coffee anyway. I played for time, holding up my end of a conversation in which he was silent but for gestures. No coffee anywhere? I've been all over the city looking for coffee. Nobody has any. I really like coffee. You know what I mean? "Cubans drink a lot of coffee," he finally said. Our bond established, I wiggled my head back and forth and asked, Wasn't there somewhere to get coffee? "No," he said. Really? Maybe someone had some? A little bit? He wiggled his head. The *maybe* gesture.

Who?

"Mrs. ——," he said.

Where was that?

As though guiding a blind man, he came out from behind the counter, took my arm, and led me out onto the street. We went only ten steps down the sidewalk. He turned into the first doorway and absentmindedly grabbed the ass of a passing woman. ("Hey!" she cried, furious. "Who's that?") We stopped at an apartment located directly behind the ration store. He knocked. A woman with a baby answered.

"Coffee," he said.

I produced a 20-peso bill. She handed me one satchel of the Hola and 5 pesos back.

"That's all?" It was three times the price listed at the counter a few steps away, but I found later that Cubans also paid this markup.

He nodded. His name was Jesús.

We went back to the store. "Bread?" I asked. He consulted with his supervisor, who gave a "No" loud enough for the whole store to hear.

I asked again. He asked his boss again. No *no* this time. I handed over the 5-peso note and got five rolls.

From then on, I could buy whatever I wanted. With Jesús on my side, no questions were asked. I never needed a ration book for the common staples, and for the rest of the month I paid the same price as Cubans for the same shit food.

On the sixth day I walked to the suburbs, strolling out of my neighborhood, Plaza, through Vedado and to the west, past the immense *Colón* cemetery, home to the mausoleums and soaring angels of Cuba's once-rich families, as well as the concrete sepulchers of her middle class. A young man named Andy fell into step with me for a while, excited to hear about America ("We all want to go there") and inviting me to a barbershop owned by his friend. Alone again, I passed the occasional café, studying each of these tiny stands. One offered "bread with hamburger" for 10 pesos, the lowest price I had seen yet. But that was still too much for today.

I joined the world of the long-range pedestrian, working my way down a dozen avenues and more than twenty streets in the course of an hour and finding a small bridge over the *Almendares* River that separates Havana proper from Havana greater. Exiles wax nostalgic about the *Almendares*, whose twisting route is overgrown with vines and immense trees, but I always found it depressing or even frightening: a humid, muddy border between the gritty city and the expansive (and expensive) houses of the western suburbs. From a low Oceanside bridge I could see what remained of the sailor scene: a dozen sunken hulls, a few collapsing houseboats, and abandoned boat shacks. Only two boats were in motion: a police launch and a dismasted micro-yacht of twenty feet or so, apparently incapable of reaching Florida.

I made a right turn into Miramar, passing some of Cuba's grandest mansions and many embassies. This was "the zone of the moneybags, foreign firms, and people with lineage," a prostitute says in the book *Havana Babylon*. "Living in Miramar, even in a toilet, is a sign of distinction."

I was pursued by two women waving a gigantic can of tomato sauce and shouting "Fifteen pesos! It's for our children!" I went on but later realized I had made a mistake. At 15 pesos for a restaurant-size container, the tomato sauce had been good value. Stolen food was the cheapest food. And nothing could be more normal here than wandering around with a huge can of something.

A few blocks later I stumbled on the Museum of the Interior Ministry. The museum was staffed by women in khaki MININT uniforms, with green shoulder boards and knee-length skirts. The entrance fee was 2 CUC, they told me. I couldn't pay that, of course. How much was it for a Cuban, I asked? Wrong question. You don't bargain with MININT.

I said I would come back another time, but dawdled in the entrance hall, which had its own exhibits: racks of machine guns, photos of the big MININT headquarters near my apartment, and oversized quotes from Raúl Castro and other officials praising the patriots at MININT for protecting the nation.

One of the women, hair in a tight bun, watched me. Although I took no notes or pictures, she was shrewd.

"Who are you?" she asked.

I smiled and turned to leave.

"Are you a journalist?" she demanded.

"Tourist," I said, over my shoulder, and racewalked away.

"Are you accredited here?" she called after me.

I continued westward on foot for another half hour. I was coated in sweat by the time I reached the house of Elizardo Sánchez, one of MININT's targets.

When I told Sánchez I had walked here, as part of spending thirty days living and eating as a Cuban, he showed me his *libreta*. "They call this the supply booklet, but it's a rationing system, the longest-running one in the world. The Soviets didn't have rationing for as long as Cuba. Even the Chinese didn't ration this long." Shortages began soon after the revolution; a system for the controlled distribution of basic goods was in place by 1962.

After fifty years of progress, the country was effectively bankrupt. In 2009, peas and potatoes had been removed from the ration, and cheap workplace lunches had been shrunk down to snack-size portions. "There was talk of removing things from the ration, or getting rid of it entirely," Sánchez told me, repeating the rumor that captivated all Cubans. But the talk had died on January 1, 2010, when the new *libretas* were handed out, like always.

Sánchez was happily ignorant of the domestic arts. "Four pounds of rice at 25 centavos," he said, trying to recall his monthly allotment. "I think. And, uh, a fifth pound at 90 centavos, I think. Let's consult the women. They dominate on this matter." He called to his common-law wife, Barbara. Aside from being a lawyer who worked on prisoners' cases, she cooked and was helping her mother and another woman run a bakery out of the kitchen. They had bought a bag of flour "on the left," meaning it was stolen or bought from a connection. This cost 30 pesos. With this and some ground beef purchased under the counter at the butchers, they made tiny empanadas that they sold for 3 pesos apiece, or about eight for a dollar. This was how Cuba got along: the ration stores were staffed by neighbors, who stole and resold ingredients, which were then reworked into finished products and sold back to these same neighbors. Eight empanadas would make a lunch, but a dollar was inconceivably beyond my budget. Barbara gave me two, each of which I demolished in a bite.

She listened blankly as I explained my attempt to live on the ration. "It's a great diet plan," she said. Another dissident visiting the house, Richard Rosello, piped in. He'd been filling a notebook with the prices of goods on the parallel markets, also called the clandestine or black-bag markets. "One problem is food," Richard said, "but another is how do you pay your light bill, the gas, the rent? Electricity has gone up four to seven times in cost compared with before." Elizardo was paying nearly 150 pesos a month for electricity—a quarter of the typical salary.

How to get by, then? "Cubans invent something," Barbara said. One trick was "overselling" your cheap, rationed goods at market prices. I'd finally scored my allotment of ten eggs this way. Without a ration book I could not buy the eggs legally. But at dusk the night before, I had waited near my local egg shop and made eyes at an elderly woman who'd emerged with thirty eggs—a month's supply for three people. She'd bought them for 1.5 pesos each and sold me ten of them for 2 pesos apiece. She immediately spent the money on more, turning a profit of three eggs and change. We both walked home gingerly, afraid of smashing a month's protein with a single misstep.

Barbara now pointed out a terrible mistake in my plan. In recent years, most sources outside Cuba reported that the ration includes five pounds of black beans. But it had been years since this was true. This month, the allotment was just eight ounces.

Ten thousand calories had just evaporated from my month.

To make up for this blow, Barbara decided to treat me to a "typical" Cuban lunch. This began with rice, at four or five dry pounds per person each month the mainstay of Cuba's diet. Each citizen could eat about as much cooked rice per day as fits in a condensed-milk can. It was low-quality Vietnamese rice and variously called "creole," "ugly," or "microjet" rice, the last a mocking reference to one of Fidel's plans to boost agricultural production with drip irrigators. A typical lunch included half a can of cooked rice (the other half saved for dinner); it was a gooey mash, but it tasted good enough, sauced by my hunger.

Next was a bowl of bean soup. It had only a handful of beans, but the broth was rich, flavored with beef bones. ("Ten pesos a pound for bones," Barbara noted. "Many people can't afford it.")

I hadn't tasted meat in six days.

Then she gave me half a small sweet potato. "Much better nutritionally than potato!" Elizardo called from somewhere down the hall.

There was also a fried egg, although, as Elizardo noted with another shout, "Eat that egg today and you won't eat one tomorrow." Or the day after.

The egg was wonderful. With my shrunken stomach, the whole meal, including the two little empanadas, was perfectly adequate. I chewed on the bones, extracting small bits of meat. This was the best I'd eaten in days. Barbara carefully preserved the oil from the frying pan.

Richard, with his little notebook of prices, pointed out the math of eating this way. A "monthly basket" of rationed food (which actually lasted just twelve days) cost 12 pesos a person, by government calculation. For the next ten days, people had to buy the same food for about 220 pesos on the various free, parallel, and black markets. That still got you only to day twenty two. A month would run about 450 pesos—more than the entire incomes of millions of Cubans, and that didn't account for clothes, transport, or household goods.

No one could afford cups and plates anymore. These were stolen from state enterprises when possible and traded on the black market. Clothes had to be bought used, at swap meets called *troppings*, a play on the hard-currency *shoppings*. Those who ran out of food went rummaging in dumpsters, or became alcoholics to numb the pain, he said.

Elizardo came back in. "This isn't Haiti, or Sudan," he said. "People aren't falling over in the streets, dead of hunger. Why? Because the government guarantees four or five pounds of sugar, which is high in calories, and bread every day, and enough rice. The problem in Cuba isn't food, or clothes. It's the total lack of civil liberty, and therefore of economic liberty, which is why you have to have the *libreta* in the first place."

As in the rest of the world, the problem of food is really one of access, of money. And the problem of money is one of politics.

On the seventh day I rested. Lying in bed with Victor Hugo, lost in the test of man's goodness, I could forget for an hour at a time that my gums ached, that saliva was bathing my throat.

Havana was changing, as cities do. The historic zone had been placed under the control of Eusebio Leal Spengler, the city historian. Leal had been given special priority for building supplies, labor, trucks, tools, fuel, pipes, cement, wood, even faucets and toilets. But this was not why the people loved him. Instead, my friend explained, the "privileged" access to supplies simply meant that *there was more to steal*.

A friend of mine was renovating in hopes of renting rooms to foreigners, and indeed within a few minutes there was a screech of truck brakes and a great horn blast. Her husband signaled to me urgently, and we threw open the front door. A flatbed truck was waiting. In sixty seconds, three of us unloaded 540 pounds of Portland cement bags. The husband passed some wadded bills to the trucker, who promptly roared off. They had made money off cement destined for some construction job. We spent half an hour moving the bags to a dark corner in a back room, covering them with a tarp because they were printed with blue ink, marking them as state property. Green printing was for school construction. Only cement in red-printed bags could be bought by citizens, in state stores, at $6 a bag.

Unlike most Cuban functionaries, Leal had actually made a difference in people's lives. He rebuilt the old hotels; my friends took 540 pounds of cement for their new tourist bungalow. He restored a museum; they looted tin sheeting for roofs. He sent trucks of lumber into the neighborhood; they made half the wood vanish.

The State owned all. The people appropriated all. A ration system in reverse.

Helping to steal the cement was my first great success. For half an hour of labor, I was paid with a heaping plate of rice and red beans, topped with a banana and a small portion of picadillo. At least 800 calories.

The second week was easier, my two little shelves well stocked with bags of rice and beans, some sweet potatoes at 80 centavos a pound, and my bottle of smuggled whiskey still half full. I had nine, and then eight, and then seven eggs, though the refrigerator was otherwise barren.

I had given up luxuries like sandwiches (or sandwich, singular: I had bought only one, but the expense still haunted me). On day ten I found I had 100 pesos left. As with the eggs, could imagine a careful, slow reduction over the next twenty days, but my budget and diet could be equally ruined by a slip that left a yolk on the floor. It all came down to a question of how long the rice would last: with just 5 pesos per day remaining, I could afford no major purchases for the rest of my stay. I learned to suppress my appetite, walking past the queues of Cubans buying tiny balls of fried dough for a peso apiece. My only indulgence was a bar of stiff peanut butter, handmade by farmers, which sold for 5 pesos in the *agros*. With restraint, this little slab of about six tablespoons of crudely ground, heavily sweetened peanut could be made to last two days. The poorest *campesinos* could be seen nibbling on these packets of peanut butter, carefully rewrapping after each bite.

Another thing I had in common with most Cubans was that I did absolutely no work during my thirty days. That is to say, I worked hard and often at my own projects—I hauled cement and shoveled gravel for food, and wrote a lot—but it was not state labor, not the kind of work that is counted in the columns of official Cuba, where more than 90 percent of people are state employees. Why should I get a job? Nobody else took theirs seriously, and the oldest joke in Havana is still the best: They pretend to pay us, we pretend to work.[3]

So I had time on my hands. That night I heard music and found a series of stages set up along 23rd Street, culminating in a good rock band playing under a rising moon. I sat on the pedestal of some heroic obscurity—the statue of a mother thrusting her son toward battle. After a while a small girl, seven or eight, came and sat on the stone.

"*Caramelo?*" she said. Sweet?

"I don't have any."

"None?"

"No."

"Not one?"

"No."

Then the usuals: where are you from, where do you live, why are you here? And again: "Some money?"

"I don't have any."

"But foreigners always have so much money."

"Yes, in my country I have money. But here, I live like a Cuban."

"Give me a peso?"

I can't. I'm playing a game, my dear. I'm pretending to be broke. I'm living like your parents for a while. I haven't eaten in nine hours. In the past eleven days I've missed 12,000 calories off my normal diet. My teeth hurt so badly.

Or, in Spanish, "*No.*"

I finally strode home to a long-awaited celebration. It was Friday, and tonight was the weekly Eating of the Meat. Although the day had so far been one of my worst—less than 1,000 calories by 9 p.m., with a huge amount of walking—I was determined to make up for it with a feast. I prepared rice, put a single sweet potato in the pressure cooker—known to Cubans as The-One-Fidel-Gave-Us, because they were handed out in an energy-saving scheme—and poured a precious glass of whiskey (250 calories) on the rocks, all with a side of yesterday's beans and rice. Of necessity the portions were small.

From the freezer I drew my protein, one of four breaded chicken cutlets for the month. I fired the stove carelessly and burned the cutlet black, though at the table it proved cold and soggy on the inside. It was not chicken. It was not even the "formed chicken" it claimed to be. The principal ingredients were listed as wheat paste and soy. Close inspection revealed no chicken at all. I was eating a breaded sponge with only 180 calories. Ah, for a McNugget.

In the end, I crossed the 2,000- calorie barrier for the first time in ten days, just barely. Discounting for a huge amount of walking and a little dancing, this left me at my familiar benchmark of 1,700 calories. But my stomach was full when I went to bed.

Or so I thought. After two hours of sleep, I woke with insomnia, the companion to hunger. From 1 a.m. until dawn I lay in bed, five hours of swatting at mosquitoes, tossing, reading Victor Hugo and Alexandre Dumas *père*.

Still, I can't compare my situation to real hunger. As Hugo notes, "Behind living on a little lies the art of living on nothing." I sank into thousands of pages of nineteenth-century France, two authors describing revolution, forced marches, and real starvation. "When one has not eaten," Hugo writes, "it is very queer. . . . He chewed that inexpressible thing which is called the cud of bitterness. A horrible thing, which includes days without bread, nights without sleep." So came the dawn, my twelfth.

Suddenly, fortune and happiness. The next night, as I sat in front of my apartment watching the street, my neighbor came walking down the alley holding a phone. A phone call. For me. It was a friend of a friend, visiting Cuba with her boyfriend. They were verifiable ain't-we-grand Americans, and I instantly smelled free food. They'd landed in Havana and, unfamiliar with the city or Spanish, were inviting me to dine with them. We went for a walk around Vedado and I carefully avoided pleading for food, playing the stoic. They bought dinner at a tourist restaurant, and for the first time I ate pork. The next afternoon we met again. I took them to see a Santería initiation, an hour of steamy drumming in a tiny apartment, complete with three separate acts of possession. Another invitation to dine at a fancy restaurant followed.

More pork!

Cubans marinate *lechón*, the innocent little suckling pig, with garlic and bitter orange, and slow-cook it until you can eat it with a spoon. Along with the glistening fat and protein, we were served a platter of rice and beans, exactly what I ate twice a day in my own kitchen. The platter would make four meals for me, I explained.

"Excuse me," the boyfriend said, helping himself. "I'm just going to eat your Thursday."

Like the hundreds of Cubans whom I have fed over the years, I sang for my supper. The lore of Afro-Cuban cults. The history of buildings I had never seen before. Strolls in the shoes of Capone, Lansky, Churchill, and Hemingway. Socialism jokes. The arts of the ration. The secret of the daiquiri. Both of those nights I had some pork, rice and beans, and a pair of cocktails.

Despite the meat I was hardly better off—just 2,100 calories each day, compared with my usual 1,700. But the meals added to my psychological well-being. I had carried off a respite, a vacation, from the grinding anxiety of seeing my dry goods evaporate.

The next morning I found a woman riffling through my garbage. She wanted glass bottles or anything valuable: I gave her my broken pants. She was eighty-four years old, the same age as my mother, and lived on a pension of 212 pesos a month, or a little over $8. She scavenged in the trash for items—to the fury of my housekeeper, who considered the trash her own resource—and worked as a *colero*, or professional line-waiter, for five families on this block. She took their ration books to the bodega, collected and delivered the monthly goods, and was paid a total of about 133 pesos for this. She was sucking on an asthma inhaler that cost 20 pesos, or about 75 cents, but only the first one came at that price: others had to be bought on the black market at several dollars apiece.

In return for my pants, she mentioned that the "free" bakery was stocked. This was the non-ration bakery, where anyone could buy a loaf. The price is four times that of the ratio bakeries, but there is much more bread. I retrieved a plastic bag, walked eight blocks (passing three empty ration bakeries), and bought a loaf for 10 pesos.

As I walked home, a woman passing the other way asked, "They have bread?" She doubled her pace.

Then, as I passed a chess game under a shortleaf fig tree, a man looked up and asked the same.

"Yes, there is bread," I told him.

He toppled the pieces, rolled up the board, and both players decamped for the bakery.

Breakfast had been a tiny, hard plantain, bought from a man in an alley. With coffee and sugar, it was less than 200 calories. Lunch was an egg and two slivers of the new bread, for another 380.

There were three dollars in my wallet and seventeen days to go.

A catastrophic mistake. I had been afoot all afternoon, my blood sugar bottoming out, and when I passed an alley with a small piece of cardboard reading pizza, I stopped and bought one. The basic pizza—a six-inch disk of dough smeared with ketchup and a tablespoon of cheese—cost 10 pesos. But I impulsively supersized my order, adding chorizo. It was now a 15-peso snack.

In my apartment I set the little pizza down and stared in horror. 15 pesos was an incredible, budget-busting 60 cents. I could have bought pounds of rice for that amount. Staring at the puny thing, smaller than a single slice in America, I began trembling. I had to sit down. Then I burst into tears. For a good ten minutes I wept, cursing myself. Moron! Fool! Idiot!

I had spent a fifth of my remaining money on impulse. Now I had just 64 pesos to survive the next seventeen days. What would happen to me now? How would I eat when I ran out of beans, which were already low? What if there was another mistake? What if I was robbed? How would I get to the airport on the last day if I didn't have even a few pennies for bus fare?

Crying releases not just tension and fear but endorphins. Around the time the pizza had cooled down, I had, too. I ate it carefully, with a knife and fork, and a glass of ice water. This "meal" lasted less than two minutes. It was the low point of my month. An hour later, there was a knock on the door. The child of one of my neighbors was outside. "*Patri!*" she cried. "*Patri!*"

I went out. She handed me a shoe box. It was heavy and covered in packing tape. Someone had stopped by—another American visiting Cuba—and dropped it off. In the kitchen I cut it open and found a note from my wife and young son, and three dozen homemade tea cookies.

I ate ten cookies. Ambush to escape. Tears to peace. Damnation to joy.

I rationed the rest of the cookies: five per day until they ran low, then two per day, and finally I disassembled the box with a knife and ate the crumbs out of the corners.

Once a day I indulged my vanity, standing shirtless in front of a mirror and staring at a man I had not seen in fifteen years. I had lost four, then six, then eight pounds. But the stomach and mind adjust with frightening ease. My first week had been pained and starving. The second was pained and hungry. Now, in my third week, I was eating less than ever but was at ease both physically and mentally.

I had my worst day so far, eating just 1,200 calories. That was the intake of an American POW in Japan during WWII.

I went back to my friends the cement thieves, and after much waiting, the woman cooked me a generous dinner, cackling with laughter over "your experiment." She had fried (in oil stolen from a school) some ground chicken (bought from a friend who stole it), which she served with the "ugly" rice from the ration and a single tiny beet. After the meal, she even made me some eggnog, but in a Cuban serving—one mouthful, in an espresso cup. There were also a few spoonfuls of papaya (1 peso each, at a cheap market she recommended), cooked down in sugar syrup.

"It's impossible," she said of my attempt to be officially Cuban. For survival, everyone had to have "an extra," some income outside the system. Her husband rented a room to a Norwegian sex tourist. Her neighbor sold lunches to the workers who'd recently lost their canteen meals. Her own mother wandered the streets with pitchers of coffee and a cup, selling jolts of caffeine. Her friend around the corner stole the cooking oil and resold it for 20 pesos a pint. Another neighbor stole the ground chicken and resold it for 15 pesos a pound. ("Good quality, a very good price, you should get some," and I did.)

Her meal was the only one I ate that day, the calories undercut by an astonishing walk not just across Havana but completely around it, passing in a giant loop down the carbuncled streets, through big hotels, past dim houses, among people sleeping without roofs, sitting on packing crates, onward all the time, hours in rotation through noon, afternoon, evening, on wide avenues and in narrow alleys, across Plaza, Vedado, Centro, Old Havana, into Cerro, out through Plaza again, into Vedado again, two, four, six, eight miles, past the bus station, the sports stadium, burning holes in my shoes, and then to bed.

My feet hurt. But there wasn't the slightest complaint from my stomach.

I used to say that 10 percent of everything was stolen in Cuba, to be resold or repurposed. Now I think the real figure is 50 percent. Crime is the system. On the sidewalk in front of my ration store one day, I saw a teenager with a punk-rock haircut, idling in his shiny Mitsubishi Lancer and playing with what I mistook for an iPhone. "It's not an iPhone," he corrected me. "It's an iTouch."

These sell for $200, or 5,300 pesos. Some people have money, even here. The only certainty is that they didn't make that money in any legitimate way.

I walked to the sweeping Riviera, where the gaming floor was cleared by nationalization just a year after it opened. (Meyer Lansky, the owner, famously said he had "crapped out.") In the gym I weighed myself: 200 pounds. In 18 days I'd lost ten pounds, a rate that would result in hospitalization in the United States.

On the way home, a woman asked me where the P2 bus was found. I mangled the answer. "Oh, I thought you were a Cuban," she said.

Lose weight, change nationalities. I laughed off her mistake and went on, but a minute later she was chasing me down.

"Hey, invite me to lunch," she said. "Anyplace." I shook my head, no.

"Lunch," she called after me. "Dinner. As you like."

At home, I opened the fridge and counted: five eggs left.

Like the woman looking for the P2, I'd become direct. I walked two miles out to Cerro, a bad neighborhood. This took me right through an alley lined with rusting wrecks of trucks, past a crumbling sports stadium, through an overgrown park and a grove of trees, to the front door of the Ministry of the Interior. This is the famous building with a giant Che Guevara on it. It was guarded by a couple of red-bereted soldiers. The MININT building is constantly photographed because of its signature Che Sculpture, but you don't want to go inside. I ignored the guards and strolled out onto the vast broken asphalt of the Plaza de la Revolución. On the far side, walking carefully, I cut past the entrance of a low but massive building sitting at the top of a sweeping driveway. This was the Council of State, the nucleus of the revolutionary system, where Raúl Castro oversaw his top functionaries. Special-forces troops with pistols and batons guarded the entrance ramp; the government feels secure enough that only a couple of pistols stood between me and Raúl.

Wandering, sometimes in circles, I passed out through Cerro and other neighborhoods until I found the house of Oswaldo Payá, one of Cuba's most important dissidents. We talked about politics, culture, neoliberalism, and human rights, but what caught my attention was his own personal economy. "My salary is 495 pesos a month," he said. "That's about ten meals for four or five people. Wages don't cover a fifth of our food needs. A 10-peso sandwich, with a 1-peso drink, is half my daily salary. With me going to my job and coming home, my three kids going to school, we spend about 12 pesos a day on transport—that's 50 to 60 percent of our total income." He himself survived thanks to a brother in Spain who sent money. "The paradox is that the workers are the poorest people in Cuba. We're all worse off than the guy who sells hot dogs in the gas station on the corner" (a hard currency enterprise). Most people had no CUC and went home hungry every night. "I don't say everything in Cuba is bad, or terrible. That's because we have distribution schemes to feed the poor, to give benefits. But that's another way of domination, keeping people eternally poor. Free my hands, I'll start a business and feed myself."

I asked him where someone would get the money for an iPod Touch, or any of the other gizmos, luxury goods, modern cars, sound systems, and sleek clothes that were increasingly common in Cuba. "A salary . . . is equal to poverty," he said. "They all have to rob the system to survive. That's the tolerated corruption of survival." A tiny middle class had emerged: "Businessmen, mostly ex-officials, people who run restaurants. All of them are regime people. Most are ex-military, or from the Ministry of the Exterior, and so on. They have connections. They are inside the system. They are untouchable." And there was a third, incredibly small but "indescribably" well-off group within the leadership, "with big houses, foreign travel, everything. The Cuban people know this group exists, but you will never see them, there is no way."

During an hour of talk, his wife, Ofelia, another human-rights activist and domestic servant, brought me a glass of pineapple juice. Oswaldo began to wrap up and urged me to come back for a meal and a mojito "anytime."

I stayed in my chair. All this talk of future meals had my mouth coursing with saliva. Ofelia saw this, and soon I heard frying in the kitchen.

We ate tomato soup, tomatoes, rice, and yellow lentils. She served some protein, a gray mash that I took for government picadillo because it tasted like soybeans and scraps of something that had once been an animal. But Ofelia dug the wrapper out of the garbage can. It was "mechanically separated" turkey meat from Cargill in the United States, part of the hundreds of millions of dollars' worth of agricultural products sold to Cuba every year under an exemption to the embargo. It was almost inedible, even in my hungry state, but Ofelia was beaming. "It's much better than the turkey we used to get," she said.

On the way out, Oswaldo tried to hand me 10 pesos. "Every Cuban would do this for you," he said. He told me to spend it on food, but I declined, pushing the bills away. I couldn't take cash from a source, though I didn't scruple at the meal. He insisted. In the end, to avoid walking home, I accepted a 1-peso coin for the bus.

Oswaldo walked me out through his gritty neighborhood, full of staring adolescent boys, to a bus stop. "Wear long pants" was his final advice. Only tourists went around in shorts.

I'd long ago finished my whiskey, and I was hard-pressed to enjoy Cuba without a drink. Oswaldo Payá had put the bug in my ear, declaring, "Having a drink is one of the rights we all have." It was time to make some liquor.

The only food I possessed in superabundance was sugar—I hadn't even bothered to pick up my allotment of "crude" sugar, because in three weeks I'd gone less than halfway through my four and a half pounds of refined white sugar. The process of making rum is simple, at least in theory. Sugar plus yeast equals alcohol. Distillation equals stronger alcohol. I had never distilled before, but I'd recently toured the Bushmills distillery in Northern Ireland and, fortified by notes from *Chasing the White Dog*, by Max Watman, I blundered my way toward bliss.

The first step was making a wash, or low-alcohol solution. I already had the sugar. I walked to the free bakery, where a disappointed crowd was waiting for the machines to turn out a new batch of bread. At the back door I flagged down a baker and asked if I could buy some yeast. "No," she said. "We don't have enough ourselves." In the now-familiar ritual, I hung out for a while, chatted her up, and soon she was shoving half a bag of yeast—made in England—through the fence. I tried to pay her, but she refused.

After reverse-engineering Watman's prose with a calculator, and converting to metric, I could only hope I was in the ballpark. A kilo of sugar would require slightly more than a gallon of water. In true Havana style, the water proved the biggest obstacle: tap water in the city is thick with magnesium. My landlord had a Korean water purifier, but it was broken. It took thirty-six hours to scrounge a single gallon of purified water. Then I scrubbed out my pressure cooker, tested and repaired its rubber seals, sterilized it, and dumped the water and sugar in. Watman didn't mention how much yeast to use; I went with "half," on the theory that a screw up would still leave me enough for a second shot.

Mix, close, wait. In four hours the pressure cooker—The-One-Fidel-Gave-Us—was almost bubbling over with scummy brown foam that smelled deadly. Distilling requires a hose. I tried a large hardware store in a hard currency shopping mall on the Malecón, then a hardware *shopping*, and finally asked a gas-station attendant. He told me to look for a man standing by a small card table on 3rd Avenue. After much discussion of alcohol, this grease-covered man, a black-market plumber straight out of *Brazil*, gave me a yard of filthy plastic tubing. I spent two hours trying to clean hardened grease out of this tube. Heat, soap, a rag, and a disarranged coat hanger made no dent. I couldn't have my booze tasting like an old Chevy.

Finally I asked a gardener working on a neighbor's yard if he could *conseguir* me a bit of tubing appropriate for distilling firewater. He thought this request the most natural thing in the world and returned in half an hour, having lopped off a yard of somebody's garden hose.

For the next two days I checked the pond scum in the cooker. It attracted fruit flies and gave off a gentle hiss.

The gods were smiling, and so were the prostitutes. For more than a week I had been fending off the attentions of a young lady who walked past my apartment. She was a classic example of the Cuban economy in action: hot pants, gold chains, blue eye shadow, platform sandals, and inch-long acrylic fingernails painted the colors of the Cuban flag.

"*Psst*," she would say, calling my attention to these attributes. I often sat outside my small apartment to relieve the feeling of being trapped indoors. She would look through the iron gate along the road and summon me. *Psst.*

I resisted. But she was, like the many Cuban prostitutes I have talked with, a charming and intelligent survivor beneath the blunt *jewwannafuckeefuckee* propositions. We spoke once, then again a few days later, and then our third conversation lasted a long time. She kept trying to get into my apartment—did I have a light for her cigarette? Some coffee? a beer or soft drink?—and I kept stringing her along, enjoying her tales.

Her cleavage started ringing once, and she pulled out a cell phone. A tendentious conversation followed, in English. When she hung up she said, "He wants to fuck me in the ass." *Cogerme en el culo.* Cubans, especially prostitutes, are direct about sex. Also race. "Black guys always want to do it in the ass," she continued. "I don't like black guys, even though I consider myself black. I'm the lightest in my family, my mother is black, my sister is black, but I think black people smell bad. That guy has a lot of money. He's some kind of big man in the Cayman Islands, he's really rich. He offered me $150, but I told him no. Now he says he's going to pay me $300 just to have dinner."

"I don't think so," I observed.

"I know. I keep telling him to call my cousin. She loves black guys."

All our conversations began and ended with a proposition. Because, over a week, I had repeatedly turned her down, she now said, "I thought you were a duck." A what? "You know, *maricón. Un gay. Homosexual.*"

She was a nurse, twenty-four, from Holguín. She worked twelve hour shifts to earn vacation time, then every four or six months came to Havana for a long break to "dedicate myself to this," she said. In a rare euphemism, she said she was a *dama de acompañamiento.*

"Most of the girls have pimps, you know, but not me, so I have to look after myself." In addition to a phone, her cleavage concealed a small serrated knife, which she snapped open and waved around.

"You know why we do this," she said, "right? It's the only way to survive. I have a daughter, I love her so much, she's precious. I miss her. So I do this for her. Why don't you give me a hundred and I'll come upstairs right now?" (Eventually she offered me the "Cuban price" of $50.)

I told her I didn't have any money. I explained what I was doing. The ration. The salary. That I had already lost ten pounds. "I don't have a peso," I told her. She asked for a pen, wrote down her phone number, and handed it to me. Then she pulled, from one of the minuscule pockets of her hot pants, a single peso coin, which she handed to me.

"That's so you can call me," she said.

That was another terrible day for food, the worst yet. Between dawn and midnight I ate rice, beans, and sugar that totaled just over a thousand calories. I got up at three the next morning and finished the rice. Nothing left but a fistful of beans, two sweet potatoes, a few tiny plantains, three eggs, and a quarter of a cabbage.

Nine days to go.

I went to the ration shop, found Jesús, and bought coffee, a pound of rice, and some bread, all at Cuban prices—14 pesos total, or about 60 cents. That was the end of the money. But with the scraps of food, and the generosity of various Cubans, and a stomach shrunk to the size of a walnut, it would be enough. I knew I was going to make it.

I walked the next day to the house of Elizardo Sánchez, the human rights activist. An hour and ten minutes each way. "Everything is fine now," I told him, delirious with low blood sugar. "Even the prostitutes are giving me money."

I was in his house for an hour. He offered me a glass of water.

At last the great day of escape was here. Not my departure, which was still eight days away, but the alcohol. The brown wash had stopped bubbling after four days—when the alcohol content reaches about 13 percent it kills off the remaining yeast. I sterilized the garden hose and, using a bent hanger, fixed it to the vent on top of the pressure cooker. I struck a match, and in ten minutes I had alcohol vapor, and then a steady drip of condensation into the empty whiskey bottle sitting in a bowl of ice.

Ignorant, and a disgrace to my Virginia roots, I cooked the wash too hot and failed to throw away the initial stripping run of low wine—a harsh and even toxic alcohol. But after four hours the heart run had produced a liter of milky booze, and I had the naive sense to quit before the dregs could poison it. I should have made a second distillation, a spirit run, but couldn't be bothered. At four in the afternoon I finally sat down with a glass of warm white dog.

Thirty seconds after I started drinking I had a stomachache. The alcohol content was low, but so was my tolerance, and I was quickly giggling. The gardener came by and tasted some, with a sad face. I woke up at midnight with a headache, and this pattern continued for the last week of my residence. Instant stomachache; mild drunk; headache. The two or three hours in the middle were well worth it. When I left Havana there wasn't a drop of lightning left.

There wasn't much of me left either. In mid-February I walked one last time to the Riviera, weighing myself in the gym. I was down eleven and a half pounds since my arrival. More than eleven pounds gone in thirty days. I'd missed about 40,000 calories. At this rate I would be as lean as a Cuban by spring. And dead by autumn.

I finished out with a few tiny meals—the last of the ugly rice, a last sweet potato, and the quarter of a cabbage. On the day before my departure I broke into my emergency stash, eating the sesame sticks from the airplane (60 calories), and opening the can of fruit punch I'd smuggled in from the Bahamas (180). The taste of this red liquid was a shock: bitter with ascorbic acid, and flooded with sugar, to imitate the flavors of real juice. It was like drinking plastic.

My total expenditures on food were $15.08 for the month. By the end I'd read nine books, two of them about a thousand pages long, and written much of this article. I'd been living on the wages of a Cuban intellectual, and, indeed, I always write better, or at least faster, when I'm broke. My final morning: no breakfast, on top of no dinner. I used the prostitute's coin to catch a bus out toward the airport. I had to walk the last 45 minutes to my terminal, almost fainting on the way. There was a tragicomic moment when I was pulled out of line at the metal detectors by men in uniform because an immigration officer thought

I had overstayed my thirty-day visa. It took three people, repeatedly counting it out on their fingers, to prove that I was still on day thirty.

I ate a dinner and a breakfast in the Bahamas and gained four pounds. Back in the States, I put on another seven before the month was out. Put on nationality, change weight.

End Notes

1 *For their protection from the Cuban state, certain persons in this article will go unnamed.*

2 *Cuba has two currencies, the valuable peso, officially called the CUC, and known as the* kook, fula, chavita, and convertible*; it was introduced to eliminate the presence of foreign currency and to be valued roughly equivalent to the U.S. dollar, at least before the 20 percent exchange fee. Then there is the lowly peso (known as the peso). Cubans are paid in the regular peso, and to get anything important they must trade twenty-four of these for one CUC. A tiny box of stir-fried noodles in Havana's Chinatown was priced at "75/2.5," in regular pesos and CUC, in either case representing about 15 percent of the average monthly income.*

3 *Those Cubans who ignore the summons to official labor can be charged with "dangerousness," a vague offense punishable by up to four years in jail. Dangerousness is "pre-crime," Elizardo Sánchez said—the police nipping your bad attitude in the bud before you have a chance to commit an actual crime. There are regular campaigns to arrest young people who try to avoid work or the draft, and this year it was particularly relentless, a sign of nervousness. "It's not easy to hide from the government," Sánchez told me. "Boys are required to register themselves for military service at fifteen. They change their address sometimes, but it doesn't work. It's very hard for a young person to hide. Cuba is a dossier society. From first grade onward, the police stop children and ask for I.D. They can radio in and get everything."*

1. In what ways are Cuba's rations comparable to the U.S.'s government food programs? How are they different?

2. Is it better to have rations that must be supplemented through criminal income or to have a portion of the population that receives less than the equivalent of Cuba's rations?

3. What has influenced Cuba to keep its rationing program intact longer than other countries around the world?

Yasmin Alibhai-Brown is a British journalist and author and a regular columnist for the British newspapers The Independent *and* The Evening Standard. *Born in Uganda to an East African mother and an Indian father, she chose to immigrate to Britain before Idi Amin began his campaign against Ugandan Asians. Alibhai-Brown studied philosophy at Oxford University and is now known for her writing related to issues of race, ethnicity, multiculturalism, diversity, and immigration.*

HOORAY FOR BOLLYWOOD: 100 YEARS OF INDIAN CINEMA

BY YASMIN ALIBHAI-BROWN

The Indian film industry is the biggest and loudest on the planet. Eight hundred films are produced every year for domestic audiences of a billion-plus and a burgeoning overseas market. Although regional and independent films have always done their own thing, and brilliantly, the most prodigious sector is Bollywood, the ultimate dream factory in Mumbai.

Burhan Wazir, director of the Doha Film Institute, finds the films formulaic, featuring "gym-fit actors, exotic locations and rampantly consumerist lifestyles." Which is true, but it is such a winning formula that glitzy Bollywood is now outshining Hollywood—no mean feat, when one considers how American cultural hegemony has dominated and disabled the European film industries.

Beautiful megastars Shah Rukh Khan and Aishwarya Rai appear on the covers of *Forbes* and *Time* magazine and are considered more famous globally than Tom Cruise or Julia Roberts. Michael Ellis of the Motion Picture Association admits that U.S. studios have not penetrated the Indian market. Until 2008, American cinemas did not screen Hindi movies. Now they do, big time.

In Los Angeles, dance studios teach Bollywood dancing to wannabe starlets while Columbia, Disney, Fox et al. seek out co-production deals with Bollywood. Hitherto narcissistic Hollywood was oblivious to its eastern counterpart. Now it is sprinting to catch up with the rest of the world. Bollywood patriarch and superstar Amitabh Bachchan is jubilant that they who ignored or ridiculed his industry are eating humble (American) pie: "We always knew and believed in our films. The uniqueness of Hindi cinema has been its content... It has survived almost 100 years and is still growing [so] it must be doing something right."

So what is the secret of this success? According to the buoyant director Karan Johar, it is, "A mixture of music, love, family values, comedy, fantasy... [and an] adventurous choice of film location." Discerning audiences know that films are not real life but allegories which give hope because good triumphs over evil, poetic justice prevails.

Nasreen Munni Kabir, curator of Channel 4's annual season of Hindi movies, writes: "They are unquestionably the most-seen movies in the world... [watched] well beyond the Indian continent and the diaspora, in such unlikely places as Russia, China, the Middle East, the Far East, Turkey and Africa. People from very different cultural and social worlds have a great love for Indian popular cinema, and many have been Hindi film fans for over 50 years." Mao Tse-tung was a fan, as were millions of others in communist countries. Bollywood was a globalised phenomenon long before our age of globalisation.

It all started exactly 100 years ago when DJ Phalke, a nerdy-looking, bespectacled Indian Brahmin made the first ever Indian feature film, *Raja Harishchandra*, about a noble king guided by Hindu gods, some frolicsome, some deadly and full of wrath.

In 1895, the French Lumière brothers had created the first motion pictures, and by 1911, moving images had been shown in Mumbai venues, creating a buzz and palpable anticipation. A vast audience was prepped for this new medium, its possibilities and magic, and Phalke's first big filmic adventure. He became king of the silent era, producing dozens of mythological films with actors gesticulating wildly, backed by some live music and crude sound effects. The film-maker was populist and subversive, a storyteller with messianic resolve.

Let us go back to India in 1912. The British Raj was full of pomp and hubris, and natives were getting restive. Two years later, Gandhi would launch his liberation movement. Phalke had studied art and architecture, tried printing, photography, archaeology and various other ventures. And then, in Mumbai, he watched a French film, *The Life of Christ*, and was gripped "by a strange spell. I bought another ticket and saw the film again. Could we, the sons of India, ever be able to see Indian images on the screen?" He had found his calling. He would put those images on screen to awaken Indian nationalism.

Ironically, however, Phalke knew he couldn't fulfil his mission without western technology and British expertise. He travelled to Europe, met directors, bought a Williamson camera and, in London, was trained by the English director Cecil Hepworth in his Walton-on-Thames studios. Creative Indian and European film-makers then were mutually respectful collaborators who circumvented political partition, defied colonial and societal strictures.

Phalke thrilled audiences and subliminally aroused his compatriots to resist unjust power and inequality. Other silent films chose their own targets. As early as 1921, *England Returned* mocked pretentious, Anglicised Indians. (*Goodness Gracious Me* picked on similar characters in their hit BBC TV series in the 1990s.) Risqué and sexually daring films seemed to herald new personal freedoms. One of the boldest was *Shiraz* (1928), about ill-fated, royal lovers, directed by Franz Osten, a German. The producer and leading actor was the Indian trailblazer, Himansu Rai. It was shown in Germany and England to great acclaim.

Fearing films could incite dissidence and high emotion, colonial administrators imposed strict censorship. Any character wearing a loin cloth was deemed dangerous because it was Gandhi's chosen attire; so, too, any expression of patriotism. To beat the bans, anti-British messages were embedded in song lyrics. Post-imperial India kept the scissors and state censorship. The Brits cut seditious messages; Indian controllers expurgated "licentiousness"—kisses and bedroom antics. So smart directors used dance and suggestive dialogue to make highly charged, erotic films. Just don't tell the censors.

Gorgeous Devika Rani, an Indian actress trained at Rada, met Rai in London in 1928, married him and starred in his films. One of these, *Karma* (1933), was in English, shot in a London studio and premiered in Leicester Square. Rani received rave reviews, but the film bombed, and the couple moved back home. Two years earlier, the sound era had arrived with Alam Ara, a historical musical made by Ardeshir Irani, and Rai and Rani, the hot and ambitious couple, set up the Bombay Talkies studio. One of its early hits was *Achhut Kanya*, about untouchables, starring Rani and directed by Osten, who made 18 films in India—yet joined the Nazi Party while doing so. Inexplicable.

Lalit Mohan Joshi, founder of the South Asian Cinema Foundation in London, was born in India, and used to bunk off school to sneak into cinemas, like the boy in *Cinema Paradiso*. He tells me that in the 1930s and 1940s, common themes were female rights, hypocritical social mores and caste prejudice, always done beautifully through compelling stories and acting.

Idealistic and artistic directors won prizes at Cannes and Venice. They used the popular art form to create unity in a multilingual, disparate, often conflicted nation. Muslims were key players, and astonishingly, Jewish and Christian actresses—some European—were employed by the studios, usually to play red-lipped vamps. The influence of cinema in India, says Joshi, is immeasurable: "It has more of an impact than books, art and even religion."

Adulated stars join the limitless pantheon of Hindu deities. When Bachchan was seriously injured while filming in 1982, millions stopped work, fasted and prayed. PM Indira Gandhi cancelled a foreign trip to go to his bedside. Shah Rukh, Aamir and Salman Khan (unrelated) are today's top male idols. All three are of Muslim heritage and immensely powerful. Aamir created and hosts a TV programme which confronts unjust and corrupt practices in public and domestic life. Six hundred million people watch the show, which terrifies and chastens the powerful and rich. Several Bollywood luminaries have gone into politics.

The golden age of Hindi cinema was, arguably, from the 1950s to the mid-1960s. And again, British technical expertise was enlisted by some celebrated Indian producers. Among the actors who emerged then were Prithviraj Kapoor and his sons Raj, Shammi and Shashi; also, Dev Anand, Dilip Kumar and, among others, Raj Kapoor, also a director, replicated Chaplin's hapless characters in memorable films. The Kapoor acting dynasty is still going strong in Bollywood.

Wonderful actresses such as Nargis and Waheeda Rehman (both Muslims), Meena Kumari and Geeta Bali, meanwhile, were not always good, obedient Asian women. They were rule-breakers, some mistresses and hard drinkers in real life, all defiant and free on screen. Nargis wore revealing ballgowns and short tennis skirts and played feisty characters.

In the remarkable film *Guide* (1965), Rehman, a dancer, was stuck with an archaeologist husband much like Casaubon in *Middlemarch*. A sexy tourist guide came along and the heroine went off with him. That, though, didn't end her deep unhappiness. In her most famous film *Pakeezah* (1972), Meena Kumari played a dignified courtesan exposing society's duplicities.

Moral concerns were depicted with such feeling that they stayed with you, within you. The Oscar-shortlisted *Mother India* (1957) was about tough, maternal love and the unwinnable fight for peasant land rights. The usually glam Nargis played the heroine. That powerful drama seeded my socialist principles. In 1960, another immortal masterpiece was released—*Mughal-e-Azam*, about a Mughal prince and a dancing girl, an epic tussle between love and duty. My English husband has watched it five times.

From the late 1960s, Bollywood changed, perhaps forever. Flamboyant films arrived, with ridiculous story-lines, foreign locations, lovers running around trees and gyrating women breaking into song and dance for no good reason. And bad jokes. Movies such as *An Evening in Paris* and *Love in Tokyo* were cringe-making but box-office hits. Then in the 1970s, came the Indian Rambo, ballsy Bachchan, playing volcanic young men and breaking all box-office records. The actor seemed to channel the people's anger under the authoritarian PM Indira Gandhi.

Through the good and bad times, India's independent sector has produced internationally lauded films with low budgets. Satyajit Ray, of course, and Shyam Benegal, Aparna Sen (an actress too, who starred in Ray's films), Mrinal Sen and others have made classics without Bollywood's razzmatazz. Benegal's Ankur starred the subtle and versatile actress, Shabana Azmi, who played an adulterous wife. It is among my 10 favourite films.

Modern director Onir, famous for his touching films on homosexuality and other taboo subjects, has compared Bollywood to a shopping mall, calling it mindless and regressive, and is part of a confident new wave which is making its mark at home and internationally. As are diasporic Indian film-makers such as Mira Nair (*Salaam Bombay!, Monsoon Wedding, The Reluctant Fundamentalist*) and Deepa Mehta, director of Rushdie's *Midnight's Children*.

For post-war Asian migrants to the UK, Hindi movies were cheap entertainment and gave them solace, an identity as they coped with racism and dreadful weather. The multi-talented Meera Syal remembers going to Hindi films at Wolverhampton picturehouses with her family: "This was the only time and place we saw an art form that was ours. People dressed up and it was as exciting as it must have been for Elizabethan audiences going to the theatre. It was a window into a country I didn't really know, a living link. And I felt proud. To see people who looked like us acting and dancing was amazing. Remember, TV here then had no place for us. The films also had good messages—about families being sacred."

Gurinder Chadha, renowned director of *Bend it Like Beckham* and *Bride & Prejudice*, was brought up in Southall and went on Sundays with her family to the temple, then a Bollywood film—"The singing and dancing, big musical numbers, bright colours, big emotions!"—followed by samosas and sweets at a local café. She too admires early Hindi films because they had social commentary and defiant messages, all dressed up with songs and music: "A lot of it was about installing pride and unity in this new, freshly independent nation. They were trying to define who they were."

The kitsch came later and carries on, but every decade, she believes, has produced remarkable films reflecting political, economic and social shifts and moods. Interestingly, Chadha's best work is influencing some Indians in the business.

So where are we now? In the words of the novelist Hari Kunzru, "Bollywood has taken a contemporary turn and production values often overshadow narrative. Social-conscience movies dissolved during the 1980s into a torrid orgy of wet-sari clad violence and were overtaken by a new generation of super-glossy love stories with big budgets and international locations."

I tire of the bling and Lamborghinis, the vast mansions, super-lavish weddings and in-house gods covered in real gold leaf. Joshi, too, finds these developments disheartening: "Most of today's films are not deep. They are pseudo, plastic, have no originality or integrity. Whereas before, directors were progressive, today they are regressive." He is right: previously movie-makers were unabashedly Indian, used their own idiom, with integrity and without trying too hard to impress or emulate America or Europe.

Modern global capitalism has changed all that. Indians in the US and UK are upwardly mobile, über-aspirational and getting wealthy. They disdain moralising stories about dirt-poor rural Indian villagers or oppressed women. In India itself, too, the rapidly growing urban middle- and upper-classes want movies which cast them as heroes of a brave new world, not tearful folk tales.

In India this January, the shrill daughter of a wealthy financier gave me an earful: "I mean, you arty types like all those sad films with the poor and weeping women and all that. Why? Is it that you can't accept that India is now a superpower? That you want us to stay backward for your entertainment? Why do you hate and mock Indians who walk tall in Jimmy Choos?" Maybe she has a point. Are those who fetishise old, socially concerned movies refusing to acknowledge, new, shining India? Perhaps, but only because those old divides and injustices have become worse.

And anyway, there is no turning back: Bollywood in the 21st century is a rising brand. Of 12 white students interviewed at Middlesex University for this article, most recognised the "product" and big names and some had watched the movies. That never happened before. Of the Asian students also interviewed, trendy and irreversibly British, almost all watched the films and felt affirmed by them, just as Syal did way, way back.

Though there is too much dross, Bollywood has, in this decade, been making movies of real substance, displaying innovation, high production values, courage and artistry. Examples include *Omkara*, based on *Othello*, a multi-layered film of the destructive love between a gullible outlaw and his lover from a respectable family; and *Barfi!*, a story of a dumb-and-deaf charmer, the highest-grossing movie in India in 2012. The most highly paid stars are now choosing to act in non-glam films with meaning.

So the future looks bright. My American friend, married to an Indian, is unsettled by that: "These movies are great, but they tell me power is moving away from the U.S., going east. And you know that's hard for us Americans." Her husband cut in, "It's time things were hard for you all. Hollywood will be humbled by Bollywood. Watch this space." Someone should make a movie about the clash of these two titans.

1. In the article, Alibhai-Brown discusses some Indian filmmakers' perceptions that Bollywood has become "mindless" and "regressive," and that the influence of globalization and commercialism has degraded the film industry. In 2013, American director Stephen Soderbergh gave a keynote address to the San Francisco Film Festival, in which he decried similar problems in American, Hollywood cinema. After listening to Soderbergh's speech, do you see explicit connections between the two industries? Do the problems share a common source, or do these problems and complaints spring from different sources and bear differing results?

   http://www.indiewire.com/article/watch-full-video-recording-of-steven-soderberghs-impassioned-state-of-cinema-address-from-the-san-francisco-film-festival

2. Alibhai-Brown quotes many in the Indian Film Industry who fear that materialistic, spectacular depictions of Indian culture and life in Bollywood films are degrading and should give way to films that tackle social realism. However, others argue that the spectacle in these films is part of what has made them popular with global audiences and helped the industry to grow. Would abandoning this spectacle help or harm the industry? Do these considerations play out differently for an emerging industry than they would for Hollywood?

Jon Kelly is the feature writer for the BBC News. He has previously reported for Guardian, Observer, Daily Record, The Scotsman, The Tablet, *and* The List. *He was educated at City University and the University of Edinburgh in Britain. He has an honors Masters in Politics and was awarded Critic of the Year from Guardian Student Media Awards in 2000.*

WHY BRITISH POLICE DON'T HAVE GUNS

By Jon Kelly

The deaths of two female police constables have brought into focus the unarmed status of most British police. Why does Britain hold firm against issuing guns to officers on the beat?

It's the single most obvious feature that sets the British bobby apart from their counterparts overseas.

Tourists and visitors regularly express surprise at the absence of firearms from the waists of officers patrolling the streets.

But to most inhabitants of the UK—with the notable exception of Northern Ireland—it is a normal, unremarkable state of affairs that most front-line officers do not carry guns.

Unremarkable, that is, until unarmed officers like Nicola Hughes and Fiona Bone are killed in the line of duty. There are always those who question why Britain is out of step with most of the rest of the world, with the exceptions of the Republic of Ireland, New Zealand, Norway and a handful of other nations.

VIEW FROM A BOBBY

A police constable serving in a city in southern England gives his view:

"I have been in the police for 12 years, before that I was in the Army. I would happily carry a gun if the decision was made but it won't ever happen.

"I don't think practically it could work because of the training. Officers in this country are highly trained and this would extend to firearms training, too. But, at the moment, with all the cuts, we can't put enough officers in the cars, let alone give them firearms training.

"Also, the police in this country are always under so much scrutiny. Look at the issue of Tasers, the civil liberty groups think they are one of the most inhumane things going.

"I was previously injured badly in an assault. My colleague and I feared for our lives—thankfully other officers came to our aid. I don't think a gun—or a Taser for that matter—would have helped us in that situation. Communication is one of the best tools, and to be honest, having a gun could make an officer feel over-confident."

For a heavily urbanised country of its population size, the situation in Great Britain is arguably unique.

Film director Michael Winner, founder of the Police Memorial Trust, and Tony Rayner, the former chairman of Essex Police Federation, have both called for officers to be routinely armed.

But despite the loss of two of his officers, Greater Manchester Chief Constable Sir Peter Fahy was quick to speak in support of the status quo.

"We are passionate that the British style of policing is routinely unarmed policing. Sadly we know from the experience in America and other countries that having armed officers certainly does not mean, sadly, that police officers do not end up getting shot."

But one thing is clear. When asked, police officers say overwhelmingly that they wish to remain unarmed.

A 2006 survey of 47,328 Police Federation members found 82% did not want officers to be routinely armed on duty, despite almost half saying their lives had been "in serious jeopardy" during the previous three years.

It is a position shared by the Police Superintendents' Association and the Association of Chief Police Officers.

The British public are not nearly so unanimous.

An ICM poll in April 2004 found 47% supported arming all police, compared with 48% against.

In 2007, the centre-right think-tank Policy Exchange found 72% of 2,156 adults wanted to see more armed police patrols.

INTERNATIONAL MODELS

All major police forces in Europe, as well as the U.S., Canada and Australia routinely carry firearms, says Prof. Peter Waddington. The exceptions are Britain, the Irish Republic, and New Zealand. In Norway, officers carry arms in their cars but not on their person, he says.

New Zealand has adopted an armed response model similar to Britain, says the International Law Enforcement Forum. There was considerable debate there in 2010 when two officers were shot, and commissioner Peter Marshall wrote: "International experience shows that making firearms more accessible raises certain risks that are very difficult to control."

These considerations included:

- risk of police having weapons taken from them
- risk of greater use of weapons against the public and/or offenders
- and ambush can never be controlled, whether or not officers are armed

For decades there have been incidents that have led to calls for issuing all officers with firearms. Cases like those of Sharon Beshenivsky, shot dead during a robbery in 2005, or of the three plain-clothes officers murdered by Harry Roberts in west London in 1966, or the killing of PC Sidney Miles in the Derek Bentley case of 1952.

Few expect the system to change even after widespread public horror at the deaths of PCs Bone and Hughes.

For one thing, incidents such as that in Greater Manchester are extremely rare. Overall gun crime, too, remains low.

In 2010-11, England and Wales witnessed 388 firearm offences in which there was a fatal or serious injury, 13% lower than the previous 12 months. In Scotland during the same period, there were two fatal and 109 non-fatal injuries during the same period, a decade-long low.

Additionally, officers, chief constables and politicians alike are wary of upsetting an equilibrium that has been maintained throughout Britain's 183-year policing history.

"There's a general recognition that if the police are walking around with guns it changes things," says Richard Garside, director of the Centre for Crime and Justice Studies.

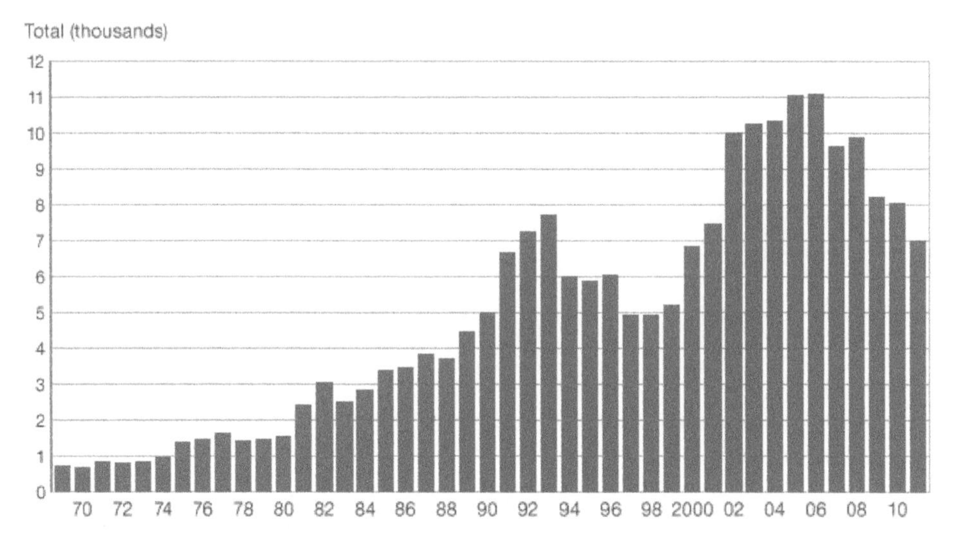

Arming the force would, say opponents, undermine the principle of policing by consent—the notion that the force owes its primary duty to the public, rather than to the state, as in other countries.

This owes much to the historical foundations of British criminal justice, says Peter Waddington, professor of social policy at the University of Wolverhampton.

"A great deal of what we take as normal about policing was set out in the early 19th century," he says.

POLICE USE OF FIREARMS 2010-11

- Authorized in 17,209 operations, says Home Office figures for England and Wales—a decrease of 1,347 (7%) on previous year
- 6,653 authorized firearms officers—(5% decrease)
- 13,346 operations involving armed response vehicles (6% decrease)
- Three incidents in which police discharged a conventional firearm (down from six incidents)

"When Robert Peel formed the Metropolitan Police there was a very strong fear of the military—the masses feared the new force would be oppressive."

A force that did not routinely carry firearms—and wore blue rather than red, which was associated with the infantry—was part of this effort to distinguish the early "Peelers" from the Army, Waddington says.

Over time, this notion of guns being inimical to community policing—and, indeed, to the popular conception of the Dixon of Dock Green-style bobby—was reinforced.

While some in London were issued with revolvers prior to 1936, from that date only trained officers at the rank of sergeant or above were issued with guns, and even then only if they could demonstrate a good reason for requiring one.

Today only a small proportion of officers are authorized to use firearms. Latest Home Office figures show there were just 6,653 officers authorized to use firearms in England and Wales—about 5% of the total number.

None of which implies, of course, that the British police are somehow gun-free. Each police force has its own firearms unit. Police armed response vehicles have been deployed since 1991.

VIEW FROM LOUISIANA

Colonel Richie Johnson West Baton Rouge Sheriff's Office

"What does a British police officer do if someone comes out with a knife? Is he supposed to get out his knife and fight him?

"Our citizens are armed—even the bad ones. The criminal element here is better armed than the police departments most of the times, due to budget constraints.

"It would be impossible for us to do our job if we weren't armed. I'd have to quit. I worked narcotics for 20 years and definitely in that field, how would you do that job without being armed? Even as a patrolman, you're reactive. The other guy knows what he's going to do. It definitely has to be armed when you have to be reactive.

"The public expects us to be armed—when they call in the cavalry that's exactly what they want. The general public, because of television, they believe that we're a lot better armed than we really are. You respond to a call and they say 'Where's your machine gun?'"

In addition, trained officers have had access to Tasers since 2004 despite controversy about their use. Met Commissioner Bernard Hogan-Howe called for police response officers to be routinely armed with the weapons in November 2011.

Particularly in London, the sight of armed officers at airports, embassies and other security-sensitive locations has become a familiar one, especially since the 11 September attacks.

However much firearms become an accepted part of British life, former Met deputy assistant commissioner Brian Paddick doubts police themselves will ever support a universal rollout.

For one thing, the sheer cost of equipping all personnel with weapons as well as providing regular training would be prohibitive at a time of public spending cuts, he says.

In addition, Paddick adds, front-line officers would not be keen to face the agonising, split-second decisions faced by their counterparts in specialist firearms units.

"In terms of the police being approachable, in terms of the public being the eyes and ears of the police, officers don't want to lose that," he says.

"Every case in which a police officer has shot someone brings it home to unarmed officers the sheer weight of responsibility that their colleagues face."

Cases like that of Jean Charles de Menezes, shot dead by a Met firearms officer after he was wrongly identified as a terrorist, illustrate Paddick's point.

For now, at least, that starkest of all distinctions between British officers and those abroad looks secure.

What are some of the recent societal attitudes that have contributed to the British population being in favor of armed police?

What is your reaction to the statement " . . . policing by consent—the notion that the [police] force owes its primary duty to the public, rather than to the state, as in other countries?"

Jamey Keaten currently writes for the Associated Press *as their Paris correspondent. He specializes in politics, foreign affairs, defense, and security.*

MUSLIMS WORRY ABOUT BROADER FRANCE HEADSCARF BAN

By Jamey Keaten

LE BOURGET, France—Because of her choice to wear a headscarf, Samia Kaddour, a Muslim, has all but abandoned trying to land a government job in France. Soon, some private sector jobs could be off limits, too.

French President Francois Hollande says he wants a new law that could extend restrictions on the wearing of prominent religious symbols in state jobs into the private sector. His new tack comes after a top French court ruled in March that a day care operator that gets some state funding unfairly fired a woman in a headscarf, sparking a political backlash.

As Christians celebrated Easter on Sunday, Kaddour attended the four-day Annual Meeting of Muslims of France in Le Bourget, north of Paris. The convention, which last year drew some 160,000 faithful and was expected to grow this year, is billed as the largest annual gathering of its kind in Europe. It is in its 30th year and ended Monday.

French law bars state employees from wearing prominent religious symbols such as Muslim headscarves, Jewish skullcaps or large Christian crosses in public schools, welfare offices or other government facilities. Two years ago, France banned Muslim veils that cover faces, such as the niqab, which has a slit for the eyes, or the mesh-screen burqa, from being worn anywhere in public.

Meeting leaders say France has made progress in accepting Muslims and noted that, unlike 30 years ago, women wearing headscarves today rarely draw suspicion, scowls or curiosity. Still, many Muslims—and even some Roman Catholics and Jews—fear France's insistence on secular values first enshrined in the French Revolution more than two centuries ago is unfairly crimping their ability to express their religious beliefs freely.

They also worry that Hollande's Socialist government, like a conservative one before it, wants to score political points.

"Islam has become a political instrument," said Kaddour, 26, who is a community activist from the English Channel port city of Le Havre and one of 10 children of Algerian-born parents who moved to France for plentiful jobs during its economic boom times decades ago. "Islam is always brandished whenever there is internal political discord."

Most mainstream politicians insist Islam is not being targeted. But a backlash erupted after the Court of Cassation ruled in March that Baby Loup, a private-sector day care operator that gets some state funding, unfairly fired a woman who wore a headscarf to work. The far-right railed at the decision, and even Interior Minister Manuel Valls expressed regret over it.

Wading into the debate in a prime-time TV interview on Thursday, Hollande suggested new limits are needed on Muslim headscarves, saying that "when there is contact with children, in what we call public service of early childhood ... there should be a certain similarity to what exists in (public) school.

"I think the law should get involved," he added.

Many Muslims fear an encroaching Islamophobia, while proponents of such measures insist they counter extremism and act as a rampart to protect France's identity against inequality. Polls show that most French people support at least some restrictions on religious symbols.

France, with an estimated 5 million-6 million Muslims whose families mostly have origins in former French colonies in north Africa, is at the forefront of addressing the challenges that many European countries are facing about how to integrate their sizeable ethnic and religious minorities on a continent where white Christians have dominated the political landscape for centuries.

Bristling against stereotypes in many corners of the West that Muslims are closet radicals or even terrorists, leaders of the convention in Le Bourget preached peace and justice. And after prayers and praise of Islam's Prophet Muhammad, convention leaders led a song in Arabic in a vast meeting hall with thousands in the audience — and some up on the dais waved French flags.

In another convention hall, vendors offered items such as headscarves, sweet pastries or T-shirts emblazoned with the saying 'Don't Panic, I'm Muslim,' while mothers pushing strollers and others wandered through the crowd. Several other stalls took up political issues such as support for Palestinians or war-weary Syrians. Nearby, men kneeled in rhythmic unison for afternoon prayers.

Kaddour said many Muslims regret that their faith is in the political crosscurrents again in France. But she said she's not discouraged enough yet to want to leave.

"Many others feel that way too: We are French and we have our place to claim and our future to establish in France," she said. "I'm not a foreigner. I'm French. I want to live in France; I love this country. Even if it has trouble liking us, we are going to do what's necessary to live serenely in France."

Kaddour says she plans to go back to school to get a higher degree but has all but given up hopes for a state job. And in France, that matters: the European Union says more than half of France's gross domestic product comes from government spending—potentially curbing the work options for headscarf-wearing Muslims such as Kaddour if the ban is broadened.

"A state job, unfortunately..." she said, her voice trailing off. "When I go into job interviews, I wear my headscarf. No results." She admits that she doesn't always know why—it could just be her skill set isn't sufficient—but suspects her religion plays a role, too.

Kaddour says her future career seems increasingly limited to independent, private practice work. She currently works for a small community group devoted to improving understanding of Islam, called Le Havre de Savoir, or The Haven of Knowledge.

At a time of double-digit unemployment rates in France, a nation of 65 million, such restrictions to job access hit headscarf-wearing women especially hard: Muslim men in France don't usually wear visible religious garb.

Ahmed Jaballah, the head of the Union of Islamic Organizations of France, a major Muslim group that helped organize the conference, said the "rather morose ambiance" over France's sluggish economic growth recently hasn't helped Muslims' aspirations, suggesting that a search for scapegoats is politically appealing. He said he's concerned about the government's plans.

"Unfortunately, Muslims have the impression today that secularism is being shaped based on Muslim practices, and that's worrisome," he said in an interview. "Everybody always talks about secularism, how it's not just about Muslims. But in fact, Muslims are targeted. Nobody is fooled.

"Muslims wonder: Can we trust secularism?" he said. "Remember the French slogan: 'Liberte, Egalite, Fraternite.' Today, we want this fraternity to be real."

1. Should headscarves be banned in all businesses, federal and private?

2. Using the "Cui Bono" handout, describe the gains and losses and the groups involved if France legally bans religious symbols from private businesses. Then do the same if these religious symbols are not banned.

Anu Partanen is a Finnish journalist, freelance writer, visiting reporter, and columnist based in New York City. She has written for the New York Times *and* The Atlantic *and has been a visiting staff writer for* Helsingin Sanomat, *Scandinavia's largest daily subscription newspaper. Anu Partanen holds a master's degree in Social Science and has studied in France and Australia. She is married to the American writer and educator, Trevor Corson.*

WHAT AMERICANS KEEP IGNORING ABOUT FINLAND'S SCHOOL SUCCESS

By Anu Partanen

The Scandinavian country is an education superpower because it values equality more than excellence.

Everyone agrees the United States needs to improve its education system dramatically, but how? One of the hottest trends in education reform lately is looking at the stunning success of the West's reigning education superpower, Finland. Trouble is, when it comes to the lessons that Finnish schools have to offer, most of the discussion seems to be missing the point.

The small Nordic country of Finland used to be known—if it was known for anything at all—as the home of Nokia, the mobile phone giant. But lately Finland has been attracting attention on global surveys of quality of life—*Newsweek* ranked it number one last year—and Finland's national education system has been receiving particular praise, because in recent years Finnish students have been turning in some of the highest test scores in the world.

Finland's schools owe their newfound fame primarily to one study: the PISA survey, conducted every three years by the Organization for Economic Co-operation and Development (OECD). The survey compares 15-year-olds in different countries in reading, math, and science. Finland has ranked at or near the top in all three competencies on every survey since 2000, neck and neck with superachievers such as South Korea and Singapore. In the most recent survey in 2009 Finland slipped slightly, with students in Shanghai, China, taking the best scores, but the Finns are still near the very top. Throughout the same period, the PISA performance of the United States has been middling, at best.

Compared with the stereotype of the East Asian model—long hours of exhaustive cramming and rote memorization—Finland's success is especially intriguing because Finnish schools assign less homework and engage children in more creative play. All this has led to a continuous stream of foreign delegations making the pilgrimage to Finland to visit schools and talk with the nation's education experts, and constant coverage in the worldwide media marveling at the Finnish miracle.

So there was considerable interest in a recent visit to the U.S. by one of the leading Finnish authorities on education reform, Pasi Sahlberg, director of the Finnish Ministry of Education's Center for International Mobility and author of the new book *Finnish Lessons: What Can the World Learn from Educational Change in Finland?* Earlier this month, Sahlberg stopped by the Dwight School in New York City to speak with educators and students, and his visit received national media attention and generated much discussion.

And yet it wasn't clear that Sahlberg's message was actually getting through. As Sahlberg put it to me later, there are certain things nobody in America really wants to talk about.

* * * * *

During the afternoon that Sahlberg spent at the Dwight School, a photographer from the *New York Times* jockeyed for position with Dan Rather's TV crew as Sahlberg participated in a roundtable chat with students. The subsequent article in the *Times* about the event would focus on Finland as an "intriguing school-reform model."

Yet one of the most significant things Sahlberg said passed practically unnoticed. "Oh," he mentioned at one point, "and there are no private schools in Finland."

This notion may seem difficult for an American to digest, but it's true. Only a small number of independent schools exist in Finland, and even they are all publicly financed. None is allowed to charge tuition fees. There are no private universities, either. This means that practically every person in Finland attends public school, whether for pre-K or a Ph.D.

The irony of Sahlberg's making this comment during a talk at the Dwight School seemed obvious. Like many of America's best schools, Dwight is a private institution that costs high-school students upward of $35,000 a year to attend—not to mention that Dwight, in particular, is run for profit, an increasing trend in the U.S. Yet no one in the room commented on Sahlberg's statement. I found this surprising. Sahlberg himself did not.

Sahlberg knows what Americans like to talk about when it comes to education, because he's become their go-to guy in Finland. The son of two teachers, he grew up in a Finnish school. He taught mathematics and physics in a junior high school in Helsinki, worked his way through a variety of positions in the Finnish Ministry of Education, and spent years as an education expert at the OECD, the World Bank and other international organizations.

Now, in addition to his other duties, Sahlberg hosts about a hundred visits a year by foreign educators, including many Americans, who want to know the secret of Finland's success. Sahlberg's new book is partly an attempt to help answer the questions he always gets asked.

From his point of view, Americans are consistently obsessed with certain questions: How can you keep track of students' performance if you don't test them constantly? How can you improve teaching if you have no accountability for bad teachers or merit pay for good teachers? How do you foster competition and engage the private sector? How do you provide school choice?

The answers Finland provides seem to run counter to just about everything America's school reformers are trying to do.

For starters, Finland has no standardized tests. The only exception is what's called the National Matriculation Exam, which everyone takes at the end of a voluntary upper-secondary school, roughly the equivalent of American high school.

Instead, the public school system's teachers are trained to assess children in classrooms using independent tests they create themselves. All children receive a report card at the end of each semester, but these reports are based on individualized grading by each teacher. Periodically, the Ministry of Education tracks national progress by testing a few sample groups across a range of different schools.

As for accountability of teachers and administrators, Sahlberg shrugs. "There's no word for accountability in Finnish," he later told an audience at the Teachers College of Columbia University. "Accountability is something that is left when responsibility has been subtracted."

For Sahlberg, what matters is that in Finland all teachers and administrators are given prestige, decent pay, and a lot of responsibility. A master's degree is required to enter the profession, and teacher training programs are among the most selective professional schools in the country. If a teacher is bad, it is the principal's responsibility to notice and deal with it.

And while Americans love to talk about competition, Sahlberg points out that nothing makes Finns more uncomfortable. In his book, Sahlberg quotes a line from Finnish writer named Samuli Paronen: "Real winners do not compete." It's hard to think of a more un-American idea, but when it comes to education, Finland's success shows that the Finnish attitude might have merits. There are no lists of best schools or teachers in Finland. The main driver of education policy is not competition between teachers and between schools, but cooperation.

Finally, in Finland, school choice is noticeably not a priority, nor is engaging the private sector at all. Which brings us back to the silence after Sahlberg's comment at the Dwight School that schools like Dwight don't exist in Finland.

"Here in America," Sahlberg said at the Teachers College, "parents can choose to take their kids to private schools. It's the same idea of a marketplace that applies to, say, shops. Schools are a shop and parents can buy what ever they want. In Finland parents can also choose. But the options are all the same."

Herein lay the real shocker. As Sahlberg continued, his core message emerged, whether or not anyone in his American audience heard it.

Decades ago, when the Finnish school system was badly in need of reform, the goal of the program that Finland instituted, resulting in so much success today, was never excellence. It was equity.

* * * * *

Since the 1980s, the main driver of Finnish education policy has been the idea that every child should have exactly the same opportunity to learn, regardless of family background, income, or geographic location. Education has been seen first and foremost not as a way to produce star performers but as an instrument to even out social inequality.

In the Finnish view, as Sahlberg describes it, this means that schools should be healthy, safe environments for children. This starts with the basics. Finland offers all pupils free school meals, easy access to health care, psychological counseling, and individualized student guidance.

In fact, since academic excellence wasn't a particular priority on the Finnish to-do list, when Finland's students scored so high on the first PISA survey in 2001, many Finns thought the results must be a mistake. But subsequent PISA tests confirmed that Finland—unlike, say, very similar countries such as Norway—was producing academic excellence through its particular policy focus on equity.

That this point is almost always ignored or brushed aside in the U.S. seems especially poignant at the moment, after the financial crisis and Occupy Wall Street movement have brought the problems of inequality in America into such sharp focus. The chasm between those who can afford $35,000 in tuition per child per year—or even just the price of a house in a good public school district—and the other "99 percent" is painfully plain to see.

* * * * *

Pasi Sahlberg goes out of his way to emphasize that his book *Finnish Lessons* is not meant as a how-to guide for fixing the education systems of other countries. All countries are different, and as many Americans point out, Finland is a small nation with a much more homogeneous population than the United States.

Yet Sahlberg doesn't think that questions of size or homogeneity should give Americans reason to dismiss the Finnish example. Finland *is* a relatively homogeneous country—as of 2010, just 4.6 percent of Finnish residents had been born in another country, compared with 12.7 percent in the United States. But the number of foreign-born residents in Finland doubled during the decade leading up to 2010, and the country didn't lose its edge in education. Immigrants tended to concentrate in certain areas, causing some schools to become much more mixed than others, yet there has not been much change in the remarkable lack of variation between Finnish schools in the PISA surveys across the same period.

Samuel Abrams, a visiting scholar at Columbia University's Teachers College, has addressed the effects of size and homogeneity on a nation's education performance by comparing Finland with another Nordic country: Norway. Like Finland, Norway is small and not especially diverse overall, but unlike Finland it has taken an approach to education that is more American than Finnish. The result? Mediocre performance in the PISA survey. Educational policy, Abrams suggests, is probably more important to the success of a country's school system than the nation's size or ethnic makeup.

Indeed, Finland's population of 5.4 million can be compared to many an American state—after all, most American education is managed at the state level. According to the Migration Policy Institute, a research organization in Washington, there were 18 states in the U.S. in 2010 with an identical or significantly smaller percentage of foreign-born residents than Finland.

What's more, despite their many differences, Finland and the U.S. have an educational goal in common. When Finnish policymakers decided to reform the country's education system in the 1970s, they did so because they realized that to be competitive, Finland couldn't rely on manufacturing or its scant natural resources and instead had to invest in a knowledge-based economy.

With America's manufacturing industries now in decline, the goal of educational policy in the U.S.—as articulated by most everyone from President Obama on down—is to preserve American competitiveness by doing the same thing. Finland's experience suggests that to win at that game, a country has to prepare not just some of its population well, but all of its population well, for the new economy. To possess some of the best schools in the world might still not be good enough if there are children being left behind.

Is that an impossible goal? Sahlberg says that while his book isn't meant to be a how-to manual, it is meant to be a "pamphlet of hope."

"When President Kennedy was making his appeal for advancing American science and technology by putting a man on the moon by the end of the 1960s, many said it couldn't be done," Sahlberg said during his visit to New York. "But he had a dream. Just like Martin Luther King a few years later had a dream. Those dreams came true. Finland's dream was that we want to have a good public education for every child regardless of where they go to school or what kind of families they come from, and many even in Finland said it couldn't be done."

Clearly, many were wrong. It is possible to create equality. And perhaps even more important—as a challenge to the American way of thinking about education reform—Finland's experience shows that it is possible to achieve excellence by focusing not on competition, but on cooperation, and not on choice, but on equity.

The problem facing education in America isn't the ethnic diversity of the population but the economic inequality of society, and this is precisely the problem that Finnish education reform addressed. More equity at home might just be what America needs to be more competitive abroad.

1. How do cultural ideologies inform our attitudes about the aims of education?

2. How do current models of accountability in education in the U.S. reflect Western values?

3. How is "quality" defined in education in the United States? In other countries/cultures?

4. Is competition the best motivator in educational programs?

Kevin Slaten is program coordinator at China Labor Watch. In 2012, he completed a master's thesis on Chinese labor rights at Ohio State University. He also worked as an intern at New Urban Home in Qingdao, China, in 2012; he received a Fulbright Grant to study in Taiwan in 2009; and he was a Junior Fellow at the Carnegie Endowment for International Peace in 2008. He has written for publications such as Foreign Policy, South China Morning Post, *and* The Diplomat. *Xue Chao was the program director for five years at New Urban Home, a labor NGO in Qingdao, China. He is currently studying law and plans to become a labor lawyer.*

WAGES RISING IN CHINESE FACTORIES? ONLY FOR SOME

By Kevin Slaten and Xue Chao

If we are to take recent news reports at face value, the collective conscience of the world's consumers can be eased, because conditions at Chinese factories are improving.

Last year, *The New York Times* told us that these workers are "cheap no more," and just this February, the Heritage Foundation, touting the virtues of global free trade, claimed that Chinese factory wages have risen 20 percent per year since 2005. Foxconn, Apple's major supplier and the manufacturer of approximately 40 percent of the world's consumer electronics, says it will hold free union elections every five years.

But Pollyannas should take pause: The average migrant worker's $320 monthly salary in 2011 was actually 43 percent less than the $560 national average, according to government statistics. And though it's true that Foxconn will permit the election of union leaders, we have yet to see how much China's so-called democratic unions can empower the workers they purport to represent.

Skepticism and caveats aside, the reality is that the lot of formal production workers in China is indeed advancing, however slowly and painfully. But that is true only for *formal* workers. What many consumers and observers fail to note are the perilous conditions of

China's *temporary* production workers and the increased tendency among Chinese factories to use such workers to manufacture the brand-name products that fill your home.

Factories supplying Apple and Samsung, for example, make heavy use of temp workers. According to official statistics, temp workers make up 20 percent of China's urban workforce of 300 million, though the proportion in individual factories often tops 50 percent. As China turns into a land of short-term workers, there are grave implications for labor, companies, and Chinese society.

WHAT IS A CHINESE TEMP WORKER?

The two most common Chinese terms for temp workers are *linshigong* (临时工), literally "short-term workers," and *paiqiangong* (派遣工), "dispatch workers."

The second term is instructive. Temp workers in China are primarily recruited and assigned via *laowu paiqian gongsi* (劳务派遣公司), "labor dispatch companies." These are conceptually similar to America's staffing agencies.

Another thing Chinese and American temp workers share is a lack of benefits. Temp workers in a Chinese factory do not receive any type of insurance from the factories, leaving them with neither a health care safety net beneath them nor a retirement net ahead.

But working *sans* benefits is one of the few things all that American and Chinese temp workers have in common. While an American temp may be employed only 30 hours per week, a Chinese dispatch worker might spend 12 hours per day in a factory six or seven days a week.

What makes Chinese temp workers both unique and their plight urgent is the illegality of their conditions. Article 68 of Chinese labor law defines non-full-time workers as those employed no more than 24 hours per week and an average of four hours per day, filling a company's short-term temporary needs. But the reality is that such workers do more overtime than the law permits, lack a contractual relationship with their employers, and are often paid sub-minimum wages.

Labor dispatch companies are also often the channel through which child workers—under the age of 16 in China—end up in factories. Dispatch companies charge workers $50 to $100 in service fees, so to the company a child worker is simply another source of revenue.

WHY DO TEMP WORKERS EXIST?

Businesses gain considerable cost-saving benefits by using temp workers in their factories. Temp workers do not sign a contract with the factories, relieving the company of responsibility for providing these workers with the five types of insurance mandated by Chinese law. In a mid-sized factory with 500 temp workers, the company could save tens of thousands of dollars per month in insurance payments alone.

Another long-term benefit for companies is that they do not have to employ veteran workers who might require higher pay. Rather, the company can let temp workers come and go, then hire the next batch of cheap young temps. In cases where workers are injured, the company is less likely to be forced to pay compensation because the worker does not have evidence of a contractual relationship. Finally, factories can skimp on making their facilities more pleasing for workers since the workers are not expected to stay.

Temp workers do gain some benefits, however short-sighted they may be. Using the temp route, workers have a sense of freedom. Factories make promises during recruiting that end up being distant from the true working and living conditions within, and managers are often unkind or condescending toward workers, most of whom have less than a high school education. For these reasons, workers may understandably wish to avoid dealing with the stresses of being a formal employee in the factory. The thinking is, "If the supervisor has it in for me, I can simply leave and get assigned elsewhere."

Another reason one may prefer to be a temp worker is the frequency of pay. In China, where factory profit margins are often thin, employees commonly get stuck working without pay. Temp workers can sometimes avoid the wage-arrears headache when they get paid daily or weekly.

Poor governance in China has played a major role in the rise of the temp phenomenon. The text of Chinese law is generally pro-labor. But in reality, collusion between local government and business interests—and the oiled gears of bribery—have led to severely sub-par law enforcement.

THE RISKS OF A TEMP WORKER EMPIRE

The most apparent victims of an economy that relies on temp workers are, of course, the workers themselves. The price they pay for the freedom to walk away is unequal treatment under law, a lack of economic security, and a weakened ability to defend their rights. Unlike formal employees, temp workers are often paid less and do not usually receive insurance. If they are injured on the job, they must depend on their own meager savings, those of their economically disadvantaged families, or the benevolence of the factory. If a worker wants to take a job-injury or rights-violation case to court, her legal standing is diminished because she lacks a contract with her employer.

The system also presents risks to business. First and foremost, the conduct surrounding the employment of temp workers is illegal in China, and businesses risk being sued or criminally indicted for their behavior. Economically, while the up-front savings for a company may seem obvious, temp workers will be unfamiliar with the production process and less committed to the factory; the result is inefficiency and a greater number of deficient products.

At a broader political level, with intermittent work and illegally unequal wages, the growing temp worker population contradicts the Chinese government's professed commitment to reducing economic inequality (Chinese). On the government's priority list, social stability comes a close second to development, and the growth of a transient, marginalized social group is not conducive to stability.

TURNING BACK THE TIDE OF TEMPS

When the numbers are crunched, businesses using temps can perhaps improve their bottom lines. But this wanton pursuit of profit is illegal, unethical, and a poor standardization of business practices. Chinese factories and the global brands they supply have a social responsibility to respect the value of full-time jobs and eradicate the illegal use of temp workers.

Workers and labor-rights NGOs, for their part, must continue to increase awareness among the worker community of the risks of temp work and the rights of labor.

The Chinese government has an obvious responsibility to strengthen the enforcement of its own laws. Indeed, in December the government strengthened restrictions on the use of temp workers, but without effective enforcement, these are empty expressions and may only serve to further diminish the respect for law.

Lastly, the duty of foreign governments is clear: The U.N. Guiding Principles on Business and Human Rights, unanimously endorsed by developed countries, states that a government has the duty to prevent companies operating in its jurisdiction from violating laws and impinging on human rights in other jurisdictions. The U.S. and others should pass national laws that punish companies for labor violations in foreign territories. Such a law would have the support of Americans, who know that "injustice anywhere is a threat to justice everywhere."

1. The authors state, "Workers and labor-rights NGOs, for their part, must continue to increase awareness among the worker community of the risks of temp work and the rights of labor." What exactly are the risks of temp workers as outlined in the article? Why might workers prefer temp positions?

2. As one of their solutions, the authors write, "The U.S. and others should pass national laws that punish companies for labor violations in foreign territories." What implications could this have on our consumer industry or foreign relations? Remember that the article notes, "Factories supplying Apple and Samsung, for example, make heavy use of temp workers." Do you support this idea? Why or why not?

Natasha Trethewey is the Robert W. Woodruff Professor of English and Creative Writing at Emory University, where she also directs the Creative Writing Program. She won the 2007 Pulitzer Prize in Poetry for her 2006 collection Native Guard *and was appointed United States Poet Laureate in June 2012.*

ON WHITMAN, CIVIL WAR MEMORY, AND MY SOUTH

BY NATASHA TRETHEWEY

O magnet-South! O glistening perfumed South! my South!
O quick mettle, rich blood, impulse and love! good and evil!
O all dear to me!

—Walt Whitman

I. THE NEW SOUTH

A few years ago I was interviewed for the *Atlanta Journal-Constitution*—a newspaper whose slogan used to be "Covering Dixie Like the Dew"—and later, when the article appeared, the headline read, "Poet Digs at Secrets in Her South." Not long after that, I received several e-mail and phone messages from a marketing representative who wanted to get a few lines from me about "my South." In the messages, he said it wouldn't take long and that his firm couldn't pay me for my comments. Well, I was busy, and besides that, I figured he didn't want to hear what I really think about the South. Most likely, he probably wanted some sound-bite clichés about how I like my grits, sweet tea, or barbecue, about how we southerners like sitting on porches and after-church visiting.

Some time after that, I started seeing advertisements for Turner South Network on the sides of buses all around Atlanta. Usually the ads featured a photograph of a man or woman next to a quote about his or her South. The text suggested the kinds of things I suspect that marketing representative was looking for when he tried to contact me; and though I don't know whether it had been the network calling me or not, I couldn't help thinking that there might be some connection. Not only were these images of the New South appearing on buses, they were showing up in some clever and entertaining television commercials too.

In one commercial, a long-haired teenager is driving fast down a dusty road—until he gets pulled over by a police officer. The officer appears menacing behind his metallic aviator sunglasses, and he has the kind of belly and demeanor that are reminiscent of some country sheriff straight out of Hazzard County. Approaching the car, the police officer stands—almost threateningly—for a moment, then says, lifting his shades, "Son, don't forget to pick your sister up from ballet." This is the new South—a riff on the stereotypes of the not-so-new South—and the message is certainly one of change. It's a comforting thought—if not completely true. Watching it, I thought of Walt Whitman and his South: how even his love for this place is underscored by something we'll never see in these commercials or on buses rolling through Atlanta.

The South of Whitman's time was not without its stunning beauty or its stunning cruelty. Writing "O Magnet South" in 1860, Whitman praised the landscape—its rivers, lakes, trees, the native flora and fauna:

> O the cotton plant! The growing fields of rice, sugar, hemp!
>
> The cactus guarded with thorns, the laurel tree with large
> white flowers . . .

His love for the South, however, was complex, and in the poem he acknowledges, too, the darker side of it—"the piney odor and the gloom, the awful natural stillness." When he goes further to mention "the fugitive" and his "conceal'd hut," it is hard not to think of fugitive slaves. Whitman's take on the South is much like my own; it is a love/hate relationship. Later, he would write: "I would be the last one to confuse moral values—to imagine the South impeccable. I don't condone the South where it has gone wrong—its Negro slavery, I don't condone that—far from it—I hate it." Because of his open-armed enthusiasm, his inclusiveness and celebration of everyone, even the lowliest prostitute or degraded slave, Whitman's work has come to represent a poetics of democracy, a humane tradition of antiracism. Even now, there is much more to be learned from him and from his conflicted relationship to his subject matter—especially as Americans near and far are still fighting, ideologically, the Civil War.

II. THE LOST WAR

E. O. Wilson has written, "Homo Sapiens is the only species to suffer psychological exile." I've been thinking about that a lot lately, particularly in relation to all the panels I have been on at conferences on contemporary southern literature and culture. I began to notice, after several of these panels, that someone in the audience almost always raised a question about the psyches of southern writers—why we write the way that we do. It seemed to me that just as often, someone on the panel would answer that question by saying something like, "We southerners write the way that we do because, after all, we lost the war." Each time I've heard this I've had to say, "My South didn't lose the war." On each of these occasions, the other panelists—most likely unintentionally—had responded to the question in a manner that seemed to suggest they had forgotten I was there, and that seemed to define the southern psyche and the southern experience as if they were monolithic. In a sense, their responses echo a type of erasure that has affected the documenting of public history and the dedication of public monuments and has continued to affect our public memory. I'm sure my fellow panelists never meant to exclude me when they said "we." I am a southerner too, but these occurrences are evidence of the public memory of the war and its aftermath that still makes outsiders of black Americans—even as nearly 200,000 fought for freedom in the Civil War—and leaves out many narratives which would give us a fuller, richer understanding of our American experience.

A champion of American experience—the diversity of its people and their labors—Whitman feared that the "real war" would not get written. He believed that war existed in the alternative narrative that might be offered by so many anonymous soldiers—most dead and buried, often in unmarked graves—whose stories would never be told. Whitman's Specimen Days becomes a kind of monument to the common soldier—

the harsh facts of war recorded in his honest language. And yet, there is still little written of black soldiers, though he mentions tending to them as well: "Among the black soldiers, wounded or sick, and in the contraband camps, I also took my way whenever in their neighborhood, and did what I could for them." This is only a slight acknowledgment from the poet who wrote with great inclusiveness of blacks in such poems as "I Sing the Body Electric" and "Song of Myself." Perhaps a more telling poem, however—one that suggests the complexity of Whitman's conflicted relationship to the South and all her citizens—is "Reconciliation."

> Word over all, beautiful as the sky!
>
> Beautiful that war, and all its deeds of carnage, must in time be utterly lost;
>
> That the hands of the sisters Death and Night incessantly
> Softly wash again, and ever again, this soil'd world;
>
> . . . For my enemy is dead, a man divine as myself is dead;
>
> I look where he lies white-faced and still in the coffin—I draw near;
>
> Bend down and touch lightly with my lips the white face in the coffin.

Here, Whitman suggests the reunion of the nation, men on opposite sides of the war drawn together beneath the banner of reconciliation. However, in the final image of the dead, "white-faced" in the coffin, Whitman leaves out the reality of so many dead soldiers whose faces were not white. And further, according to historian David Blight, the poem highlights—in the "kinship" of the dead white brothers—"the ultimate betrayal of the dark-faced folk whom the dead had shared in liberating." This kind of erasure would continue to dominate Civil War memory as monuments to only part of the story inscribed a narrative on the American landscape—particularly in the South. The lost war, then, is the narrative of black Americans whose stories were often subjugated, lost, or left out of public memory and the creation of public monuments.

III. MEMORY AND FORGETTING

Just off the coast of my hometown, Gulfport, Mississippi, is a series of barrier islands—Cat, Horn, Deer, and Ship—that separate the dirty waters of the coastal area, with its dead fish and debris, from the clearer waters out in the Gulf. Ship Island is a Civil War site, and during the warmer months, anyone can buy passage on one of the small cruisers making daily trips out there and take a brief tour offered by the National Park Service.

The island's history is an interesting one. The first regiments of the Louisiana Native Guards were mustered into service in September, October, and November of 1862—the 1st regiment thus becoming the first officially sanctioned regiment of black soldiers in the Union Army, and the 2nd and 3rd made up of men who had been slaves only months before enlisting. During the war, the fort at Ship Island, Mississippi, called Fort Massachusetts, was maintained as a prison for Confederate soldiers—military convicts and prisoners of war—manned by the 2nd regiment. In his wartime reminiscences, Whitman pointed out that "few white regiments [made] a better appearance on parade than the 1st and 2nd Louisiana Native Guards." And yet, visitors to the fort today will learn almost none of this history. Instead, they will see first the plaque placed at the entrance by the Daughters of the Confederacy listing the names of the Confederate men once there. Nowhere is a similar plaque memorializing the names of the Native Guards, and if tourists don't know to ask about the history of these black soldiers, most likely the park ranger will overlook this aspect of the fort's history in his tour, mentioning only that this was a fort taken over by Union forces and that Confederate prisoners were kept there. Even the brochures leave out any mention that the troops stationed on the island were black. This omission serves to further the narrative that blacks were passive recipients of the freedom bestowed upon them by white "brothers" who fought and died in the Civil War.

Monuments all around the South serve to inscribe a particular narrative onto the landscape while at the same time subjugating or erasing another. Fortunately, there are several organizations and historians trying to restore the history of the role of black soldiers to the public memory through monuments. Last February, in the Vicksburg

National Military Park, the first monument of its kind in a national park was erected, though not without certain omissions. According to the Jackson Advocate, during the earlier ground-breaking ceremony, "Park Superintendent Bill Nichols and Park historian Terry Winschel begrudgingly labeled the black regiments as 'supply guards' in the text on display rather than giving the men their full measure of respect as the fully-recognized infantry, artillery and cavalry units that they were."

That a more inclusive history of black soldiers is not given on Ship Island or in the Vicksburg Military Park, and that certain facts are often left out of local historical narratives and (perhaps until most recently) were likely to be given only a small part in larger histories, is emblematic of ideological contests about how to remember the Civil War, how we construct public memory with its omissions and embellishments. As David Blight asserts in *Race and Reunion: The Civil War in American Memory*, "Deflections and evasions, careful remembering and necessary forgetting, and embittered and irreconcilable versions of experience are all the stuff of historical memory." Though Whitman had acknowledged black soldiers in his letters and reminiscences, ultimately he often left blacks out of his larger concerns: "When the South is spoken of," he wrote, contrasting the roles of the ruling class and the masses, "no one means the people, the mass of freemen." Here Whitman is referring to the free white masses, even as his language reminds us of the invisible "freedmen" all around the South. In fact, according to Daniel Aaron in The Unwritten War:

> the Negro did not figure significantly in his calculations for America's future, the Grand Plan of History; and it is just as mistaken to confuse Whitman's prose opinion of the Negro and the poetic use he made of him in "Leaves of Grass" as it is to identify his antislavery position with abolitionism.

At the ground-breaking ceremony for the new monument, historian Jim Woodrich's words seemed to echo Whitman's more-than-a-century-old prediction that the real war would not get into the books: "By being here today," Woodrich began, "we acknowledge the valor and honor" of the black Union troops. Their story, he said, "yearns to be known."

IV. "THE REAL WAR WILL NOT GET INTO THE BOOKS"

William Faulkner has said, "the past isn't dead; it isn't even past." All around us debates about the memory of the Civil War and its aftermath continue to shape contemporary concerns. In many states, the battle over the meaning of the Confederate flag is ongoing, with revisionist versions abounding. Here in Georgia, the battle connects us not only to the Civil War but also to public opposition to desegregation. In Mississippi, my home state, the flag still flies on the beach between Gulfport and Biloxi as a monument to only part of our shared history, whereas an equally significant history is overlooked—that of other southerners, black former slaves who were stationed at Ship Island and who fought for their own freedom and citizenship in contests not far away, thus helping the nation come a bit closer to realizing the full democratic potential outlined in the Constitution. These issues are, ultimately, fights about remembrance—how we see ourselves as Americans within the context of history.

When the Daughters of the Confederacy mounted the plaque at Ship Island, they were working to inscribe their exclusive version of history into the public memory, leaving out the other population on the island. C. Vann Woodward, in his preface to *Jumpin' Jim Crow: Southern Politics from Civil War to Civil Rights*, asserts that during the last two decades of the 19th century and the first two of the 20th it was "white ladies . . . who bore primary responsibility for the myths glorifying the old order, the Lost Cause, and white supremacy." Woodward is referring, specifically, to the United Daughters of the Confederacy, the Daughters of the American Revolution, Daughters of Pilgrims, and Daughters of Colonial Governors; they were considered "guardians of the past." "Non-daughters," he writes, "were excluded." The efforts of the Daughters of the Confederacy extended beyond the erecting of monuments and the naming of roads; indeed, they commissioned the history textbooks written for southern schools and oversaw the material contained within them in order to control the narrative of the South's role in the war—that is, to tell a story that was rife with omissions and embellishments, that sought to cast the causes of the war only in terms of states' rights and not at all in terms of the matter of slavery.

It would seem that Whitman, in his conflicted attitudes toward the roles of both North and South, toward slavery and black suffrage (he hated slavery but did not believe blacks capable of exercising the vote), could foresee such one-sided narratives and the need for a fuller understanding of the roots of the conflict—a history more inclusive than what would be told and written for several generations: "But what of the main premonitions of the war?" he asked. Decades later, W. E. B. DuBois would begin to answer him—furthering Whitman's own ideas about the war's origins—and in so doing, point out the embellishments and omissions in the history put forth by a generation of scholars. In his essay "The Propaganda of History," DuBois would take to task American historians, asserting that among the profession, "we have too often made a deliberate attempt so to change the facts of history that the story will make pleasant reading for Americans."

Whitman knew all too well that the real war he feared would not get written was not a pleasant one. Referring primarily to the "seething hell and the black infernal background of countless minor scenes," he nonetheless foreshadows another backdrop—the narratives of blacks relegated to the margins of public memory. "Long, long hence," he anticipated, "when the grave has quenched many hot prejudices and vitalities, and an entirely new class of thinkers and writers come to the argument, the complete question, can perhaps be fairly weighed."

V. WHAT WOULD WHITMAN DO?

On billboards around the South and on church marquees proclaiming the theme of upcoming sermons, a frequent question stands out: What Would Jesus Do? I ask, instead, what would our earthly father—father of modern American poetry, father of the poetry of a democratic vision—what would our Whitman do? OK, so this question is overly speculative. I can hear the voices out there saying that people are products of their historical moment. The defenders of Thomas Jefferson as well as his detractors are getting their guard up. I'm not interested in arguing the omissions of the past, only the restoration of those omissions in the present. Perhaps not restoration: acknowledgment is a better word. When Robert Penn Warren returned to his South to write *Segregation*, he was a man in the midst of change—he was rethinking his position as a contributor to the anthology *I'll Take My Stand.* The nation was changing, and he was changing along with it.

When Whitman took on the task of setting down on paper some of his thoughts about the Civil War, its causes and its aftermath, he probably did not have the image of the black soldier in the foreground of his thinking. Though his wartime reminiscences would consider regiments of black troops, his poem "Ethiopia Saluting the Colors" focuses on a "dusky woman, so ancient hardly human," and not black soldiers who were participants in the war rather than bystanders. However, the omissions, inherent even in his later writings about the war, underscore the questions of historical memory with which future generations would contend:

> Probably no future age can know, but I well know, how the gist of this fiercest and most resolute of the world's warlike contentions resided exclusively in the unnamed, unknown rank and file; and how the brunt of its labor of death was, to all essential purposes, volunteered.

Here, Whitman directs us to the unnamed, unknown rank-and-file white soldier and, inadvertently, to black soldiers as well—the legions of runaway slaves and freedmen who flocked to Union camps, first as contraband and then later as men (and women) eager to enlist—whose story has been left out of public memory of the Civil War and has only begun to be inscribed onto the man-made, monumental American landscape.

VI. CODA

A lot of things have changed since Whitman declared his love for the South and her contradictions. Some have not. Contradictions abound in this landscape of beauty and ugliness, this cauldron of nostalgic remembrances and willed forgetting. In Mississippi and Alabama, lawyers and concerned citizens are continuing to work to bring to trial the perpetrators of heinous crimes—Byron de la Beckwith; the bombers who blew up a church in Birmingham, killing four little girls; the men responsible for the murders of Cheney, Schwerner, and Goodman. An exhibit about the history of lynching is touring the country, even as opponents of this necessary remembering here in Atlanta opine in letters to the editor that some things are best left buried, forgotten. I live with the ghosts of the past every day; when Halloween comes around, I see in the decorative skeletons hanging from my neighbors' trees the specter of lynching. And even worse, I encounter the specter of what put real bodies in trees still lingering in the kind of willed forgetting and intolerance we haven't yet overcome. From where I stand, it's easy to feel the kind of contradictions evident in Whitman's work, those things he revealed both intentionally and inadvertently.

Like him, I love my South. And I hate it too.

1. Trethewey writes about the way society views the past. What role does memory play in the perception of history in the United States?

2. Trethewey discusses different historical perspectives of the South. Consider the region where you or your family grew up, and list some notable historical events associated with that region. Then write about how memory and what is recorded in history might have affected the region's historical identity. Can you identify any possible gaps in history?

Thomas Rogers is a translator currently living in Berlin. He is a freelance journalist with Slate, *was the former editor of* Salon, *and has also contributed to* NY Mag, TNR, *and* The Awl. Slate *is a United-States-based English language online current affairs and culture magazine.* Slate *is a division of the Washington Post Company.*

FOR HELP IN OLD AGE, HOW ABOUT A NEW AGE OF ROBOTS?

By Thomas Rogers

Early in the new science-fiction film *Robot & Frank*, Frank, an elderly man, gets a visit from his son, Hunter. Worried about his father's apparent decline, Hunter takes a gift out of the back of his car: a white robot with a humanlike body and a polite speaking voice. The machine, Hunter promises, will keep his dad healthy and focused—and the house clean. Frank is not so sure, though: "That thing's going to kill me in my sleep," he worries.

But before long, the "health care" robot is cooking his meals, planting a garden and planning activities to keep his human overlord occupied.

The film's depiction of robot-human relations may still be a fantasy, but it's also a reminder we've been expecting elder care robots like Frank's in the real world for several years now, and so far, they're nowhere to be seen. So what's the hold-up?

It's no secret that America is getting older. By 2030, thanks to the baby boomers, one in five Americans will be 65 or older, stressing the health care system and economy. Half of those over 85 require assistance in everyday activities, and, if 2009 numbers hold up, more than 13 percent of people over 85 will spend time in nursing homes. It's unclear who will pay for this and how. And more importantly, it's unclear who will take care of all of these old people.

The solution, the robotics industry hopes, is technology. In Japan, where panic over an aging population is nothing new, elder care robots have been a priority for more than a decade. One of the Japanese researchers' bigger successes is Paro, a touch-sensitive companion robot—a sort of high-tech stuffed animal, shaped like a seal—for elderly people with cognitive disorders like Alzheimer's. Japanese Nursebots can lift up elderly patients and bring them breakfast in bed, and this year, researchers from Japan's Chukyo University released Babyloid, a baby-like robot similar to Paro that looks like something that crawled out of a Miyazaki movie.

In recent years, Japanese tech giant Panasonic has created a hair-washing robot, a drug delivery robot, a robotic bed, and HOSPI-Rimo, a robot with a touchscreen that helps hospital patients communicate with doctors and family.

In the next decade, the selection of personal elder care robots is expected to expand dramatically in the United States as well. "Full robots with arms are still very expensive," says Ashutosh Saxena, a professor in the department of computer science at Cornell, "but they are getting cheaper by the day."

He predicts that armless robots—capable of communicating verbally with the elderly and observing them in case of accidents—will hit the market within the next five years. These kinds of robots, which could even monitor a person's medication intake, should allow elderly people to live independently and healthily longer, like a very sophisticated Life Alert bracelet.

There's just one hiccup: the elderly themselves.

Despite manufacturers' hopes, robotic technology has proven to be alienating for many older people—even, the BBC reports, in Japan, a country with an intense, long-term love of all things robotic. Alexander Libin, scientific director of simulation and education research at Medstar Health Research Institute, argues that one of the biggest challenges is that the elderly need to be able to communicate easily with them. Although many robots (and mobile phones) can now recognize voice commands, nonverbal cues pose a much bigger challenge. Libin, who has worked extensively on robot-patient interaction, believes that touch-sensitive technology—like the one used by Paro, the therapeutic seal robot—will play a large role in making robots palatable to seniors. DARPA, the government-funded research institute, is working on neural robot limb communication, a technology that, Libin believes, could be applied to robots.

Given the elderly population's diverse needs, elder care robots will also likely be far more specialized than *Robot & Frank's* robotic helper suggests. "People with chronic illnesses like diabetes need a robot that can help them with shots, people with bad vision need guidance, people with cancer that are in pain will need a robot to entertain them by having a conversation or reading a book," says Libin. The coming generation of robots, he says, will be created with those specific goals in mind.

Unlike the Japanese, American engineers have been focusing on robots that are more practical and less humanoid. "The Japanese want robots to be like them," says Libin, noting Japan's long tradition of treating inanimate objects like living beings. In the United States, we're more comfortable treating machines as machines. "We want things we can control."

The path toward robot acceptance may also require something very simple and, for robot manufacturers, frustrating: patience. The process of getting old people to be comfortable with robots, Saxena argues, will be a question of gradual acclimatization. Elderly people will have to get used to having small, nonthreatening observer robots watching them in their homes before they'll allow robots do tasks on their behalf—or even touch them.

And the truth is, boomers who grew up long before the rise of computers or smartphones may never be comfortable with the idea of replacing a human being with a machine. Like other forms of social change, robot acceptance may simply require one generation to replace the previous one.

Robots can be a technology that is difficult for the elderly to accept. Apart from the technology, what are some of the human relationship challenges associated with the elderly relying on robotic assistance? Is there a limit to their effectiveness? Is there a trade-off between independence and isolation when the elderly rely on robots?

Judy Lin is a writer with the UCLA Today *news site www.today.ucla.edu. She has also freelanced for* Prevention *magazine and other publications.*

HONOR OR ABANDON: SOCIETIES' TREATMENT OF ELDERLY INTRIGUES SCHOLAR

By Judy Lin

When people grow old in traditional villages in Fiji, family and friends care for them at home until their dying days. In America, the elderly are more typically sent to nursing homes—a contrast that may appear unfeeling, even cruel. But the ways in which societies around the world treat their elderly span a vast and varied range, according to Jared Diamond, UCLA professor of geography and physiology.

Why this differs so drastically from culture to culture is an intriguing question that Diamond, 72, a Pulitzer Prize-winning author of *Guns, Germs, and Steel: The Fates of Human Societies* and recipient of a MacArthur Foundation "genius" award, is currently researching. Recently, he shared some of his thoughts on the subject with a standing-room-only audience in the Neuroscience Research Building auditorium in a lecture, "Honor or Abandon: Why Does Treatment of the Elderly Vary so Widely Among Human Societies?"

The idea that it's human nature for parents to make sacrifices for their children and, in turn, for their grown children to sacrifice for their aging parents—turns out to be a "naïve expectation," said Diamond. This assumption, he said, ignores undeniable conflicts of interest between generations.

From a common sense perspective, "Parents and children both want a comfortable life—there are limits to the sacrifices that they'll make for each other." And from a scientific perspective—natural selection—Diamond noted, "It may under some circumstances be better for children to abandon or kill their parents and for the parents to abandon or kill their children."

Those circumstances include life's often heart-wrenching realities—from the threat of starvation among indigenous tribes to the difficult choices posed by modern societies' life-prolonging medical care, Diamond said.

Traditional nomadic tribes often end up abandoning their elderly during their unrelenting travels. The choice for the healthy and young is to do this or carry the old and infirm on their backs—along with children, weapons and necessities—through perilous territory. Also prone to sacrificing their elderly are societies that suffer periodic famines. Citing a dramatic example, Diamond said Paraguay's Aché Indians assign certain young men the task of killing old people with an ax or spear, or burying them alive.

"We react with horror at these stories, but upon reflection, what else could they do?" Diamond asked. "The people in these societies are faced with a cruel choice."

Those of us in modern cultures face cruel choices of our own, he added. "Many of you have already faced or will face a similar ordeal when you are the relative responsible for the medical care of an old person—the one who has to decide whether to halt further medical intervention or whether to administer painkillers and sedatives that will have the side effect of hastening death."

Yet the fact remains, Diamond said, that many societies treat their elderly better than Americans do. In some cultures, he said, children are so devoted that when their aging parents lose their teeth the children will pre-chew their food. A closer look at how traditional societies value (or don't value) their old people might teach us what to emulate and what to avoid.

The elderly's usefulness in a society plays a big part in determining their fate, Diamond said. While old people in traditional societies can no longer spear game or battle enemies, they can still gather food to care for children. They are also often expert at making tools, weapons, baskets and clothes. In many societies they serve as "tribal elders" in medicine, religion and politics.

Perhaps most important, in cultures lacking written records of history, song and other forms of culture, older people are invaluable sources of information.

"The repositories of knowledge are the memories of old people," Diamond said. "If you don't have old people to remember what happened 50 years ago, you've lost a lot of experience for that society," from communal history to advice on how to survive a cyclone or other natural disaster.

Societies also vary in how much they respect their old people—or don't. In East Asian cultures steeped in a Confucian tradition that places a high value on filial piety, obedience and respect, Diamond said, "it is considered utterly despicable not to take care of your elderly parents." The same goes for Mediterranean cultures, where multigenerational families live together in the same house—in stark contrast to the United States, "where routinely, old people do not live with their children and it's a big hassle to take care of your parents even if you want to do it."

While modernization has brought many benefits to the elderly—most notably improved health and longer life spans—it has also led to a breakdown of traditions. For example, multigenerational families are becoming a thing of the past in many modern cities in China, Japan and India, Diamond said, where "today's young people want privacy, want to go off and have a home of their own."

In America, Diamond said, a "cult of youth" and emphasis on the virtues of independence, individualism and self-reliance also make life hard on older people as they inevitably lose some of these traits. Then, there's America's Protestant work ethic, "which holds that if you're no longer working, you've lost the main value that society places on you." Retirement also means losing social relationships, which, coupled with

America's high mobility, leaves many old people hundreds or even thousands of miles away from longtime friends and family.

Modern literacy and its ties to technology are also putting the elderly at a disadvantage.

"Modern literacy means that we look up things in books or on the Internet—we don't go ask an old person," Diamond said. "Formal educational systems, such as UCLA, replace old people with highly trained professors for transmitting specialized knowledge."

And lightning-speed technological advances "mean that the things that old people do understand got technologically outdated," Diamond said, adding that his ability to multiply two-digit numbers in his head has now been superseded by pocket calculators. He even admitted to having to consult his teenage sons to use the TV's "remote with 47 buttons on it."

Still, steps can be taken to improve the lives of our elderly, Diamond said. Understand their changing strengths and weaknesses as they age, he advised, and appreciate their deeper understanding of human relationships and their ability to think across wide-ranging disciplines, to strategize, and share what they've learned.

"So if you want to get advice on complicated problems, ask someone who's 70; don't ask someone who's 25," Diamond concluded. "Old people can have new value ... although we often don't recognize that this is possible."

1. Do some research to find out how the elderly are treated in different countries around the world. Reflect on your reaction by considering your cultural norms and how they differ from the culture you've studied.

2. "Virtues of independence, individualism and self-reliance" are highly valued in the United States. Reflect on highly valued character traits in your culture or sub-culture and how they have affected your treatment of the elderly.

Gene Luen Yang is a Chinese American writer who currently teaches at Hamline University in Minnesota. He is a well-known voice in comics and literature, having published work with Marvel, Dark Horse, and Harper Collins. In 2007, Yang's book American Born Chinese *became the first graphic novel to win the Michael L. Printz Award.*

AMERICAN BORN CHINESE

By Gene Luen Yang

1. What are some of the misconceptions about different groups living in the United States? Why do people have these ideas?

2. What is the significance of the school Jin attends being called Mayflower Elementary?

Elizabeth Kolbert was a writer for the New York Times *from 1984 to 1999 and has been writing for* The New Yorker *ever since. She grew up in New York, attended Yale University, and received the Fulbright Scholarship to study at the Universität Hamburg, in Germany. Her book about global warming,* Field Notes from a Catastrophe, *won the 2006 National Magazine Award for Public Interest, the 2006 National Academies Communication Award, and the 2005 American Association for the Advancement of Science Journalism Award. She now resides in Massachusetts with her family.*

SPOILED ROTTEN: WHY DO KIDS RULE THE ROOST?

By Elizabeth Kolbert

In 2004, Carolina Izquierdo, an anthropologist at the University of California, Los Angeles, spent several months with the Matsigenka, a tribe of about twelve thousand people who live in the Peruvian Amazon. The Matsigenka hunt for monkeys and parrots, grow yucca and bananas, and build houses that they roof with the leaves of a particular kind of palm tree, known as a *kapashi*. At one point, Izquierdo decided to accompany a local family on a leaf-gathering expedition down the Urubamba River.

A member of another family, Yanira, asked if she could come along. Izquierdo and the others spent five days on the river. Although Yanira had no clear role in the group, she quickly found ways to make herself useful. Twice a day, she swept the sand off the sleeping mats, and she helped stack the *kapashi* leaves for transport back to the village. In the evening, she fished for crustaceans, which she cleaned, boiled, and served to the others. Calm and self-possessed, Yanira "asked for nothing," Izquierdo later recalled. The girl's behavior made a strong impression on the anthropologist because at the time of the trip Yanira was just six years old.

While Izquierdo was doing field work among the Matsigenka, she was also involved in an anthropological study closer to home. A colleague of hers, Elinor Ochs, had recruited thirty-two middle-class families for a study of life in twenty-first-century Los Angeles. Ochs had arranged to have the families filmed as they ate, fought, made up, and did the dishes.

Izquierdo and Ochs shared an interest in many ethnographic issues, including child rearing. How did parents in different cultures train young people to assume adult responsibilities? In the case of the Angelenos, they mostly didn't. In the L.A. families observed, no child routinely performed household chores without being instructed to. Often, the kids had to be begged to attempt the simplest tasks; often, they still refused. In one fairly typical encounter, a father asked his eight-year-old son five times to please go take a bath or a shower. After the fifth plea went unheeded, the father picked the boy up and carried him into the bathroom. A few minutes later, the kid, still unwashed, wandered into another room to play a video game.

In another representative encounter, an eight-year-old girl sat down at the dining table. Finding that no silverware had been laid out for her, she demanded, "How am I supposed to eat?" Although the girl clearly knew where the silverware was kept, her father got up to get it for her.

In a third episode captured on tape, a boy named Ben was supposed to leave the house with his parents. But he couldn't get his feet into his sneakers, because the laces were tied. He handed one of the shoes to his father: "Untie it!" His father suggested that he ask nicely.

"Can you untie it?" Ben replied. After more back-and-forth, his father untied Ben's sneakers. Ben put them on, then asked his father to retie them. "*You* tie your shoes and let's *go*," his father finally exploded. Ben was unfazed. "I'm just *asking*," he said.

A few years ago, Izquierdo and Ochs wrote an article for *Ethos*, the journal of the Society of Psychological Anthropology, in which they described Yanira's conduct during the trip down the river and Ben's exchange with his dad. "Juxtaposition of these developmental stories begs for an account of responsibility in childhood," they wrote. Why do Matsigenka children "help their families at home more than L.A. children?" And "Why do L.A. adult family members help their children at home more than do Matsigenka?" Though not phrased in exactly such terms, questions like these are being asked—silently, imploringly, despairingly—every single day by parents from Anchorage to Miami. Why, why, why?

With the exception of the imperial offspring of the Ming dynasty and the dauphins of pre-Revolutionary France, contemporary American kids may represent the most indulged young people in the history of the world. It's not just that they've been given unprecedented amounts of stuff—clothes, toys, cameras, skis, computers, televisions, cell phones, PlayStations, iPods. (The market for Burberry Baby and other forms of kiddie "couture" has reportedly been growing by ten percent a year.) They've also been granted unprecedented authority. "Parents want their kids' approval, a reversal of the past ideal of children striving for their parents' approval," Jean Twenge and W. Keith Campbell, both professors of psychology, have written. In many middle-class families, children have one, two, sometimes three adults at their beck and call. This is a social experiment on a grand scale, and a growing number of adults fear that it isn't working out so well: according to one poll, commissioned by *Time* and CNN, two-thirds of American parents think that their children are spoiled.

The notion that we may be raising a generation of kids who can't, or at least won't, tie their own shoes has given rise to a new genre of parenting books. Their titles tend to be either dolorous ("The Price of Privilege") or downright hostile ("The Narcissism Epidemic," "Mean Moms Rule," "A Nation of Wimps"). The books are less how-to guides than how-not-to's: how not to give in to your toddler, how not to intervene whenever your teenager looks bored, how not to spend two hundred thousand dollars on tuition only to find your twenty-something graduate back at home, drinking all your beer.

Not long ago, Sally Koslow, a former editor-in-chief of *McCall's*, discovered herself in this last situation. After four years in college and two on the West Coast, her son Jed moved back to Manhattan and settled into his old room in the family's apartment, together with thirty-four boxes of vinyl LPs. Unemployed, Jed liked to stay out late, sleep until noon, and wander around in his boxers. Koslow set out to try to understand why he and so many of his peers seemed stuck in what she regarded as permanent "adultescence." She concluded that one of the reasons is the lousy economy. Another is parents like her.

"Our offspring have simply leveraged our braggadocio, good intentions, and overinvestment," Koslow writes in her new book, *Slouching Toward Adulthood: Observations from the Not-So-Empty Nest* (Viking). They inhabit "a broad savannah of entitlement that we've watered, landscaped, and hired gardeners to maintain." She recommends letting the grasslands revert to forest: "The best way for a lot of us to show our love would be to learn to un-mother and un-father." One practical tip that she offers is to do nothing when your adult child finally decides to move out. In the process of schlepping Jed's stuff to an apartment in Carroll Gardens, Koslow's husband tore a tendon and ended up in emergency surgery.

Madeline Levine, a psychologist who lives outside San Francisco, specializes in treating young adults. In *Teach Your Children Well: Parenting for Authentic Success* (HarperCollins), she argues that we do too much for our kids because we overestimate our influence. "Never before have parents been so (mistakenly) convinced that their every move has a ripple effect into their child's future success," she writes. Paradoxically, Levine maintains, by working so hard to help our kids we end up holding them back.

"Most parents today were brought up in a culture that put a strong emphasis on being special," she observes. "Being special takes hard work and can't be trusted to children. Hence the exhausting cycle of constantly monitoring their work and performance, which in turn makes children feel less competent and confident, so that they need even more oversight."

Pamela Druckerman, a former reporter for the *Wall Street Journal*, moved to Paris after losing her job. She married a British expatriate and not long after that gave birth to a daughter. Less out of conviction than inexperience, Druckerman began raising her daughter, nicknamed Bean, *à l'Américaine*. The result, as she recounts in *Bringing Up Bébé* (Penguin Press), was that Bean was invariably the most ill-behaved child in every Paris restaurant and park she visited. French children could sit calmly through a three-course meal; Bean was throwing food by the time the apéritifs arrived.

Druckerman talked to a lot of French mothers, all of them svelte and most apparently well rested. She learned that the French believe ignoring children is good for them. "French parents don't worry that they're going to damage their kids by frustrating them," she writes. "To the contrary, they think their kids will be damaged if they can't cope with frustration." One mother, Martine, tells Druckerman that she always waited five minutes before picking up her infant daughter when she cried. While Druckerman and Martine are talking, in Martine's suburban home, the daughter, now three, is baking cupcakes by herself. Bean is roughly the same age, "but it wouldn't have occurred to me to let her do a complicated task like this all on her own," Druckerman observes. "I'd be supervising, and she'd be resisting my supervision."

Also key, Druckerman discovered, is just saying *non*. In contrast to American parents, French parents, when they say it, actually mean it. They "view learning to cope with 'no' as a crucial step in a child's evolution," Druckerman writes. "It forces them to understand that there are other people in the world, with needs as powerful as their own."

Not long ago, in the hope that our sons might become a little more Matsigenka, my husband and I gave them a new job: unloading the grocery bags from the car. One evening when I came home from the store, it was raining. Carrying two or three bags, the youngest, Aaron, who is thirteen, tried to jump over a puddle. There was a loud crash. After I'd retrieved what food could be salvaged from a Molotov cocktail of broken glass and mango juice, I decided that Aaron needed another, more vigorous lesson in responsibility. Now, in addition to unloading groceries, he would also have the task of taking out the garbage. On one of his first forays, he neglected to close the lid on the pail tightly enough, and it attracted a bear. The next morning, as I was gathering up the used tissues, ant-filled raisin boxes, and slimy Saran Wrap scattered across the yard, I decided that I didn't have time to let my kids help out around the house. (My husband informed me that I'd just been "kiddie-whipped.")

Ochs and Izquierdo noted, in their paper on the differences between the family lives of the Matsigenka and the Angelenos, how early the Matsigenka begin encouraging their children to be useful. Toddlers routinely heat their own food over an open fire, they observed, while "three-year-olds frequently practice cutting wood and grass with machetes and knives." Boys, when they are six or seven, start to accompany their fathers on fishing and hunting trips, and girls learn to help their mothers with the cooking. As a consequence, by the time they reach puberty Matsigenka kids have mastered most of the skills necessary for survival. Their competence encourages autonomy, which fosters further competence—a virtuous cycle that continues to adulthood.

The cycle in American households seems mostly to run in the opposite direction. So little is expected of kids that even adolescents may not know how to operate the many labor-saving devices their homes are filled with. Their incompetence begets exasperation, which results in still less being asked of them (which leaves them more time for video games). Referring to the Los Angeles families, Ochs and Izquierdo wrote, "Many parents remarked that it takes more effort to get children to collaborate than to do the tasks themselves."

One way to interpret these contrary cycles is to infer that Americans have a lower opinion of their kids' capacities. And, in a certain sense, this is probably true: how many parents in Park Slope or Brentwood would trust their three-year-olds to cut the grass with a machete? But in another sense, of course, it's ridiculous. Contemporary American parents—particularly the upscale sort that "unparenting" books are aimed at—tend to take a highly expansive view of their kids' abilities. Little Ben may not be able to tie his shoes, but that shouldn't preclude his going to Brown.

In "A Nation of Wimps: The High Cost of Invasive Parenting" (Broadway), Hara Estroff Marano argues that college rankings are ultimately to blame for what ails the American family. Her argument runs more or less as follows: High-powered parents worry that the economic opportunities for their children are shrinking. They see a degree from a top-tier school as one of the few ways to give their kids a jump on the competition. In order to secure this advantage, they will do pretty much anything, which means not just taking care of all the cooking and cleaning but also helping their children with math homework, hiring them S.A.T. tutors, and, if necessary, suing their high school. Marano, an editor-at-large at *Psychology Today*, tells about a high school in Washington State that required students to write an eight-page paper and present a ten-minute oral report before graduating. When one senior got a failing grade on his project, his parents hired a lawyer.

Today's parents are not just "helicopter parents," a former school principal complains to Marano. "They are a jet-powered turbo attack model." Other educators gripe about "snowplow parents," who try to clear every obstacle from their children's paths. The products of all this hovering, meanwhile, worry that they may not be able to manage college in the absence of household help. According to research conducted by sociologists at Boston College, today's incoming freshmen are less likely to be concerned about the rigors of higher education than "about how they will handle the logistics of everyday life."

One of the offshoots of the L.A. family study is a new book, *Life at Home in the Twenty-First Century* (Cotsen Institute of Archaeology), which its authors—the anthropologists Jeanne Arnold, of UCLA, Anthony Graesch, of Connecticut College, and Elinor Ochs—describe as a "visual ethnography of middle-class American households." Lavishly illustrated with photographs (by Enzo Ragazzini) of the families' houses and yards, the book offers an intimate glimpse into the crap-strewn core of American culture.

"After a few short years," the text notes, many families amass more objects "than their houses can hold." The result is garages given over to old furniture and unused sports equipment, home offices given over to boxes of stuff that haven't yet been stuck in the garage, and, in one particularly jam-packed house, a shower stall given over to storing dirty laundry.

Children, according to *Life at Home*, are disproportionate generators of clutter: "Each new child in a household leads to a 30 percent increase in a family's inventory of possessions during the preschool years alone." Many of the kids' rooms pictured are so crowded with clothes and toys, so many of which have been tossed on the floor, that there is no path to the bed. (One little girl's room contains, by the authors' count, two hundred and forty-eight dolls, including a hundred and sixty-five Beanie Babies.) The kids' possessions, not to mention their dioramas and their T-ball trophies, spill out into other rooms, giving the houses what the authors call "a very child-centered look."

When anthropologists study cultures like the Matsigenkas', they tend to see patterns. The Matsigenka prize hard work and self-sufficiency. Their daily rituals, their child-rearing practices, and even their folktales reinforce these values, which have an obvious utility for subsistence farmers. Matsigenka stories often feature characters undone by laziness; kids who still don't get the message are rubbed with an itch-inducing plant.

In contemporary American culture, the patterns are more elusive. What values do we convey by turning our homes into warehouses for dolls? By assigning our kids chores and then rewarding them when they screw up? By untying and then retying their shoes for them? It almost seems as if we're actively trying to raise a nation of "adultescents." And, perhaps without realizing it, we are.

As Melvin Konner, a psychiatrist and anthropologist at Emory University, points out in "The Evolution of Childhood" (Belknap), one of the defining characteristics of *Homo sapiens* is its "prolonged juvenile period." Compared with other apes, humans are "altricial," which is to say immature at birth. Chimpanzees, for instance, are born with brains half their adult size; the brains of human babies are only a third of their adult size. Chimps reach puberty shortly after they're weaned; humans take another decade or so. No one knows when exactly in the process of hominid evolution juvenile development began to slow down, but even *Homo ergaster*, who evolved some 1.8 million years ago, seems to have enjoyed—if that's the right word—a protracted childhood. It's often argued by anthropologists that the drawn-out timetable is what made humans human in the first place. It's the fact that we grow up slowly that makes acquiring language and building complicated social structures possible.

The same trend that appears in human prehistory shows up in history as well. The farther back you look, the faster kids grew up. In medieval Europe, children from seven on were initiated into adult work. Compulsory schooling, introduced in the nineteenth century, pushed back the age of maturity to sixteen or so. By the middle of the twentieth century, college graduation seemed, at least in this country, to be the new dividing line. Now, if Judd Apatow is to be trusted, it's possible to close in on forty without coming of age.

Evolutionarily speaking, this added delay makes a certain amount of sense. In an increasingly complex and unstable world, it may be adaptive to put off maturity as long as possible. According to this way of thinking, staying forever young means always being ready for the next big thing (whatever that might be).

Or adultesence might be just the opposite: not evidence of progress but another sign of a generalized regression. Letting things slide is always the easiest thing to do, in parenting no less than in banking, public education, and environmental protection. A lack of discipline is apparent these days in just about every aspect of American society. Why this should be is a much larger question, one to ponder as we take out the garbage and tie our kids' shoes.

1. Do you consider your upbringing "spoiled"? Why or why not? Did your view change after reading about Yanira at the beginning of the article?

2. What features of American culture might lead to a more spoiled upbringing?

ANALYZE, DON'T SUMMARIZE

By Michael Berubé

The first time a student asked me about my "grading system," I was nonplused—and a bit intimidated. It was an innocent question, but I heard it as a challenge: I was a 25-year-old graduate student teaching my first section in an English-literature class at the University of Virginia, and I really didn't know *what* my grading system was. Nor did I feel comfortable saying, "Well, it's like Justice Stewart's definition of pornography, really—I simply know an A paper when I see one."

I fumbled my way through a reply, but I was unsettled enough by the exchange to seek the advice of the professor in charge of the course (and roughly a dozen teaching assistants). He went on a sublime rant that I've never forgotten, though I'm sure I've embellished it over the years. "These students come in here," he fumed, "with the idea that *you* have to explain yourself. 'You gave me a B-plus,' they say. 'What did you take points off for?' I tell them, 'Your paper was not born with an A. Your paper was born with a "nothing," and I made up my mind about it as I read it. That's what the marginalia are—they're the record of my responses to your arguments.'"

Today I've incorporated versions of that rant into my own teaching handouts: I try to explain the differences among superior, mediocre, and failing papers, and I tell students that my skills as a reader have been honed by my many experiences with professional editors, who attend carefully to paragraph transitions, dangling modifiers, and inaccurate citations. But I've never been able to give my students a visceral idea of what goes through my head as I read their work—until now.

Like many sports fans, I've grown a bit tired of ESPN's 25th-anniversary hyper-self-awareness of itself as a sports medium. While it's great to see the network poke fun at its early years, when its anchors wore dorky sports coats and weren't always sure when they were on the air, it's really quite tedious to be reminded of how sports-television hype helped hype TV sports.

The show *Around the Horn* has come to epitomize the general decline to me. Another half-hour program with which it's paired, *Pardon the Interruption*, gives us two volatile, opinionated sportscasters disagreeing with each other in rapid-fire fashion, with but a handful of seconds devoted to each topic. *Around the Horn* takes that format and makes a game show of it, offering us sportswriters competing for whose commentary will "win" by the end of the show.

I still play an organized sport—ice hockey—and as an amateur (and aged) player, I have to say that sports talk shows like this make me wonder whether some people don't see sports as simply an opportunity for endless metacommentary...and, of course, as gainful employment for an entire entourage of chattering parasites. In all that noise, I think, where are the games themselves?

Imagine my surprise, then, when I watched *Around the Horn* one afternoon and realized that here, at last, was my grading system in practice.

The idea behind *Around the Horn* is simple. There are a host and four contestants, each of whom speaks briefly on a series of up-to-the-moment sports topics. Points are awarded for smart—or merely plausible—remarks, and points are deducted for obviously foolish or factually inaccurate ones. There's a mute button involved, too, and players get eliminated as the show progresses (but those aspects of the game, so far as I can tell, have no counterpart in the world of paper-grading). And—of course, for this is the point of all such sports metacommentary—the viewers at home get to disagree with and complain about the commentary, as well as the officiating.

My standard undergraduate survey-course for paper-writing tells students things like this: "Assume a hypothetical readership composed of people who have already read the book. That means you shouldn't say, 'In class, we discussed the importance of the clam chowder in Chapter five.' But more important, it means *you don't have to summarize the novel.* We're your readers, and we've read the book. However, we haven't read it in quite the way *you're* reading it. We haven't focused on the same scenes and passages you're bringing to our attention, and we haven't yet seen how your argument might make sense of the book for us."

But not all of my students see the point. Every semester I'm approached by some who don't quite understand why they're being asked to make an *argument* out of literary criticism. Why shouldn't they simply record their impressions of the works before them? When I tell them that an observation is not a thesis, and that their thesis isn't sufficiently specific or useful if they can't imagine anyone plausibly disagreeing with it, they ask me why they can't simply explain *what happens in the novel.*

But in what world, exactly, would such an enterprise count as analysis? Not in any world I know—not even in the ephemeral pop-culture world of sports metacommentary. Can you imagine someone showing up on *Around the Horn* and saying to host Tony Reali, "Well, Tony, let me point out that last night, the Red Sox swept the Tigers and crept to within three games of the Yankees."

"And?"

"And nothing. I'm just pointing out that the Sox won, 3-1, on a four-hitter by Schilling, while the Yanks blew another late-inning lead."

No one does that, because no one in the sports world confuses summaries with analyses.

I also tell students that an essay of 2,000 words doesn't give them all that much space to get going.

"You've only got a few pages to make that argument of yours. You don't need a grand introductory paragraph that begins, 'Mark Twain is one of Earth's greatest writers.' It's far better to start by giving us some idea of what you'll be arguing and why. If you like, you can even begin by pointing us to a particularly important passage that will serve as the springboard for your larger discussion: 'Not long after the second scaffold scene in *The Scarlet Letter*, when Arthur Dimmesdale joins hands with Hester Prynne and her daughter Pearl, Nathaniel Hawthorne asks us to reconsider the meaning of the scarlet A on Hester's breast.'"

On *Around the Horn*, commentators have to make their points in 15 seconds, which, as people who know me can testify, just happens to be roughly the amount of time it takes me to utter 2,000 words. So here, too, the analogy holds up.

Seriously, the sports-talk analogy is useful simply as a handy way of distinguishing between summary and analysis—and, more important, as an illustration of what happens in my grading process when a student paper cites textual evidence so compelling and unusual that it makes me go back and reread the passage in question (good!), suggests that a novel's conclusion fails to resolve the questions and tensions raised by the rest of the narrative (interesting!—possibly good, depending on the novel we're talking about), or makes claims that are directly contradicted by the literary text itself (bad! the mute button for you!).

So in a sense, I do "take off" points as I go—but then I add them back on as well, sentence by sentence, paragraph by paragraph, as I weigh the claims my students advance and the means by which they advance them.

The rules for literary analysis are the same rules in play for any kind of analysis: mastery of the material. Cogency of supporting evidence. Ability to imagine and rebut salient counterarguments. Extra points for wit and style, points off for mind-numbing clichés, and permanent suspension for borrowing someone else's argument without proper attribution.

And yet, every year, I'm left with a handful of students who tell me that if *that's* what I want, I should simply assign topics to each student. "Not a chance," I reply. "Most of the mental labor of your paper takes place when you try to figure out just what you want to argue and why." As books like Thomas McLaughlin's *Street Smarts and Critical Theory* and Gerald Graff's *Clueless in Academe* have argued (with wit and style), students seem to understand this principle perfectly well when it comes to music, sports, and popular culture. It's our job to show them how it might apply to the study of literature.

My students, too, are often suspicious of what they regard as an idiosyncratic and subjective enterprise that varies from English professor to English professor. But I can tell them there's really nothing mysterious about its mechanics. In fact, if they want to watch it in action, they can tune in to ESPN any weekday afternoon, 5 p.m. Eastern.

WORKS CITED

Alibhai-Brown, Yasmin. "Hooray for Bollywood: 100 Years of Indian Cinema." *The Independent*. Independent Digital News and Media, 17 Mar. 2013. Web. 09 July 2013.

Carreiro, Heather. "Matador Network." *Matador Network*. Matador Network, 30 Apr. 2010. Web. 09 July 2013.

Fisher, Max. "Welcome to America, Please Be On Time." *The Atlantic*. The Atlantic, 1 June 2012. Web. 09 July 2013.

Flanagan, Jane. "Drunk Baboons Plague Cape Town's Exclusive Suburbs." *The Telegraph*. The Telegraph, 29 Aug. 2010. Web. 9 July 2013.

Hochschild, Arlie R. "The Nanny Chain." *The American Prospect*. The American Prospect, 3 Jan. 2000. Web. 09 July 2013.

Keaten, Jamey. "The Big Story." *Associated Press*. Associated Press, 1 Apr. 2013. Web. 09 July 2013.

Kelly, Jon. "Why British Police Don't Have Guns." *BBC News*. BBC, 19 Sept. 2012. Web. 09 July 2013.

Kolbert, Elizabeth. "Spoiled Rotten." *The New Yorker*. The New Yorker, 2 July 2012. Web. 09 July 2013.

Lin, Judy. "Honor or Abandon: Societies' Treatment of Elderly Intrigues Scholar." *UCLA Today*. University of California Los Angeles, 7 Jan. 2010. Web. 09 July 2013.

"Man Already Knows Everything He Needs To Know About Muslims | The Onion - America's Finest News Source." *Man Already Knows Everything He Needs To Know About Muslims. The Onion - America's Finest News Source*. The Onion, 30 Aug. 2010. Web. 09 July 2013.

Menzel, Peter, and Faith D'Aluisio. "Introduction." *Hungry Planet: What the World Eats*. Berkeley, CA: Ten Speed, 2007. 11-18. Print.

Miner, Horace. "Body Rituals Among the Nacirema." *Body Rituals Among the Nacirema*. N.p.: Irvington Publications, n.d. 50. Print.

Nafisi, Azar. "Chapter 1." *Reading Lolita in Tehran: A Memoir in Books.* New York: Random House Trade Paperbacks, 2008. 3-6. Print.

Partanen, Anu. "What Americans Keep Ignoring About Finland's School Success." *The Atlantic.* The Atlantic, 29 Dec. 2011. Web. 09 July 2013.

Rogers, Thomas. "For Help in Old Age, How about a New Age of Robots?" *HeraldTribune.com.* Herald Tribune, 17 Aug. 2012. Web. 09 July 2013.

Slaten, Kevin, and Xue Chao. "Wages Rising in Chinese Factories? Only for Some." *Wages Rising in Chinese Factories? Only For Some -.* In These Times, 18 Mar. 2013. Web. 09 July 2013.

Symmes, Patrick. "Thirty Days as a Cuban." *Harpers Magazine.* Harpers Magazine, Oct. 2010. Web. 09 July 2013.

Trethewey, Natasha. "On Whitman, Civil War Memory, and My South." *VQR On Whitman, Civil War Memory, and My South.* Virginia Quarterly Review, n.d. Web. 09 July 2013.